During the nineteenth century, the trans-Atlantic slave trade was made illegal and eventually suppressed, and superseded by alternative forms of 'legitimate' trade with western Africa, especially in vegetable products such as palm oil. This commercial transition marks the beginning of the modern economic history of the region.

This book considers the implications of that process for the African societies involved, through ten case-studies written by leading specialists in the field. These studies address the central issue of continuity and change in economic structures, and critically assess the argument that the transition posed a 'crisis of adaptation' for African rulers by undermining their control over the income from overseas trade. Also highlighted are the effects of transition on slavery and gender relations within Africa and its links to the growth of European imperialism, culminating in the Partition of Africa at the end of the nineteenth century. The book is a major contribution to the interpretation of nineteenth-century African history.

From slave trade to 'legitimate' commerce

African Studies Series 86

A list of books in this series will be found at the end of the volume.

From slave trade to 'legitimate' commerce

The commercial transition in nineteenth-century West Africa

Papers from a conference of the
Centre of Commonwealth Studies,
University of Stirling

Edited by

Robin Law

CAMBRIDGE
UNIVERSITY PRESS

PUBLISHED BY THE PRESS SYNDICATE OF THE UNIVERSITY OF CAMBRIDGE
The Pitt Building, Trumpington Street, Cambridge, United Kingdom

CAMBRIDGE UNIVERSITY PRESS
The Edinburgh Building, Cambridge CB2 2RU, UK
40 West 20th Street, New York NY 10011–4211, USA
477 Williamstown Road, Port Melbourne, VIC 3207, Australia
Ruiz de Alarcón 13, 28014 Madrid, Spain
Dock House, The Waterfront, Cape Town 8001, South Africa

http://www.cambridge.org

First published 1995
First paperback edition 2002

A catalogue record for this book is available from the British Library

Library of Congress Cataloguing in Publication data
From slave trade to legitimate commerce: the commercial transition in
nineteenth-century West Africa / edited by Robin Law.
     p.   cm. – (African studies series: 86)
Includes bibliographical references (p.　).
ISBN 0 521 48127 9
1. Africa, West – Commerce – History – 19th century.
2. Slaves – Emancipation – Economic aspects – Africa,
West – History – 19th century.
3. Africa, West – Economic conditions.
I. Law, Robin.　II. Series.
HF3920.F76　1995 2002
382′.0666′009034–dc20　95-3428　CIP

ISBN 0 521 48127 9　hardback
ISBN 0 521 52306 0　paperback

Contents

Contributors

GARETH AUSTIN   Lecturer in Economic History, London School of Economics; editor (with K. Sugihara) of *Local Suppliers of Credit in the Third World, 1750–1960* (1993); currently preparing a book on the history of cocoa-farming in Ghana.

A. G. HOPKINS   Smuts Professor of Commonwealth History, University of Cambridge; author of *An Economic History of West Africa* (1973) and (with P. J. Cain) *British Imperialism* (2 vols., 1993); editor (with Clive Dewey) of *The Imperial Impact: Studies in the Economic History of Africa and India* (1978); formerly co-editor of the *Journal of African History* and of the *Economic History Review*.

RAY A. KEA   Professor of History, University of California, Riverside; author of *Settlements, Trade and Polities in the Seventeenth-Century Gold Coast* (1982); currently preparing a book on the cultural and social history of the Gold Coast in the eighteenth and nineteenth centuries.

ROBIN LAW   Professor of African History, University of Stirling, Scotland; author of *The Oyo Empire c. 1600–c. 1836* (1977), *The Horse in West African History* (1980) and *The Slave Coast of West Africa 1550–1750* (1991); co-editor of the *Journal of African History*

PAUL E. LOVEJOY   Professor of History, York University, Ontario; author of *Caravans of Kola* (1980), *Salt of the Desert Sun* (1986), *Transformations in Slavery: A History of Slavery in Africa* (1983) and (with Jan Hogendorn), *Slow Death for Slavery: The Course of Abolition in Northern Nigeria, 1897–1936* (1993); editor of several collections of essays on the history of slavery and African economic history, including most recently (with Toyin Falola) *Pawnship in Africa* (1994); co-editor of *African Economic History*.

MARTIN LYNN   Senior Lecturer in History, Queen's University, Belfast; author of several articles, in the *Journal of African History* and elsewhere, on British trade with West Africa in the nineteenth century.

E. ANN McDOUGALL   Associate Professor of History, University of Alberta; editor of *Sustainable Agriculture in Africa* (1990); currently preparing a book on the salt industry and economic development in the pre-colonial southern Sahara.

KRISTIN MANN   Associate Professor of History, Emory University, Atlanta; author of *Marrying Well: Marriage, Status and Social Change among the Educated Elite in Colonial Lagos* (1985); editor (with Richard Roberts) of *Law in Colonial Africa* (1991).

SUSAN MARTIN   Formerly Lecturer in History, School of Oriental and African Studies, University of London; author of *Palm Oil and Protest: An Economic History of the Ngwa Region, South-Eastern Nigeria, 1800–1960* (1988).

DAVID RICHARDSON   Reader in Economic History, University of Hull; editor of *Bristol, Africa and the Slave Trade to America* (4 vols., from 1986); author of several articles on the history of the Atlantic slave trade.

ELISÉE SOUMONNI   Assistant Professor of History, Université Nationale du Bénin; author of several articles on the history of Dahomey in the nineteenth century.

Abbreviations

AEH	*African Economic History*
CEA	*Cahiers d'Etudes Africaines*
CJAS	*Canadian Journal of African Studies*
EHR	*Economic History Review*
IJAHS	*International Journal of African Historical Studies*
JHSN	*Journal of the Historical Society of Nigeria*
JEH	*Journal of Economic History*
JAH	*Journal of African History*
JICH	*Journal of Imperial and Commonwealth History*

Introduction

Robin Law

The ending of the Atlantic slave trade and its replacement by what contemporaries called 'legitimate' (i.e. non-slave) trade – principally in agricultural produce, such as palm oil and groundnuts[1] – during the nineteenth century has been one of the central themes in the historiography of western Africa since the beginnings of serious academic study of African history in the 1950s.[2] Basil Davidson, in his classic study of the impact of the Atlantic slave trade on Africa, published originally in 1961, held that the slave trade had had a profound and essentially destructive effect on the African societies involved in it. Paradoxically, however, he argued that the ending of the trade in the nineteenth century was also negative and disruptive in its impact:

The ending of the trade was of tremendous significance for Africans and Europeans on the Guinea Coast. It upset the trading habits of four full centuries, undermined systems of government, disrupted social customs and opened the way for European intervention.

In Davidson's analysis, the ending of the slave trade caused an 'economic crisis' for African societies, leading to 'political upheaval' in them, which in turn provoked imperialist intervention and ultimately annexation.[3]

When Davidson was writing in 1961, there was little detailed research on the impact of the ending of the slave trade in Africa to sustain the apocalyptic picture which he painted. Essentially, he generalized from the one specific case-study which was then available, Kenneth Dike's pioneering monograph on the trading states of the Niger Delta (and more especially Bonny), published in 1956.[4] Dike argued that the shift from slaves to palm oil in this region's export trade had politically and socially disruptive effects on the African communities involved in it, weakening the authority of existing ruling elites and enabling men of slave origin (such as the famous Jaja, who eventually seceded from Bonny to establish his own kingdom at Opobo) to acquire wealth and bid for political power. These tensions were allegedly reflected in the civil wars (interpreted by Dike as 'slave revolts') which occurred in Bonny in

1

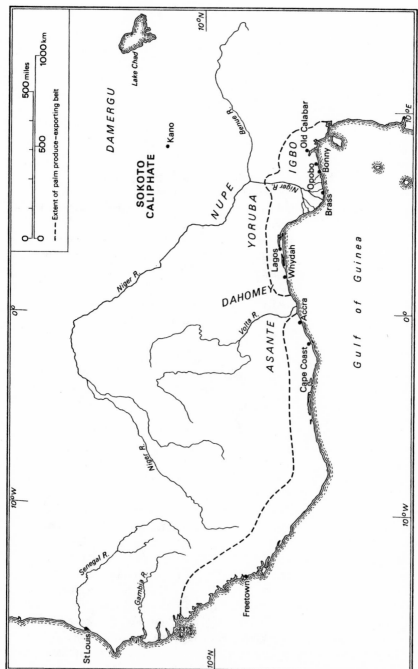

Map 1   West Africa in the nineteenth century, showing the extent of the palm produce exporting belt.

1855 and 1869. Dike himself, however, while noting the growth of
consular interference in the troubled politics of these states, did not very
clearly link the strains of the commercial transition to the ultimate
annexation of the area by Britain in the 1880s.

The development of the historiography of this issue since the 1960s has
been surveyed elsewhere.[5] Detailed rehearsal would be out of place in the
present context, but some of the salient steps in the progression of the
debate may be noted. In the early stages, the tendency was to extend the
scope of the argument geographically, identifying more or less analogous
processes of social and political upheaval in other West African societies.
Especially critical was the extension of the argument from the coastal
middleman states studied by Dike to societies in the hinterland which
were involved in the actual production, as well as marketing, of goods
for export. Tony Hopkins, in an article published in 1968 dealing with
Yorubaland, sought to link the endemic wars of that area in the nineteenth century, and especially their final phase in 1877–93, to the shift
from slaves to palm oil, arguing that this commercial transition had
undermined the wealth and power of existing rulers, causing them to
resort to warfare and plunder to maintain their incomes. Since these wars
in turn, by disrupting the export trade, provoked the British annexation
of Yorubaland in the 1890s, the strains of the commercial transition were
held to have contributed to the European Partition of Africa. This article
was also noteworthy for coining the phrase 'crisis of adaptation' to refer
to these problems.[6] A similar analysis was subsequently applied by
Martin Klein to the rise of groundnut exports from Senegambia, where
the commercial transition was held to have contributed to the overthrow
of the existing political order in the 'Muslim Revolution' which occurred
there from the 1860s onwards.[7]

More clearly than Dike, both Hopkins and Klein explained that the
military chiefs who had dominated the slave trade were less able to
control the new trade in agricultural produce, because the latter was
readily open to participation by small-scale traders and farmers. In a
notable epigram of Klein (much quoted or adapted for examination
questions in African history courses), 'whereas the slave trade strengthened the elite, the peanut trade put money, and thus guns, in the hands of
peasants'.[8] Hopkins also stressed the significance of the collapse of West
African produce prices in the 'Great Depression' of 1873–96, which
compounded the problems facing local rulers by reducing their income
from exports, and also created conflicts between African suppliers and
European merchants. Both the 'crisis of adaptation' and the origins of
Partition, therefore, were to be sought not in the strains arising from
structural change in West Africa's export trade alone, but in their

exacerbation by the adverse movement in the terms of trade in the late nineteenth century. In his *Economic History of West Africa* published in 1973, Hopkins generalized his analysis of the 'crisis of adaptation' and its relevance to European imperialism to the whole of coastal West Africa. Again emphasizing the opening-up of the export trade to small-scale enterprise, he now added the reflection that this development could be regarded as

the start of the modern economic history of West Africa ... In so far as firms of this type and size are the basis of the export economies of most West African states today, it can be said that modernity dates not from the imposition of colonial rule, as used to be thought, but from the early nineteenth century.[9]

This view has not, of course, commanded universal support among historians of Africa. It has been contested in two rather different ways, which need to be distinguished (although they are not mutually incompatible, and may be combined). On the one hand, some historians have argued that the Atlantic trade was, in fact, of only marginal significance for the African societies involved in it, with the implication that the transformation of the character of that trade in the nineteenth century can likewise have had little effect on their development: the most systematically argued case along these lines has been made by David Eltis.[10] Alternatively (or additionally), it has been argued that, in fact, existing ruling elites were able to dominate the new trade, as they had the old; this view has been propounded perhaps most influentially by Ralph Austen, originally in an article published in 1970.[11] According to this view, West African economic and political structures remained substantially intact until they were destroyed by the European colonial conquest at the end of the nineteenth century; 'modernity' (in Hopkins' terminology) thus came only with colonial rule. The breakdown of indigenous structures is seen as a consequence rather than a cause of the European Partition; implicitly, indeed, it was the continued resilience of these indigenous structures, seen as inimical to European capitalist interests, rather than their weakening (as Hopkins proposed) which required the European colonial takeover.

Although many aspects of the debate remain contested, something of a consensus may be said to have emerged on at least one central point, the need to distinguish between conditions in the coastal middleman states (such as Bonny) and the hinterland producing societies (such as Yorubaland). Although often presented as a criticism of Hopkins' concept of a 'crisis of adaptation', this distinction was, in fact, incorporated by him into the revised (and generalized) version of his thesis propounded in the *Economic History* of 1973, which conceded that 'the traditional unit of trade was less affected by the structural changes brought about by legitimate commerce than was the traditional unit of production'.[12] The critical contribution in this area was the research conducted (under Hopkins' supervision) by John Latham on the case of Old Calabar, which argued that the existing ruling elite there retained their dominance of the new trade in palm oil; although some ex-slaves in Calabar (as in Bonny) were able to become substantial merchants, they rose through the patronage of their masters rather than in competition with them, effectively from within the existing political and commercial structure rather than through its overthrow.[13] Other research showed that this was also true of the rise of ex-slaves such as Jaja in Bonny itself.[14] Dike's argument linking the rise of such ex-slaves, and political disorder in the Delta states more generally, to the shift from slaves to palm oil, is now generally held to be unsustainable – though there remain questions about the degree to which, in practice, existing merchants faced small-scale competition, elsewhere on the coast if not in Bonny itself, as will be seen later in this introduction.

While a 'crisis of adaptation' is generally held not to have materialized (or at least to have been successfully surmounted) in the coastal middleman communities, the subsequent extension of the argument to areas of palm oil and groundnut production in the hinterland, associated with Hopkins and Klein, although criticized, has not been so decisively refuted.[15] Some recent research on the case of Dahomey, for example, tends to support the idea of a 'crisis of adaptation' arising from the inability of the ruling elite to control and profit from the new 'legitimate' trade to the same extent as they had from the earlier trade in slaves.[16]

It also seems clear that distinctions have to be made between different periods within the nineteenth century, as well as between different societies within West Africa. Patrick Manning, in particular, has stressed the need to periodize the development of 'legitimate' trade, in order to grasp its impact upon social and political structures. On his view, conditions in the early nineteenth century, when the slave trade was in decline and the palm oil trade, although expanding, remained limited, 'favoured powerful monarchs and wealthy slave merchants'; the middle decades, when the volume and price of oil exports soared, were marked by 'free-swinging competition and unusual upward social mobility'; but the later nineteenth century, when the trade was stagnant (because of the collapse of oil prices) again saw a trend towards 'consolidation' of political and economic power.[17]

A conference organized by the Centre of Commonwealth Studies of the University of Stirling in April 1993 provided an opportunity both to take stock of the state of the debate on the impact of the ending of the Atlantic slave trade, and to present new detailed research bearing upon that debate. Revised versions of the papers from that conference are presented in the present volume. Where, then, does the debate now stand, after over twenty years of discussion and research? And more particularly, how do the contributions assembled in this collection advance understanding of these issues? This seems best approached not through summary and assessment of each individual contribution, but rather through consideration of certain general aspects of the commercial transition which were highlighted in the discussions, as well as in the papers presented, at the conference.

The market for slaves

Although the decline of the trans-Atlantic slave trade broadly coincided with the rise of 'legitimate' trade in agricultural produce, analytically these two processes have to some degree to be considered separately. As Hopkins pointed out, not all West African societies experienced a transition from exporting slaves to exporting 'legitimate' products, since some former slave-supplying societies were unable to get involved in the new trade in agricultural produce, and others which had been marginal to the slave trade became significant suppliers for 'legitimate' commerce.[18] The distinction is especially important in considering those societies in the West African interior (represented in this volume by Ann McDougall's study of the western Sahel region), which had supplied slaves for the Atlantic trade but were effectively excluded (by the high cost of transport) from the new trade in agricultural produce.

Assessment of the impact of the decline of trans-Atlantic exports of slaves is complicated, first, by the fact that this decline was a very protracted process: despite the legal abolition of the trade in the early nineteenth century, trans-Atlantic exports remained at a high level until at least the mid nineteenth century.[19] This persistence of slave exports involved, not only straightforwardly illegal trade, but also legal evasions promoted by some European governments, such as the scheme for the recruitment of supposedly 'free emigrants' from Africa to the West Indies pursued by the French government in 1857–61, discussed in Elisée Soumonni's contribution to this volume.[20] There was, moreover, an alternative export market for slaves, across the Sahara to northern Africa: although smaller in scale than the Atlantic trade, the trans-Saharan slave trade probably did not suffer significant decline until the end of the nineteenth century, and may indeed even have been increasing in volume.[21]

Even more critically, account has to be taken of the demand for slaves within West Africa itself, which was also expanding at this period. The general study of slavery in Africa by Paul Lovejoy, published in 1983, documents a growth of the use of slaves throughout West Africa (and in other regions of the continent) during the nineteenth century.[22] In part, this growth of slavery within West Africa reflected the increased use of slave labour in the production and transport of exports for the growing 'legitimate' trade. In addition to their use in production directly for export, slaves were also employed extensively, in coastal areas of West Africa, to produce food for the commercial and urban centres involved in overseas trade. In Old Calabar, for example, as Latham showed, slaves on agricultural plantations were producing for local consumption rather than for export;[23] and in this volume, Ray Kea's study of plantations on the south-eastern Gold Coast shows that many of these were likewise oriented to the local market. To a large degree, therefore, directly or indirectly, the growing demand for slaves was a consequence of the growth and transformation of the character of the Atlantic trade. Since, however, the expansion of slavery also occurred in areas relatively uninvolved in exports of 'legitimate' produce, such as the West African interior, this cannot be a complete explanation.

The existence of this growing demand for slaves within West Africa tended to cushion the effects of the ending of the overseas trade, since slaves could be diverted from export to the local market (as noted, for example, in the case of Asante, in Gareth Austin's contribution to this volume). It may even be argued on this basis, as is done by Ralph Austen, that the ending of overseas exports in practice posed 'little problem' for slave suppliers, since 'it did not diminish the total regional market for servile labour'.[24] Against Austen, it has generally been held that the price of slaves in West Africa fell in the early nineteenth century, reflecting a glut in local markets caused by the collapse of overseas exports.[25] It has commonly been supposed, indeed, that the expansion of slavery in West Africa during the nineteenth century was largely supply-driven, as slaves became cheaper to acquire. This was certainly an observation often made by contemporary observers: the missionary Samuel Crowther in the 1850s, for example, noting the 'accumulation of slaves' by wealthy persons in the the towns of Aboh, Idah and Igbegbe on the lower Niger, explained that 'since the slave-trade has been abolished in the Bight of Biafra, slaves have become very cheap; and ... they have the means of purchasing a great many slaves'.[26] At the same time, however, the supply of slaves within West Africa may well have been increased by factors not directly related to the ending of the overseas slave trade, such as the wars occasioned by the *jihads* or 'Islamic Revolutions' in the interior.[27]

Whatever its causes, a fall in the price of slaves must be presumed to have reduced the profitability of slave-raiding and slave-trading, and undermined the incomes of those involved in them. There have been different views as to the likely consequences of this. The more usual assumption has been that the reduced profitability of slaving would have encouraged those involved to withdraw from it, and seek alternative sources of income – as Ivor Wilks, for example, argued for Asante.[28] Claude Meillassoux, however, with regard to the West African interior, suggested that the effect there was quite the contrary, the response of local rulers being to increase the scale of their slaving activities, in order to offset the decline in price.[29] Perhaps these alternative analyses are not, strictly, contradictory, but may each be applicable to different cases, depending on the degree to which viable alternatives to slaving were available. Withdrawal from the slave trade would have been a rational option for those who could transfer their energies into other forms of exports, while an increase in output to compensate for falling prices would have made sense for those for whom no such alternative was on offer.

The basic assumption that slave prices fell in the nineteenth century is, however, now seen to be more problematical than hitherto appreciated. This question is treated, in this volume, by Paul Lovejoy and David Richardson, who argue that the evidence for falling slave prices in the early nineteenth century is, in fact, far from clear-cut. The ostensible decline in slave prices, as expressed in European currencies, appears to have reflected falls in the cost of the imported goods exchanged for slaves (in part, a consequence of the cost-reducing changes asscociated with the 'Industrial Revolution' in Western Europe); the real price of slaves, in terms of quantities of imports, shows little sign of long-term decrease, at least down to the mid nineteenth century. Although there was indeed a collapse of slave prices (and to that extent, presumably a 'crisis of adaptation' for West African slave suppliers) in the years immediately following the legal abolition of the British and USA slave trades in 1807/8, this was only temporary, with slave prices in real terms recovering by the 1820s. These findings are complemented by McDougall's contribution to this volume, which examines slave prices in the Sahelian interior, and likewise concludes that, far from declining, if anything they probably increased during the course of the nineteenth century.

If this evidence for the continued buoyancy of slave prices is accepted, how does it affect assessment of the impact of the ending of the overseas slave trade? One possible inference is that the Atlantic trade was, in fact, of only marginal significance for West African societies, the major market for slaves (and therefore the major determinant of slave prices) residing within the domestic economy. Alternatively, however, the rapid recovery of slave prices after the initial impact of declining overseas sales might reflect the expansion of local demand for slaves arising from the expansion of 'legitimate' exports. Such an inference can be supported by at least some contemporary comment, which recorded rising rather than falling slave prices: in Sierra Leone in the 1860s, for example, an officer of the British navy engaged in anti-slave trade patrols reported that the local price of slaves had risen to a level where it was more profitable to sell them on the local market than for export:

The reason is the great increase of trade, and all labour being required for the cultivation principally of ground nuts, palm nuts, and palm oil ... the legal trade and the increasing communication has made the slaves much more valuable, so many being required for home slavery that the increased price would not pay any one exporting slaves from this part of the coast.[30]

If this was so, the recovery of slave prices would illustrate the continuing importance, rather than the marginality, of trans-Atlantic demand for West African domestic economies.

Comparative profitability

Whatever the explanation for the recovery of slave prices, the implication remains that West African slave suppliers, although certainly from time to time suffering severe temporary price falls due to localized gluts of slaves caused by disruption of overseas exports, may not have faced any substantial long-term decline in profitability. Since, however, nominal prices for palm oil in the first half of the nineteenth century were actually increasing, the *relative* profitability of slave-trading, by comparison with 'legitimate' alternatives, was presumably falling. In this context, as Lovejoy and Richardson note, it may have become more profitable for African slave-holders to employ their slaves in production for export than to sell them. Such calculations were already being made in the Sierra Leone area, at least, by the 1830s, where a chief of the Bulom, who was using slave labour on his farms (to produce rice for the Freetown market, rather than strictly for export), declared that each of his slaves earned him, over and above the cost of their subsistence, about £7 10s. annually, whereas the average selling price of a slave was only £10, suggesting that greater profits might be obtained by retaining than by exporting slaves.[31]

The question remains whether, more generally and in the long run, 'legitimate' trade was an adequate substitute for the slave trade. Part of Hopkins' argument for a 'crisis of adaptation' is that the new forms of trade were generally less remunerative than the export of slaves.[32] Although this issue is not addressed in detail in any of the contributions to this volume, it warrants some further comment here.

This is not, it should be stressed, merely a question of aggregate export earnings, but also of relative profit rates, since the costs of gathering/ producing slaves and agricultural produce and delivering them to the coast probably differed substantially. On this, it must be conceded that there has as yet still been little detailed research. There is, however, an abundance of impressionistic evidence, in the form of statements reported from West African traders and rulers, most of which tends to support the suggestion that the new trade was less profitable. The trading chiefs of Abeokuta, inland from Lagos, in 1855, for example, complained that

From that time [when] they began to sell this oil, those that have 300 slaves, now [have] left 50; and they that have 200, left 40; and that of 100, left 20; that of 50, left 5. So they remember that it would have been better if they have been trading slaves as they used to.[33]

Such self-interested testimony, of course, is clearly not by itself decisive. One area, however, in which it does seem possible to demonstrate that costs were higher in the new trade is that of transport, especially where goods had to be moved overland. Slaves required feeding in transit, but were themselves self-transporting, needing only to be guarded. On the basis admittedly of a single illustrative example, it may be suggested that one armed guard could supervise around five slaves.[34] Agricultural produce, on the other hand, had to be transported, which in the absence of wheeled vehicles or (in most coastal areas of West Africa) of pack animals, meant that it was carried on human heads. The normal head-load (of around 40–50 lbs), corresponded to only about 5 gallons of palm oil.[35] A rough comparison of transport costs can be based on the statement that in the Niger Delta in the 1830s a slave commanded the same price as a ton of palm oil, or 320 gallons.[36] To deliver five slaves to the coast would involve the cost of subsistence for six persons (five slaves + one guard); but to deliver five tons of oil would require over 300 porters, incurring subsistence costs over fifty times as great.[37]

The difference was less where, as in the Niger Delta, waterborne transport was available, since both slaves and palm oil were carried in canoes. Even here, however, the transport costs for oil were clearly significantly greater than for slaves. The great trading canoes of Bonny, requiring up to 40 rowers, could carry probably up to 80 slaves each.[38] By contrast, in the oil trade the great canoes carried only around 12 puncheons (equivalent to 9 tons) of palm oil.[39] In order to deliver oil in quantities which would realize the same gross return as in the slave trade, a trader in oil would therefore need nine times as many canoes (or, of course, the substitution of larger for smaller canoes). In terms of subsistence costs, while transporting 80 slaves required subsistence for 120 persons (80 slaves + 40 rowers), oil of an equivalent value (80 tons, or 106–7 puncheons) would require 360 paddlers in 9 canoes, and costs around three times greater.

The profitability of the oil trade varied, of course, from area to area within West Africa, reflecting differential yields of palm trees in different regions as well as differing transport costs. Two modern estimates of the labour required to produce a ton of palm oil in pre-colonial conditions give around 315 person/days per ton in Dahomey, but only around 250 in Igboland, suggesting that oil was nearly 20 per cent cheaper to produce in the latter.[40] Profitability also varied through time, with fluctuations in palm oil prices. If the profits from 'legitimate' trade were considered insufficient in the early stages of the trade, when European prices for palm oil were rising, they presumably became even less adequate with the fall in prices which set in from the 1860s onwards and reached catastrophic proportions in the 'Great Depression' of the 1880s. On Hopkins' view, the profit margins and incomes of African suppliers were then significantly eroded, compounding the already existing problems of the commercial transition and bringing the 'crisis of adaptation' to a head.[41] On this, however, some caution is needed, since the precise relationship between European and local prices of West African produce is not yet wholly clear. It has been suggested that, at least in the Lagos area, prices paid for oil in West Africa did not fall in line with those in Europe, thus squeezing the profit margins of the European purchasers but leaving those of African suppliers relatively intact.[42] African resistance to European attempts to force down prices in the Depression of the 1880s, and European merchants' inability to overcome it, was one of the factors which brought the latter to favour imperialist annexation.

Large-scale and small-scale enterprise

The central element in Hopkins' conception of the 'crisis of adaptation' was that the slave trade had been effectively monopolized by a small number of large entrepreneurs, often the political and military chiefs of West African societies, whereas the new trade in agricultural produce was open to the generality of the populace. The argument was partly related to economies of scale: it was suggested that whereas slave-trading was most profitably carried out on a large scale, in agricultural production large-scale enterprise enjoyed no competitive advantage. The domination of large-scale enterprise in the slave trade was not absolute, since records of slave-ships document many purchases of slaves in ones and twos, which presumably implies the involvement of relatively small-scale traders;[43] but the validity of the general point does not seem in doubt. In any case, quite apart from the question of economies of scale, a trader selling even a single slave was dealing in a relatively large unit of value. As Hopkins noted, by their physical natures, whereas a slave is indivisible, oil could be produced and marketed in small quantities.[44] If (as noted earlier) a slave was equivalent in value to 320 gallons of oil, and if we take the pot of 5 gallons which formed the normal head-load as the smallest unit in which oil was likely to be marketed, oil could be traded in units of less than one-sixtieth of the value of a single slave.

The involvement of small-scale producers and traders in the new 'legitimate' trade, and the contrast with conditions under the slave trade, was frequently noted by contemporary observers of the nineteenth century. For example, in the hearings of the Select Committee of the British Parliament on the Slave Trade in 1848, the question was put to some of the witnesses, whether the oil trade was done with the chiefs, or with the generality of their subjects. A naval officer of the anti-slavery patrol, Commander Matson, replied that 'it is sold by the different families; different families cultivate the berry'. Pressed as to whether he meant that 'each family trades in palm oil on its own account', he agreed: 'Yes; sometimes they come down with a canoe with a small quantity, and they come alongside a vessel laying in the river to sell it for anything they can get'. The trader William Hutton likewise deposed that whereas 'it is only the chiefs and better classes of the inhabitants of the coast of Africa that can be slave merchants', on the contrary 'the palm oil trade is pursued by all classes; whoever takes a pot of palm oil into a factory gets an equivalent for it in the shape of British goods'.[45]

Despite such contemporary testimony, as was noted earlier, it has generally been held, following Latham's study of the case of Old Calabar, that the coastal marketing (as opposed to the hinterland production) of agricultural produce continued to be dominated by existing large-scale traders. The distinction was, in fact, clearly made in some contemporary accounts of trade in the Delta, which noted that, although the palm oil was originally purchased (at least in large part) from small-scale producers, it was bulked up by the coastal traders before being transported to the coast. A British trader at Bonny in the early 1840s, for example, noted that 'The Bonny men buy the oil in small quantities from the growers, and sell it by the puncheon to the masters of the ships.'[46] Likewise in the 1860s, Winwood Reade described the collection of oil up-country by the Bonny traders in similar terms: 'The oil is brought to them little by little in calabashes. This they pour off into barrels.'[47] The smallest unit in which oil was normally traded at Bonny was evidently the 'puncheon', of 240 gallons, or three-quarters of a ton of palm oil. It is not entirely clear, however, whether this was true of trading conditions elsewhere on the coast. At Old Calabar to the east also, oil seems normally to have been traded in puncheons.[48] At Brass, however, the smallest unit in which oil was traded was apparently the 'angbar', of only 30 gallons.[49] A standard measure of 30 gallons was also employed at Badagry, west of Lagos; but at Lagos itself the measure was even smaller, of only 10 gallons.[50] In Dahomey, it was 18 gallons.[51] Outside Bonny and Old Calabar, therefore, it was possible to trade palm oil on a relatively small scale, in units which were (at the rate cited earlier, of one slave to one ton, or 320 gallons, of oil) equivalent to between about one-thirtieth (10 gallons) and one-tenth (30 gallons) of the value of a slave.

Even in places such as Bonny and Calabar, in so far as larger-scale trading remained dominant, this did not reflect merely the superior competitive efficiency of large-scale merchants (or the preference of European traders for dealing with them), but was enforced through prohibitions on small-scale enterprise. In Old Calabar, it is explicitly reported that the slaves in charge of the trading canoes, while receiving a commission on their trade, were not permitted to trade on their own account in palm oil.[52] In the last resort, small-scale enterprise could be excluded by legislative action. The best-known instance of this in Calabar was in 1862 when, after 'young men and boy [i.e. slave?] traders' had begun selling oil in smaller measures – barrels (i.e. 32 gallons), hogsheads (63 gallons) and rum puncheons (72 gallons?) – the governing Ekpe society decreed that oil should not be sold in smaller quantities than 'the usual trade-cask or puncheon'. The British traders complained that this measure discriminated against 'the young traders, many of whom are at present unable to command the requisite means for conducting a wholesale trade, but if allowed to go on gradually would in time become useful and extensive traders', and served the interests only of 'the King and a few men of position, who thus monopolize the whole trade of the interior markets to the exclusion of all others'. The British Consul Richard Burton intervened to negotiate a treaty which stipulated that anybody should be free to trade 'in any quantities whatever ... in his own name'.[53] It is doubtful whether this removal of restrictions was wholly effective, but the provision was reiterated in a second treaty imposing free trade on Calabar in 1878, which stipulated that people should be 'permitted to buy in large or small quantities as suits them, whether puncheons, hogsheads, barrels or any lesser measure'.[54]

Similar disputes about access to the market occurred in other communities of coastal West Africa also. For example, Kosoko, the king of Lagos expelled by the British in 1851 for refusing to accept a treaty banning the slave trade, established himself at Epe, across the lagoon to the north-east. Although he initially tried to continue to sell slaves, within a few years he had entered the palm oil trade. It was noted in 1856, however, that 'he wishes to carry into this, to him, new trade, the same arbitrary and monopolizing policy that he pursued with the Slave Trade at Lagos', which he did by requiring all imported goods to be delivered to himself (on credit, moreover), enabling him to re-sell them at 'monopolizing prices'. But by 1859 it was reported that 'many' of Kosoko's slaves had been granted 'the privilege of trading for themselves', and the freedom they had gained was held to be a constraint on Kosoko resuming the slave trade, as he was then disposed to do.[55]

In this volume, the question of continuity of economic structures at the coast is most directly addressed by Martin Lynn, primarily with regard to the Niger Delta/Old Calabar region. Unlike most earlier analyses, however, Lynn looks mainly at the European rather than the African end of the trade – in effect, asking whether there was a 'crisis of adaptation' for Europeans, as well as for Africans. He concludes that in the initial stages of the development of the new 'legitimate' trade there was an essential continuity of structures, with both the personnel and the trading methods of the slave trade carried over into the new trade, and that the entry of new traders was inhibited by the high capital costs of entry into the trade as then organized. Structural change did occur, from the 1850s, with the entry of new (including smaller-scale) traders, some of whom were 'Krio' from Sierra Leone; and Lynn identifies, if not exactly a 'crisis of adaptation', at any rate a 'crisis of restructuring'. This was due, however, not to the move from slaves to palm oil as such, but to subsequent technical and managerial innovations, notably the introduction of steamship services and the commission house system, which lowered the costs of entry. In an interesting parallel to the strategies pursued by their African suppliers, existing European traders sought to use extra-economic means to exclude this developing competition. In Old Calabar in 1856, for example, when a Court of Equity was established to regulate the affairs of foreign traders, it was stipulated that traders had to pay a fee of 20,000 'coppers' (£1,000) for permission to operate, a provision which seems to have been aimed especially at excluding the Sierra Leonean petty traders.[56] The British Consul who authorized this regulation, when it was queried by the Foreign Office, admitted that 'on the face of it, this may seem to be protecting a monopoly'.[57]

The eventual break down of the established European traders' monopoly and opening up of the trade to wider competition presumably had implications for African suppliers, since the entry of additional (including smaller-scale) purchasers of oil would potentially have offered opportunities for new (including smaller-scale) traders on the African side also. The fall of palm oil prices and profitability in the 1870s and 80s, however, prompted a movement towards amalgamation into larger firms among European traders (as, for example, in the formation of the African Association in 1889), which parallels the trend of 'consolidation' which Manning postulated during the same period on the African side of the trade.

As regards the African suppliers, the question of large- and small-scale enterprise in the palm oil trade is touched upon in this volume by Kristin Mann (with regard to Lagos) and Robin Law (on Dahomey and Yorubaland). In these areas, it seems clear that both large- and small-scale enterpreneurs were involved in the production and trading of oil, though the balance between them is difficult to establish. Mann, however, suggests that in Lagos, as in Old Calabar or Bonny, petty traders could advance into larger-scale enterprise only through the patronage of existing big traders; and further (again, consistently with Manning's argument) that opportunities for profitable petty trading became more restricted in the commercial depression of the 1870s and 80s.

The issue is more systematically explored by Susan Martin, with respect to Igboland. Martin does somewhat qualify Hopkins' assumption that there no economies of scale in palm oil production, identifying innovations in the production process which facilitated larger-scale operations (involving the treading out of oil in canoes or hollowed-out tree trunks, as opposed to the earlier method of squeezing it out by hand). But she concludes, in corroboration of Hopkins' model, that most of the oil exported from this area was produced by small households using family labour and that, contrary to some earlier research, there was far less use of slave labour here than in the Niger Delta. In the hinterland, the traders who had dominated the slave trade (members of the Okonko society, associated with the Aro merchants) were less successful than those at the coast in maintaining their position in the new 'legitimate' trade. Although thus vindicating the central premise of Hopkins' concept of a 'crisis of adaptation', however, Martin queries his emphasis on this entry of small-scale producers into the export trade as marking the beginning of the 'modern economic history' of West Africa. She argues that even where, as in the Igbo case, little use was made of slave labour, lineage heads were able to use their authority over their juniors and wives to exploit their labour for palm oil production and transport, and thus circumscribed the autonomy of individual 'households' which Hopkins emphasized as an index of 'modernity'.

Slavery and gender

The growth of 'legitimate' trade had significant implications for two important aspects of West African social organization: the institution of slavery and the position of women. These two issues are, indeed, closely connected, in so far as a majority of the slaves held within West Africa were probably women – as, conversely, a majority of those sold for trans-Atlantic export were men.[58]

The institution of slavery within West Africa was affected by the commercial transition in various ways. First, as has been seen, the decline of overseas demand led to a fall in the price of slaves within West Africa – even if this was only temporary, or restricted to certain areas. Such a cheapening of slaves would evidently have facilitated the expansion of their use locally, and may also have tended to encourage worse treatment of them, since it became more economical to work slaves to death and replace them than to restrict the burden of their work in order to keep them alive. This was certainly claimed to be the case by some contemporary observers in the Niger Delta. Consul Burton, for example, told the British Select Committee on the Western Coast of Africa in 1865 that slaves had fallen in price there, and that consequently 'it is worth while for a native gentleman to buy those men at a cheap rate, and work or starve them to death in a few months to buy others'.[59]

In a second respect, however, the ending of overseas sales probably tended to ameliorate slaves' conditions, inasmuch as the threat of sale overseas had operated as an important mechanism of social control over slaves (much like sale 'down the river' in the USA). It was reported of Old Calabar, for example:

While the foreign slave trade prevailed, the masters easily got quit of their troublesome people, and the fear of it had a deterring effect on the rest. Often therefore was the wish expressed that it could be resumed, if only to the extent of one ship in the year, to let them sell off their bad people.[60]

Initially, human sacrifice (for which slaves formed the principal victims) may have served as an alternative method of social control; the scale of human sacrifice did, in fact, increase in Calabar in the years immediately following the ending of the Atlantic slave trade, although it was itself legally abolished there in 1851.[61]

Thirdly and most important, as was noted earlier, slaves were extensively used in the production and transport of 'legitimate' exports such as palm oil and groundnuts. One aspect of this which is easily overlooked is that Europeans, as well as Africans, made use of slave labour in the production of agricultural exports, slavery itself of course being still legal in the period immediately following the banning of the trans-Atlantic slave trade.[62] Coffee was cultivated in Angola, for example, by Portuguese planters using slave labour, as well as by free African peasants.[63] In this volume, Ray Kea offers a detailed study of slave plantations established by the Danes and by Africans under their influence on the Gold Coast, in the period between the abolition of the Danish slave trade and the Danish withdrawal from the Gold Coast in 1850.

Those slaves owned by Africans might be employed on large-scale plantations broadly similar to the European or American model, or incorporated (in smaller numbers) into households. However, in some cases slaves operated as independent producers or traders, working on their own account while paying a duty (or, it might be said, a rent, for their own labour power) to their owner: this was clearly the situation of the trader-slaves of Bonny or Old Calabar, and similar arrangements existed elsewhere (for example, in Yorubaland and Dahomey, as shown in Law's contribution to this volume). The implications of these different forms of relations of production for the living conditions and opportunities for upward mobility of the slaves involved were, evidently, very different. Slaves on plantations producing for the market might expect to suffer intensified exploitation and harsher conditions, as (in a different historical context) Karl Marx suggested;[64] while those incorporated into households would normally have received better treatment (and, in principle, ultimately assimilation among its free members). Those who could operate as independent entrepreneurs, however, could potentially accumulate wealth, and might thus even be able to achieve their own freedom by redeeming themselves (as noted, again, in Law's contribution on Dahomey and Yorubaland). Even where slaves were theoretically prohibited from such independent enterprise, they might engage in it illegally: in Brass, for example, it is reported that one of the duties of the 'head slaves' who delivered oil to the European shipping was to ensure that the rowers did not steal any oil, presumably with a view to selling it on their own account.[65]

In this volume, although the question of slavery is touched upon in several of the contributions, it is most centrally dealt with by Kristin Mann, for the case of Lagos. Mann documents a tendency towards the weakening of owners' control over slaves during the second half of the nineteenth century, with slaves seeking independence, re-negotiating their relations with their masters, or transferring their allegiance to other patrons. This is attributed in part to the commercial changes of the period, with the trade in palm oil seen (in corroboration of Hopkins' analysis) as offering expanded opportunities for small-scale enterprise, including independent trading by slaves. In the case of Lagos, however, evaluation of the impact of the commercial transition is complicated by the legal changes which occurred there after the British annexation in 1861, which brought the abolition (or more accurately, non-recognition) of the status of slavery, and it must therefore be uncertain how far Mann's analysis of developments in Lagos can be generalized to other areas which remained outside European jurisdiction until the end of the nineteenth century. Moreover, it is suggested that the more difficult trading conditions in the 1870s and 1880s, when palm oil prices fell, restricted opportunities for independent accumulation by slaves, and stimulated a reassertion of control over their labour by owners.[66]

The commercial transition impacted upon gender relations also, not only because many slaves were female, but also because of the importance of specifically female labour in 'legitimate' trade. Whereas the slave trade was an overwhelmingly male occupation, agricultural labour and the marketing of produce were, at least in many coastal societies, predominantly female tasks. The distinction was explicitly noted, for example, in somewhat colourful and censorious terms, by the British expedition on the lower Niger in 1832: 'The women and children are employed in collecting palm-oil; the men, in trading to Brass and Eboe [Aboh], kidnapping their neighbours, and drinking the worst description of spirits'.[67] (The reference here to the role of children's labour, it may be noted, points to the possible significance of the commercial transition for relations between generations, as well as between the sexes, which would merit detailed research in the future.)[68] This issue, which has hitherto attracted little attention, is treated in this volume by Susan Martin and Robin Law, with regard to Igboland and Dahomey/Yorubaland respectively. Although the predominance of female labour in the production and trading of palm oil is clearly established in both these areas, the consequences for relations between the sexes were apparently different. In Igboland, Martin argues that the new commercial opportunities caused men to move into the production of palm oil and seek to appropriate the product to their own profit, leading therefore to greater exploitation of women's labour rather than to their enrichment (though the trade in palm kernels, which developed later in the nineteenth century, remained in female hands and did give women opportunities for independent accumulation). In Yorubaland, however, as interpreted by Law, women were more generally able to operate as independent small-scale producers and traders, and thereby achieved both greater wealth and (presumably) greater independence *vis-à-vis* their menfolk. These different hypothesized outcomes need not, perhaps, be regarded as problematical, since the distribution of benefits from changing commercial opportunities was not pre-determined in any mechanistic fashion, but surely depended to some degree on the contingencies of particular struggles, as well as upon the nature of the pre-existing social structures.

A 'crisis of monarchy'?

As was noted earlier, the structural changes associated with the transition from the slave trade to 'legitimate' trade were held by Hopkins and others to have undermined the position of existing West African ruling elites. Borrowing a concept from the history of seventeenth-century England, Hopkins spoke of a 'crisis of the aristocracy';[69] John Lonsdale, however, in a more recent historiographical survey, noting the emergence of conflict within West African ruling elites, as well as opposition from below, suggested that there was rather a 'crisis of monarchy', a challenge more specifically to the authority of central (and centralizing) government.[70] In Hopkins' analysis, rulers' incomes, and hence their effective power, were supposedly undermined by a combination of the lower profitability of the new trade, and of their smaller share in it, as they now faced competition from ordinary farmers and petty traders. It can be suggested, indeed, that ruling elites suffered increased competition, not from small-scale enterprise alone, but from the private sector more generally, including wealthy merchants operating on a large scale; whereas the slave trade depended on violence (capture in warfare being the principal source of slaves for export), and therefore favoured the domination of the chiefs who controlled military forces, the new trade in agricultural produce offered no special advantages to warrior elites, and enabled private individuals of wealth, such as merchants, to strengthen their position by moving into large-scale production for export.[71] Existing rulers might, as Hopkins acknowledged, seek to maintain their incomes by taxation of private-sector enterprise, but he argued that since 'legitimate' trade was more dispersed in its operation (because of the involvement of a multiplicity of small producers), it was likely to be more difficult to monitor and tax effectively. In addition, such attempts to increase taxation (like the attempts to enforce monopolies of trade mentioned earlier) were likely to be resisted, and thus to provoke political problems of their own.[72]

That 'legitimate' trade generally yielded lower revenues than the slave trade was, certainly, frequently asserted by West African rulers. King Ghezo of Dahomey in 1848, for example, fending off British pressure for the abolition of the slave trade, complained that the palm oil trade was 'a slow method of making money, and brought only a very small amount of duties into his coffers'.[73] The Yevogan, or official in charge of European trade at Whydah, the principal port of Dahomey, in discussion with a British naval officer in 1850, dramatically emphasized the point by comparing the capacity of a tumbler and a wine-glass: 'The tumbler is the slave, the wine-glass the palm oil trade.'[74] Such statements need, of course, to be treated with caution, since in the context in which they were made (making a case for the continuation of the slave trade, or at least for substantial compensation for its abolition) there was good reason to exaggerate the fiscal difficulties posed by the transition. Although, in the case of Dahomey at least, there is apparently corroborative evidence for the relative impoverishment of the royal court by the 1870s,[75] this might reflect the decline in palm oil prices at that time, rather than the problems of the original move from slaves to oil.

In this volume, the problems allegedly posed by the commercial transition for African states are studied especially by Elisée Soumonni and Gareth Austin, for the cases of Dahomey and Asante respectively. For Dahomey, Soumonni argues that the transition from slaves to palm oil down to the 1850s was a relatively smooth process, and to that extent the 'crisis of adaptation' here was successfully surmounted. This was possible partly because, contrary to the assumption often made by British abolitionists in the nineteenth century, the slave and palm oil trades were compatible rather than contradictory, and the new trade could thus be developed alongside the old.[76] Even more critically, King Ghezo of Dahomey was able to resist or evade British pressure for the abolition of the slave trade, in large part because the French, although theoretically also committed to abolition, in practice adopted a much less demanding attitude on this issue, and Ghezo was therefore able to develop trade in palm oil with them while still continuing the slave trade. (To some extent, indeed, as was noted earlier, the French themselves traded in slaves, under the guise of 'free emigrants'.) It is acknowledged that, in the longer run, when the overseas slave trade came to an end (in Dahomey, effectively in the 1860s), the Dahomian state had difficulty in realizing an adequate revenue from the export of palm oil alone. Dahomey was not, however, destabilized by these problems, and remained a strong polity down to the French conquest in the 1890s.

The case of Asante, studied by Austin, was more complex than that of Dahomey since its heartland lay north of the palm oil belt, and it was therefore for most of the nineteenth century (until the development of rubber exports from the 1880s) unable to participate directly in the supply of agricultural produce to the coast. Asante responded by a reorientation of its foreign trade, selling gold at the coast to obtain necessary European imports (such as firearms) and compensating for the decline of its trans-Atlantic trade by increasing exports of kola nuts to the West African interior. Although questioning the degree of state control over trade suggested in some earlier work, Austin argues that overall Asante was successful in accommodating to the changing commercial environment, and in securing adequate revenues under the new conditions – at any rate down to the catastrophic military defeat which it suffered at the hands of the British in 1874. In the aftermath of that defeat, Asante did suffer a major political crisis, collapsing into civil war in the 1880s, and some role was played in this by tensions arising from increases in government regulation and taxation of private-sector enterprise.[77] The immediate cause of this crisis, however, was clearly the defeat of 1874, which undermined the authority of the Asante state and led to the loss of territories which eroded its tax base (thereby necessitating increases in taxation of those areas which it still controlled). On the face of it, therefore, Austin's analysis appears to suggest that, without the intervention of the British, the Asante state might have survived the commercial transition intact. Austin also, however, raises the question (which has a relevance beyond the case of Asante, as will be argued later in this Introduction) of whether, in fact, it is realistic to see the British intervention as an entirely 'exogenous' factor, since it was itself, in part, provoked by Asante commercial policies; the official regulation and taxation of trade which had enabled the Asante state to cope with the commercial transition were condemned by the British as interference in the free operation of the market.

Whether it remains appropriate to speak of a 'crisis of adaptation' in these cases is, ultimately, a semantic as well as an empirical question; for some historians, a 'crisis' successfully surmounted may not merit the title at all. Both Dahomey and Asante were, however, by West African standards, exceptionally strong states, with relatively effective centralized administrations, and caution is therefore required in generalizing from their experience. Weaker or more decentralized states may have been less able to contain the strains of the commercial transition. The different perceptions of Hopkins and Martin Klein, in the cases of Senegambia and Yorubaland, may well reflect differing realities on the ground in West Africa, as well as the differing perspectives of these authors.

The interior

Analysis of the 'crisis of adaptation' has, naturally enough, tended to concentrate upon the coastal societies which were most directly and intensively involved in the Atlantic trade. Account needs to be taken also, however, of conditions in the West African interior, which was less involved in the sale of slaves to the coast, and for the most part unable to participate directly in the new 'legitimate' trade. In general, societies in the interior were precluded from direct participation in the export of agricultural produce by the high cost of overland transport, noted earlier. The point is illustrated by the development, by the mid nineteenth century, of seasonal migration from the interior to the valley of the River Gambia to cultivate groundnuts for export: it was easier to move the labour force nearer the coast than to cultivate crops in the interior and transport them.[78] Societies in the interior could only export bulk agricultural produce profitably if situated close to navigable rivers which provided relatively cheap access to the coast. An important example is Nupe, on the lower Niger, which exported shea-butter in the second half of the nineteenth century.[79] The export of gum arabic from the southern margins of the western Sahara was likewise made possible by the navigable waterway of the River Senegal.[80]

The question of the impact of the ending of the Atlantic slave trade on the West African interior is addressed in this volume by Ann McDougall, with regard to the western Sahel region. Although the scale of this region's involvement in the supply of slaves to the Europeans was evidently marginal, by comparison with coastal societies such as Dahomey or Asante, McDougall argues that the impact of the abolition of the trans-Atlantic slave trade was nevertheless significant. Adjustments to trading patterns were necessary, as in Asante, to secure the continued importation of European firearms, which had now to be purchased with exports of gum arabic rather than slaves. The growth of the export trade in gum here provides a parallel with 'legitimate' trade in palm oil and groundnuts in coastal areas – though McDougall stresses that this expansion of the gum trade was not directly linked to the ending of the Atlantic slave trade, and had begun before the abolition of the latter. Although these changes involved shifts in economic power among groups within the region, overall the transition was managed smoothly; in Hopkins' terminology, there was successful 'adaptation' here, but no 'crisis'. Moreover, in this successful adaptation, McDougall emphasizes, rather than the impact of the Atlantic trade, the dominant importance in this case of internal regional networks, especially the exchange of slaves for Saharan salt. This reminder that there were other factors than the

Atlantic trade affecting the development of West African economies is salutary. Its significance, moreover, extends beyond the interior itself, since the autonomous internal dynamism of the economies of the Sudan/ Sahel region had important effects on at least certain parts of coastal West Africa also. As Austin notes in this volume, the relatively successful response of Asante to the ending of the Atlantic slave trade was only possible because of the contingent circumstance that, owing to the 'Islamic Revolution' which created the Sokoto Caliphate in the early nineteenth century, the internal West African demand for kola from Asante was expanding.[81]

It may be, indeed, that if a parallel to the coastal 'crisis of adaptation' is to be sought in the interior, it is to be found, not in the impact of the ending of the Atlantic slave trade, but rather in the subsequent ending of trans-Saharan exports, around the end of the nineteenth century. There is even a parallel here to the development of 'legitimate' trade at the coast, with the increasing importance in the late nineteenth century of commodities other than slaves, such as ivory, ostrich feathers and goat skins. An explicit attempt to apply Hopkins' analysis to the trans-Saharan trade has, in fact, been made by Stephen Baier, with regard to the central Sahelian state of Damergu. The new forms of trade here, Baier argues, like the trade in agricultural produce at the coast, lacked economies of scale and were accessible to 'commoners' as well as chiefs, so that the trade acquired 'a broader social base'. As at the coast, the warrior aristocracy tried to tighten control over the new trade, leading to tensions and conflicts. While hesitating to speak of a 'crisis' (because foreign trade accounted for 'only a very small fraction' of rulers' incomes), Baier suggests that these commercial changes did tend to 'shift the balance of social and economic power' within Damergu.[82]

Imperialism

Hopkins' analysis was concerned not only to elucidate the internal dynamics of African states and economies but also to link these to the European conquest of West Africa in the late nineteenth century. In this volume, the connections between commercial change and European imperialism are touched upon by Martin Lynn, with reference mainly to the case of the Niger Delta, and by Gareth Austin, for that of Asante; and also, in a broader overview, by Tony Hopkins himself.

The links between the commercial transition and European imperialism can be conceived at two levels. First, the project of suppressing the slave trade and promoting 'legitimate' trade by its nature tended to draw Europeans into political interference in West Africa, since it involved

European governments (primarily the British) in seeking to impose economic change on African rulers who were often unwilling to comply, and to use diplomatic and sometimes military pressure to coerce them – as, for example, in the British intervention at Lagos, to depose a ruler who refused to end slave exports, in 1851. The commercial transition was thus inherently 'imperialist', not because it necessarily led to actual annexation (though this did, in fact, occur in Lagos ten years after the original intervention), but in the looser sense of involving the exercise of political power to promote approved forms of commercial development – what has come to be called, though arguably infelicitously, 'informal imperialism'.[83]

The second dimension of the problem relates to the move from 'informal imperialism' to formal annexation, with the Partition of Africa among rival European colonial powers in the late nineteenth century. Hopkins, as has been seen, sought to connect this shift in policy also to the West African 'crisis of adaptation'. The connection was partly that 'informal' methods were now perceived as insufficiently effective in bringing about the desired transformation of African economies and societies, but partly also that the difficulties posed by the transition for West African rulers themselves obstructed the healthy development of European commerce. In this context, it should be stressed that it was not necessary for the 'crisis of adaptation' to have occasioned local disorder obstructive of trade (though this was the scenario posited for Hopkins' original case-study in Yorubaland). Even 'successful' responses to the crisis, in the sense of ones where West African ruling elites remained in effective control, presented threats to European commercial interests. Whatever else the European conquest of West Africa was intended to effect, it was centrally concerned to impose free trade on West Africans, with the elimination of the monopolies enjoyed by coastal middlemen such as Jaja of Opobo, and more generally of the duties levied on trade by African rulers.[84] More broadly, imperialism aimed to modernize African economic structures, an objective symbolized by the issue of slavery, whose abolition was a central concern of European powers, reaffirmed at the Congress of Brussels in 1890.[85] In so far, therefore, as African rulers had responded to the commercial transition by asserting monopolies of trade, increasing taxes, and by the more extensive and intensive use of slaves for export production, they were reinforcing the very practices whose abolition, in the longer run, European capitalism would demand. African states, it may be suggested, could not win. Where the commercial transition had a disintegrative effect on political structures, as Hopkins suggested in Yorubaland, European commercial interests would demand intervention for the imposition of order; but where local states kept effective control of the situation, as Austin shows in the case of Asante, this might provoke intervention in the interests of free trade. From this longer perspective, even a 'successful' response to the commercial transition, therefore, could be so only in the short term.

The difficulty here, it may be suggested, is not so much whether these problems have any bearing upon the ultimate Partition of West Africa, as what weight of emphasis to place upon them. It is possible to argue, as Lynn does in his contribution to this volume, that both the difficulties of West African rulers and their conflicts with European traders were due more to the decline of produce prices in the 'Great Depression' than to the original commercial transition. The Hopkins thesis, however, does not require a choice between the two, but a dialectical interaction between them.

Wider perspectives

In conclusion, it should be stressed that the debate on the impact of the commercial transition in nineteenth-century West Africa is, or should be, of interest to others than specialists in this particular region in this particular period. As Hopkins argues in his contribution to this volume, the topic has a broader relevance, both chronologically (in relation to longer-term issues of economic development in Africa) and geographically (by comparison with similar processes elsewhere in the world). As regards Africa's economic development, it is evident that the reality (if not the terminology) of 'imperialism', in the sense of the power relations between local and foreign governments (and also, nowadays, trans-governmental agencies, such as the World Bank) and the constraints in economic policy which these impose on the former, is as critical in the contemporary situation was it was in the nineteenth century. Moreover, the transition from the slave trade to 'legitimate' commerce, as is shown in this volume, raised questions about the relative advantages of large-and small-scale enterprise and about the role of the state in relation to the private sector, which were actively contested and debated on the African as well as the European side of the trading frontier, and which remain central to discussion of African economic development today. Indeed, if the analysis of commercial change in nineteenth-century West Africa is extended beyond the specific issue of changing export staples on which this volume focuses, to include the coincident (or rather, indirectly related) problems of currency instability (with the depreciation and ultimate collapse of local currencies, such as the cowry shell)[86] and of the expansion of European credit to African traders (with consequent conflicts over the enforcement of debt repayment),[87] the contemporary resonance of West Africa's nineteenth-century experience may well seem uncanny. If the present really can learn from the past, there must surely be lessons of significance here.

At the same time, what occurred in West Africa has to be seen against the wider background of commercial change and the growth of European imperialism throughout the world. This aspect of the question is explicitly explored in Tony Hopkins' contribution to this volume, which shows that the British government's promotion of commercial change on the western coast of Africa in the nineteenth century was merely one local application of a much wider project, applying to other regions of Africa and indeed to other continents, which sought to reconstruct the world in the image and interests of British liberal capitalism. Although the issue of the suppression of the Atlantic slave trade gave this process a special character in West Africa, British policy there had much in common with other areas of the world, and study of the West African case needs to be viewed in this broader context. The specificity of West Africa's experience will be clarified by a comparative perspective; and conversely, historians of other areas, and especially of other regions of Africa, may gain fruitful insights from more explicit and sustained engagement with the abundant literature which already exists on the 'crisis of adaptation' in West Africa.

NOTES

1　The term 'legitimate trade' is clearly open to objection, both because it is Eurocentric (since the slave trade itself initially remained 'legitimate' in African societies, although now illegal for Europeans), and because it tends to obscure the fact that commodities other than slaves (including agricultural produce such as palm oil) had been exported from Africa even before the legal abolition of the slave trade; it remains, however, so deeply embedded in the literature that it is difficult to avoid.

2　It should be acknowledged that the subject had also attracted some attention earlier, from historians working from an 'imperial' rather than an Africanist perspective: see esp. Allan McPhee, *The Economic Revolution in British West Africa* (London, 1926), ch. 2; W. K. Hancock, *Survey of British Commonwealth Affairs, Vol. II: Problems of Economic Policy 1918–1939, Part 2* (London, 1942), ch. 2.

3　Basil Davidson, *Black Mother: Africa, The Years of Trial* (London, 1961), pp. 222, 224.

4　K. O. Dike, *Trade and Politics in the Niger Delta 1830–1885* (Oxford, 1956).

5　Robin Law, 'The historiography of the commercial transition in nineteenth-century West Africa', in Toyin Falola (ed.), *African Historiography: Essays in Honour of Jacob Ade Ajayi* (Harlow, 1993), pp. 91–115.

6 A. G. Hopkins, 'Economic imperialism in West Africa: Lagos, 1880–92', *EHR*, 21 (1968), 580–606.

7 See esp. Martin Klein, 'Social and economic factors in the Muslim Revolution in Senegambia', *JAH*, 13 (1972), 419–41. The argument was already adumbrated, although not elaborated, in Klein, *Islam and Imperialism in Senegal: Sine-Saloum 1847–1914* (Edinburgh, 1968), pp. 44–5.

8 'Social and economic factors', p. 424.

9 A. G. Hopkins, *An Economic History of West Africa* (London, 1973), ch. 4.

10 See esp. David Eltis, *Economic Growth and the Ending of the Transatlantic Slave Trade* (Oxford, 1987), pp. 62–77. For a counter-argument, cf. Paul E. Lovejoy, 'The impact of the Atlantic slave trade on Africa: a review of the literature', *JAH*, 30 (1989), 365–94.

11 Ralph A. Austen, 'The abolition of the overseas slave trade: a distorted theme in West African history', *JHSN*, 5/2 (1970), 257–74; recently reiterated, in *African Economic History* (London, 1987), esp. pp. 101–2.

12 Hopkins, *Economic History*, pp. 145–7.

13 A. J. H. Latham, *Old Calabar 1600–1891: The Impact of the International Economy upon a Traditional Society* (Oxford, 1973).

14 See esp. Susan Hargreaves, 'The political economy of nineteenth-century Bonny: a study of power, authority, legitimacy and ideology in a Delta trading community from 1790–1914', PhD thesis, University of Birmingham, 1987. For Jaja, cf. also Sylvanus Cookey, *King Jaja of the Niger Delta: His Life and Times, 1821–1891* (New York, 1974). The dynamics of social mobility in the Delta, including the dependence of slaves on the permission and support of their owners to enter the palm oil trade, are also, in fact, clear from the contemporary published account (relating mainly to Brass) of C. N. de Cardi, 'A short description of the natives of the Niger Coast Protectorate', in Mary Kingsley (ed.), *West African Studies* (London, 1899), esp. pp. 471–2.

15 Hopkins' analysis of the transition in Yorubaland was criticized especially by J. F. Ade Ajayi and Ralph A. Austen, 'Hopkins on economic imperialism in Africa', *EHR*, 25 (1972), 303–6 (with rejoinder by Hopkins, ibid., 307–12). Klein's analysis of developments in Senegambia, however, is supported (or maybe repeated) in the most recent published research: Mamadou Diouf, *Le Kajoor au XIXe siècle: pouvoir ceddo et conquête coloniale* (Paris, 1990), esp. pp. 154–5, 293.

16 John Reid, 'Warrior aristocrats in crisis: the political effects of the transition from the slave trade to palm oil commerce in the nineteenth century kingdom of Dahomey', PhD thesis, University of Stirling, 1986; also Robin Law, 'Dahomey and the end of the Atlantic slave trade' (African Studies Center, Boston University, Working Papers in African Studies No. 165, 1992). See, however, the different emphasis of Elisée Soumonni, in this volume.

17 Patrick Manning, 'Slave trade, "legitimate" trade, and imperialism revisited: the control of wealth in the Bights of Benin and Biafra', in Paul E. Lovejoy (ed.), *Africans in Bondage: Studies in Slavery and the Slave Trade* (Madison, 1986), pp. 203–33.

18 Hopkins, *Economic History*, p. 140.

19 See, most recently, Eltis, *Economic Growth*, Appendix A, pp. 241–54.
20 Another instance was the recruitment of soldiers for the Dutch colonial army in Asante in 1831–42: Larry W. Yarak, *Asante and the Dutch 1744–1873* (Oxford, 1990), pp. 107–11.
21 See, most recently, Ralph A. Austen, 'The Mediterranean Islamic slave trade out of Africa: a tentative census', in Elizabeth Savage (ed.), *The Human Commodity: Perspectives on the trans-Saharan Slave Trade* (London, 1992), pp. 214–48.
22 Paul E. Lovejoy, *Transformations in Slavery: A History of Slavery in Africa* (Cambridge, 1983), ch. 8.
23 Latham, *Old Calabar*, pp. 92–5.
24 Austen, *African Economic History*, p. 102.
25 E.g. Lovejoy, *Transformations*, p. 139.
26 Samuel Crowther and John Taylor, *The Gospel on the Banks of the Niger* (London, 1859), p. 438.
27 Note, however, the arguments that at least certain specific *jihads* were themselves, in part, a consequence of the decline of the slave trade: see Martin Klein for Senegambia (cited above, n7) and Claude Meillassoux for the western Sudan more generally (below, n29).
28 Ivor Wilks, *Asante in the Nineteenth Century* (Cambridge, 1975), pp. 679–83.
29 Claude Meillassoux, *The Anthropology of Slavery* (Chicago, 1991), pp. 62–3. Meillassoux linked this need to increase the scale of slaving with the nineteenth-century *jihads*; see, however, criticisms of this view in Ann McDougall's contribution to this volume.
30 Parliamentary Papers [hereafter, PP]: Correspondence relating to the Slave Trade 1864, I, Inclosure 4 in No. 110: Commander Cochrane, Sierra Leone, 9 Jan. 1864.
31 Public Record Office, London: CO267/132, Governor Campbell, Freetown, 11 July 1836. Cf. the argument of MacGregor Laird and R. A. K. Oldfield, *Narrative of an Expedition into the Interior of Africa* (London, 1832), II, p. 361, that a slave retained in Africa could produce one ton of palm oil a year, which allegedly fetched twice as much as could be obtained by selling him for export (though this takes no account of the slave's subsistence costs).
32 Hopkins, *Economic History*, p. 142.
33 PP: Correspondence relating to the Slave Trade 1855–6, II, Inclosure in No. 17: S. B. Williams, Report [of Meeting 17–18 Sept. 1855].
34 Hugh Clapperton, *Journal of a Second Expedition into the Interior of Africa* (London, 1829), p. 33, referring to slave caravans going from Oyo to Badagry, speaks of 10–12 armed guards to each batch of fifty slaves.
35 This was the normal head-load of oil in Dahomey: Reid, 'Warrior Aristocrats', p. 346. On the Gold Coast, oil was transported in pots of 5–6 gallons: Brodie Cruickshank, *Eighteen Years on the Gold Coast of Africa* (London, 1853), II, p. 180. On the lower Niger, it was collected in gourds containing 2–4 gallons: Laird and Oldfield, *Narrative*, I, p. 103.
36 Laird and Oldfield, *Narrative*, I, p. 106, referring to Aboh. Elsewhere, the same source says that a ton of oil fetched twice as much as a slave, £8 as opposed to £4 (II, p. 361); but this seems to confuse the price of oil at the coast with that at Aboh, where it was only £4 per ton (cf. ibid., I, p. 103).

37 This ignores the fact that porters would receive pay as well as subsistence; on the other hand, slaves might be moved over longer distances.

38 In the early nineteenth century, the Bonny canoes sent up-country for slaves are described as capable of carrying 120 persons, but this figure presumably includes rowers as well as slaves: John Adams, *Remarks on the Country Extending from Cape Palmas to the River Congo* (London, 1823), p. 130. In the seventeenth century, Kalabari canoes carried 40 rowers, and had space for 60–80 additional passengers: Olfert Dapper, *Naukeurige Beschrijvinge der Afrikaensche Gewesten* (Amsterdam, 1668), quoted in Thomas L. Hodgkin, *Nigerian Perspectives* (2nd edn, London, 1975), p. 175.

39 Richard Burton, *Wanderings in West Africa* (London, 1863), II, p. 277. The size of a 'puncheon' varied, but at Bonny the standard puncheon was of 240 gallons, or three-quarters of a ton: ibid. II, p. 270.

40 Patrick Manning, *Slavery, Colonialism and Economic Growth in Dahomey 1640–1960* (Cambridge, 1982), p. 99; David Northrup, *Trade without Rulers: Pre-Colonial Economic Development in South-Eastern Nigeria* (Oxford, 1978), p. 186.

41 Hopkins, *Economic History*, p. 148.

42 Colin Newbury, *The Western Slave Coast and its Rulers* (Oxford, 1961), p. 87.

43 Marion Johnson, 'The Atlantic slave trade and the economy of West Africa', in Roger Anstey and P. E. H. Hair (eds.), *Liverpool, the African Slave Trade, and Abolition* (Historic Society of Lancashire and Cheshire, 1976), pp. 24–5.

44 Hopkins, *Economic History*, p. 125.

45 PP: Report from the Select Committee on the Slave Trade, 1848, Minutes of Evidence, 1638–9: Commander H. J. Matson; 2620, 2627: W. M. Hutton.

46 PP: Report from the Select Committee on the West Coast of Africa, 1842, Appendix No. 3: Report of Her Majesty's Commissioner of Inquiry on the State of the British Settlements on the Gold Coast, at Sierra Leone, and the Gambia, 1841, Appendix B, No. 22: Queries addressed to Captain Gentle Brown, 2 Feb. 1841.

47 Winwood Reade, *Savage Africa* (London, 1863), quoted in Hodgkin, *Nigerian Perspectives*, p. 347.

48 At least by the mid nineteenth century. But note that earlier in the century, oil is said to have been sold at Old Calabar by the 'tub, or crue, of ten gallons': Adams, *Remarks*, p. 247.

49 De Cardi, 'Short description', p. 472.

50 Newbury, *Western Slave Coast*, p. 59.

51 E.g. PP: Correspondence relating to the Slave Trade 1850–1, I, Inclosure 3 in No. 198, Lieutenant Forbes, At sea, 6 Apr. 1850.

52 Hope Masterton Waddell, *Twenty-Nine Years in the West Indies and Central Africa* (London, 1863), pp. 319–20.

53 PP: Correspondence relating to the Slave Trade 1862, II, Inclosures 2 & 4 in No. 44: Supercargoes in Old Calabar River, 28 Apr. 1862; Agreement between Supercargoes & Native Traders of Old Calabar, 5 May 1862 (article 13).

54 Treaty with Kings and Chiefs of Old Calabar, 6 Sept. 1878, text in Ekei

Essien Oku, *The Kings and Chiefs of Old Calabar (1785–1925)* (Calabar, 1989), pp. 257–61 (article IX); cf. Latham, *Old Calabar*, pp. 81–2.

55 PP: Correspondence relating to the Slave Trade 1856–7, II, No. 38: Consul Campbell, Lagos, 1 Oct. 1856; 1859–60, II, No. 1: and, 4 March 1859.

56 This episode is treated more fully in Martin Lynn, 'Technology, trade and "a race of native capitalists": the Krio diaspora of West Africa and the steamship, 1852–95', *JAH*, 33 (1992), 434–5.

57 Thomas J. Hutchinson, *Ten Years' Wandering among the Ethiopians* (London, 1861), p. 199.

58 See esp. Claire Robertson and Martin A. Klein (eds.), *Women and Slavery in Africa* (Madison, 1983).

59 PP: Report from the Select Committee on the State of the British Settlements on the Western Coast of Africa, 1865, Minutes of Evidence, 2167. Another report of this period claims that in Bonny 'an able-bodied slave is only calculated to stand three years' work in consequence of the ill-usage he receives': Correspondence relating to the Slave Trade 1862, I, No. 124: Commodore Edmonstone, Sierra Leone, 22 Oct. 1862.

60 Waddell, *Twenty-Nine Years*, p. 321.

61 See further Robin Law, 'Human sacrifice in pre-colonial West Africa', *African Affairs*, 84 (1985), 53–87.

62 This was not entirely new, since there had been European attempts to develop agricultural plantations using slave labour in West Africa even before the legal abolition of the slave trade: see, most recently, Robin Law, 'King Agaja of Dahomey, the slave trade and the question of West African plantations: the embassy of Bulfinch Lambe and Adomo Tomo to England, 1726–32', *JICH*, 19 (1991), 137–63.

63 David Birmingham, 'The coffee barons of Cazengo', *JAH*, 19 (1978), 523–38.

64 Karl Marx, *Capital*, I (London, 1974), p. 226.

65 De Cardi, 'Short description', p. 472. Theft of palm oil by slaves is also reported as a problem in Dahomey, as noted in Law's contribution to this volume.

66 This is at least broadly paralleled in Old Calabar, where in the later nineteenth century there was an effort by freemen to curb the influence of wealthy traders of slave origin, by asserting owners' rights to inherit slaves' estates on their deaths: Latham, *Old Calabar*, p. 102.

67 Laird and Oldfield, *Narrative*, I, 105.

68 As urged by Tony Hopkins, in his contribution to this volume.

69 Hopkins, *Economic History*, p. 143. The allusion is to Lawrence Stone, *The Crisis of the Aristocracy, 1558–1641* (Oxford, 1965); the parallel is not exact, since the English aristocracy were threatened by the growth of the central power of the state, rather than from below.

70 John Lonsdale, 'States and social processes in Africa: a historiographical survey', *African Studies Review*, 24 (1981), 180.

71 As argued by Claude Meillassoux, 'Introduction', in Meillassoux (ed.), *The Development of Trade and Markets in West Africa* (London, 1971), pp. 56–7.

72 Hopkins, *Economic History*, p. 145.

73 Quoted in Hopkins, *Economic History*, p. 142.

74 PP: Correspondence relating to the Slave Trade 1849–50, I, Inclosure 1 in
    No. 198: Journal of Lieutenant Forbes, 15 March 1850. For an attempt to
    assess state revenues from the palm oil trade in Dahomey in the 1850s
    (which supports the view that they were an inadequate substitute for the
    slave trade), see Reid, 'Warrior Aristocrats', pp. 353–8.
75 Reid, 'Warrior Aristocrats', pp. 489–93.
76 Soumonni here develops the argument originally articulated (in the case of
    Igboland) by David Northrup, 'The compatibility of the slave and palm oil
    trades in the Bight of Biafra', *JAH*, 17 (1976), 353–64.
77 See further Wilks, *Asante in the Nineteenth Century*, pp. 703–5, 712–17;
    Thomas J. Lewin, *Asante before the British: The Prempean years, 1875–1900*
    (Lawrence, Kansas, 1979), pp. 53–9.
78 Ken Swindell, 'SeraWoollies, Tillibunkas and strange farmers: the develop-
    ment of migrant groundnut farming along the Gambia River, 1848–95',
    JAH, 21 (1980), 93–104.
79 See Michael Mason, *The Foundations of the Bida Kingdom* (Zaria, 1981),
    p. 101.
80 In addition, gum was of significantly higher value relative to bulk than palm
    oil or groundnuts: see James L. A. Webb, Jr, 'The trade in gum arabic:
    prelude to French conquest in Senegal', *JAH*, 26 (1985), 149–68.
81 For the kola trade, see esp. Paul E. Lovejoy, *Caravans of Kola: The Hausa
    Kola Trade, 1700–1900* (Zaria, 1980). Like gum arabic, kola could bear the
    cost of long-distance transport because it had a high value relative to bulk.
82 Stephen Baier, 'Trans-Saharan trade and the Sahel: Damergu, 1870–1930',
    JAH, 18 (1977), 37–60.
83 The terminology seems infelicitous, because this sort of imperialism often
    involved formal agreements – such as the anti-slave trade treaties imposed
    on Lagos and Dahomey in 1852, or indeed (outside Africa) that imposing
    free trade in the Ottoman Empire in 1838, and the 'Unequal Treaties' with
    China in 1842 and 1860. It should also be stressed that the existence of a
    policy of 'informal imperialism' does not necessarily mean that an 'informal
    empire', in the sense of effective control, was actually established: on this, see
    Martin Lynn, 'The "Imperialism of Free Trade": and the case of West
    Africa, *c.*1830–*c.*1870', *JICH*, 15 (1986), 22–40.
84 Hopkins, *Economic History*, p. 156.
85 Suzanne Miers, *Britain and the Ending of the Slave Trade* (London, 1975).
86 See esp. Jan Hogendorn and Marion Johnson, *The Shell Money of the Slave
    Trade* (Cambridge, 1986); and more generally, Jane I. Guyer (ed.), *Money
    Matters: Instability, Values and Social Payments in the Modern History of
    West African Communities* (Portsmouth NH, 1994).
87 See esp. Colin Newbury, 'Credit in early nineteenth century West African
    trade', *JAH*, 13 (1972), 81–5.

1   The initial 'crisis of adaptation': the impact of British abolition on the Atlantic slave trade in West Africa, 1808–1820

Paul E. Lovejoy and David Richardson

Since 1956, when Dike argued that abolition involved 'a drastic change' for Africa, with Britain's withdrawal from slaving in 1807 precipitating 'an economic crisis among African traders',[1] the impact of British abolition on Africa has been the subject of controversy. What impact, if any, did British abolition have on the economies of West Africa? Most historians now agree that the transition from the export trade in slaves to the export of primary products such as palm oil, peanuts and gum arabic, was a major transformation in West Africa, which Hopkins equates with the emergence of the modern economy of West Africa.[2] There is, however, considerable disagreement over the timing and nature of economic change that was associated with this transition. Much of the recent scholarly literature has tended to agree with Dike that there were significant adjustments after 1807, but there is considerable doubt about the extent and timing of these adjustments. Whether or not they constitute a 'crisis' is another matter.

Much of this debate depends upon an analysis of the volume and value of the slave trade in the first half of the nineteenth century. It is now generally recognized that there was a sharp drop in the number of enslaved Africans leaving West Africa in the decade or two after 1807 and that the price for slaves at the Atlantic coast of Africa experienced a sudden drop in nominal and real terms during the same period. Average prices quickly fell to less than a quarter of their level in the decade before 1807. The numbers of slaves being exported to the Americas had been declining since about 1793 and after 1810 dropped even further, averaging in the 1810s only about half the level reached during the peak years of the 1780s. Such a drop in prices and volume usually indicates the onset of a major crisis for economies dependent upon revenues from the trade in commodities so affected, and it is therefore reasonable to hypothesize that British abolition may have caused severe economic dislocation in Africa. The purpose of this study is to identify where this crisis was concentrated and to determine how long it lasted.

As we demonstrate below, the trend in volume and prices applied unequally to different sections of the Atlantic coast of Africa, the price collapse being confined to West Africa and especially to the Gold Coast and the Bights of Benin and Biafra, where much of the decline in the volume of the trade was also concentrated. Slave prices did not drop in Senegambia, where prices remained relatively constant through c.1780–1830, perhaps even rising towards the end of this period. Prices held steady in Angola, too, as did the number of slaves being exported to the Americas. Prices at Angola neither experienced the rise to unprecedented heights as in West Africa in the decade before British abolition nor fell after 1807. When these regional variations are examined, it is clear that British abolition had a striking impact on the slave trade 'above the line', while Senegambia and the region 'below the line' that was exempt from naval intervention reveal no significant change in the volume or value of the export trade in slaves to the Americas. If there was a 'crisis of adaptation' at the time of British abolition, to use the phrase adopted by Hopkins, then it is to the Gold Coast and the Bights that we must look.

Based on our analysis of price data and export volume, we suggest that abolition had an initial severe impact on the commercial elites of the Gold Coast and the Bights in the form of a sudden decline in income from the trans-Atlantic slave trade. The severity of the decline in export earnings almost certainly had a strong, negative impact on the coastal economies and societies until the 1820s when real prices recovered strongly and the number of slaves being exported to the Americas, particularly in the Bights, also increased to former levels. The lower slave prices that characterized the slave trade on the Gold Coast and in the Bights of Benin and Biafra prevailed for only a decade or two, therefore. This initial 'crisis of adaptation' to British abolition of the trans-Atlantic slave trade was localized and relatively brief.

Prices for slaves at the Atlantic coast of Africa, 1783–1850

The trend in the price of slaves at the Atlantic coast of Africa between 1783 and 1850 suggests that there was a steep rise in prices in the eighteenth century, followed by a sudden collapse after 1807. Slave prices were relatively steady at £5–6 in the first half of the eighteenth century but then rose sharply during the period after 1760. In 1783–7, current prices at the Atlantic coast of Africa averaged £15.6, rising to £33.2 in the years preceding British abolition in 1807.[3] This rapid increase in the average price of slaves at the African coast reflected the great expansion of sugar production in the West Indies before 1793 and then the uncertainties of war and the anticipated abolition of the British slave trade in 1807. After abolition, prices dropped to a quarter of the level of

1803–7; the average cost of slaves in 1815–1825 was £8.5. Current prices remained low, fluctuating between approximately £8 and £11 until 1850.[4]

This trend in current prices has led some scholars to conclude that prices for slaves never regained their high levels. Thus Eltis has contended that the fall in slave prices in Africa was both substantial and permanent after 1807, but he believes that this collapse had very little impact on Africa because the slave trade was marginal to the exporting economies.[5] For Eltis, there was no crisis following abolition. By contrast, Manning and Lovejoy have argued that the drop in the prices for slaves shipped to the Americas made available a reservoir of slaves for redeployment in the internal economy of West Africa.[6] Low prices for slaves fuelled the domestic economies of the region, thereby averting an economic crisis in the adjustment to abolition. Whether the trans-Atlantic slave trade is considered marginal or significant, both interpretations use price data to demonstrate that there was no serious economic crisis after 1807. Based on our analysis of slave prices, we would modify these interpretations of abolition by arguing that large-scale use of slaves in the domestic economies of the major states of West Africa predated abolition and that the transformation to which Manning and Lovejoy have alluded began some time before 1807. In this respect the export slave trade to America was by 1800 an extension of a large domestic market for slaves within West Africa itself.

The movement in the current prices for slaves is not an accurate indicator of the trend in the real value of slaves, as determined by the goods that were exchanged for slaves. To assess the trend in slave prices more accurately and thereby assess the impact of British abolition on the export of slaves to the Americas, we calculated the real prices for slaves based on the years 1783–87 (table 1.1). An examination of this series suggests that prices collapsed after 1807 but very soon regained levels that were similar to those before 1807. From a level of £14.8 in the mid-1780s, the average price of slaves rose to £21–22 in the decade before British abolition in 1807, but fell to £9.4 in 1815–20. Thereafter, prices rose again to £12.9 in 1821–5 and further to £18.3 in 1826–30. By the 1840s, real prices continued to be higher than the peak years of the trans-Atlantic slave trade in the 1780s.

Moreover, slave prices varied considerably among regions of the Atlantic coast of Africa, and hence the trend in real prices disguises regional differences. For instance, the slave prices in Angola provided by Miller and Curto did not decline after 1807. Slave prices at Luanda tended to remain steady between the 1780s and early 1820s and then began to move upward.[7] Angolan prices were about £12.2 in 1783–7, rising slightly in the next decade, and averaging between £13 and £14

Table 1.1 *Slave prices (£ sterling) on the Atlantic coast of Africa, 1783–1850*

Period	Current price West Africa	Real prices West Africa	Real prices Atlantic Coast
1783–87	15.6	15.6	14.8
1788–92	19.5	19.1	17.6
1793–97	18.0	17.5	16.8
1798–1802	27.3	23.3	21.0
1803–7	33.2	25.3	22.3
1808–14	17.2	14.2	13.9
1815–20	8.5	7.7	9.4
1821–5	8.5	11.0	12.9
1826–30	11.5	17.2	18.3
1831–5	7.5	12.9	12.9
1836–40	10.0	18.5	18.5
1841–5	8.2	16.7	16.7
1846–50	11.3	23.1	23.1

Sources: Paul E. Lovejoy and David Richardson, 'British Abolition and its impact on slave prices along the Atlantic coast of Africa, 1783–1850', *JEH*, forthcoming. Current prices are converted to real prices based on the evidence of Ralph Davis on market prices of exports and re-exports at 10 yearly intervals, beginning in 1784–6 and ending in 1854–6 (*The Industrial Revolution and British Overseas Trade* (Leicester, 1979), p. 86). We used his prices for 1784–6 to deflate slave prices in 1783–7; prices for 1794–6 to deflate slave prices for 1793–7; and so on. To deflate slave prices in the intervening periods we took the average of the 10-yearly prices.

through 1807, remaining at that level until *c*.1820. Prices then increased to £18.7 in 1821–5 and £21.6 in 1826–30. Since Angola and the region of west-central Africa in general exported more slaves to the Americas in the nineteenth century than all of West Africa, the trend in prices recorded for Angola is particularly significant in analysing the impact of British abolition on the trans-Atlantic slave trade. Since Angola diverged from the trend, then the trend must have been set in West Africa, and indeed have been more pronounced there. That is, slave prices rose more steeply in West Africa in the late eighteenth century and fell more steeply after 1807 than for the trans-Atlantic trade as a whole.

Not all West Africa followed the same trend. Data on Senegambia compiled by Curtin suggest that real slave prices at St Louis and Gorée averaged around £27 in the 1780s and 1790s, dropping only slightly in the 1810s and early 1820s, before rising sharply after 1826, reaching over £40 in 1827–8 and seemingly averaging well over £30 during the 1830s.[8] Prices were noticeably higher than elsewhere on the Atlantic coast. None the less, prices appear to have fluctuated considerably. Mollien was under the impression that slave prices had dropped in 1818. He learned that 'Moors' from the desert were paying only half the amount for slaves that European merchants had paid before abolition.[9] Whether or not there was a temporary decline in slave prices here, it should be observed that, unlike Angola, Senegambia sent very few slaves across the Atlantic and therefore did not affect the general pattern of export prices very much. The high local prices probably were a major factor in keeping the volume of slave exports across the Atlantic at a modest level.

By contrast with Angola and Senegambia, slave prices elsewhere at the West African coast rose from an average of £15.6 in 1783–7 to a peak of £23–25 in 1798–1807. The collapse in prices in the next decade was considerable, reaching a low of £7.7 in 1815–20, about half the level in Angola at the same time. Thereafter, real prices rose to £11 in the first half of the 1820s and over £17 in the second half of the decade. Despite a modest reduction in the early 1830s, the price of slaves at the West African coast continued to rise through 1850.

The sharp drop in prices after 1807 which is reflected in our price data was of relatively short duration. Although an English traveller observed in 1817 that Portuguese and Spanish traders had taken advantage of 'the drop in purchases and prices occasioned in Africa by the withdrawal of the English', paying £2 to £5 per slave at the coast, he believed that the 'fall was only temporary'.[10] The impact of this fall in prices was felt some distance inland. Slaves could be bought in Asante in 1817 for 2,000 cowries, or about $1. So many slaves were said to be on the market at the capital, Kumasi, that there were fears of a slave uprising.[11] As van Dantzig has observed, 'after the abolition of the slave trade [in 1807], a glut developed ... on the Kumasi slave market'.[12] Coinciding with the first Asante-British war in 1806, abolition is seen by some therefore to have caused considerable short-term dislocation on the Gold Coast.[13] According to figures collected by LaTorre, prices fell to as low as 1.2 gold *agyiratwefa*, or 0.9 oz. trade, in Asante in 1817, but in Fante markets and Accra slave prices were 24 *agyiratwefa* (18 oz.) and at ports east of the Volta stood at 38 *agyiratwefa* (28.5 oz.) in the same year. These compare with prices for adult males at Cape Coast and Anomabo of 8–12 oz. in 1783–1803.[14]

LaTorre's series suggests that prices in Asante collapsed in the early nineteenth century but rebounded by the early 1820s at the latest. By 1823, prices had risen to 6 gold *agyiratwefa* (4.5 oz.), and by 1836 had once again reached no less than 24–32 *agyiratwefa* (18–24 oz.). Prices at Fante markets and Accra had risen to 30–40 *agyiratwefa* (22–30 oz.) by 1840–1, while prices at ports east of the Volta ranged between 30–54 *agyiratwefa* (22–40 oz.). Over the long run slave prices at the Gold Coast,

Asante and adjacent areas appear to have recovered by 1818, with prices rising even higher than those of 1783–1803.[15] It should be noted that these price increases were unrelated to the trans-Atlantic trade, since the Gold Coast no longer exported slaves to the Americas. Asante sent a few slaves to Whydah for export, but overall the price rise on the Gold Coast and in Asante reflected local demand, not the export trade.

While we think that slave prices fluctuated most on the Gold Coast and in the Bights, the price of slaves, in bars, on the upper Guinea coast also declined somewhat after 1807–8. At least, the fall in price at the Galinhas was by no means as severe as that reported elsewhere on the coast.[16] Most slave exports from West Africa after 1807 came from the Bights of Benin and Biafra, which were the areas that experienced the sharpest drop in prices. Hence, if there was a 'crisis of adaptation' in the decade or so following British abolition, it is to the Bights of Benin and Biafra that we must look. The fact that the Gold Coast no longer exported slaves in appreciable numbers is sufficient proof of a crisis in Asante.

Demography of slave exports from West Africa reconsidered

In light of the identification of the Gold Coast and the Bights of Benin and Biafra as the principal areas affected by the rise in prices in 1783–1807 and the dramatic collapse in the decade or so after 1807, it is worthwhile to reconsider the demographic patterns that characterized the trans-Atlantic slave trade from West Africa in this period. After peaking at almost 47,000 slaves per year in the last quarter of the eighteenth century, slave shipments from West Africa fell back to 27,000 a year in the second decade of the nineteenth century, before rising again to about 34,000 a year by the end of the 1820s. The total number of slaves exported in the four decades before British abolition was considerably higher than the number exported in the four decades following abolition, the volume declining almost a quarter from 1,312,000 to 986,000. The Bights of Benin and Biafra accounted for a considerable proportion of these exports, together providing almost two-thirds of the total before 1807 and three-quarters after 1807.[17] Slave departures from the Bights declined 26 per cent from a peak of 346,300 slaves in the 1780s to 256,300 slaves in the 1790s. The fall in the volume of exports continued into the first decade of the nineteenth century; the number of exported slaves fell an additional 22 per cent to 198,700 in the 1800s and a further 5 per cent to 187,500 in the 1810s, which was a little over half the number of slaves deported from the Bights in the 1780s. Because of rising prices, the value of the trade remained high through 1807 even though fewer slaves were being exported.

The decline in the volume of the slave trade can be attributed to the elimination of French and Dutch shipping during the Wars of the French Revolution and the successful slave revolt in St Domingue in the 1790s, which reduced demand. The French and Dutch had been major carriers of slaves in the eighteenth century, particularly on the Gold Coast and in the Bight of Benin. Their absence after 1793 reduced the carrying capacity of the trade. Until 1807 British and USA shipping was able to replace much of this lost capacity, but the trade could not withstand the pressures of British and USA withdrawal after 1807. The decade following 1807 was, therefore, a critical period of adjustment in West Africa. Of the various changes between the early 1790s and 1807, British abolition was clearly the most significant factor in the collapse of the trade.

The slight decline in the number of slaves exported in the second decade of the nineteenth century (a 5 per cent reduction over the first decade) in the context of the virtual collapse in prices suggests that there was a substantial supply of slaves in the interior of the Bights. That is, the drop in price has to be explained in terms of virtually constant external demand. Seen in this light, the price collapse indicates a sudden infusion of slaves on the market, which is not surprising given the intense fighting of the Sokoto *jihad* between 1804–12 and again in 1817, the intermittent slave-raiding in other years in the far interior and the annual slave-raids of Dahomey and Oyo in the south. There are indications that the trans-Saharan trade to the north was also substantial in this period. The existence of these alternative markets makes the price drop appear even more pronounced.

By the 1820s, the volume of the export trade from the Bights recovered, but apparently a rise in demand for slaves within West Africa limited the availability of slaves for export, thus putting upward pressure on prices at the coast. In the 1820s, 242,000 slaves were exported to the Americas from the Bights while in the 1830s another 200,800 slaves left. Thereafter, the Bight of Biafra was no longer a significant factor in the export trade in slaves; 98,700 of the 110,800 slaves exported from the Bights in the 1840s came from the Bight of Benin.[18] The rise in real prices, in the context of the revival of the number of slaves exported to the Americas, suggests that internal demand and the external market were combining to push prices up. With the break-up of the Oyo Empire, the resultant dislocation of population, endemic warfare and the aggression of the Sokoto Caliphate, there is every reason to believe that the supply of slaves continued to be substantial.

The long-term trend is clear. The number of slaves leaving the Bights peaked in the 1780s, experienced a steady decline through the 1810s, and recovered to levels in the 1820s and 30s that were comparable to those at the peak of the trade. A final decline occurred in the 1840s and 50s. As a comparison of these figures with the trend in prices indicates, the slave trade from the Bights was declining exactly at the time when the price of slaves was increasing on two occasions, first in the 1790s and then again in the 1830s and 40s. Whereas declining slave volumes had been matched by rising prices before 1807, British abolition ushered in a decade or more of low volume and low prices. Slave prices recovered their previous levels by the 1820s at the same time as the number of slaves being exported also rose, so that export earnings from the trade were also restored, at least until the 1830s in the Bight of Biafra and in the Bight of Benin for the 1840s as well. Earnings from the slave trade by interior states, particularly the Sokoto Caliphate, apparently were substantial for the whole period.

The rise in coastal slave prices after 1783 and especially in 1795–1807 corresponded with the diminishing importance of the region as a source of slaves in the trade as a whole. Overall exports were tailing off by 1793–1807. However, the fact that prices were rising suggests that there were constraints on slave supply, including the possibility of rising internal demand for slaves. One result of this rise in prices was to encourage the inward expansion of slaving. Beginning in the 1770s and 1780s, slaves from the Central Sudan became a recognizable category of the exported population for the first time, distinguished usually as Hausa, Nupe or Borno and occasionally as Muslims. Moreover, the vast majority of these exported slaves from the far interior were adult males.

The re-export of male slaves from the interior through the Bight of Benin was part of a trend towards higher proportions of males in the trans-Atlantic slave trade. By the end of the eighteenth century, increasing numbers of males comprised the slave cargoes destined for the Americas. The ratio of males in slave cargoes rose from 0.66 in the eighteenth century to 0.71 in the nineteenth century at the Bight of Benin. Comparable figures for Upper Guinea were 0.61 in the eighteenth century, increasing to 0.68 in the nineteenth century, while in the Bight of Biafra the proportion of males rose from 0.57 to 0.65. For the Bight of Benin, at least, the higher proportion of males in the nineteenth century included re-exports from the interior.[19]

Recognizable numbers of slaves from the far interior first appear with the increase in coastal slave prices in the 1770s and 1780s. Before c.1780, very few slaves from the far interior appear to have boarded ships for the Americas. By c.1790 through 1825, as many as 25 per cent of the slaves leaving the Bight of Benin were identified as Hausa, Nupe or some other ethnicity from the Central Sudan.[20] Moreover, these slaves tended to be prime adult males in their 'teens or early twenties. Information on the age and gender composition of the exported slave population between c.1805–50 indicates that approximately 95 per cent of the exported slaves were adult males. The total number of slaves from the Central Sudan who were transported to the Americas in the nineteenth century may have reached 200,000.

Bearing in mind that slaves from the Central Sudan who left the Bight of Benin for the Americas were almost entirely adult males, it is possible to draw a more accurate picture of the age and gender structure of the exported slave population whose origins were from areas near the coast. Virtually all of the women and children who were exported from the Bight of Benin in the late eighteenth and early nineteenth centuries came from near the coast. The proportion of children was increasing dramatically. The ratio of children among slave cargoes in the Bight of Benin before 1810 was only 0.17, doubling to 0.33 for the period after 1810. Other exporting areas in West Africa experienced this shift to more children; the proportion of children among the exported slaves rose from 0.25 to 0.40 on the upper Guinea coast, and from 0.21 to 0.36 at the Bight of Biafra. In general, therefore, the proportions of slave children exported from West Africa rose by some 70–95 per cent after 1810, with the proportion of boys rising faster than that of girls. Since virtually none of these child slaves came from the far interior, the supply of slaves from near the coast was even more balanced in terms of age and gender than the total figures for the Bight of Benin indicate.

By contrast, the interior trade was skewed towards adult males and hence was more in line with the usual pattern in the international flow of unfree labour, as analysed by Eltis and Engerman.[21] The proportion of interior slaves in the total number of slaves exported from the Bight of Benin and the Gold Coast seems to have been especially significant in 1790–1825, before the surge in Yoruba war prisoners arising from the collapse of Oyo. The women and children exported in the 1820s and 1830s account in large measure for the increase in slave exports in these years. Their presence in the exported population indicates that local African merchants could not supply enough prime male slaves for export, despite the operation of a trade in this very category of slave from the Central Sudan. Even though the recovery in prices from the mid-1820s provided an incentive for maintaining and even increasing the flow of prime adult male slaves, many women and children from near the coast were sold off. The flow of adult males from the far interior, corresponding as it did with higher prices for slaves, appears to have been a major factor in the determination of export earnings for African merchants after 1825. Of course, this re-export trade was an important dimension of the internal trade of West Africa as well. It drew on the domestic demand for slaves of any age and both genders and balanced the trans-Saharan demand for pretty girls and young women.

The penetration of the slave catchment area inland checked the demographic shift to a younger population being exported from the Bights to some extent but accentuated its increasing maleness. The increased proportion of males in the exported population included the high concentration of males from the Central Sudan, but the trend towards a younger population reflected a great increase in the number of children for sale near the coast. The far interior had a negative impact on this trend. The trade from the interior began as a highly specialized trade in prime adult males in the late eighteenth century and continued as such after *jihad* erupted in the Central Sudan in 1804. Thereafter, the expansion and consolidation of the Sokoto Caliphate was associated with the export of adult males, often war captives of the *jihad*. The availability of these prime slaves probably contributed to the recovery of the slave trade in the Bights of Benin and Biafra after the lean years of the 1810s. Prime males from the interior continued to represent a substantial proportion of adult male exports from the Bight of Benin for several decades thereafter.

Crisis and recovery, 1807–1850

The most obvious consequence of abolitionist measures in 1807–8 was a sharp drop in West African export earnings from slaves. Despite the price recovery by the 1820s, total earnings for slave exporters in the Bights must have been down considerably, with losses being heaviest in the 1810s and earnings off significantly after the virtual withdrawal of the Bight of Biafra from the trans-Atlantic slave trade in the 1840s. A precise calculation of such losses is impossible, for data on regional slave prices are weak and figures on slave exports from individual regions are less than perfect. Moreover, we do not know what exports and prices would have been in the absence of abolition in 1807. If, however, we assume equality in prices across regions and, without abolition, exports and prices at the same levels prevailing in the 1780s and 90s, then we may estimate that abolition reduced earnings from slave exports in the second decade of the nineteenth century by nearly 60 per cent in upper Guinea and the Bight of Benin and by as much as 85 per cent at the Bight of Biafra. In the case of the first two regions, the fall in earnings occurred despite maintaining slave shipments roughly at pre-abolition levels. On the Gold Coast, almost all the revenue earned from exporting slaves, amounting to perhaps £150,000 or more a year in the 1790s and first few years of the nineteenth century, was lost after abolition.[22] Overall, earnings from slave exports to America from the four principal slave-exporting regions in West Africa in 1807 may have fallen by about three-quarters, with slave exporters at the Gold Coast and the Bight of Biafra bearing the largest losses.

Such calculations are, of course, extremely crude. But if the trans-Atlantic traffic in slaves was a vital source of state revenues and private wealth in some of the major states of West Africa at this time, it is difficult to believe that losses of export earnings on such a scale did not produce severe short-term economic and political problems. All the states in the immediate interior of the Gold Coast and the Bights of Benin and Biafra appear to have experienced political unrest in this period. In 1806, Asante fought a war with Britain over relations with the Fante states, whereafter Asante economic policy was directed at developing its northern trade. The emergence of a Muslim faction in Asante attests to the success of Asante in redirecting its economy northward.[23] Similarly, the 'reign of terror' preceding Ghezo's *coup d'état* in Dahomey in 1818 may well have related to the economic strain caused by the collapse in slave prices in the Bight of Benin.[24] And it is likely that economic crisis exacerbated the constitutional troubles of Oyo in the first two decades of the nineteenth century. The culmination of these troubles was Afonja's attempted *coup d'état* and the uprising of Muslim slave soldiers at Ilorin in 1817.[25] In the Bight of Biafra, the first two decades of the nineteenth century are associated with the emergence of the large canoe-houses, which may well be associated with the shift to palm oil in the 1820s. By abolishing its own slave trade in 1807 and seeking to suppress the trade of other nations after 1815, Britain appears to have contributed to the political and financial crises of several states in West Africa.

The available data on slave exports and prices suggests that some easing of the problems facing slave exporters may have occurred after about 1820, particularly for those in the Bight of Benin and Bight of Biafra. Thus, as table 1.2 shows, real prices of slaves at the coast tended to rise quite sharply in the 1820s. Similarly, figures compiled by Eltis show that exports of slaves in the Bight of Benin remained buoyant after 1820.[26] The earnings of exporters at the Bight of Benin perhaps matched pre-abolition levels in the late 1820s. The real price of slaves rose further in the late 1830s and 1840s, which helped to maintain earnings from the export of slaves at high levels through to 1850. Exports from the Bight of Biafra reached their post-1807 peak in the decade or so after 1824,

Table 1.2   *Real prices of slaves, West Africa and Angola, 1783–1830* *(£ sterling, base 1783–7)*

Period	West Africa	Angola	Atlantic coast
1783–1787	15.6	12.2	14.8
1788–1792	19.1	13.3*	17.6
1793–1797	17.5	14.6*	16.8
1798–1802	23.3	13.9	21.0
1803–1807	25.3	13.1	22.3
1808–1814	14.2	12.9	13.9
1815–1820	7.7	14.6	9.4
1821–1825	11.0	18.7	12.9
1826–1830	17.2	21.6	18.3

Sources: Lovejoy and Richardson, 'Slave prices along the Atlantic coast of Africa, 1783–1850'. Interpolated prices are indicated with an asterisk.

but earnings appear never to have fully recovered. By 1830, slave-exporters at the Bight of Biafra seem to have received about three times the level of their earnings in the 1810s (though still only about half of their level before 1807). These relatively low earnings may account for the willingness of exporters to shift from slaves to palm oil in the 1820s and 30s. The partial recovery in slave exports by the early 1830s was not sufficient to halt the move to palm oil, which now replaced slaves as the principal export. Earnings at the Bight of Biafra remained at about the level reached around 1830 until the final collapse of slave exports from the region after 1840.

In summary, the Gold Coast failed after 1807 to achieve significant earnings from supplying slaves to the Americas, but improvements in coastal prices of slaves combined with modest increases in slave shipments brought about major recoveries in earnings from slave exports in 1820–40 at the Bight of Benin and the Bight of Biafra. Moreover, at the Bight of Benin this recovery extended through to 1850, while at the Bight of Biafra increased earnings from slave exports were supplemented by earnings from exports of palm oil by the 1830s. Central to the recovery of income from slave sales was an increase in slave prices, with prices rising particularly strongly in 1826–30, 1836–40 and 1846–50. Along the upper Guinea coast, earnings from slave exports appear to have risen in the 1820s after a decade or so of relatively low export levels, even surpassing their pre-abolition levels in the late 1830s.

The movements in prices in 1820–50, like those before and after 1807, partly reflected events outside Africa. Slave-exporters at the coast benefited from rising industrial productivity in Britain and improvements in Afro-European terms of trade that derived from this productivity and cheaper transport costs on the Atlantic. These helped to cushion the effects of British and USA abolition on slave-dealers. As earlier, the periods of major price increases at the coast after 1807 coincided to some degree with increases in prices of imported slaves at Cuba, Bahia and Rio de Janeiro, the principal markets for African slaves in America after 1815.[27] In this respect trends in African slave prices after 1820 paralleled changes in 1793–1807, when a surge in coastal prices mirrored increases in slave prices in the British Caribbean islands.[28]

The coastal prices of slaves after 1820 were not solely determined by changes in Afro-European terms of trade or demand for slave labour in Cuba and Brazil, however. As noted above, slave prices seem to have risen sharply in Asante during the 1820s and 30s despite the fact that trans-Atlantic shipments of slaves from the Gold Coast had largely ceased by 1807. Unlike in the Bights of Benin and Biafra, the recovery of prices in Asante was probably related to changes in the domestic economy and the development of export sectors to the north after 1815.[29] Because Asante was able to export kola nuts and purchase imports from Europe with gold, the decline of the trans-Atlantic slave trade was minimized accordingly. Furthermore, kola and gold production seem to have depended heavily on slave and pawn labour.

British and USA abolition appear to have caused fewer problems in Senegambia than in other regions because the Atlantic slave trade was not very important.[30] The interior market for slaves, which was closely connected with Saharan and trans-Saharan demand, was apparently much larger than the trans-Atlantic trade. As data from Gajaaga demonstrates, there was considerable stability in prices for slaves in the interior. African merchants are reported to have charged £7–9 per slave in 1785–6, a level maintained through 1814–26, whereafter the price rose to £11–15 per slave in the late 1820s.[31] Furthermore, the region had historically produced a range of exports other than slaves and, in addition to the Atlantic, its 'shore' facing the Sahara provided access to markets for slaves in and across the desert.[32] Exports of gum from Senegambia rose sharply, from £10,000 per year in the 1780s to £250,000 a year in the 1830s, in response to buoyant international prices. This in turn probably led to an expansion in internal demand for slaves as gum production depended heavily on slave labour.[33] At the same time, the trans-Saharan trade appears to have expanded. Because some reorientation of the Senegambian economy was already taking place before 1807, adjustments to further falls in trans-Atlantic slave shipments were perhaps less difficult than in other parts of West Africa.

Available evidence points to the likelihood that slave prices remained relatively stable at markets throughout the interior of West Africa between about 1780 and 1850, not just at Gajaaga in Senegambia. Prices were most often quoted in silver dollars, usually Maria Theresa thalers or Spanish dollars, or in cowry shells, which also circulated widely in the interior. According to our calculations, prices for females ranged from $15–25 (£3–5) for much of the period from 1780–1850, with prices falling below this range in the region of the Niger-Benue confluence in the early 1840s and rising to as much as twice these levels in some years. Prices for males were consistently less than for females, although these also fluctuated, generally between $10–15 (£2–3), but falling as low as $5–7 (£1–1.5) in some years, especially in the early to mid-1840s.[34]

As these prices reveal, female slaves tended to fetch much higher prices than males in the interior markets. By comparison, prices of males were almost invariably higher than for females at the coast of West Africa. Given that the labour of women, slave and free, probably underpinned much agricultural production in West Africa, including production of export crops such as palm oil, the existence of premiums on prices of female slaves within West Africa would suggest that the Atlantic slave trade had to compete to some degree with an internal and probably expanding market for slaves by the early nineteenth century, if not earlier. At the very least, therefore, internal demand for slaves, as Manning has observed, may have placed a floor under export prices of slaves in West Africa by the nineteenth century.[35] By competing with overseas buyers, rising demand for slaves within West Africa increased inflationary pressures on slave prices at the coast.

If we are right in concluding that the real price for slaves in the Bights of Benin and Biafra returned to previous levels by the 1820s, then the interpretations of some scholars of the impact of abolition on West African society and economy have to be revised. Abolition may have been a factor in the shift of newly enslaved Africans from the export sector to the domestic economy, but it appears that there was already a large, internal trade for slaves before abolition. Hence, the 'transformation' of the 'social formation' into one based largely on slave labour appears to antedate abolition. The collapse in the price of slaves at the Atlantic coast of Africa was temporary, thereby making available low-cost slaves for local use for a brief period, but by the 1820s internal demand, in combination with the recovery in the volume of slave exports to the Americas, was sufficient to drive prices back up to previous levels.[36]

In the light of the price data, it appears that the internal economies of West Africa were able to absorb substantial numbers of new slaves who were regularly captured in raids, kidnapping and war. Evidence of relative stability in the price of slaves in the interior during the first half of the nineteenth century suggests that there was little if any difficulty in adjusting to the vicissitudes in price and volume of the trans-Atlantic trade. Unfortunately, there are few data on the crucial decade after 1807 and hence it is not possible at this stage of research to determine whether or not the rise in slave prices in $c.1785-1807$ and sudden collapse of prices after 1807 was reflected in the slave markets of the interior of West Africa. Available evidence does not preclude such an inference, but all that can be concluded at this point in research is that if the 'crisis of adaptation' extended into the interior, it was largely over there in the 1820s as well.[37]

The West African slave trade: external and internal sectors

The relative size of the internal and external markets for West African slaves remains unclear and is a continuing source of debate among historians. However, contemporary reports suggest that in some places slaves may have constituted a third or even a half of the population before 1850.[38] Moreover, expanding production of commercial crops, whether for export overseas, as in the case of gum arabic and palm oil, or consumption within West Africa, as in the case of kola nuts, grain and cotton, provided a major impetus to slavery within Africa in the nineteenth century, precisely at the time that British and USA abolition came into effect.[39] Plantation production of crops with slaves employed as agricultural labourers was widespread, especially in the major states, although the development of this sector is poorly documented. Slaves were also used extensively in many capacities other than agricultural labour. They were particularly important in the transport of crops to market and in the gathering and distribution of firewood, thatch, fertilizer and water. The indigenous textile industry employed slaves at many levels of production, especially in growing cotton and indigo and in carding and spinning. Slave-holding within the households of merchants (and merchant-princes in coastal societies) seems to have increased with the growth of commercial agriculture, especially in the towns along the trade routes of the interior. Indeed, the Sokoto Caliphate and other Muslim states of the interior depended extensively on slave labour, besides exporting slaves into and across the Sahara and southward to the states bordering the Guinea coast. The scale of the internal traffic in slaves that was required for the expansion of agricultural production and other activities in the nineteenth century must have been considerable.

The rise of palm oil exports, the major 'legitimate' export from West

Africa by 1850, suggests that the market for slaves within the Bight of Biafra, the principal exporter of oil before 1850, probably was large enough to influence the export price of slaves in 1820–50. The oil trade grew substantially both in volume and value from 1820–50, with ports in the Niger Delta supplying perhaps 85 per cent of all palm oil exports from Africa in the late 1820s and about three-quarters in the 1840s, the relative decline largely reflecting the entry of the Bight of Benin into the export market.[40] Among the Delta ports, Old Calabar was the leading oil port before 1830, but was then overtaken by Bonny and Kalabari. Together the last two supplied over half of West African palm oil exports between the 1830s and the early 1850s. The oil was shipped to Europe, and some may have gone to Bahia, particularly after the Bight of Benin became an important producer in the 1840s. Because Britain, and especially Liverpool, was, in Hopkins' words, 'by far the largest importer of palm oil in Europe',[41] figures on British oil imports from West Africa probably provide a reasonably reliable indicator of trends in oil exports from West Africa, particularly the Bight of Biafra, up to the 1840s. Indirectly, the rise in these figures at a time when slave prices were high is a measure of the local demand for slaves.

Between 1815–20 and 1846–50, the volume of British oil imports from West Africa rose from less than 2,000 tons a year to over 22,000 tons. During the same period, the value of oil imports rose from about £90,000 to £725,000 a year.[42] Prices of palm oil in Britain reached a pre-1850 peak in 1818–19, when they averaged £47–64 per ton. They then declined sharply to about £23–27 per ton in the early 1820s, before stabilizing at this level for the rest of the decade. Prices then rose to over £31 per ton in 1831 and apart from 1834–5 and 1843–5 remained at or over £30 per ton through to 1850, reaching peaks of over £40 per ton in 1838–9. On the whole therefore palm oil prices in Britain were higher in the 1830s and 1840s than in the 1820s but lower than in the years immediately after 1815. Significantly, particularly sharp increases in the value of oil imports into Britain occurred in 1826–30, 1832–3, 1835–9 and 1844–7. Evidence presented in table 1.1 shows that slave prices at the coast of West Africa also rose in some of these years, notably in the late 1820s, the late 1830s and the mid- to late 1840s. These figures on the value of British imports are only an imperfect indicator of earnings from oil by African exporters, since British prices include transport and other costs.

Although the data are sparse, there are some coastal prices of oil, f.o.b, that allow an estimate of African earnings from oil exports. At Calabar oil cost about £7–15 per ton in 1820–1, £5–14 per ton in 1832, and £7–11 per ton in 1836–9, while prices were £17–20 per ton at Bonny in 1839–40.[43] Why prices at Bonny were higher than at Calabar is unknown, but on the basis of the available data it appears that coastal prices of oil at Calabar were about 20–40 per cent of Liverpool prices around 1820, 15–40 per cent in 1832 and 18–28 per cent in the late 1830s, while prices at Bonny in 1839–40 were just over 50 per cent of Liverpool prices. Mark-ups on prices between Calabar and Liverpool appear to have risen between 1820 and 1840, but since the amount of oil shipped from Bonny increased after about 1830 the overall mark-up on oil between the Delta ports and Liverpool perhaps changed little, with income from palm oil in the Bight of Biafra averaging about 30–40 per cent of the value of British oil imports between 1815 and 1850. Based on these figures, income from oil at the Bight of Biafra may have been about £30,000 a year in the late 1810s, rising to £55–70,000 a year in the late 1820s, before reaching £160–210,000 a year in the late 1830s, a level that was apparently maintained through to 1850. It is not possible to disaggregate the figures for West Africa, but it seems reasonable to assume that most of the additional income from oil in the 1840s probably accrued to merchants in the Bight of Benin. It should, however, be noted that the data on prices of oil at the coast are based on the prime cost in Britain of the goods used to purchase oil and prices of such goods fell by some 60 per cent in 1815–50, most of this fall occurring before 1840.

Measured in terms of the quantities of goods received per ton of oil, the real price of oil at the coast probably rose quite significantly between 1815 and 1840, with the result that the rise in earnings of oil exporters in the Bight of Biafra was almost certainly much greater than the figures given above suggest. It seems likely, therefore, that by the late 1830s the earnings of merchants in the Bight of Biafra from oil were greater than from slave exports. Moreover, if as Laird and Oldfield claimed in 1832–4 a slave commanded the same price as a ton of oil, then it may well have seemed as profitable to African slave-holders in the Bight of Biafra to put slaves to work producing and transporting oil as to export them.[44] The sharp rise in oil exports from the Bight of Benin after 1840 suggests that slave-holders in that region were making similar choices in switching to palm oil production.

The growth of 'legitimate' trade was an important factor in the apparent expansion in slavery in West Africa in the nineteenth century, but its importance relative to other sectors of the West African economy for the internal demand for slaves is difficult to discern. To judge by the sharp rise in real prices of slaves at the West African coast *before* 1807, slavery may have been expanding in the region prior to British and USA abolition and the rise of 'legitimate' trade. Our price data (see table 1.2) suggest that slave prices collapsed temporarily between c.1807–20 but then recovered strongly in real terms, despite the fact that the number of

Table 1.3   *Slave exports from the Bights of Bénin and Biafra, 1750–1850*

Period	Bight of Bénin	Bight of Biafra	Total
1750–1759	86.6	106.1	192.7
1760–1769	98.3	142.6	240.9
1770–1779	111.5	160.4	271.9
1780–1789	121.0	225.3	346.3
1790–1799	74.6	181.7	256.3
1800–1809	75.7	123.0	198.7
1811–1820	93.8	93.7	187.5
1811–1815	34.6	33.1	
1816–1820	59.2	60.6	
1821–1830	114.7	127.3	242.0
1821–1825	44.2	60.6	
1826–1830	70.5	66.7	
1831–1840	88.1	112.7	200.8
1831–1835	37.7	71.9	
1836–1840	50.4	40.8	
1841–1850	98.7	12.1	110.8
1841–1845	45.3	4.4	
1846–1850	53.4	7.7	

Source: For the period before 1810, David Richardson, 'Slave exports from West and West-Central Africa, 1700–1810: new estimates of volume and distribution', *JAH*, 30 (1989), p. 10; for the period after 1810, Eltis, *Economic Growth*.

enslaved Africans who were exported (cf. table 1.3) generally remained below pre-1807 levels. Increased production of palm oil, gum, kola and other products may well have had a strong influence on the movement in slave prices in West Africa after 1820. The decline in slave exports to the Americas tended to correspond with the move to an alternative export – gum in Senegambia (1780–1830), gold and kola in Asante (1800–20), and palm oil in the Bight of Biafra (1820–35). As suggested above, slave prices recovered in each of these former regions of slave export to the Americas independently of the trans-Atlantic slave trade. Although fewer slaves were exported from West Africa, the Bight of Benin and some places on the upper Guinea coast reached levels in the 1830s and 40s that were close to or even higher than those reached at the peak of the export slave trade half a century earlier, thereby continuing their dependence on income derived from slave exports for a decade or two longer.

The indications are that many of the newly enslaved from this period were women, a feature of the trade that requires further analysis because female slaves were generally worth more than male slaves. As some historians have noted, conditions within Africa, in particular patriarchal structures, affected the composition of slave shipments to America after

1800.[45] The trend in slave prices in 1780–1850 should be given greater weight in assessing African influences on the trans-Atlantic slave trade. We would certainly agree with Eltis and Engerman that 'less attention [should] be paid to the Americas', particularly to the patterns of demand for slaves among planters, and more attention to trans-oceanic transport costs and to conditions of slave supply in Africa.[46] In searching for connections between conditions in Africa and changes in the trans-Atlantic trade in slaves, however, historians should perhaps give greater attention to the growth of slavery within West Africa and, in particular, the factors that promoted its expansion in the nineteenth century.

Implications of slave prices for the study of the slave trade

This study is a preliminary attempt to treat the slave trade as a series of inter-related markets, consisting of several regions along the Atlantic coast of western Africa and in the interior of West Africa. In suggesting that there may have been linkages among these different sectors, we follow Manning's lead in recognizing 'a web of interactions that may fairly be labelled a world market for forced labor'.[47] Regional variations are to be expected within and among these different sectors, but the concordance of patterns in the trend in slave prices presents the possibility that international market forces affected the price of slaves across broad regions. The recognition of such market conditions may assist in further analysis of the slave trade and the impact of abolition on Africa. We differ from Manning's interpretation of this world market in slaves in suggesting that the price drop after 1807 was only temporary. A decade or more of collapsed prices was followed by a period of recovery which matched the last years of large-scale exports of slaves from Africa to the Americas. In the long run, slave prices may well have fallen off, but for West Africa, at least, there was a period of recovery that lasted until 1850, if not later.

As Richardson has observed, the steep rise in slave prices at the end of the eighteenth century, which affected North Africa as well and may have occurred in the interior of West Africa too, suggests that the demand for enslaved Africans may have outstripped the ability of West African merchants to supply slaves within existing price schedules.[48] The internal market for slaves also appears to have put pressure on the supply mechanism. That crisis seems to have subsided by c.1810, whereupon there were excessive numbers of slaves available within parts of West Africa, at least, for more than a decade. Over-supply was reflected in the temporary collapse in slave prices at the Atlantic coast, apparently in North Africa as well, and perhaps within West Africa too.

Prices appear to have returned to the same levels as in the 1780s and 1790s in all sectors by the 1820s, even though West Africa was contributing a smaller proportion of slaves to the trans-Atlantic trade than previously. It seems likely, therefore, that the recovery in the slave market, as reflected in the trend in prices, indicates that internal West African markets, as well as the trans-Saharan sector, began to put pressures on the ability of West Africa to supply new captives and that the supply mechanism once again became over-stretched, despite the apparent increase in the size of the newly enslaved population. Slave prices remained relatively constant at levels that were similar to those at the end of the eighteenth century.

We believe that there was strong growth in the use of slaves within West Africa, possibly beginning in the late eighteenth century and reflected in to the rise in prices in the Bights of Benin and Biafra. The preference for females in the internal markets of West Africa corresponded to the increasing maleness of the export trade at this time. The price data and demographic structure of the trade confirm the general impression that the purchase and retention of female slaves were central to the expansion of slavery within West Africa. Hence, one important adaptation to the decline in slave exports from the Bights was greater use of female slaves in productive activities, while proportionately more adult males and children were exported to the Americas. In this sense, a division of slave labour on the basis of gender seems to have emerged, with women being retained and men exported.

There were at least three main influences on the price of slaves in West Africa after 1807, therefore. First, expansion in slave shipments to Brazil and Cuba almost certainly helped to raise the real price of slaves at the coast after 1820, as did the fall in the prices of goods exported to Africa to exchange for slaves, which partly reflected lower transport costs.[49] Furthermore, a shift in the terms of trade seems to have benefited suppliers of 'legitimate' exports as well. Secondly, internal West African demand for slaves appears to have been considerable in the period, despite the fact that it is difficult to measure. The export of slaves across the Sahara was in itself a substantial trade. Thirdly, growing British demand for soap and other oil-based commodities provided an important stimulus to the use of slave labour within West Africa between 1820 and 1850, and perhaps earlier in some places.

The buoyancy of the market for slaves might indicate that the external trade across the Atlantic was a smaller proportion of the total slave trade than previously thought. The return of prices to levels that were as high as the late eighteenth century indicates that the demand for slaves within West Africa may have increased at a sufficient rate to offset the relative decline of West Africa as a source of slaves for the Americas. There is no reason to assume a decline in the supply of slaves in West Africa at this time. As west-central Africa and south-eastern Africa became more and more important as sources of slaves for the Americas, the economies and societies of West Africa were absorbing the newly enslaved population that was being generated locally. As a result, slave prices remained relatively constant within West Africa. To the extent that demand for slaves in North Africa and in the Sahara increased in the nineteenth century, the decline in demand in the Americas was further offset. Again, slave prices in North Africa remained relatively stable until the late nineteenth century, which suggests that sufficient slaves were available for that market.

On the basis of our analysis of slave prices, we conclude that the initial 'crisis of adaptation' was largely confined to West Africa, principally to the Gold Coast and the Bights of Benin and Biafra, and then only to the decade or so after 1807. As our data indicate, the trend in slave prices at the Atlantic coast varied among regions, with prices in Angola remaining relatively steady between 1790 and 1820, while prices in West Africa rose substantially in the 1790s and first decade of the nineteenth century to levels considerably above those in Angola. But with British abolition, prices of slaves in West Africa collapsed to a level that was only half the average price in Angola. These lower prices lasted for a decade or so, but in the 1820s prices of slaves at the West African coast began to rise again, thereby bringing them back into line with those in Angola.

The price decline after 1807 suggests that there was a glut of slaves in coastal West Africa. With the withdrawal of the French, the Dutch, the USA and above all Britain from the trade between 1793 and 1808, there was insufficient capacity to carry slaves to the Americas. Smaller export earnings resulting from fewer slaves being exported and lower prices caused a 'crisis of adaptation' to abolition, which lasted through the 1810s, until the depressed market for slaves had revived by the late 1820s. Competing demand for slaves within West Africa and from the trans-Saharan sector eventually pushed prices up, so that from 1826–30 until 1850, prices were high, even though trans-Atlantic exports from West Africa were significantly lower than in the late eighteenth century. The sharp rise in slave prices in West Africa at the end of the eighteenth century made the collapse in prices after 1807 all the more serious, especially when fewer slaves were being exported. The ensuing crisis proved brief, however, as growing markets for slaves in Cuba and Brazil, into and across the Sahara, and, most importantly, within West Africa itself, brought about a recovery in slave prices at the coast from about 1825 onward.

NOTES

We acknowledge with thanks the generosity of a number of scholars in sharing their data with us, most notably David Eltis but also including Joseph C. Miller, José Curto and Robin Law. We have combined their data with our own to generate a computer file with full citations, which is available upon request, either on disk or hard copy.

1 K. O. Dike, *Trade and Politics in the Niger Delta 1830–1885* (Oxford, 1956), p. 47.
2 A. G. Hopkins, *An Economic History of West Africa* (London, 1973).
3 David Richardson, 'Prices of slaves in West and West-Central Africa: toward an annual series, 1698–1807', *Bulletin of Economic Research*, 43 (1991), 21–56. For earlier assessments of slave prices in the eighteenth century, see Richard N. Bean, *The British Trans-Atlantic Slave Trade 1650–1775* (New York, 1975), which was revised following the discovery of new data, in B. J. Wattenberg (ed.), *The Statistical History of the United States from Colonial Times to the Present* (New York, 1976). Other data on eighteenth-century West coast prices are to be found in Marion Johnson, 'The ounce in eighteenth-century West African trade', *JAH*, 7 (1966), 197–214; E. P. LeVeen, 'British slave trade suppression policies 1821–1865: impact and implications', PhD thesis, University of Chicago, 1971, p. 10; Robert L. Stein, *The French Slave Trade in the Eighteenth Century* (Madison, 1979); Alison Jones, 'The Rhode Island slave trade: a trading advantage in Africa', *Slavery and Abolition*, 2 (1981), 225–44; Adam Jones, *From Slaves to Palm Kernels: A History of the Galinhas Country (West Africa) 1730–1890* (Wiesbaden, 1983); J. M. Postma, *The Dutch in the Atlantic Slave Trade 1600–1815* (Cambridge, 1990); Joseph C. Miller, 'Slave prices in the Portuguese southern Atlantic 1600–1830', in Paul E. Lovejoy (ed.), *Africans in Bondage* (Madison, 1986), p. 67; and Philip D. Curtin, *Economic Change in Precolonial Africa: Senegambia in the Era of the Slave Trade* (Madison, 1975), II, pp. 48–53.
4 Richardson, 'Prices', pp. 21–56; Paul E. Lovejoy and David Richardson, 'British abolition and its impact on slave prices along the Atlantic coast of Africa, 1783–1850', *JEH*, 55 (1995), 98–119.
5 Basing his analysis on a price series for slaves between 1815–67 which he constructed, David Eltis suggested that 'the African coast slave prices fell by a little more than half and remained generally below the pre-1807 price for as long as the traffic lasted'. Some of this decline may have been due to the changing age structure of slave shipments at this time, but for Eltis the collapse in prices after 1807 and their continuation at relatively low levels primarily reflected a market adjustment at the coast to over-supply of slaves in West and west-central Africa in the face of declining exports to the Americas: *Economic Growth and the Ending of the Transatlantic Slave Trade* (Oxford, 1987), pp. 41, 227. We subsequently reinterpreted the data used by Eltis in the construction of our series; see Lovejoy and Richardson, 'British abolition'.
6 Paul E. Lovejoy, *Transformations in Slavery: A History of Slavery in Africa*

(Cambridge, 1983); Patrick Manning, *Slavery and African Life: Occidental, Oriental, and African Slave Trades* (Cambridge, 1990).

7   Miller, 'Slave prices', p. 67; and Curto, personal communication. We greatly appreciate the assistance of both Miller and Curto in providing data for our analysis.

8   Curtin, *Economic Change*, II, pp. 48–53. Also see Curtin, 'The abolition of the slave trade from Senegambia', in David Eltis and James Walvin (eds.), *The Abolition of the Atlantic Slave Trade: Origins and Effects in Europe, Africa and the Americas* (Madison, 1981), p. 88; and *The Rise and Fall of the Plantation Complex: Essays in Atlantic History* (New York, 1990), p. 116.

9   Gaspard Théodore Mollien, *L'Afrique Occidentale en 1818* (Paris, 1967), p. 76.

10 Cited in Fernand Braudel, *Civilization and Capitalism from the Fifteenth to the Eighteenth Century: Volume III, The Perspectives of the World* (London, 1984, trans. Sian Reynolds), p. 440.

11 Thomas Edward Bowdich, *Mission from Cape Coast Castle to Ashantee* (London, 1819), p. 333. Also see Albert van Dantzig, 'Elmina, Asante and the Abolitionists: morality, security and profits', in S. Daget (ed.), *De la traite à l'esclavage du Ve au XIXème siècle: Actes du colloque international sur la traite des Noirs, Nantes 1985* (Nantes and Paris, 1988), II, p. 592; Ivor Wilks, *Asante in the Nineteenth Century* (Cambridge, 1975), pp. 177–78, 262–63.

12 Van Dantzig, 'Elmina', p. 592; Wilks, *Asante*, p. 262.

13 For an excellent summary of this 'crisis of adaptation', see Edward Reynolds, *Trade and Economic Change on the Gold Coast, 1807–1874* (New York, 1974), pp. 43–71, although it should be noted that Reynolds concludes that 'abolition was not very damaging to the Asante economy'. His assessment is perhaps correct over the long run, but his discussion makes it clear that in the short term there was considerable dislocation.

14 J. R. LaTorre, 'Wealth surpasses everything: an economic history of Asante, 1750–1874', PhD thesis, University of California, Berkeley, 1978, pp. 426, 440, 470. In converting gold *agyiratwefa* to trade ounces we assumed that 4 *agyiratwefa* equalled 3 oz. trade, following evidence supplied by LaTorre for 1777–1803.

15 LaTorre, 'Wealth', pp. 426, 440, 470.

16 Thus, figures given by Adam Jones show that in 1807–8 adult males cost 137–140 bars at Galinhas and Rio Pongo, whereas average prices of all slaves, including women and children, at Galinhas were 104–119 bars in 1819: *Slaves to Palm Kernels*, p. 31.

17 For a summary of recent work on the volume of the Atlantic trade in slaves see Paul E. Lovejoy, 'The impact of the Atlantic slave trade on Africa: a review of the literature', *JAH*, 30 (1989), 365–94 For specific figures on the period 1780–1850, see David Richardson, 'Slave exports from West and West-Central Africa, 1700–1810: new estimates of volume and distribution', *JAH*, 30 (1989), 10; Eltis, *Economic Growth*, pp. 250–2.

18 Virtually all of the rest of the slaves exported from West Africa in 1811–50 came from the upper Guinea coast.

19 David Eltis and Stanley L. Engerman, 'Fluctuations in sex and age ratios in the transatlantic slave trade, 1663–1864', *EHR*, 46 (1993), 308–23; David

Eltis, 'Fluctuations in the age and sex ratios of slaves in the nineteenth-century transatlantic slave traffic', *Slavery and Abolition*, 7 (1986), 257–72. As with other aspects of the trade, there were considerable regional variations. The regions that attained the greatest proportion of males and the youngest age set were south-eastern Africa and west-central Africa. The various parts of West Africa followed the trend towards more and younger males, but the shift in West Africa was not as extreme.

20 Paul E. Lovejoy, 'The Central Sudan and the Atlantic slave trade', in Robert Harms, Joseph C. Miller, David S. Newbury and Michelle D. Wagner (eds.), *Paths to the Past: African Historical Essays in Honor of Jan Vansina* (Atlanta, 1994); 'Background to rebellion: the origins of Muslim slaves in Bahia', in Lovejoy and Nicholas Rogers (eds.), *Unfree Labour in the Development of the Atlantic World* (London, 1994).

21 Eltis and Engerman, 'Age and sex ratios'.

22 According to Behrendt's figures, British ships took 4,000–5,000 slaves per year from the Gold Coast in the 1780s; that number increased to 5,000–6,000 from 1793 through the early years of the nineteenth century. See Stephen D. Behrendt, 'The British slave trade, 1785–1807: volume, profitability, and mortality', PhD thesis, University of Wisconsin, 1993, pp. 318–27.

23 Wilks, *Asante*; Paul E. Lovejoy, *Caravans of Kola: The Hausa Kola Trade, 1700–1900* (Zaria, 1980).

24 See Elisée Soumonni's contribution to this volume.

25 Robin Law, *The Oyo Empire*, c.1600–c.1836 (Oxford, 1977).

26 Eltis, *Economic Growth*.

27 Eltis, *Economic Growth*.

28 Richardson, 'Prices'. For the Caribbean islands, see Roger Anstey, *The Atlantic Slave Trade and British Abolition, 1760–1810* (Cambridge, 1975), pp. 416–18; John R. Ward, *British West Indian Slavery, 1750–1834: The Process of Amelioration* (Oxford, 1988).

29 LaTorre, 'Wealth'; Lovejoy, *Caravans*, pp. 11–18, and *Transformations*, pp. 163–9.

30 The most recent study of the slave trade from Senegambia is James F. Searing, *West African Slavery and Atlantic Commerce: The Senegal River Valley, 1700–1860* (Cambridge, 1993). Also see Curtin, *Economic Change*.

31 Curtin, *Economic Change*, II, pp. 48–53.

32 On the expansion of the demand for slaves in the far western Sahara and Sahel, see Dennis D. Cordell, 'The Saharan slave trade and the demographic reproduction of commercial societies in the Sahara in the nineteenth century', paper presented at the Eleventh International Economic History Conference, Milan, 1994; James L. A. Webb, Jr., *Desert Frontier: Ecological and Economic Change along the Western Sahel, 1600–1850* (Madison, 1994); and E. Ann McDougall, 'Salt, Saharans and the trans-Saharan slave trade: nineteenth-century developments', in Elizabeth Savage (ed.), *The Human Commodity: Perspectives on the Trans-Saharan Slave Trade* (London, 1992), pp. 61–88. For the latest figures on the trans-Saharan slave trade, see Ralph Austen, 'The Mediterranean Islamic slave trade out of Africa: a tentative census', in Savage (ed.), *Human Commodity*, p., 227.

33 James L. A. Webb, Jr., 'The trade in gum arabic: prelude to French conquest

in Senegal', *JAH*, 26 (1985), 149–68; and 'The horse and slave trade between the Western Sahara and Senegambia', *JAH*, 34 (1993), 221–46; McDougall, 'Salt', p. 74; and Martin Klein, 'The impact of the Atlantic slave trade on the societies of the Western Sudan', *Social Science History*, 14 (1990), 246.

34   Paul E. Lovejoy and David Richardson, 'Competing markets for male and female slaves: slave prices in the interior of West Africa, 1780–1850', *IJAHS*, forthcoming. Prices can be converted to sterling at the current rate of $4.80 per £.

35   Patrick Manning, *Slavery, Colonialism and Economic Growth in Dahomey 1640–1960* (Cambridge, 1982), p. 49.

36   Lovejoy, *Transformations*; Klein, 'Impact'; Manning, *Slavery and African Life*.

37   Lovejoy and Richardson, 'Competing markets',

38   For a summary of some estimates, see Lovejoy, *Transformations*, chs. 7–9.

39   See, e.g., David Northrup, *Trade without Rulers: Pre-Colonial Economic Development in South-Eastern Nigeria* (Oxford, 1978), ch. 7. Also see Lovejoy, *Transformations*; and Manning, *Slavery and African Life*.

40   Dike, *Trade and Politics*, p. 50; Manning, *Slavery, Colonialism and Economic Growth*; A. J. H. Latham, *Old Calabar, 1600–1891: The Impact of the International Economy upon a Traditional Society* (Oxford, 1973); and Northrup, *Trade without Rulers*.

41   Hopkins, *Economic History*, p. 129.

42   Figures on volume and prices are cited in Latham, *Old Calabar*; and 'Palm oil exports from Calabar 1812–1887 (with a note on price formation)', in G. Liesegang, H. Pasch, and A. Jones (eds.), *Figuring African Trade* (Berlin, 1986), pp. 265–91.

43   Latham, *Old Calabar*; Dike, *Trade and Politics*; Martin Lynn, 'The profitability of the early nineteenth-century palm oil trade', *AEH*, 20 (1992), 77–97.

44   MacGregor Laird and R. A. K. Oldfield, *Narrative of an Expedition into the Interior of Africa by the River Niger* (London, 1837), I, p. 106.

45   David Eltis and Stanley L. Engerman, 'Was the slave trade dominated by men?' *Journal of Interdisciplinary History*, 23, 2 (1992), 237–57; Herbert S. Klein, 'African women in the Atlantic slave trade', in Claire C. Robertson and Martin A. Klein (eds.), *Women and Slavery in Africa* (Madison, 1983), pp. 29–38; Herbert S. Klein, *The Middle Passage: Comparative Studies in the Atlantic Slave Trade* (Princeton, 1978). It should be noted that our conclusions differ from those of Inikori, who has argued that 'export demand determined the sex ratios of the populations exported as well as those of the slave populations left in tropical Africa ... rather than domestic demand determining the sex ratios of the populations exported'; see Joseph E. Inikori, 'Export versus domestic demand: the determinants of sex ratios in the transatlantic slave trade', *Research in Economic History*, 14 (1992), 158.

46   Eltis and Engerman, 'Sex and age ratios', p. 321.

47   Manning, *Slavery and African Life*, p. 102; also pp. 103–109.

48   Richardson, 'Prices'.

49   For a discussion of transport costs and their possible influence on prices, see Manning, *Slavery and African Life*.

2 The West African palm oil trade in the nineteenth century and the 'crisis of adaptation'

Martin Lynn

The idea that parts of West Africa experienced a 'crisis of adaptation' in the nineteenth century with the transition from the slave trade to what was termed at the time 'lawful commerce', has been one of the most debated issues in West African historiography.[1] This concept goes back a long way but in recent years it has been the writings of A. G. Hopkins that have most fully spelt out what it entailed. For Hopkins, the transition from slave-trading to produce-trading had serious political consequences for parts of West Africa, which culminated in a 'crisis of adaptation' which in turn led on to British imperial intervention.[2] As is well known, however, not all historians of the area have been convinced by Hopkins' analysis. Austen, indeed, describes the transition as 'adaptation without revolution', and many writers have questioned whether it amounted to a 'crisis' in any meaningful sense.[3] The ensuing debate has been a compelling one for historians of the region, with numerous case studies being produced to show the validity of one side or other. However, as Law has implied in his recent survey of writings on this topic, something of a consensus might now be said to have developed. Few historians, he suggests, now argue for a 'crisis of adaptation' in the coastal trading states of West Africa in the nineteenth century. For the interior producers, however, the debate remains far more open, with persuasive evidence from both sides of the argument to support or refute the idea of a 'crisis of adaptation' inland.[4]

Whatever the case concerning the interior producers, the aim of this chapter is to look at the growth of the export palm oil trade in nineteenth-century West Africa and to see how far this produced a 'crisis of adaptation'. For these purposes, the export palm oil trade is defined in the admittedly limited sense of the trade between coastal brokers and British traders; production and marketing of oil in the interior will in this instance be left to others to consider. The chapter will first look briefly at the coastal trading states of West Africa before moving on to examine in more detail the often neglected British side of the trade. The intention will be to show how a case for a 'crisis' – though with a different emphasis to that usually postulated – can be made.

In doing this, there is an important distinction in Hopkins' analysis of the 'crisis of adaptation' that we need to keep clear.[5] In postulating a crisis in West Africa in this period, Hopkins distinguishes in effect between *two* distinct problems: that caused by the transition from slave- to produce-trading and that caused by the adverse shift in the terms of trade between Europe and Africa in the last quarter of the century.[6] These two problems had different origins; that they coincided in Yoruba- land when they did was contingent as much as anything else. For Hopkins it is the latter element in the crisis, rather than the former, which is the vital one for explaining – as he was attempting to do – the development of British imperialism in parts of West Africa.

How far, then, did the transition to palm oil exporting produce a 'crisis of adaptation'? Certainly this was a period of some change in West Africa's external trade. While it is of course wrong to see a sudden decline in slave exports in the early nineteenth century following British abolition, none the less West Africa's external trade was undergoing important changes in this period.[7] According to the calculations of Eltis and Jennings, Africa's Atlantic exports (effectively West Africa's) at current values fell between the 1780s and 1820s from £31.7m to £27.7m, while combined exports and imports fell from £50.2m to £38.3m, a fall of nearly 24 per cent. This is by no means a negligible figure and on the face of it must have posed considerable difficulties of adjustment for many traders in West Africa – though by the 1860s, according to the same source, Africa's Atlantic trade (exports and imports combined) had reached £93.1m, more than making up for the shortfall resulting from abolition and the Anglo-French wars.[8]

How far did this adjustment cause problems for West African brokers? The conventional answer to this has been to look at the coastal states most centrally involved in the transition, namely the trading states of the Niger Delta area where the palm oil trade emerged during the early nineteenth century to replace slave-exporting. This is well-traversed ground and need not detain us long.[9] Certainly historians have found much to suggest a political crisis in these states in the nineteenth century, arguably derived from the emergence of new forces dependent on the transition from slaving to produce trading, such as Oko Jumbo and Jaja in Bonny, Will Braid and George Amakiri in Elem Kalabari, or the so- called 'Order of Bloodmen' in Old Calabar.[10] Yet, as is also often stated, more persuasive research, whether by Alagoa on Bonny, Latham on Old Calabar or Wariboko on Elem Kalabari, suggests that these events were far more complex than they appear and few historians would now accept without qualification the view that they were primarily due to the transition to the palm oil trade.[11] This is not to argue that the transition did not cause difficulties for these states. Indeed, there was very clearly a crisis concerning control of the Delta oil trade in the later part of the century: one can see evidence for this in the series of wars in the area that were fought over the interior oil markets in the 1870s–80s, which very neatly mirror the picture Hopkins drew for Yorubaland at the same time.[12] But these problems are more closely related to the difficulties that accompanied the fall in oil prices from the 1860s onwards and, while real enough, should not be put down to the transition itself.

This view that the transition was not necessarily responsible for the political problems of this period in the Delta area is of course echoed elsewhere in West Africa. Adam Jones' work on the Galinhas country, a major source of palm produce, especially kernels, in the latter part of the nineteenth century, suggests that it was 'big men' in the form of the traditional rulers that benefited from the trade, not 'new men'.[13] Similarly on the Gold Coast, where Sanders argues that the growth of palm oil exports was to have a major impact on Fante society, with wealth becoming more dispersed and cheap imports coming within reach of the 'masses'.[14] Yet even so, it is hard to see here the emergence of a mass of small-scale traders challenging established power in a political 'crisis'.[15]

The reason why there is little to suggest that the transition to the oil trade caused a 'crisis of adaptation' in the coastal broking states of West Africa lies in Hopkins' stress on the key issue as being access to the market.[16] The existing rulers of the coastal states in practice found it relatively easy to control entry into the market. As the work of various historians suggests, there were two ways in which this occurred. Firstly, these ruling groups were able to use political weapons to shore up their position in the palm oil trade. Latham's work on Old Calabar shows how successful was the ruling oligarchy there in using institutions like the Ekpe society to do this. Far from being overwhelmed by small-scale traders, the existing merchants were able to use Ekpe regulations to stop the sale of oil in small quantities in 1862 and again against the sale of kernels in 1872; similar regulations were used by the chiefs of Brass in 1867.[17] The oil trade, writes Latham, 'did not of itself alter the structure of Efik society which had been established in response to the demands of the slave trade, because both trades were similarly organized'.[18] Similarly, Hargreaves has shown how the transition to the oil trade in Bonny was accompanied by House Heads reinforcing their control over the market.[19] The capital required to enter the oil trade was too great for small-scale traders effectively to challenge the existing oligarchy of merchants. Moreover, their long-established ties with British traders meant that there was in practice a community of interest between the two groups, with British traders keen to maintain the one advantage which they had against their own competitors, namely their long-established relationship with the traders of the Delta states.[20] This was reinforced by British Consuls who, fearing instability and disruption in the area, were keen, in the various treaties they signed with Delta rulers, to reinforce the power over access to the trade, and particularly trust, of traditional authorities whom they could thereafter hold responsible for the conduct of the trade.[21]

Secondly, there were economic reasons for this continued dominance by the large-scale coastal brokers. Economies of scale, especially in transport from the interior, gave such brokers a considerable advantage *vis-à-vis* smaller-scale traders; the advantage continued to lie with those traders who could utilize large canoes and large numbers of canoemen to transport their oil.[22] Transport remained a major barrier to entry on the African side of the trade, just as it did on the British side. Moreover, as often pointed out, the key issue in the development of the oil trade for brokers was access to trust.[23] Those traders who received trust from the Europeans were the ones who could exploit economies of scale; it remained in the interest of British traders to ensure that trust went to large-scale traders whose credit was well-established and who could be held accountable for it.

These points are long-established. However, there was a more fundamental reason, quite apart from the continued political and economic powers of traditional elites, that explains why the transition to oil trading among the coastal brokers was characterized by adaptation rather than crisis. This was that the oil trade did not in practice represent a break with the slave trade. There is more to this than the well-known argument of Northrup that the slave and oil trades in the Bights were 'compatible'.[24] Rather, it was precisely because the oil trade represented continuity rather than change and because its structures and practices were a continuation of the old, that it grew so rapidly in the early nineteenth century.

The commercial palm oil trade had, after all, been long established in West Africa. This was partly an internal trade between different parts of the region, but also an export trade, being imported into England from 1588 and, according to Pacheco Pereira, exported from the Forcados River a century earlier.[25] It was extensively used, as is well known, as a foodstuff on the slave ships crossing the Atlantic throughout the slave trade era. It was also in demand in Britain at this period: Britain was importing from Africa some £2,000 of oil (unspecified) p.a. in the first half of the eighteenth century. Indeed, the first major increase in imports

of oil into Britain from West Africa can be dated to the 1790s, well
before the British abolition of the slave trade; by the end of the eighteenth century Britain was importing up to £10,000 p.a.[26] Moreover, as
Northrup suggests, the growth of the oil trade thereafter, at least from
the Bight of Biafra, was not at the cost of the slave trade; rather, the two
trades grew 'in tandem until the 1830s'.[27]

Furthermore, while Northrup may be right to stress the differences
between these two trades in their inland organization, as far as export
structures are concerned, the palm oil trade grew organically out of the
slave trade and derived most of its early features from it. This is not just
the obvious fact that the same areas and ports were central to the
nineteenth-century palm oil trade as to the late eighteenth-century slave
trade. Rather, the same trading organization and techniques were used in
the palm oil trade as in the slave trade. Like the slaver, the British palm
oil trader relied on the trading voyage and direct negotiation with the
African broker. The same mechanisms of buying and selling, the same
utilization of the 'unit of account', the same processes of bargaining, the
same reliance on coastal brokers and the same use of 'trust' applied to
both slaving and oil trading. It was particularly the last that reflected this
continuity, for trust reinforced the authority of rulers and large-scale
traders. It was the fact that, like the slave trade, the export palm oil trade
was heavily dependent on personal contacts and experience that lay at
the heart of this, for such experience determined who received trust.
Moreover, it ensured, in the absence of other mechanisms, the British
trader's reliance on the ruling authority of the broking state to supervise
the trade. Thus the same trading institutions in broking states survived
the transition and it was precisely because of this that it was so relatively
easy for the new produce trade to be established, at least in the Delta
area.[28]

Thus, as far as the coastal states of West Africa are concerned, it is
difficult to find a general 'crisis of adaptation' covering the transition
period. This is not to say that there were no localized problems of
adjustment, but as far as the African side of the export palm oil trade is
concerned, 'adaptation without revolution' does appear the most appropriate description.[29] What, however, about the British side of the trade?
For slave-traders in the leading British slaving ports (Liverpool and
Bristol), the ending of the British slave trade in 1807 threatened its own
'crisis of adaptation'. Moreover, for these traders there was little chance
of a continuing illicit trade to cushion the impact of abolition. The threat
was such that British traders utilized extensive political means to try to
prevent abolition.[30] When the Bill to end the British slave trade finally
received the royal assent in 1807, wrote Gomer Williams,

the whole [Liverpool] community was terror stricken. The docks were to become fish-ponds, the warehouses to moulder into ruins, grass was to grow on the local Rialto, the streets were to be ploughed up ... and Liverpool's glorious merchant navy, whose keels penetrated to every land, and whose white sails wooed the breeze on every ocean, was to dwindle into a fishing vessel or two.[31]

However, the most detailed study of the impact of abolition on Liverpool's trade, the thesis by B. K. Drake, suggests that 'continuity and flexibility' rather than a 'crisis of adaptation' characterized the experience of abolition for most Liverpool traders.[32] He writes of Liverpool's trade with Africa as being 'a long continuing composite ... rather than as two distinct and independent trades, one rising to pre-eminence in the wake of the other's decline'. 'There was', says Drake, 'an essential continuity in the African export trade [with Liverpool] of the periods before and after Abolition.'[33] The reasons for this, suggests Drake, lay in two factors. Firstly, abolition had been on the horizon for so long that Liverpool traders were able to re-deploy their slave fleets well in advance. Slave-traders did not renew their fleets as ships became aged, or diversified them into other trades, particularly the direct West Indies trade.[34] 'The slave fleet appears to have been re-deployed with relative ease', he notes, and suggests that Liverpool's African commerce kept a roughly constant position in this period relative to the general expansion of the port's trade.[35] According to Drake, this reflects the fact that, while clearly important, slave trading was not of crucial significance for the fortunes of the port as a whole by the end of the eighteenth century: in 1791, for example, only 3 per cent of Liverpool shipping was involved in the African trade; in 1805 only 112 voyages out of 2,349 (5 per cent) leaving Liverpool were to Africa.[36]

Secondly, Liverpool's 'legitimate' African commerce, far from being suddenly born with abolition, 'was rooted firmly in the pre-Abolition period'.[37] Indeed, it was an integral part of the slave trade before 1807: 'In the last years of the slave trade few slave ships returned to Liverpool without some African cargo on board'. As much as 20–30 per cent of net profits on a slave voyage in the last years of the slave trade, suggests Drake, came from produce imports into Liverpool.[38] This was not least because the Dolben Act of 1788 had restricted the numbers of slaves that could be carried on board ship, pushing slavers towards produce-trading. 'Slaving and legitimate trading on the West African coast', notes Drake, 'were inextricably interrelated' and had long been so.[39] Thus, abolition did not lead to the crisis that the prophets of doom anticipated. 'By 1809 the port had shaken off the effects of Abolition – such as they were.'[40] Indeed, Liverpool traders found it relatively easy to develop a significant

market in 'legitimate trade' from West Africa after 1807, first in timber
and then by the late 1820s in palm oil.

Drake's argument for continuity in Liverpool's trade with Africa
carries much conviction. Indeed, looking at Britain's trade with West
Africa more broadly what is striking is the degree of continuity over the
period of abolition that marks it. This applies whether we look at the
ports, the traders or the structures and techniques involved. On the most
simplistic level, the same British ports – Liverpool, Bristol and London –
were involved in the post-1807 trade as in the slave trade. Liverpool, the
leading British slaving port at the end of the eighteenth century,
continued to lead Britain's African trade throughout the nineteenth;
indeed, over three-quarters of Britain's palm oil imports arrived through
Liverpool for much of the century.[41]

Similarly, the same traders were involved in 'legitimate trading' after
1807 as in slaving earlier. Of the 22 Liverpool ships involved in the
African trade in 1809, 17 were former slave ships; of the 17 firms
responsible for these 22 ships every one had been slavers before.[42]
Indeed, examination of the careers of the leading Liverpool 'legitimate
traders' in the early nineteenth century shows that most owed their
origins to the slave trade. This is seen most famously in the careers of the
Tobin brothers, John and Thomas. John Tobin (1763–1851) was originally a slave-ship captain, but following his marriage into the Aspinall
family – major slavers – of Liverpool he was to establish a successful
slaving firm of his own after 1799, operating as John Tobin & Co.[43]
Thomas Tobin (1773–1863) similarly began his career as a sailing master
in the slave trade in the 1790s sailing between Bonny and Jamaica, also
for the Aspinalls, before moving into business on his own account.[44] The
two Tobins were to be central figures in Liverpool's post-abolition trade
with Africa. As Latham has shown, John Tobin was the trader on the
Liverpool side involved in the first major growth of the palm oil trade
after 1807. His links with Duke Ephraim of Old Calabar were central to
this; by the 1820s he was one of Liverpool's largest importers of oil.[45]
Meanwhile, Thomas Tobin was deeply involved in the growth of oil
exports from Bonny – the port he had slaved from in the 1790s/1800s –
as that port came to replace Old Calabar as the new centre of the trade
during the 1830s and 40s. By the 1840s Thomas Tobin was among the
largest importers of palm oil in Liverpool.[46] Nor were the Tobins
exceptional in this. George Case, Jonas Bold and James Penny were
other Liverpool slavers who successfully turned to the oil trade after
abolition. Similar was Charles Horsfall, founder of the largest palm oil
firm in Liverpool in the early nineteenth century and deeply involved in
the West Indian trade before 1807.[47]

Nor was this continuity restricted to Liverpool. The firm of R. & W. King of Bristol was another of the large African traders of nineteenth-century Britain who owed their origins to involvement in the pre-1807 trade, in this case growing out of the career of Thomas King in the 1790s. The fortunes of his sons, Richard and William, were to be made with the great increase in the oil trade in the 1830s; they were to be one of the very largest importers of palm oil in Britain by the middle of the nineteenth century.[48] In passing we may note that the continuing role of such ex-slaving firms in the oil trade meant that continuity rather than crisis also marked the local politics of Britain's ports in the African trade. It is well known how Liverpool slave traders in the years before 1807 played a major role in the borough's politics, but it is often forgotten how African traders continued to have a significant place in Liverpool politics after 1807, with Thomas Case, Sir John Tobin, Thomas Littledale, Charles Horsfall and (later) Thomas Horsfall (MP for Liverpool for twenty-one years) but the most obvious of African traders to play central roles in the port's politics until the ousting of the Tory elite in the 1830s; similarly in Bristol, Richard King was 'in effect, the head of the [City] Council' until his death in 1874.[49]

This continuity in the British ports and traders involved in the African trade over 1807 should hardly surprise us. It had its origins in the fact that the British side of the post-1807 trade relied on the existing techniques of trading with Africa: in these terms 1807 was no break. As in the slave trade era, trade continued to focus around the voyage of a ship, outfitted from Liverpool or Bristol by a single trader or partnership. The accounts of the slaver *Africa*, detailed for the 1770s by Minchinton, for example, are little different from those of any of the ships of W. A. & G. Maxwell sailing to Old Calabar for palm oil in the 1830s.[50] These ships, having reached the coast, would then either wait up-river for a cargo to be collected or, along the Windward or Gold Coasts, use the 'coasting' technique of collecting numerous small quantities of produce before returning home. Trade would, as in the slaving era, be undertaken by an experienced captain or supercargo. The trade still relied on personal knowledge of the market in West Africa and personal contacts with African brokers. This was because of the final feature of continuity in the trade's techniques, the use of credit. Trust was, of course, as much at the heart of the organization of legitimate trading as it had been in the later years of the slave trade era.[51]

These methods of trading in West Africa, evolved in the slave trade era, continued to the mid nineteenth century. Their significance is that they all represented formidable barriers to entry into the market and this was the real continuity over 1807. As Newbury says, this was a trade 'characterised by large outlay of capital and a lengthy seasonal turnover'. The capital costs of outfitting a ship, maintaining it over a long voyage (especially if 'coasting'), the need for experience of the African market, and the costs of trust – which could take a year or more before being redeemed – all were major barriers. Trust, the institution at the centre of the trade, was especially so, and was the key way existing traders could maintain their hold over the new produce trade; the great increase in the prevalence of trust noted in the second half of the century reflects this. As Nzemeke notes, trust was 'truncated protectionism ... [that] guaranteed the continued commercial ascendancy of the old hands in the trade of the area'.[52] This continuity in trading techniques meant that the African trade continued to be dominated in Britain by a handful of large traders who could afford the costs of shipping and trust and thus could rely, as before 1807, on the high costs of entry to keep rivals out. The pattern of the British side of the trade – with a handful of long-established traders at its heart and a plethora of smaller-scale traders at its margins – reflects the imperfect competition that characterized the trade in this period.

This continuity of organization and methods of trade after 1807 could hardly be otherwise. Geographical factors – in particular the absence of deep-water harbours – inevitably meant that methods of trade would not change until the shipping technology used in the trade changed; and 1807, whatever else it might have represented, did not mark a change in the technology of the trade. Equally, until European conquest at the end of the century, Africans remained the essential determinants of the techniques of trading.[53] British traders found it extremely difficult to impose new methods of trade on the African side before the 1850s. Continuity with the slaving era was therefore the central feature of the British side of the African trade in the early nineteenth century, just as it was on the African side. Yet change did come. From the 1840s the structure and techniques of the oil trade began to change significantly and it is here that we can find much more compelling evidence for a 'crisis'. From the 1840s the palm oil trade underwent a major reorganization: in this writer's view, a 'crisis of restructuring'. At the heart of this restructuring lay changes in the capital costs of entry that had hitherto kept out small-scale traders.

This reorganization of oil trade in the middle of the century had three features. The first of these was the influx of new British traders who entered the palm oil trade from the 1840s onwards. If the establishment and early growth of the oil trade in West Africa lay in the hands of the Tobin brothers, the King family, Charles Horsfall and other ex-slavers, then the second great expansion in volume of oil imports into Britain, in the 1840s and 50s, lay with a new generation of British traders who entered the trade in this period and went on to dominate it. Many examples can be given of major oil-importing firms that entered the trade in the 1830s/40s: Thomas Harrison & Co. (established 1837), Stuart & Douglas (established 1843), Wilson & Dawson (established in the 1830s) and Hatton & Cookson (established 1838), to name but a few.[54] This new generation did not rely on its slaving experience to enter the oil trade, rather it was a product of the growth in palm oil trading. Some, like Peter Douglas, had been ship's surgeons to West Africa and gained experience working for other oil traders. Others, like Peter Stuart, were coopers for the oil trade; while Hatton & Cookson were ironmongers.[55] These and others like them could use their contacts with the oil trade to overcome the barriers to entry that had hitherto kept out interlopers.

Why did this influx of new traders occur around 1840? Partly it was due to generational change as former slave traders reached retirement. Sir John Tobin, for instance, retired from the trade in the early 1840s and died in 1851; Charles Horsfall probably left the trade in the late 1830s.[56] J. O. Bold had also retired in the 1840s. But largely this influx of new names was due to the high prices that palm oil gained in Britain in these years. British palm oil prices reached a peak in the late 1830s and again in the war boom of the 1850s, while in terms of value the trade continued to grow through to the early 1860s.[57] This was clearly a boom period for the trade. While we have little evidence to suggest profit rates in the palm oil trade, one study of the firm of W. A. & G. Maxwell in the late 1830s – when prices were at their pre-1850s peak – suggests net operating profits of up to 100 per cent per voyage were possible for oil cargoes.[58] It is important to note that such profits would not have been sustained across the whole period, but they do suggest a reason why the period of high British prices in the 1830s/40s saw so many new names enter the trade.

Such an influx of new participants does not necessarily imply strains in the trade, particularly while, as was the case here, the oil market continued to grow in terms of its overall value and there was plenty of oil for everyone. But the new generation of traders did have a major impact, for they brought with them a willingness of develop new techniques which were in turn to lead to major changes in the trade's structure. The new trading techniques of the 1840s and after are the second new feature of these years. Hitherto the oil trade had continued the slave trade practice of relying on the ship-board trade, whether the 'coasting voyage' along the Windward Coast or the 'river voyage' to the Niger Delta area. In either case trading was the responsibility of the master or a supercargo accompanying the ship and trade was invariably undertaken on board. While traders might pass time on land, they would not remain on the coast for longer than it took to fill their ship's cargo. Only on the Gold

Coast, where long-established trading forts existed and resident traders were semi-permanently based, and on the 'South Coast' around the Congo, was this pattern not followed. Elsewhere, and particularly at its heart, the Niger Delta, the trade remained, as it had been during the slave trade era, an essentially ship-board trade.

However, the middle of the century was to see the start of the move 'from ship to shore' in the Delta, as the inherited techniques of the trade began to alter. From the 1840s British traders began to take up a larger presence on land in the Delta states. With the expansion in the volume of the trade the need for greater storage facilities on land grew and with it the need to keep staff in the rivers over a long period; the development of malaria prophylaxis after 1854 facilitated this. This began with the development of a 'rotational system' for shipping, whereby one ship would stay out in the Delta rivers for an entire trading 'season', filling other ships belonging to the firm as cargoes became available, before, with the season ended, it would return home itself.[59] With this went the use of smaller tenders to collect oil from other rivers for the firm's main ship, though this was a long-established practice.[60] This led to the expansion in the existing use of 'beaches' and 'cask houses', as traders occupied areas on land to store oil.[61] From this it was a short step to the use, from around 1850, of hulks in the trade: that is, the placing of rotting ships in the Delta rivers to remain there permanently as a base for a particular firm.[62] Finally, with hulks came resident agents, clerks and other staff placed in the river for long periods. In the Delta area, resident agents began first on the Benin River, where around 1850 a Mr Henry could be found trading on his own account, as well as as an agent for Harrisons. From here, resident agents spread elsewhere across the Delta.[63]

Certainly, by increasing costs as new techniques had to be introduced, these innovations might be said to have reinforced existing structures in the trade. However, the move 'from ship to shore' was a prerequisite for a final change in trading technique, namely the arrival in the Delta in the second half of the century of the Commission Houses, which were to lead to dramatic long-term changes. The Commission Houses were firms based in Britain that agreed to advance goods to traders based permanently in West Africa in return for selling those traders' produce in Britain at a commission. They had been long established in Sierra Leone and the Gold Coast, with Forster & Smith of London (established c.1817) the most well-known.[64] From the middle of the century the number of Commission Houses involved in the African trade mushroomed as the institution moved eastwards from the Gold Coast to Lagos and then to the Delta.[65] Not only did this reduce invoicing costs, it allowed small-scale traders to enter the oil trade without the need for large capital requirements in terms of stocks, thereby removing a further capital barrier to entry. The shift to the use of currency that soon followed was also part of this.[66]

The third feature of the restructuring of the oil trade in the middle of the century was the most important of them all. This was the technological revolution represented by the move 'from sail to steam'. As is well known, from 1852, with the establishment of Macgregor Laird's African Steam Ship Co., and 1869, with the British and African Steam Navigation Co., steamship services became the prevalent form of communication between Liverpool and the West Coast.[67] In time all the British palm oil traders, including the long-established, large-scale operators, turned to use the steamship services for their transport. This technological revolution was to destroy the last vestiges of the structures and practices the oil trade had inherited from the slave trade era. Not least of its long-term consequences was its destruction of African brokers' ability to dictate the commercial practices of the trade.

The most important consequence of the introduction of the steamship services was its impact on the capital costs of entry. Hitherto the major barrier to entry into the oil trade was the cost of transport. Though by no means unknown, very little freighting occurred in the African trade before the arrival of steam in 1852.[68] Instead, traders had to provide their own shipping; the cost of buying or chartering a ship, as stated above, acted as the main barrier to entry into the trade. With the arrival of the regular steamship services, however, cargo space on the steamers could be hired relatively cheaply. The large sailing fleets the older firms had built up, and which were their chief weapon against intruders, were made redundant.[69] The result of this was a further influx of new traders, this time of very small-scale operators, into the oil trade after 1852. The numbers of traders in the oil trade rose from 21 in 1830 to 37 in 1850 to over 100 by the 1860s.[70] Many of these small firms were British-based traders, such as Banner Bros, Edwards Bros or A. & M. Herschell, now able to use to steamers to compete effectively against the large-scale businesses like Horsfalls or Harrisons. These 'white traders of limited capital', as Consul Livingstone described them, were to go on to greater things: John Holt would be one such example.[71] Others were Krio traders who now flocked to the Delta ports, using the steamers to enter the export trade and freight to Britain small quantities of oil.[72] Vital for this was of course the spread of the Commission Houses and the move 'from ship to shore' that coincided with the arrival of the steamship services: the former to provide them with the trade goods they needed, the latter to allow them to settle in the Delta states and put themselves under the protection of the Missions or the Consul. This 'goodly number of black traders', with their low costs and low profit margins, were to prove immensely successful at pushing into the oil trade during the 1850s and 60s.[73]

However, these newcomers, whether black or white, were by no means welcome in the trade. As Livingstone noted in 1872, 'Steam has brought new firms and a keen competition', adding that 'there are too many traders ... for the yield of palm oil'.[74] These traders brought new competition to the trade at a time when the market was contracting, and their success threatened the trading positions of the long-established traders. While the large-scale traders could rely on economies of scale and the prevalence of trust, the large influx of new traders in this period shows the extent to which these advantages were being eroded. The result was what has been described as 'the European traders' counter-attack'.[75] The established traders attempted to prevent these new competitors becoming established by both fair means (such as price-cutting) and foul (by violence and subterfuge). Dike talks of a 'savage trade war lasting till the 1880s', and Nair of the 1870s as a period of 'serious economic stress', and there is much to bear this out.[76] Violent incidents in the trade, between white trader and black broker, became much more common from the 1860s as traders pressed their African suppliers for more oil or a reduction in price. Sums of trust given out to brokers appear to have inflated significantly from the 1850s as the large-scale traders tried to use their capital resources to squeeze out the interlopers.[77] Similarly, attempts were made to use the Court of Equity to make traders pay large deposits before they could trade in Old Calabar.[78] Oil was frequently 'chopped' from smaller-scale traders, and beatings of such traders were not uncommon.[79]

The three changes that marked the reorganization of the oil trade in the middle of the nineteenth century – the influx of a new generation in the 1840s, the new trading techniques accompanying the move 'from ship to shore', and the consequences of the move 'from sail to steam' – all had the same effect. That was, to erode the capital barriers to entry that had hitherto, as in the slave trade era, kept the African trade as the preserve of the few. The increased competition that ensued was to lead to major changes in commercial organization – in Newbury's words, 'a crisis in commercial organization' – in the 1870s and 80s, as traders were forced to restructure their businesses.[80] Firms went bankrupt – most famously Irvine & Woodward, John Holt's suppliers; others merged, moved into other trades, or left the trade altogether, like Wilson & Dawson, or Horsfall & Son. Some, like the Tobin family, turned to the establishment of joint-stock companies to raise capital in place of their traditional family or partnership organization.[81] By the 1880s, when prices had fallen to their lowest point in the second half of the century, the big firms were attempting pooling arrangements in individual ports like Old Calabar, seeking new entrepots along the coast, looking at moves inland, and trying to remove brokers like Jaja who opposed their attempts to control access to the trade.[82] It was these pressures that culminated in the amalgamation of the African Association Ltd, involving the nine largest firms in the Delta area, in 1889.[83]

By the end of this process of reorganization in the 1890s the palm oil trade looked very different from how it had looked after abolition of the British slave trade in 1807. In place of a few relatively large-scale family-based firms or partnerships, operating their own shipping on single voyages to the coast, trading from on deck and reliant on the capital costs of starting-up to keep competitors out, the trade was now a land-based commerce, reliant on the steamship services for transport and having been through a period of fierce restructuring. An ex-slaver could flourish in the oil trade in the 1830s by using the old slaving techniques; quite apart from age, this would not have been the case by the 1870s. In this sense, the real break in the West African trade occurred not at the time of transition from slaving, but rather with the arrival of the steam-ship and its associated changes in the 1850s.

But how difficult a process was this mid-century restructuring? Did it amount to a 'crisis'? Much depends, of course, on what is meant by 'crisis', but it is the argument of this chapter that one can indeed talk of a 'crisis of restructuring' for the oil trade from the middle of the century. This was because of the consequences of this increase in competition in the trade. At its simplest level, it contributed to the severe fall in oil prices which hit British traders and interior producers in this period. The Liverpool price of palm oil fell from around £46 a ton at the start of the 1860s to £20 a ton in the late 1880s, before recovering slightly by the end of the century. Prices of palm kernels also fell severely, to a similar pattern.[84] There were many factors contributing to this fall in prices – from new oils entering the market (especially mineral oils) to changes in freight rates – but the new competitiveness that characterized the oil trade in this period was central to it and ensured that traders in the West African trade would not be able to avoid severe pressure on their profit margins.[85] The various attempts to restructure palm oil businesses in this period, outlined above, were the result.

Furthermore, since this fall in price was not accompanied by an increase in volumes, the value of the trade with Britain fell too, from nearly £2m p.a. in the early 1860s to £1m in 1890. Newbury estimates a fall in the value of all British imports from West Africa of 20 per cent in the late 1880s alone.[86] The result was the sharply adverse movement in the terms of trade (both barter and income) between Britain and West Africa in the late nineteenth century that hit African producers, exacerbated the Delta wars of the 1870s-80s and contributed to the problems affecting the Yoruba.[87] Moreover, the increase in competition in the trade resulting from this restructuring led to increased violence between white traders and between white and black traders, the surest sign of growing pressures. For all the talk of problems in the trade before 1850, it was the second half of the century that was the real era of the 'palm oil ruffian', floating to the top of the trade 'with the other scum of the palm oil'.[88] As Nair argues, the 1860s and 70s were the lawless period in the trade, with 'chopping' of oil becoming all too prevalent and supercargoes stepping up their 'arbitrary and illegal conduct' to pressurize brokers and rival Krio traders as prices began to fall.[89] 'This river ... has literally been managed by the revolver for the last 6 months', wrote Burton of Old Calabar in 1862.[90] 'Our traders are ready enough to demand protection and to insist upon the native chiefs performing their part ... but they will shirk their own liabilities if they have an opportunity and still claim to be protected', noted Wylde in 1868; while Livingstone observed four years later that 'most of the outrages in the oil rivers have been caused by the traders taking the law into their own hands'.[91] The clash with Jaja of Opobo in the late 1880s came at the end of a period of such incidents that stretched back to the late 1850s.[92]

Perhaps most importantly, the tensions generated by this restructuring and the shift in the terms of trade it accompanied lay behind the calls for British intervention in the Delta area that became so prevalent in the 1880s and 90s. It has been conventional, following the work of Gertzel, to stress that British Delta traders in the 1880s and 90s were not keen on encouraging political intervention into the interior.[93] After all, they had extensive investments in plant and contacts and preferred to rely on existing Delta structures, particularly of labour and transport, to bring oil to the coast. This, however, is not the full story, and much depends on what is meant by 'British Delta traders'. It may possibly have been true of the larger firms, but others had very different views of the role of government. British traders certainly remained committed to free trade to a very late date. Yet firms were also keen on aggressive consular activity, both against African brokers such as Jaja and to keep a German or French presence at bay. Newbury stresses how French activity in the early 1880s led traders to re-assess their vies of governmental action, while Hynes shows how from the mid-1880s Chambers of Commerce were calling for intervention in West Africa to defend British trading interests, if need be at the price of colonial occupation.[94] From the mid-1880s, traders were demanding that the government occupy the coast from the Gold Coast to Lagos, demanding the protection of British trade on the Niger and, following the declaration of the Protectorate over the Delta in 1885, urging governmental intervention into its interior. By the late 1880s, says Hynes, traders were emphatically in favour of annexation, with urgent demands for the establishment of 'law and order' throughout the interior and not just in Yorubaland.[95] Whatever the larger firms felt, smaller firms welcomed the establishment of the Oil Rivers Protectorate in 1891; indeed, some traders had called for such a protectorate in the face of French action as early as 1862, while repeated calls were made for an increase in the Delta Consul's powers throughout this period.[96] Moreover, while the larger firms may, as Gertzel suggested, have preferred the status quo, they were none the less vehement in calls for a royal charter over the Delta to be granted to the African Association in the late 1880s – calls only defeated by the strenuous political lobbying of A. L. Jones and the steamship companies. The failure of the charter campaign was followed by the African Association's welcome for the establishment of a Protectorate in 1891.[97] British traders' attitudes to political intervention changed considerably during the 1880s.

It is here that we see the consequences of the pressures that developed in the oil trade after the middle of the century. Thus, while the transition from the slave trade at the start of the century led to very little change in practice in the trade between West Africa and Britain, one can find much greater changes – a 'crisis of restructuring' rather than a 'crisis of adaptation' – later in the century. It is here that the African commerce went through its nineteenth-century 'crisis', and this was largely due to the reorganization of the trade that set in from about 1850. This is not to undermine Hopkins' thesis, however, since for him it was not simply the transition from slaving that was the cause of the problems facing Yorubaland in the second half of the century. In terms of explaining the origins of British imperial control in the 1890s, the immediate problems in Yorubaland were generated by the fall in oil prices in the 1880s and the accompanying shift in the terms of trade. It is the argument of this chapter that as far as the oil trade is concerned it was indeed this – exacerbated by the tensions set up from commercial restructuring – and not the transition from the slave trade that was the real crisis in nineteenth-century Anglo-West African economic relations.

NOTES

1 Robin Law, 'The historiography of the commercial transition in nineteenth-century West Africa', in Toyin Falola (ed.), *African Historiography: Essays in Honour of Jacob Ade Ajayi* (Harlow, 1993), pp. 91–115.

2 A. G. Hopkins, 'Economic imperialism in West Africa, Lagos 1880–92', *EHR*, 21 (1968), 580–606; *An Economic History of West Africa* (London, 1973), pp. 125–6, 135–64.

3 R. A. Austen, 'The abolition of the overseas slave trade: a distorted theme in West African history', *JHSN*, 5/2 (1970), 261; this is also argued by D. Eltis, 'Precolonial western Africa and the Atlantic economy', in B.L. Solow (ed.), *Slavery and the Rise of the Atlantic System* (Cambridge, 1991), pp. 97–119. Among the critics of the idea of a 'crisis of adaptation' are J. F. A. Ajayi and R. A. Austen, 'Hopkins on economic imperialism in West Africa', *EHR*, 25 (1972), 303–6; J. F. Munro, *Africa and the International Economy, 1800–1960* (London, 1976), p. 46; P. Wickins, *An Economic History of Africa* (Cape Town, 1981), p. 267; P. Manning, 'Slaves, palm oil and political power on the West African coast', *African Historical Studies*, 2 (1969), 279–88. However, Manning in 'The slave trade, "legitimate" trade and imperialism revisited: the control of wealth in the Bights of Benin and Biafra', in P. E. Lovejoy (ed.), *Africans in Bondage: Studies in slavery and the slave trade* (Madison, 1986), pp. 203–33, argues that a focus on the control of wealth rather than access to trade gives evidence for a form of 'crisis of adaptation' in this area.

4 Law, 'Historiography', pp. 103–12.

5 See esp. C. Chamberlin, 'Bulk exports, trade tiers, regulation and development: an economic approach to the study of West Africa's "legitimate trade"', *JEH*, 39 (1979), esp. 431–4.

6 This is made explicit in Hopkins, *Economic History*, pp. 124, 154.

7 G. Liesegang, 'Introduction', in G. Liesegang, H. Pasch and A. Jones (eds.), *Figuring African Trade* (Berlin, 1986), p. 2; though Eltis, 'Precolonial western Africa', p. 119, takes a contrary view.

8 D. Eltis and L. C. Jennings, 'Trade between western Africa and the Atlantic world in the pre-colonial era', *American Historical Review*, 93 (1988), 936–59.

9 Law, 'Historiography', pp. 95–8, 103–6.

10 K. O. Dike, *Trade and Politics in the Niger Delta 1830–1885* (Oxford, 1956).

11 E. J. Alagoa, 'Nineteenth century revolutions in the eastern Delta states and Calabar', *JHSN*, 5/4 (1971), 565–73; A. J. H. Latham, *Old Calabar 1600–1891* (Oxford, 1973); W. E. Wariboko, 'New Calabar and the forces of change, c.1850–1945' PhD thesis, University of Birmingham, 1991.

12 It is surprising that the Eastern Delta wars of 1871–84 involving Bonny, Opobo, Okrika, Brass and Elem Kalabari have not received much attention from historians of this area.

13 A. Jones, *From Slaves to Palm Kernels: A History of the Galinhas Country, 1730–1850* (Wiesbaden, 1983), esp. pp. 107–9.

14 J. Sanders, 'Palm oil production on the Gold Coast in the aftermath of the slave trade: a case study of the Fante', *IJAHS*, 15 (1982), 49–63.

15 E. Reynolds, *Trade and Economic Change on the Gold Coast 1807–1874* (London, 1974), pp. 103–38.
16 However, Chamberlin, 'Bulk exports', pp. 431–4, interprets Hopkins' argument solely in terms of the impact of moves in the terms of trade.
17 Public Record Office, London [hereafter, PRO]: FO 84/1176, Supercargoes to Burton, 28 April 1862, in Burton to FO, 22 May 1862; FO 84/1277, Livingstone to FO, 21 Dec. 1867; Latham, *Old Calabar*, pp. 81–2.
18 Latham, *Old Calabar*, p. 111.
19 S. Hargreaves, 'The political economy of nineteenth-century Bonny', PhD thesis, University of Birmingham, 1987, pp. 369, 376–9, 394–456, shows how this changed at the end of the century as British traders started to distribute trust more widely.
20 For one example of how such close ties could be of mutual benefit, see A. J. H. Latham, 'A trading alliance: Sir John Tobin and Duke Ephraim', *History Today*, 24 (1974), 862–7.
21 M. Lynn, 'Factionalism, imperialism and the making and breaking of Bonny kingship, c.1830–85', *Revue Française d'Histoire d'Outre-Mer*, 82 (1995), 1–24.
22 Law, 'Historiography', pp. 104–5.
23 Law, 'Historiography', p. 105.
24 D. Northrup, 'The compatibility of the slave and palm oil trades in the Bight of Biafra', *JAH*, 17 (1976), 353–64.
25 D. Pacheco Pereira, *Esmeraldo de Situ Orbis* (ed. G. H. T. Kimble, London, 1937), pp. 126–8; N. H. Stilliard, 'The rise and development of legitimate trade in palm oil with West Africa', PhD thesis, University of Birmingham, 1938, pp. 8–9.
26 Parliamentary Papers [hereafter, PP]: 1845, XVLVI (187), 481; M. Johnson, *Anglo-African Trade in the Eighteenth Century* (ed. J. T. Lindblad and R. Ross, Leiden, 1990), p. 56.
27 Northrup, 'Compatibility', p. 359.
28 This is the theme of Latham, *Old Calabar*, pp. 89–90, 111–12.
29 This is neatly encapsulated in Munro, *Africa and the International Economy*, pp. 45–6.
30 W. O. Henderson, 'The Liverpool Office in London', *Economica*, 42 (1933), 473–9.
31 G. Williams, *History of the Liverpool Privateers and Letters of Marque* (Liverpool, 1897), p. 621.
32 B. K. Drake, 'Liverpool's African commerce before and after the abolition of the slave trade', MA thesis, University of Liverpool, 1974.
33 B. K. Drake, 'Continuity and flexibility in Liverpool's trade with Africa and the Caribbean', *Business History*, 18 (1976), 85–97; 'Liverpool's African commerce', pp. 12–13.
34 Drake, 'Liverpool's African commerce', pp. 91–121. Drake suggests that some Liverpool traders did in fact continue a clandestine slave trade, especially with Brazil, after 1807: pp. 112–16.
35 Drake, 'Liverpool's African commerce', pp. 104, 123.
36 Drake, 'Liverpool's African commerce', pp. 94–7.
37 Drake, 'Liverpool's African commerce', p. 12; B. K. Drake, 'The Liverpool–

African voyage c.1790–1807: commercial problems', in R. Anstey and P. E. H. Hair (eds.), *Liverpool, the African Slave Trade and Abolition* (Historic Society of Lancashire and Cheshire, 1976), p. 137.

38 Drake, 'Liverpool's African commerce', pp. 61–2.
39 Drake, 'Liverpool's African commerce', p. 195.
40 Drake, 'Liverpool's African commerce', p. 111.
41 M. Lynn, 'Change and continuity in the British palm oil trade with West Africa, 1830–55', *JAH*, 22 (1981), 337; 'From sail to steam: the impact of the steamship services on the British palm oil trade with West Africa, 1850–90', *JAH*, 30 (1989), 236.
42 Drake, 'Liverpool's African Commerce', pp. 106–7.
43 R. C. Reid, 'Annals of the Tobin family of Liverpool' (ms. in Liverpool Central Library); B.G. Orchard, *Liverpool's Legion of Honour* (Liverpool, 1893), pp. 138–9, 676; Williams, *History*, pp. 307, 360, 645, 679, 682–3.
44 PP: 1847–8, XXII (536), 472–3.
45 Drake, 'Liverpool's African commerce', pp. 248–50; Latham, 'Trading alliance', pp. 862–8.
46 PP: 1847–8, XXII (536), 474; Stilliard, 'Legitimate Trade', p. 24; Drake, 'Liverpool's African commerce', pp. 248–50.
47 PP: 1847–8, XXII (536), 467, 482; Drake, 'Liverpool's African commerce', pp. 248–50; Williams, *History*, p. 613; Dike, *Trade and Politics*, pp. 49–50; R. Anstey, *The Atlantic Slave Trade and British Abolition 1760–1810* (New Jersey, 1975), p. 291; Lynn, 'Change and continuity', p. 344.
48 M. Lynn, 'British business and the African trade: Richard & William King Ltd of Bristol and West Africa, 1833–1918', *Business History*, 34 (1992), 20–37.
49 T. Baines, *History of the Commerce ... of Liverpool* (Liverpool, 1852), pp. 11–12; *Bristol Times & Mirror*, 28 Sept. 1874. This the theme of M. Lynn, 'Trade and politics in nineteenth century Liverpool: the Tobin and Horsfall families and Liverpool's African trade', *Transactions of the Historic Society of Lancashire & Cheshire*, 142 (1993), 99–120.
50 W. E. Minchinton, 'The voyage of the scow "Africa"', *Mariners' Mirror*, 37 (1951), 187–96; 'Memoranda of the African trade' ascribed to W. A. & G. Maxwell, 1830–40 (Sydney Jones Library, University of Liverpool).
51 The origins of trust are difficult to determine, but it was certainly established in Old Calabar by 1760: Latham, *Old Calabar*, p. 27. Interestingly, Bristol ships on the Windward Coast in the 1880s still took 'pawns' from coastal brokers as guarantees for repayment of trust: J. C. Langdon, 'Three voyages to the West Coast of Africa, 1881–4' (ms. in Bristol Central Library), p. 22.
52 C. Newbury, 'On the margins of empire: the trade of western Africa 1875–1890', in S. Forster, W.J. Mommsen and R. Robinson (eds.), *Bismarck, Europe and Africa: The Berlin West Africa Conference and the Onset of Partition* (Oxford, 1988), p. 39; A. D. Nzemeke, 'Free trade and territorial partition in nineteenth century West Africa: course and outcome', ibid., p. 61.
53 This does not necessarily mean that they were the determinants of prices.
54 Anon., 'Builders of the African Trade', *Elder Dempster Magazine*, 6 (1927), 133–4; Lynn, 'Sail to steam', pp. 234–5.
55 'Builders of the African Trade', pp. 133–4; L. Finigan, *The Life of Peter*

Stuart (privately printed, 1920), p. 68; P.N. Davies (ed.), *Trading in West Africa* (London, 1976), p. 174.

56 Lynn, 'Tobin and Horsfall families', pp. 106–7.

57 PP: 1866, LXXIII (3675), 26–7, 32–3; 1876, LXVII (1573), 34–5, 74–5; 1890–1, LXXXIX (6457), 64–5, 134–5; *Journal of the Royal Statistical Society*, 49 (1886), 641; A. J. H. Latham, 'Palm oil exports from Old Calabar 1812–87 (with a note on price formation)', in Liesegang, Pasch and Jones (eds.), *Figuring African Trade*, p. 292.

58 M. Lynn, 'The profitability of the early nineteenth century palm oil trade', *AEH*, 20 (1992), 77–97.

59 F. J. Pedler, *The Lion and the Unicorn in Africa* (London, 1974), p. 71.

60 R. M. Jackson, *Journal of a Voyage to Bonny River*, (London, 1934), p. 94.

61 These were long-established in the trade but came to be more extensively used in this period: E. Bold, *The Merchants' and Mariners' Guide* (London, 1822), p. 78; Jackson, *Journal*, p. 67.

62 For early examples see PRO: FO 84/858, Beecroft to Palmerston, 1 Sept. 1851; FO 84/920, Mitchell to Beecroft, 18 Aug. 1853, in Beecroft to Clarendon, 6 Sept. 1853; W. N. Thomas, 'On the oil rivers of West Africa', *Proceedings of the Royal Geographical Society*, 17 (1873), 148–9.

63 PRO: FO 84/858, Beecroft to Palmerston, 24 Feb. 1851.

64 PP: 1842, XI (551), 205.

65 A. G. Hopkins, 'An economic history of Lagos, 1880–1914', PhD thesis, University of London, 1964, p. 64.

66 Hopkins, 'Economic history', pp. 87–88; A. G. Hopkins, 'The currency revolution in South-West Nigeria in the late nineteenth century', *JHSN*, 3/3 (1966), 471–83.

67 P. N. Davies, *The Trade Makers: Elder Dempster in West Africa 1852–1972* (London, 1973), pp. 35–69.

68 Drake, 'Liverpool's African commerce', pp. 138–41, 148.

69 Though sail continued to be used for some time to transport cheaper, coarser goods to West Africa: PRO: FO 84/1343, Livingstone's memo. of 8 Dec. 1871.

70 Lynn, 'Sail to steam', pp. 241–2.

71 PP: 1873, LXV (828), 4; C. Gertzel, 'John Holt: a British Merchant in West Africa in the Era of Imperialism', DPhil thesis, University of Oxford, 1959.

72 M. Lynn, 'Technology, trade and a race of native capitalists": the Krio diaspora of West Africa and the steamship, 1852–95', *JAH*, 33 (1992), 421–40.

73 *Journal of the Society of Arts*, 22 (1874), 118.

74 PP: 1873, LXV (828), 3–4; PRO, FO 84/1356, Livingstone to Granville, 9 July 1872.

75 Lynn, 'Technology', p. 433.

76 Dike, *Trade and Politics*, p. 115; K. K. Nair, 'Trade in southern Nigeria from 1860 to the 1870s: expansion or stagnation?', *JHSN*, 6/4 (1973), 429.

77 Dike, *Trade and Politics*, p. 119; C. W. Newbury, 'Trade and authority in West Africa from 1850 to 1880', in L.H. Gann and P. Duignan (eds.), *Colonialism in Africa*, I (Cambridge, 1969), pp. 81–2.

78 PRO: FO 84/1001, Hutchinson to Clarendon, 24 Sept. 1856.

79 Lynn, 'Technology', pp. 433–9.
80 Newbury, 'Margins of empire', p. 57.
81 The Tobins formed the Company of African Merchants in 1863. PP: 1864, XLI (424), 581. The way these pressures to restructure affected an individual firm can be seen in Lynn, 'Richard & William King'.
82 For pooling arrangements see 'Old Calabar Agreement', c.1885, in John Holt Papers, Rhodes House, Oxford, 3/11.
83 Pedler, Lion and Unicorn, p. 139.
84 PP: 1880, LXVII (2484), 74–5; Journal of the Royal Statistical Society, 55 (1892), p. 119; W. G. Hynes, The Economics of Empire: Britain, Africa and the New Imperialism 1870–95 (London, 1979), p. 94.
85 A. McPhee, The Economic Revolution in British West Africa (London, 1926), pp. 32–6; Hopkins, Economic History, p. 133.
86 PP: 1876, LXXVII (1573), 34–5; 1890–1, LXXXIX (6457), 64–5; Newbury, 'Margins of empire', p. 42.
87 Hopkins, Economic history, pp. 131–4, 154.
88 PRO: FO 84/1377, Livingstone to Granville, 10 June 1873.
89 PRO: FO 84/1117, Hutchinson to Russell, 29 May 1860; Nair, 'Trade in southern Nigeria', 433.
90 PRO: FO 84/1176, Burton to FO, 22 May 1862.
91 PRO: FO 84/1290, Minute on Livingstone to Stanley, 25 Feb. 1868; FO 84/1356, Livingstone to Granville, 29 April 1872.
92 As examples, PRO: FO 84/1277, Livingstone to Stanley, 22 April 1867; FO 84/1308, Livingstone to Clarendon, 23 Nov. 1869; FO 84/1356, Livingstone to Stephens, 3 Aug. 1872, in Livingstone to Granville, 3 Aug. 1872.
93 C. Gertzel, 'Commercial organisation in the Niger Coast, 1852–91', Proceedings of the Intercollegiate History Conference (Salisbury, 1960), pp. 13–14; 'Relations between African and European traders on the Niger Delta, 1880–96', JAH, 3 (1962), 361–6.
94 Newbury, 'Margins of empire', p. 52; Hynes, Economics of Empire, pp. 57–87.
95 Hynes, Economics of Empire, pp. 93ff.
96 PRO: FO 84/1176, Burton to FO, 14 Jan. 1862; FO 84/1343, Hopkins to Granville, 2 Aug. 1871.
97 Gertzel, 'John Holt', pp. 373–421; Hynes, Economics of Empire, pp. 101–3.

3 The compatibility of the slave and palm oil trades in Dahomey, 1818–1858

Elisée Soumonni

One of the central issues of West African history in the anti-slave trade era is the transition from the slave trade to 'legitimate' trade. Dahomey, a major exporter of slaves and later of palm oil, has often been used as an illustrative case-study of the problems and implications of that transition.[1] In Dahomey, the reign of King Ghezo, 1818–1858, is of especial significance in this process of the substitution of palm produce exports for slaves.[2]

In fact, Ghezo came to power through a *coup d'état* with the assistance of a famous slave-trader, the Brazilian Francisco Felix de Souza, at a time when the British were leading an international crusade for the suppression of the Atlantic slave trade.[3] Throughout the forty years of Ghezo's reign, the British relentlessly put pressure on him to give up slaving and human sacrifices, two basic features of Dahomey's history. Though this pressure was resisted, palm oil progressively emerged as Dahomey's major export in place of slaves. Ghezo was therefore able to overcome the 'crisis of adaptation' resulting from the change from the slave trade to the palm oil trade, thereby proving, contrary to contemporary philanthropist assumption, that trade in human beings and in agricultural goods were compatible.

In the historiography of nineteenth-century Dahomey, the totality of factors in Ghezo's policy has not hitherto been properly assessed. Beninese scholars have perceived his reign as a turning point in the kingdom's political and economic history for two main reasons.[4] First, his accession to the throne occurred through a *coup d'état* which overthrew his predecessor Adandonzan in 1818, thus bringing to an end what is generally referred to as a reign of terror (1797–1818). Secondly, he is credited with bringing about the change from the slave trade to 'legitimate' trade in palm products. It is argued that, having realized that the slave trade had no further future, Ghezo took the initiative of encouraging the development of the palm oil trade. In other words, Ghezo was able to overcome two crises: a political crisis (Adandonzan's deposition) and an economic crisis (the transition from slave to 'legitimate' trade).

Little wonder that terms such as 'renovation', 'revival', and 'economic revolution' are often used to assess his performance. In the examination of the two aspects of the crisis, the significance of the commercial transition issue in the 1818 *coup d'état* and its implications for Ghezo's subsequent policy are hardly taken into consideration by many Beninese scholars.

Another factor that is generally yet to be properly assessed in Ghezo's policy is his clever exploitation of the rivalry between France and Britain, both responsible for suppressing the slave trade along the West African coast but not equally committed to the task.[5] While the British were putting pressure on Ghezo to give up slave-trading and human sacrifice, the French adopted a compromising attitude on the issue. The best illustration of this attitude is the official support enjoyed by Victor Régis, the businessman from Marseilles, whose firm was allowed to reoccupy the old French slave-fort in Dahomey's port of Whydah despite suspicions and accusations of slave-trading levelled against his agents.[6]

While outlining the various factors in Ghezo's policy, it will be argued in this paper that, despite the many political and economic problems it created for his regime, the 'crisis of adaptation' to the shift from the slave to 'legitimate' trade was, to a large extent, successfully overcome by King Ghezo.

Ghezo's accession, 1818

The reign of Adandozan is, without doubt, one of the most controversial issues in the political history of Dahomey. The source of this controversy is the official tradition that has completely erased his name from the list of the kings of Dahomey. Such an unprecedented measure has been justified by equally unprecedented crimes ascribed to Adandozan. Contemporary accounts and many subsequent studies have represented him as an African Nero. Thus, for the French missionary Abbé Pierre Bouche, 'he left the saddest memories among his subjects ... But for the face and name, he was hardly a human being.'[7] As if this were not enough, even the legitimacy of Adandozan's reign is questioned in some traditions. Cornevin, for example, calls him 'the king-regent',[8] while according to Herskovits 'the Dahomeans of the present time do not hesitate to speak of the cruel Adandozan who, taking the regency during the minority of Ghezo, so loved power that there was no extent to which he could not go to maintain it.'[9] The traditional picture of Adandozan as a wicked regent who had to be forced to abdicate is generally being challenged in recent studies. Akinjogbin, for example, finds it 'totally misleading', and nothing more than a means of justifying Ghezo's own irregular accession to the throne.[10]

The fact that Adandozan's name has been erased from the official king-list can be interpreted as an illustration of this conscious attempt. Akinjogbin is also of the view that the story of Adandozan's wickedness might not be unconnected with the fact that he was 'an imaginative and progressive young monarch, far ahead of his time'.[11] Djivo shares the same opinion:

> Adandozan held power. He did not lack initiatives. Some of these were audacious, and make his reign an exceptional period for a deep transformation of the traditional habits and mentality, too attached to the old customs. His mistake was to have dared to attack institutional taboos.[12]

It is against this sort of reassessment of Adandozan's reign that Maurice Glele, himself a descendant of Ghezo, appears to protest in his book. Following the official tradition, Glele explained Adandozan's deposition by two causes. The first was his sadism, which he did not question at all, since during his time Adandozan was considered 'as the very personification of devilish spirit'.[13] The second was his non-respect of tradition, because 'for twenty years he refused to make sacrifices in honour of his father Agonglo! He was committing the greatest crime of the kingdom.'[14] Glele rejects with disdain the attempt to interpret Adandozan's attitude as that of 'an imaginative and progressive monarch desiring to break with the past, with outmoded customs'.[15] What is surprising in Glele's argument is his silence about Francisco Felix de Souza, alias Chacha, the famous Brazilian slave-trader whom most of the written documents regard as Ghezo's accomplice in the *coup* against Adandozan. This significant and, I suspect, deliberate silence suggests the role that the Atlantic slave trade may have played in Adandozan's deposition.[16]

There is sufficient evidence in contemporary accounts to support such a hypothesis. Foreign traders and directors of forts in Whydah were usually roughly dealt with by Adandozan's agents. Between 1797 and 1804, for example, four Portuguese directors were 'expelled in quick succession'.[17] Many Portuguese, captured during raids against Porto-Novo and Badagry, were also held captive in the Dahomian capital Abomey. Adanzozan considered them as prisoners of war and was not prepared to release them without ransom, a condition the governor of the Portuguese fort of Whydah refused to accept.[18] It may be suggested that Adandozan's attitude *vis-à-vis* merchants established in his kingdom largely explains why contemporary European accounts contributed to publicizing his wickedness.

Such an attitude also explains why Francisco Felix de Souza, who was himself imprisoned in Abomey by Adandozan, gave his support to Ghezo.

Even Adandozan's disrespect for traditions might not be totally unconnected with the issue of the Atlantic slave trade. Irregular and unimpressive 'Annual Customs' (the principal public ceremony of the Dahomian monarchy, at which gifts were distributed to the assembled chiefs and people) during his reign can be accounted for by the abandonment, between 1797 and 1807, of the European forts at Whydah and the decline of the European trade with Dahomey. But irregular and unimpressive annual customs may also have reflected, as Akinjogbin has suggested, an attempt by Adandozan to draw his kingdom away from the slave trade.[19] In objection to this interpretation, one could of course argue that the decline of European trade with Dahomey at this period was due, not to Adandozan's deliberate policy, but to the fact that the British Abolition Act came about during his reign; but we know that this act did not have any magical or immediate effect. One might also raise the objection that Adandozan was somewhat ineffective in his military campaigns, undermining the supply of war captives for sale to the Europeans; but it might be asked to what extent his ill-treatment of slave-traders, depriving him of the necessary arms, was responsible for this military failure.

From the above, it seems that there was a dialectical relationship between the trans-Atlantic slave trade and Adandozan's internal policy. It might not be unreasonable, though there is little direct evidence for this, to see in him an innovative king, desiring to break with the traditional slave trade. The fact that Felix Francisco de Souza joined the insurrection against him and gave it its 'greatest chance of success', shows that Adandozan's political orientation was thought damaging to foreign interests in Dahomey.[20] The famous Brazilian slave-trader, it has been pointed out, 'was more an extension, an agent of the European side' of the trans-Atlantic trade, 'rather than of the African side'.[21] He was to have a great influence on Ghezo's economic policy.

In this context, it would appear that Ghezo, unlike his predecessor, was not a reluctant partisan of the slave trade. His commitment to the trade, reinforced by the blood pact with the man generally considered to be the most notorious of the slave traders on the West African coast, would remain unshakeable throughout his reign. His resistance to the British pressure to give up the slave trade, the strengthening of his armed forces by the organization of a regular corps of 'Amazons', and the impulse to military campaigns during his reign should therefore be seen in line with this commitment.

The rise of the palm oil trade

How valid is the assumption that Ghezo, having realized that the slave trade had no more future, took the initiative of encouraging the development of the palm oil trade? If the slave trade carried out throughout Ghezo's reign was part of the economic tradition of the kingdom, on the other hand, the emergence during the same period of palm oil as a main export product did indeed constitute a significant change and was to become an important factor in Dahomian internal and external policy. But how is this development to be accounted for? By the decline of the slave trade as a result of a more effective control of the seas by European powers, or by Ghezo's deliberate, conscious and wise economic policy?

The contention that the rise and growth of legitimate trade implied the decline and suppression of trade in slaves is not unquestionable. For the Bight of Biafra, David Northrup has observed that

combining the trends of the slave and the palm oil trade in the first half of the nineteenth century, the conclusion seems inescapable that the rise in the palm oil trade did not coincide with a decline in the slave trade, but that the two trades expanded in tandem until the 1830s.[22]

Likewise in Dahomey, the palm oil trade initially expanded alongside a still flourishing slave trade. According to Patrick Manning, 'export of slaves and palm products coexisted from the late 1830s to the mid-1860s: revenue from slaves and palm products were roughly equal in the 1840s, after which palm products dominated.'[23] However, the British anti-slave trade campaign in Dahomey was based precisely on the contention that the slave and 'legitimate' trades were incompatible. In order to achieve the objective of suppressing the slave trade by promoting 'legitimate' trade (and *vice versa*), the British pursued two strategies. The first was to persuade Ghezo, through special missions to Abomey, to give up the slave trade and to devote his energy towards promoting legitimate trade. The missions to Abomey of William Winniett and John Beecroft, in 1847 and 1850 respectively, were in line with this first strategy. The second strategy consisted of stronger measures, such as the blockade of Dahomian ports to stop slave exports. Thus the blockade of Whydah in 1851–2 lasted almost six months, and was lifted only after Ghezo agreed to sign a treaty (13 January 1852) by which he pledged to stop the exportation of slaves. This pledge, according to the British, he never honoured, while the Dahomian ruler was of the view that he could not be held personally responsible for the continued illegal exportation of slaves.

That the rise in the palm oil trade did not coincide with a decline in the slave trade was an illustration of the relative impact of these two strategies pursued by the British. In any case, the two strategies were certainly not the determinant factors in the transition in Dahomey, which was due rather to shifting patterns of overseas demand. As Patrick Manning has observed, 'the most basic factors in the substitution [of agricultural exports for slave exports] were the declining trans-Atlantic demand for slaves and the growing demand for palm products'.[24]

There is a need to reconsider the view according to which most of the credit for developing the palm oil trade is to be ascribed to African rulers, as a measure against an anticipated decline in the slave trade.[25] In Dahomey, as elsewhere in Africa, the move was spearheaded by external stimuli. Ghezo, like other African rulers, simply responded to these external stimuli, but he did so with the understanding that the new trade could be carried on hand in hand with the old one. The new product would simply mean an increase in revenue, supplementing that obtained from the slave trade. It was surely because of Ghezo's realization of this fact that he took positive measures to encourage the new trade in the 1840s, declaring the palm a sacred tree, which it was forbidden to cut down. He also took the crucial step of transforming the *kouzou*, a sort of royal tax on agricultural produce introduced during the reign of Wegbaja (*c.*1645–80) into a tax payable in palm oil by all palm growers and collected by an important dignitary, the Tavisa.

Slave-merchants operating in Dahomey also perceived the new trade as an additional opportunity for their business. The view that Francisco Felix de Souza opposed the trade in palm oil is questionable.[26] This view has been supported by reference to John Duncan's report that in the 1840s Ghezo was discouraging the export of shea-butter oil, on the advice of the Spanish and Portuguese slave-dealers of Whydah; it is on the basis of this account that Catherine Coquery-Vidrovitch finds the view plausible.[27] But, as Robin Law has rightly pointed out, the fact that the ban was restricted to shea-butter oil, which was grown in the northern areas of Dahomey, suggests that it may have been intended to protect the interests of the producers of palm oil near the coast at Whydah, rather than representing opposition to 'legitimate' trade as such.[28]

It is not unsafe to conclude from the above discussion that Ghezo encouraged the palm oil trade because he saw it not as a substitute for, but as a supplement to the slave trade. The two trades were assumed to be compatible, and did actually prove compatible throughout his reign. A major reason why Ghezo's strategy of combining the slave and palm oil trades proved possible was because the French, unlike the British, put little pressure on him to give up slave-trading. The factory of the French merchant Victor Régis at Whydah developed its palm oil business in this context, and its history constitutes an interesting aspect of the problems of the commercial transition in Dahomey.

The role of Victor Régis

The reoccupation of the old French slave fort of Whydah in 1841 by the firm of Régis took place, it must be recalled, in the context of the campaign against the slave trade. Against this background, it was likely to give rise to suspicion from anti-slave trade crusaders. Conscious of this danger, the French government was very cautious in dealing with the matter. The request for the reoccupation of the fort was granted only conditionally. The condition was that the factory should not be involved in the slave trade; and as a private firm it could not hoist the French tricolour flag unless it was laced with white.[29]

In fact, accusations of trading in slaves were soon levelled at the Régis factory in Whydah, and this from various quarters. To the British (traders, naval officers, explorers etc.) the French factory was not only encouraging the slave trade, but also actively engaged in it. This belief was based partly on day-to-day observations: inside the factory gallons of palm-oil coexisted with slaves.[30] It also derived from Ghezo's support to the factory, a support logically perceived as a reward for Régis' compromising attitude towards the slave trade in Dahomey. It was particularly significant that André Brue, an agent of the Régis factory, was introduced to Ghezo in 1843 by the notorious slave-trader Felix Francisco de Souza.[31] The British navy became more convinced that only a close blockade of Whydah could stop what it considered a criminal activity.

But accusations of slave-trading against the Régis factory did not emerge only from British quarters. Among the French too, there was the belief that Régis' agents' activities were not restricted to 'legitimate' trade. Reacting to Victor Régis' complaint about insufficient assistance to his agents from the French naval squadron, Montagniès de la Roque, of the *Division Navale des Côtes d'Afrique*, pointed out this trader's predilection for establishing his business in notorious slave-trading centres: 'The Squadron of Africa', he wrote, 'is daily witnessing his indirect participation in the slave trade by supplying slave markets such as Ouidah and Benguela with necessary goods.'[32] However, the most virulent accusations against the Régis factory at Whydah came from a French traveller, the naturalist Christophe Colomb, who spent two years in Dahomey (June 1847–September 1849).[33] Colomb's observations on Régis' agents' activities in Whydah reached Paris while he was still in

Dahomey. Thus, in a letter to the Minister of Trade, dated 6 December 1848, he accused the firm of Régis of openly trading in slaves. He renewed this accusation on several occasions, and particularly in 1850, when *L'Ecureuil*, a ship belonging to Victor Régis, was sold to Portuguese slave-dealers for the purpose of slave-trading.

The way these various and repeated accusations were received in official quarters is highly significant. It contradicts the caution shown in the granting of the request for the reoccupation of the old slave fort. In spite of the apparent embarrassment there was an obvious attempt to whitewash Victor Régis and present him as a worthy representative of French interests in Dahomey. Such an attitude was illustrated by the content of a letter written by the Minister of Agriculture and Trade to the Chamber of Commerce of Marseilles on 18 December 1850.[34] After denying any official character to Colomb's memoirs, the letter was concluded thus:

Moreover, I have been deeply disgusted by C. Colomb's grave accusations against one of the most respectable houses of Marseilles. The leader of this house [i.e. Victor Régis], whose experience and knowledge are, at this very moment, generously offered to the government, deserves respect and gratitude for his unselfishness and zeal.

The minister's disgust, however, could not prevent the setting up of a committee of inquiry headed by Bouet-Willaumez to look into Colomb's accusations. According to the report of this committee, local rumours rather than precise facts had contributed to the suspicions that Régis' agents were in collusion with slave-dealers. Thus, Brue was accused of slave-trading and of having accumulated by this means a fortune of 400,000 FF after only four years in Whydah! The report concluded with a suggestion: the expulsion of all traders from Whydah.

As for the sale of a ship to Portuguese slave-traders, Oddo, the captain of the ship, was brought to face charges in court and Colomb invited to testify. Victor Régis defended himself by claiming that the *Ecureuil* was attached to his factory in Gabon, which was solely concerned with trade in ivory. The crisis in this commodity, he declared, compelled him to sell it off. He dismissed Colomb's accusations in their entirety as the imaginings of an irresponsible lunatic. However, the seriousness of the charges against him compelled the Minister of Justice to submit his file to the Public Prosecutor of Aix-en-Provence for further consideration. As a result of this move a search was conducted in Victor Régis' residence in Marseilles. But the famous trader was intelligent enough not to keep compromising documents in his house. He saw the search as an affront and summoned the French government to deny, through the official gazette *Le Moniteur*, all the accusations against his factory at Whydah. The impact of this arrogant demand was immediate. The Minister of Justice wrote to the Public Prosecutor of Aix-en-Provence and urged him to act with 'the greatest discretion': 'I received', he added, 'complaints about the indiscreet police search of Régis' residence in Marseilles.'[35] After this message, it is not surprising that the case was 'lamentably lost in the sands of procedure', although, according to the Prosecutor, Régis was generally regarded as a slave-dealer.

Victor Régis' schemes to recruit 'free labourers' and 'free emigrants' provided his opponents with further evidence of his dubious role in the slave trade. In 1850 he sought the French government's permission to buy slaves back from the king of Dahomey. As 'free labourers', these redeemed slaves would have to work ten years in his factory before they became completely free.[36] The reply to this request also illustrated the dubious attitude of the French authorities *vis-à-vis* the slave trade in Dahomey. While it questioned the philanthropic motive behind Régis' proposal and the advantages Dahomeans could derive from it, the French government did not reject it. In fact, the leader of the house of Régis was implicitly encouraged to go ahead with his project if he could secure the agreement of the Dahomian authorities. In this case, the French government 'would make sure that the promise to free slaves after their service was honoured'.[37]

The basic objective of Régis' 'free labourers' scheme in Dahomey became more open to suspicion when he got involved in the subsequent (1857–61) 'free emigration' scheme. It is known that the French government, in order to recruit emigrant labourers from the West African coast for Martinique and Guadeloupe, signed a contract with Victor Régis. But as there were no free Africans anxious to emigrate the scheme could work only if slaves were disguised as emigrants. In this way, many 'free labourers' of Whydah were transformed into 'free emigrants' and conveyed by slave-ships to the West Indies. Accusations and protests against this practice from various quarters greatly embarrassed the French government, to the point that Victor Régis found it necessary to write to the Emperor Napoleon III to justify and clear himself.[38] This letter is the best illustration of Régis' views and attitude towards slavery and the slave trade.

Régis claimed that what he was involved in had nothing to do with the slave trade. According to him, the slave trade implied slavery at both departure and arrival, i.e. a slave remained a slave even in a foreign land. What he was doing, he argued, was just the opposite: 'We deliver slaves to make them citizens'. Slavery, he continued, was a very ancient and widespread institution in Africa, which could only be abolished by taking over the whole continent and imposing civilization upon it. Because this seemed impossible, the only thing to do was to wait and expect change from Providence. He was of the view that trade, more than the use of force, contributed to improving the fate of some parts of the coast, while the interior as a whole continued to live in a state of savagery. Those who thought an end to the immigration scheme would stop internecine conflicts were dreamers. Africans, Victor Régis contended, were fighting each other by instinct, not for any defined motive. No wonder the British cruisers and other means were impotent to check these conflicts. His remarks, he said, were based on practice and not on theory. Hence the following conclusion, that the immigration scheme was the only way out, the sole means of saving slaves from massacre:

Let us admit for a moment that the abolition of slavery was proclaimed everywhere, that the slave trade had lost its justification, that free emigration should cease by itself, briefly, that a tight-closed blockade of the African coasts could be established and that the dream of philanthropy be realized in all its ideal: what could slaves gain from this deadlock? They would only increase their chance of being massacred en masse or of falling one by one under the knife of fetish priests.

One is tempted, after a close examination of the above letter to Napoleon III, to wonder whether Régis' involvement in the slave trade requires any further evidence; whether it is not a matter of semantics, depending on one's definition and concept of the slave trade. And since, according to Régis, the Atlantic slave trade was nothing but a means of saving savage Africans from death and civilizing them, the rationale of a crusade for its suppression is questionable. It is not therefore surprising that the British navy regarded the Régis factory as a contributory factor in the maintenance of the slave trade in Dahomey. No wonder, either, that Régis saw the 1851 blockade of Whydah by the British navy as deliberately directed against his interests.

Victor Régis had good reasons for this belief. The 1851 blockade of Whydah followed the mission of Auguste Bouet to Abomey (May–August 1851), which Régis had initiated and the outcome of which was the signing of a Franco-Dahomian treaty on 1 July 1851.[39] A careful examination of this document shows the full extent to which Victor Régis exploited the mission in the interests of his company. As the most important of the French traders who had settled in Dahomey, he was the first to benefit from the protection and freedom of trade which Ghezo promised all French settlers in his kingdom (article 1). He also stood to gain from several other clauses of the treaty: from, for example, the special protection which the king promised to the palm oil trade (art. 4); and from Ghezo's commitment to the severe repression of fraud in the supply of palm oil which could damage this newly developing industry (art. 7). Régis benefited also from the ban on petty officials who attempted to discourage the palm oil trade on the slightest pretext (art. 8). Finally, the Régis factory was assured of a steady and permanent supply of workers employed under conditions which could be considered more than favourable, since the king undertook to punish severely anyone from the French quarter of Whydah who refused to work without a valid excuse (art. 6).

What is striking about the treaty is the significant absence of any suggestion that Ghezo should relinquish the slave trade, the point responsible for the failure of the British missions to Abomey. Obviously, the anti-slave trade crusade was far from being a central concern of either the merchant from Marseilles or, for that matter, the French government. The protection promised by the king to all French missionaries coming to settle in his kingdom (art. 10) was perhaps considered sufficient evidence of the treaty's concern with France's 'mission civilisatrice' in the area!

As far as Régis was concerned, the British blockade of Whydah was aimed at destroying the benefit of this successful French mission. On the deceitful pretext of the suppression of the slave trade, the strategy of blockade was aimed at diverting the on-going palm oil trade in Little Popo, Port-Novo and Whydah to Badagry. In his passionate appeal to the French government for a rapid end to the blockade, Régis resorted to nationalistic appeals and, in so doing, his own interests and those of France became, as usual, synonymous for him.

However, the blockade placed the French government in a very delicate position. Extremely reluctant to enter into a conflict with the British, France could, besides, hardly oppose openly a blockade which was officially justified as part of the policy to abolish the slave trade. This is why a flexible diplomatic approach, through the French embassy in London, was adopted to secure the lifting of the blockade. But this occurred only after Ghezo, conscious of the damage being done to his economy, had agreed to sign a treaty by which he pledged to stop the exportation of slaves.

Conclusion

What one may one conclude from Régis' experience in Dahomey is that the 'transition' issue raised difficulties not only for those who, like Ghezo, were committed to the slave trade despite the crusade for its suppression, but also for the self-proclaimed promoters of 'legitimate' trade. Despite suspicions and accusations, the reoccupation of the old French fort of Whydah was not intended to revive the slave trade, but the Régis factory did operate within the framework of that trade, with the support of the king's agents, and did therefore also contribute to making the trade in palm oil compatible with the continued export of human beings during the period under discussion.

This is not to say that the transition from the slave trade to 'legitimate' trade posed no difficulties for the Dahomian state. The compatibility of the two trades, successfully demonstrated by Ghezo's policy in the 1840s and '50s, could not provide a long-term solution, since the export of slaves would eventually come to an end, leaving Dahomey dependent solely on the palm produce trade. As a matter of fact, because of its long history of participation in the Atlantic slave trade, the substitution of palm products for slave exports could not be an easy process for Dahomey. The economic, ideological and political implications and strains of the transition for Dahomey have been examined in many studies, particularly in the unpublished thesis of John Reid.[40] In purely economic terms, the palm oil trade was not as profitable as the slave trade. Despite Ghezo's encouragement of it, by the mid nineteenth century, Reid concludes, 'the benefits to the monarchy from the new trade were still of relatively minor importance, particularly when compared to that derived from previously flourishing slave exports'.[41] Brodie Cruickshank's mission to Dahomey in 1848 stressed the significance of the royal income from the slave trade, estimated at about £60,000 per annum; little wonder that the British government's 'paltry offer' of £400 as annual compensation to Ghezo for the proposed ending of slave exports was contemptuously rejected.[42] It should be stressed, however, that even if it had been higher than or equivalent to the income from the slave trade, the offer would still have been rejected, because the significance of the slave trade for Dahomey cannot be assessed only in economic terms.

As a result of the nature of the slave trade, which depended upon a regular supply of war captives, because of its long participation in it, as Law has argued, 'Dahomey was a warrior state, with a deep-seated military ethos which involved a disdain for agriculture as unwarlike'.[43] It was therefore difficult and painful for the kingdom's military oligarchy to adjust to the new economic reality. It was also dangerous for any Dahomian ruler to fail to take this factor into account. Moreover, war captives were needed not only for export, but also for human sacrifice during the 'Annual Customs'. Non-respect of these customs could deprive the king of his throne. Ghezo's resistance to the British pressure for an end to the slave trade was therefore dictated by its religious and cultural implications for his kingdom.

The political strains of the transition from slave to palm oil trading were a consequence of the economic and cultural significance of the slave trade. The deposition of Ghezo's predecessor Adandozan, as discussed earlier in this essay, was an illustration of this problem. Even Ghezo's rather cautious response to the problems caused by the transition engendered dissensions within the Dahomian ruling elite, which were reflected in the disputed succession to the throne at his death in 1858, and in tensions during the reign of his successor Glele (1858–89).[44]

However, although there is no doubt that the transition from slave to 'legitimate' trade was far from being an easy one, there is a consensus in studies of Dahomey's history during the abolitionist era: the kingdom was not destabilized by the transition, and remained a relatively strong polity down to the French conquest in 1892–4. This survival of the Dahomian state, in my opinion, shows that it did, in the final analysis, successfully overcome the 'crisis of adaptation' resulting from the commercial transition.

NOTES

1   See esp. Catherine Coquery-Vidrovitch, 'De la traite des esclaves à l'exportation de l'huile de palme et des palmistes au Dahomey', in Claude Meillassoux (ed.), *The Development of Indigenous Trade and Markets in West Africa* (London, 1971), pp. 107–23; John Reid, 'Warrior aristocrats in crisis: the political effects of the transition from the slave trade to palm oil commerce in the nineteenth-century kingdom of Dahomey', PhD thesis, University of Stirling, 1986; Robin Law, 'Dahomey and the end of the Atlantic slave trade' (Centre of African Studies, Boston University, Working Papers in African Studies No. 165, 1992).

2   Cf. also Elisée Soumonni, 'Dahomean economic policy under Ghezo, 1818–1858: a reconsideration', *JHSN*, 10/2 (1980), 1–11.

3   For de Souza's role, see David Ross, 'The first Chacha of Whydah: Francisco Felix de Souza', *Odu*, new series, 2 (1969), 19–28.

4   See, in particular: Honorat Aguessy, 'Du mode de l'existence de l'Etat sous Ghezo (Danhomè, 1818–1858)', Thèse de Doctorat de 3ème cycle, Université de Paris, 1969; Jean Roger Ahoyo, 'Les marchés d'Abomey et de Bohicon: approche historique et étude géographique', Mémoire de maîtrise, Université de Paris, 1972; Joseph Adrien Djivo, *Guézo: la rénovation du Dahomey* (Dakar, 1977); Maurice A. Glélé, *Le Danxome: du pouvoir aja à la nation fon* (Paris, 1974); Leslie E. d'Almeida, 'Le Dahomey sous le règne de Dada Glèlè, 1858–1889', Thèse de Doctorat de 3ème cycle, Université de Paris, 1973.

5   Cf. A. G. Hopkins, *An Economic History of West Africa* (London, 1973), pp. 114–15. On the ambiguities of French policy, see also Serge Daget, 'France,

suppression of the illegal trade, and England, 1817–1850', in David Eltis and James Walvin (eds.), *The Abolition of the Atlantic Slave Trade* (Madison, 1981), pp. 193–217; Lawrence C. Jennings, 'French policy towards trading with African and Brazilian slave merchants, 1840–1853', *JAH*, 17 (1976), 515–28.

6   For a fuller account, see Elisée Soumonni, 'Trade and Politics in Dahomey, with particular reference to the House of Régis, 1841–1892', PhD thesis, University of Ife, 1983.

7   Abbé Pierre Bouche, *La Côte des Esclaves et le Dahomey* (Paris, 1885), p. 339.

8   Robert Cornevin, *Histoire du Dahomey* (Paris, 1962), p. 117.

9   Melville J. Herskovits, *Dahomey, an Ancient West African Kingdom* (New York, 1938), I, p. 12.

10 I. A. Akinjogbin, *Dahomey and its Neighbours 1708–1818* (Cambridge, 1967), p. 200.

11 Akinjogbin, *Dahomey*, p. 200.

12 Djivo, *Guézo*, p. 26.

13 Glele, *Le Danxome*, pp. 120–1.

14 Glele, *Le Danxome*, p. 116.

15 Glele, *Le Danxome*, p. 125.

16 'Deliberate', in the sense that the author, himself a descendant of Ghezo (as he makes clear in the introduction to his book), may find Francisco Felix de Souza's role in the 1818 *coup d'état* embarrassing for the image of his great ancestor.

17 Akinjogbin, *Dahomey*, p. 187.

18 Pierre Verger, *Trade Relations between the Bight of Benin and Biafra from the 17th to the 19th Century* (Ibadan, 1976), p. 231.

19 Akinjogbin, *Dahomey*, pp. 193–4.

20 Akinjogbin, *Dahomey*, p. 196.

21 Dov Ronen, 'On the African role in the trans-Atlantic slave trade in Dahomey', *CEA*, 11 (1971), 5–13.

22 David Northrup, 'The compatibility of the slave and palm oil trades in the Bight of Biafra', *JAH*, 17 (1976), 361.

23 Patrick Manning, *Slavery, Colonialism and Economic Growth in Dahomey, 1640–1960* (Cambridge, 1982), p. 13.

24 Manning, *Slavery*, p. 13.

25 K. O. Dike, *Trade and Politics in the Niger Delta, 1830–1885* (Oxford, 1956), pp. 68–9.

26 Maximilien Quénum, *Au Pays des Fons* (Paris, 1938), p. 296.

27 Coquery-Vidrovitch, 'De la traite des esclaves à l'exportation de l'huile de palme', p. 116.

28 Robin Law, 'Royal monopoly and private enterprise in the Atlantic trade: the case of Dahomey', *JAH*, 18 (1977), 571.

29 Bernard Schnapper, *La politique et le commerce français dans le Golfe de Guinée de 1838 à 1871* (Paris, 1964), 164.

30 Sir Richard Burton, *A Mission to Gelele, King of Dahomé* (ed. Colin Newbury, London, 1966), p. 82.

31 See Brue's own account, in 'Voyage fait en 1843, dans le royaume de Dahomey', *Revue Coloniale*, 7 (1845), 55–68.

32 Archives des Colonies, FOM, Sénégal XIII, 14b, 26 Oct. 1846.
33 Ibid., Sénégal IV, 42b.
34 Ibid.
35 Jean-Claude Nardin, 'La reprise des relations franco-dahoméennes au XIXe siècle: la mission d'Auguste Bouet à la cour d'Abomey, 1851', *CEA*, 7 (1967), p. 65.
36 Archives des Colonies, Sénégal IV, 42b.
37 Ibid.
38 Ibid.
39 Nardin, 'La reprise des relations franco-dahoméennes'; see also Schnapper, *La politique et le commerce français*, pp. 174–5.
40 Reid, 'Warrior aristocrats'.
41 Reid, 'Warrior aristocrats', p. 266.
42 C. W. Newbury, *The Western Slave Coast and its Rulers* (Oxford, 1961), p. 51.
43 Robin Law, 'The diplomacy of commercial transition: Anglo-Dahomian negotiations on the ending of the Atlantic slave trade, 1838–71' (paper presented at the Conference on the Life and Work of King Glele (1858–1889), Abomey, Dec. 1989).
44 For different interpretations of internal divisions within Dahomey in the transition era, see Reid, 'Warrior aristocrats', ch. 8; John C. Yoder, 'Fly and Elephant Parties: political polarization in Dahomey, 1840–70', *JAH*, 15 (1974), 417–32.

4 Between abolition and *Jihad*: the Asante response to the ending of the Atlantic slave trade, 1807–1896

Gareth Austin

In a series of military campaigns between 1807 and 1816, Asante, the major supplier of slaves for export from the Gold Coast, at last succeeded in overpowering the Fante 'middlemen' states and extending its political domination to virtually the whole coast. But while Asante had been thus preparing to eliminate or minimize the middlemen's rake-off from Asante slave sales to the European forts,[1] the latter had been closing their doors to human commodities. The largest slave-trading nation, Britain, withdrew from the trade in 1807. While the war in Europe lasted, the British navy ensured that the other European powers with a permanent presence on the Gold Coast, the Netherlands and Denmark, had little trade of any sort with West Africa. When it ended Britain extracted the prohibition of Dutch nationals from trading in slaves as a condition of diplomatic recognition of the post-Napoleonic Dutch regime. As the Danish authorities had already banned their merchants from participation, since 1803, within little more than a decade every fort on the Gold Coast had officially closed to slave buying. The restoration of peace in Europe made it much easier for coastal merchants to find buyers for slaves, including those sold to them by Asantes. Between 1816 and 1818 there was an intense revival of the traffic. This roughly coincided with the tenure of H. Daendels as Dutch Governor-General at Elmina. British sources accused the Dutch of connivance, while the ships themselves were Spanish and Portuguese, some with American owners. The volume of illegal slave exports from the Gold Coast proper (west of the river Volta) seems to have decreased greatly by 1830, and thereafter to have been at most a comparative trickle for several more years. It continued longer east of the Volta, with some Asante participation, at least indirectly.[2] It has been estimated that during the second half of the eighteenth century Asante supplied an average of 5,000 or perhaps 8,000 slaves a year to the Atlantic slave trade.[3] The ending of this trade deprived Asante of the corresponding means to purchase the guns and powder needed by its often busy armies as well as European textiles, ironware and other goods.

Asante faced a four-fold 'adaptive challenge'.[4] First, in foreign trade, it had to find new means of paying for purchases from Europeans, or make do with fewer. Second, the authorities had to decide what to do with the surplus of unsold slaves that was accumulating, both regularly as tributary states sent their annual quotas of slaves to Kumasi, and irregularly from victorious military campaigns. In particular, they needed to explore the possibility of using them to produce exportable goods. Third, the government had to cope with the loss of revenue from its participation in and taxation of the two-way trade with the European slave-ships. Finally, by making warfare less remunerative the ending of Asante's maritime slave exports created potential difficulties for the continued authority and economic domination of a political elite whose achievements and values were highly martial.[5] This would be particularly hard if, as apparently on the West African coast, the commercial alternatives to the slave trade offered no significant capital entry threshold and few scale economies which would make it easier for established 'big men' to reproduce their dominance in a restructured economy.[6] Because of space constraints, this essay will focus on the first three challenges, leaving the fourth to a separate paper.[7] Here, 'government' means both the central government and the paramount chief-taincies of the original Asante confederacy; 'political elite' refers to all chiefs (holders of stools) and other office-holders, whether chosen in formally hereditary succession or appointed through an Asantehene's patronage.

This essay examines the Asante response in the framework of four particular themes in the literature. The first is the debate in the 1970s between Ivor Wilks and Joseph LaTorre about the Asante economic response to the decline of the Atlantic slave market. They agreed that it was successful but differed about the means by which it was achieved. Wilks pointed to the efficiency of the central administration, which not only planned and supervised the general direction of change[8] but gave privileges to state traders which ensured them of a 'virtual monopoly' of trade before 1831, and again 'all but total protection from any form of competition' from c.1840–80.[9] LaTorre, in an important but neglected dissertation, implicitly attributed it largely to private merchants: to the 'flexibility' of Asante's external trade sector, with its 'important degree of monetarization', in responding to price signals in the pursuit of private profit.[10]

The second theme is the proposition, which is of venerable provenance but has been much strengthened by recent research, that 'Despite the aims of the abolitionists, the transition from exporting slaves to exporting other commodities resulted in the increased use of slaves in Africa'.[11] It may be illuminating to relate this to A. G. Hopkins' view that 'the new export trade saw a marked increase in the commercialization of labour and land'.[12]

The third theme is the emphasis in much of the recent research on nineteenth-century West Africa on positive aspects of the economic effects of political and military conflict in the interior of the region, away from the maritime trade: the formation of jihadist states over much of the West African savanna.[13] This applies most of all to the Sokoto Caliphate, which emerged from *jihad* between 1804 and 1808. The work of Paul E. Lovejoy and others has shown that this new political framework provided a setting which, on balance, offered favourable conditions for commercial growth and structural change in local economies both within the Caliphate and, through the stimulus of trade, to some extent outside it, including the relatively distant, forest-based economy of Asante.[14]

The fourth theme is Hopkins' proposition that the European partition of West Africa was partly a response to intensified competition brought about by the transition to 'legitimate' commerce, in the form of the entry of many new competitors on both the European and African sides of the trade, aggravated by a severe depression in the late nineteenth century.[15]

The body of the essay will consider the Asante response to each adaptive challenge. The first three sections argue that the Asante state and economy met the first three challenges with considerable success until the British raid on Kumasi in 1874. The fourth section begins by showing that this military defeat fatally undermined the foundations of Asante's previously successful adaptation and thereby brought the final challenge to a head. This begs a question, to which the rest of the section is devoted: whether the British intervention was entirely exogenous or whether it was itself in some sense a reaction to the Asante adaptation.

Reorienting and restructuring foreign trade

Possessing neither mechanized transport nor a remedy for animal trypanosomiasis, at nineteenth-century prices for palm oil Asante producers were too far from the sea to enter that export market. Political control over the palm oil exporting areas would have provided at least the resource of tax or tribute from them, but with defeat by the British at the battle of Katamanso in 1826 Asante lost effective control over the coast before palm oil exports had climbed to substantial levels (they averaged 244 tons a year during 1824–6).[16] However, when Gold Coast palm oil exports did 'take off', from the 1830s, Asante took indirect advantage by selling slaves and other commodities to the Fante, in return for European goods which the Fante had purchased with the proceeds of palm oil.[17] In the middle of the century it was reported that 'immense numbers' of slaves of savanna origin 'are being annually imported' by Fantes from Asante middlemen.[18] Asante was the main supplier of ivory as well as slaves to the Gold Coast, the former being traditionally carried on the heads of the latter. Most Asante ivory was re-exported, having been bought originally from savanna areas, notably Kong, a state north-west of Asante. The supply of tusks, being constrained by the size of the elephant population, was insufficient to make ivory into a key export and, at least after 1853, the volume was reduced towards insignificance apparently by the progressive depletion of the elephant stock.[19]

More importantly, Asante had two other valuable exports, whose supply was elastic: kola nuts and gold. Indeed, the military conquests of the previous century left the Asante state with a local monopoly of the former and a near-monopoly of the latter.[20] In the eighteenth century, as the overseas demand for slaves increased, Asante sold less gold at the coast. Now the trend was reversed, with gold exports being redirected from the savanna market. In addition, the indications are that the overall level of gold exports rose. Timothy Garrard has made the most detailed estimates, which are presented in table 4.1. They relate to the Akan region as a whole.[21] However, during the second half of the eighteenth century and the first half of the nineteenth most gold exports came from Asante and its tributaries. That share was diminished after Katamanso, but was still probably 'over half, perhaps three-quarters' of the Gold Coast total.[22] According to Brodie Cruickshank in mid-century, 'The principal supply of gold' for export from the Gold Coast 'is received from the Ashantee traders'.[23]

Meanwhile the centuries-old trade in kola nuts between what were now the Asante forests and the consumers in the savanna was launched into major growth by Uthman dan Fodio's *jihad* in 1804. Traders fleeing the jihadists helped to organize the expansion of the trade, while the formation of the Sokoto Caliphate increased the Hausa-Fulani requirement for kola in place of alcohol.[24] It also provided a political framework within which the economies of Hausaland expanded and became more integrated, so that consumer tastes were empowered with increasing purchasing power.[25] Lovejoy estimated the number of traders carrying kola from Salaga to Kano in the 1820s and early 1830s as at least 1,000–2,000 annually, probably 'much higher', with an equal number of transport animals. He also quoted an 1857 report which implied that each dry season about 6,000 donkey loads, representing about 270 tonnes, reached the Niger crossing on one of the two main routes to the Caliphate and beyond.[26] LaTorre estimated that the value of Asante's

Table 4.1. *Akan Gold Exports, 1651–1850 (ounces)*

	Northern trade	European trade	Total
1651–1700	500,000	1,500,000	2,000,000
1701–1750	400,000	1,200,000	1,600,000
1751–1800	400,000	800,000	1,200,000
1801–1850	200,000	1,400,000	1,600,000

Source: Timothy Garrard, *Akan Weights and the Gold Trade* (London, 1980), p. 163.

kola exports to Hausaland increased 'at least ten times' during the nineteenth century.[27]

The redirection of Asante's trade affected imports as well as exports. The Asante economy benefited from the growth of the Sokoto Caliphate's own output, perhaps especially in manufacturing. In return for its kola, Asante's imports from the Caliphate included not only slaves[28] and goods it could not obtain on the coast, such as natron, shea-butter, livestock and leather products (including sandals and bags),[29] but also textiles.[30] The main Asante demand for Hausa cottons was for undyed cloth,[31] though they bought finished cloth from Dagomba in exchange for kola plus ocean salt and European manufactures purchased on the coast.[32] In so far as Asante consumers did buy finished cloth from Hausaland, they may have benefited from technological advance in the Caliphate economy. Philip Shea has shown that Hausa cloth-dyers, specifically in Kano emirate, achieved technological advances during the nineteenth century which raised productivity and reduced unit production costs.[33] For Asante, the option of buying more savanna-made cloth through expanding kola sales must be set against the decline and disappearance of its capacity to pay for seaborne cloth by selling slaves to the Europeans.

The importance of seaborne textiles for Asante before 1807 is, admittedly, in some doubt. George Metcalf's study of a British trader's records during 1772–80 showed that Indian and European cloth had been the largest component of Akan purchases from the slave-traders, and he argued that this reflected the pattern of demand 'throughout the whole of the territory inhabited by the Akan peoples'.[34] Indeed, given the pre-eminence of Asante as a middleman in the supply of slaves to the British, it is reasonable to assume that it reflected Asante demand at least. However, a Danish trader reported in 1784 that at those Danish forts 'where one deals mainly with Assianthees [Asantes], one is often forced to pay for the slaves with guns and gunpowder exclusively because there is no demand for any of the other goods, apart from a piece of fine fabric or silk cloth'.[35] Both these accounts are from a relatively peaceful period in Asante military history.[36] A likely explanation of the apparent discrepancy is that Asante customers preferred the textiles sold by the British merchants to those sold by their Danish counterparts, who lacked direct access to either Indian or Lancashire cottons. The most plausible overall conclusion is that Asantes did buy much cloth from European slave-traders, but that firearms figured more largely in their imports than is indicated by the British data alone. This implies that the post-1807 adaptive challenge in Asante's foreign trade was potentially even greater than we have realized hitherto.

When European traders ceased to buy slaves, the response of Asante traders was to use gold to continue their purchases of guns and ammunition, and also of European iron, which the Asantes found superior to the savanna product.[37] Edward Bowdich explained the new pattern of Asante trade from his conversations and observations in the country in 1817:

the preference of the Ashantees for the Dagwumba and Inta [Gonja; specifically Salaga] markets, for silk and cloth, results not merely from their having been so long accustomed to them, but because they admit of a barter trade. The Boosee or Gooroo [kola] nut, salt, (which is easily procured, and affords an extravagant profit,) and small quantities of the European commodities, rum and iron, yield them those articles of comfort and luxury, which they could only purchase with gold and ivory from the settlements on the coast.[38]

In the last resort, the Hausa trade also provided a source of guns and gunpowder obtained via the Sahara: a source Asante apparently used in the early 1870s, albeit at high prices, when the British, having acquired the Danish and Dutch forts, imposed a coastal embargo on sales of war materials to Asante.[39]

However, it appears that throughout the period 1807–74, even when all the European merchants were willing to sell guns to the Asantes, textiles were the largest component by value of Asante imports from Europe. This is indicated by a preponderance of textiles in Gold Coast imports, combined with evidence that the commerce of the coast was primarily a function of the Asante trade.[40] Given that guns and gunpowder would have been the last European commodities that the Asante state would have done without, the fact that they seem never to have comprised a majority of Asante maritime imports is testimony to the successful adaptation of Asante foreign trade to the decline of the Atlantic slave market. The continued – and expanded – consumption of European textiles was stimulated by the rapid fall in the export price of European, especially Lancashire, cottons between 1817 and 1850.[41] However, the fact that Asante had purchasing power left over to buy them[42] was made possible in the first instance by the expansion of its maritime gold exports. This in turn was greatly facilitated by the growth of kola exports to the Sokoto Caliphate, which eased the release of gold which otherwise would have been required for purchases in the savanna markets.

Both the state and the private sector contributed to the successful reorientation of trade. LaTorre has noted that Wilks's argument that state traders enjoyed a virtual monopoly before 1831 and again from c.1840–80 goes beyond the evidence.[43] For example, the evidence adduced for the existence of a near-monopoly before 1831 is based on a single quotation from Dupuis which is ambiguous in itself and is contradicted, implicitly and explicitly, by other remarks in the same book.[44] I would add that Dupuis's contemporary, Bowdich, observed 'The government has no power to direct the traders to any particular market, though it interdicts the commerce with any power which may have offended it'.[45] Had the traders been government servants the government would have had the power to choose which markets they operated in. Again, Wilks' sources do not show that any state monopoly was imposed after c.1840. The biggest privilege which state traders enjoyed was first use of the Salaga market when the trading season began. Even this was shared with the free commoners who willingly carried chiefs' loads precisely in return for being allowed to sell whatever goods of their own they could carry on top.[46] The absence of a state monopoly of trade appears to be underlined by the case of the Dutch military recruitment in Kumasi between 1837 and 1842, which amounted to a disguised resumption of the slave trade, since in practice such men could only be obtained by purchase from slave-dealers, whether public or private. Whereas the Asantehene delivered only 235 of the 1,000 men he had contracted to supply, the Dutch were able to buy 1,170 slaves from other sources[47] including 'various Asante officials and merchants who would send or travel up to Salaga' to purchase captives.[48] It seems reasonable to assume that at least a substantial proportion of these retailers were trading for themselves.[49]

However, the central government's role was surely crucial too. In an environment where states contended militarily for control over markets and where banditry could be a major threat to trade, the establishment of the new market at Salaga was almost certainly by the Asantehene's decision, as Wilks contended.[50] Moreover, it can only have been the government that, between c.1840 and 1874, restricted exchanges with the Hausa to Salaga, excluding them from interior Asante markets.[51] As Lovejoy observed, this administratively created monopoly presumably improved the barter terms of trade for all Asante merchants in their dealings with the northerners.[52] The military power of the Asante state continued to underpin the ability of the economy to 'pay the bills'. Thus it really mattered economically as well as politically that the Gyaman rebellion of 1818 was put down, since the secession of Gyaman would have diminished considerably the empire's resources of gold and kola. This was all the more important in retrospect, given the loss of control over the coast in 1826. Even in relation to the coast Asante's military efforts were not wholly in vain. In the post-Katamanso negotiations which culminated in a treaty with Britain in 1831, though Asante had to renounce some of its claims to sovereignty over its southern neighbours, it achieved a long-standing object: the right of its traders to transit the Fante states to the seaside unmolested by official restrictions or banditry.

Overall, the foreign trade of Asante adjusted relatively smoothly and adequately to what one might call the 'Wilberforce shock'. This was made possible by a combination of the flexibility of the Asante economy, including the private sector; the powerful position in regional markets which had been secured by Asante military power; and the fortuitous emergence of the Sokoto Caliphate, whose economic expansion extended benefits to some of those states which remained largely unwilling to heed its religious message.

'Surplus' slaves and labour supply

For the Asante government the emergence of a surplus of slaves in Kumasi in the 1810s created a security problem in the form of unruly crowds,[53] but it also offered help with an economic problem. Increasing the exports of kola nuts required raising their output, since kola was almost a pure export crop, with no domestic market from which supplies could be diverted. Gold exports could be increased by expenditure of accumulated stock, and probably were. Gold was kept not least because gold dust was the currency in the Asante forest zone. But to minimize deflation and distress sales of stored wealth, it was desirable to increase gold production also. Garrard estimates that the annual average output of the Akan goldfields as a whole rose from 27,000 ounces a year in the second half of the eighteenth century to 35,000 in the first half of the nineteenth.[54] Since Asante controlled most of the goldfields, and had every incentive to raise output, we may assume that it accounted for much of the increase.

For both products the tools were relatively simple and widely available. Access to the right kinds of land seems not to have been a constraint on production either. A chief's subjects did not need permission to collect kola nuts or dig for gold within the chieftaincy lands, while non-subjects could usually obtain permission to do so.[55] Kola trees grew wild, and producers would clear the bush around a tree to get at the pods.[56] In Asante in general the scale of demand does not seem to have required deliberate planting of kola trees, though this may have happened by the 1880s in Dwaben, north-east of Kumasi.[57] All nuggets of gold larger than a certain size were required by law to be sent to the Asantehene's treasury, which would return part of its value, in gold dust, to be divided between the local chief and the finder.[58] In most areas strangers, and in some places subjects too, were subject to a rent on gold dust winnings of one-third or even two-thirds.[59] However, with both gold and kola it appears that the major constraint on the expansion of output was the supply, not of capital or land, but rather of labour. In this context we need to ask whether the unexpectedly unexportable slaves account for the enlarged output of kola and gold during the early nineteenth century.

Our starting point should be the fact that most of the 'surplus' slaves would been owned by the state or members of the political elite, since most of them would have been obtained from tribute or war.[60] Some were killed at the funerals of prominent members of the elite, to provide the deceased with servants in the after-life, as will be seen below. What the government did with most of them, however, was more immediately productive. It is described in the following much-quoted passage from Bowdich, referring to a law of 1817 which restricted the amount of provisions which government officials on duty could demand from the villages through which they passed. This law

was particularly consolatory and beneficial to those slaves, who, to prevent famine and insurrection, had been selected (from that fettered multitude which could no longer be driven off to the coast directly they arrived at the capital), to create plantations in the more remote and stubborn tracts; from which their labour was first to produce a proportionate supply to the household of their Chief, and afterwards an existence for themselves: of the greater part of the necessaries for the latter, they had been pilfered in common with the poorer class of Ashantees, (nominally but not virtually free), under various pretences, either in their distant plantations or on the arrival at the markets, by the public servants of the King and the Chiefs.[61]

The passage does not indicate any change in the ownership of slaves. Rather, its apparent meaning is that these slaves were incorporated into Asante society as members of chiefs' 'households' (the gyaasefoɔ)[62] and relocated in rural areas where they would support themselves without being a nuisance or threat to the government. The economic opportunity cost of employing slaves rather than selling them was very low at this time. Bowdich reported that 'so full were the markets of the interior' that the maximum price Asantes were paying to buy slaves from the north in 1817 was 2,000 cowries or one basket of kola.[63] However, Norman Klein interpreted the dispersal of surplus slaves in the 1810s as marking 'the beginnings of the large-scale spread of "domestic slavery" ', though he recognized that the 'breakup of the system of state slavery did not follow immediately' upon the decision.[64] He provides no evidence of such a transition, even if it was long term. Rather, it seems likely that slave-ownership by the political elite was at least undiminished until 1873, and may well have increased, as tribute, war and, if necessary, purchase replenished the stock of first-generation recruits to the *gyaasefoɔ*. Among the functions of the *gyaasefoɔ* was production of a marketed surplus. In the more 'remote' tracts this would have meant kola nut collection rather than food farming because commercial food production was largely concentrated around Kumasi and other large towns in central Asante,[65] whereas most of the kola trees were relatively distant from the capital.[66] As for gold, Emmanuel Terray has argued that the dominant form of mining in the Akan states, specifically including Asante, was by large groups of slaves working for chiefs.[67] Raymond Dumett has challenged this, arguing that most gold was produced by family units.[68] Whatever the contribution of chiefs' slaves to the overall level of gold production, it is reasonable to assume that a sizeable part of the increase in output of kola and gold after 1807 was the result of the redeployment of slaves by chiefs from export to use in production for the market within Asante. This applies most obviously to the surplus that accumulated in the 1810s, but there is no reason why the process should not have continued during the remaining years of slave imports into Asante.

A sidelight on chiefs' demand for slave labour is provided by the admittedly unreliable evidence on the numbers of slaves killed at funerals and other rites. The purpose of such deaths was to provide prominent ancestors, whether recently or long deceased, with servants and other companions in the after-life, as appropriate to their status in the Asante social hierarchy. Besides slaves, the oblates could comprise convicted criminals and also free Asante, some of whom were said to have volunteered.[69] It is important to note that the chiefs accounted for most of the slaves slain at funerals. The Methodist missionary T. B. Freeman 'ascertained from an Ashantee ... that the common people are *not at* liberty to sacrifice their slaves for the dead without the consent of the king, and the king seldom gives them that liberty'.[70] This may be seen as a sumptuary law against socially pretentious displays by lesser-ranked members of this highly hierarchical society. The incidence of slaves literally dispatched by chiefs to serve their ancestors, rather than retained to serve themselves, may provide a clue to the importance attached by chiefs to the utility of living slaves, which can be related to the market value of slaves.

During the middle of the century overall demand for slaves in Asante seems to have increased, though part of this is attributable to the re-export demand from the Fante states. After attempts by the Kumasi government in the early 1820s to reduce the numbers of slaves it received in tribute and replace them with other forms of wealth, its demands for human tribute stabilized at relatively high levels. Admittedly, this was partly a response to the tributaries' inability to make such a switch, and/or resistance to it, because those which could pay in gold or livestock were already doing so.[71] Despite the continued influx of new slaves through tribute, slave prices in Asante revived from c.1820 to c.1840, to judge from LaTorre's assembly of the inevitably fragmentary data.[72]

There is some evidence that the number of slaves killed at funerals had risen considerably, perhaps dramatically, in the years immediately following the withdrawal of the European forts from the slave trade.[73] But in 1848 Asantehene Kwaku Dua Panin told the visiting British governor that he was reducing the number of 'human sacrifices'. Wilks notes that his reported wording is ambiguous, in that he may have meant only fewer executions of criminals.[74] But it seems unlikely that he could have imagined that this would have sufficed to impress the governor. If the number of funerary killings fell it is reasonable to assume that non-convicted slaves were among the beneficiaries. If so, the apparent trend in the frequency with which slaves were killed at funerals, rising after 1807 and falling in the 1840s, was inversely related to the trend of slave prices within Asante. If there really was a reduction in these killings of slaves by 1848, it may have been a response not only to pressure from Britain but also to an increase in the value of living slaves, reflected in their increased price. Wilks has made essentially this point with reference to upward pressure on slave prices in Asante from the demand for slaves from palm oil exporters on the Gold Coast.[75] As this section seeks to show, however, the rising value of slaves was also – and probably primarily – a function of higher demand for their labour within Asante. The most likely link between higher slave values and fewer ritual killings of slaves is through considerations of opportunity cost. That is, the Asantehene and perhaps other masters may have preferred, at the margin, the increasingly valuable uses of slaves in this life over the personal and social satisfaction gained, within the prevailing system of beliefs, by sending them to the next. In view of the emphasis in Asante society on giving full honour to the dead and on being seen to do so, it is highly plausible, as Wilks observes, that mourners would have wished to maintain the overall value of the resources they consumed at funeary rites. But given that the market value of slaves had risen, the same total cost now represented fewer corpses.[76]

However, much of the demand for slaves in this life appears to have been from private (commoner) rather than state (or office-holder) sources.[77] That is, recruits were demanded for domestic or lineage slavery, the holding of small numbers of slaves whose descendants would be incorporated as members of cadet lineages. If Norman Klein's explanation of the origins of domestic slavery is doubtful, nevertheless he was right to emphasize the widespread extent of the institution during the nineteenth century.[78] There is much evidence of individuals and matrilineages buying slaves in the 'transit markets' where Asante forest-dwellers traded with savanna merchants. Trade was the main source of slaves available to commoners. The geographer Kwasi Boaten remarked in 1970 that 'The many domestic slaves [sic] found in practically all the Asante homes attest to the extent and popularity of the slave trade with the north'.[79] Bowdich heard that few slaves were being bought at the time of his visit,[80] but this was hardly surprising given the surplus within Asante at that time. The situation had changed dramatically by 1842 when a Dutch recruiting agent, H. S. Pel, reported that 'the greatest part of their slaves are purchased in various markets in the interior'.[81] Pel's predecessor, Jacob Huydecoper, had reported that he was in competition with substantial demand for slaves from within Asante.[82] Indeed, there is much evidence of a wholesale trade in slaves supplying local markets such as Adubease in the Adanse district of southern Asante.[83]

Commoners, as well as chiefs, appear to have used slaves in producing kola nuts and in gold mining. They also used pawns for the same purposes.[84] Indeed, referring admittedly to the last quarter of the century, Kwame Arhin's informants in Kintampo described the acquisition of pawns as the quickest way to accumulate labour in order to expand one's harvest of kola, which was in turn reinvested in slaves further to reinforce the labour force.[85] Regarding gold mining, Dumett has noted, for the Akan states generally, that the family labour unit included some slaves.[86] Indeed, we may assume that any commoner wishing to increase output beyond the capacity of the conjugal family workforce needed to use slaves or pawns. As Garrard has demonstrated, the average returns on gold digging and panning were low,[87] almost certainly too low to make it profitable to use wage labour. In 1925 the elders of an Asante village told R. S. Rattray: 'We have now stopped gold-mining because it only pays when you have slaves.'[88]

There is no evidence that the reorientation of the Asante economy, from the re-export of foreign captives to the export of commodities produced within the country, involved either technological advance or a reduction in non-export activities such as food farming. Therefore the enlarged supply of kola and gold must have required increased factor inputs. This raises the question of whether the Asante variant of 'legitimate commerce' brought about a significant increase in the commercialization of land and labour. For land, the answer is negative. There is no indication that new kinds or levels of royalties or rents were imposed on land or its natural products during 1807–73. Nor is there any sign of the mortgaging or sale of land as a factor of production, as distinct from the already-established practice of the mortgage or sale of subjects with associated land, which was in effect a transfer of sovereignty.[89] For labour, the story is different. With the available technology, both gold and kola production were highly labour-intensive. These were dry-season activities, but even in the dry season it does not appear that the Asante labour-force was significantly under-employed.[90] Much of the total output of gold and kola was produced by free subjects operating within the conjugal family unit, by pawned Asantes, by corvée labour for chiefs, by slaves imported before 1807, and by descendants of such slaves.[91] But it seems clear that much of the increased labour input was supplied by slaves who were imported when previously they would have been re-exported. Thus the decline of the Atlantic slave market was turned to advantage by Asantes aiming at gold and kola markets and, thereby, a security risk became an economic asset.

Many of these slaves reached their final owner through a market, and all possessed a market value. It can be said that the increased demand for labour, in producing for the market and in trade, increased the extent of commercialization of labour within the Asante economy. However, as before though now on an enlarged scale, labour markets in Asante, as in pre-colonial West Africa generally,[92] took the form of transactions not in labour services but in people: not in wage labour but in slaves and pawns. The growth of commercial production raised the effective demand for labour, but it was still not sufficient to permit prospective employers to offer wages high enough to attract voluntary labour from rural households all of whom had access to land themselves.[93]

Government revenue

The Asantehene derived income from a variety of sources, some of which were also tapped by chiefs: war booty; tributes paid by defeated or otherwise subordinated rulers; taxes on the income and wealth of the Asante population, ranging from market tolls and gold-mining rents to death duties, plus occasional levies to pay for war or accession; court fees and fines; the occasional labour services of all subjects (in war or public work); and the regular labour of the chiefs' servants, the *gyaasefoɔ*, who farmed, traded, escorted and in other ways served them.[94] The Atlantic slave trade had provided a major source of revenue: directly, through the state's participation in the acquisition and sale of slaves; and indirectly, in the form of that part of its receipts from tolls and death duties which derived from the turnover and profitability of this export trade and of the import trade it financed. It also enabled Asante to exact lucrative tribute from subject states who lacked gold or other valuable non-human commodities. Thus, by itself the decline of the Atlantic slave market might have caused a fiscal crisis.

As noted above, one response by the Asante government was to demand that some of its tributaries who had been paying in slaves instead supply gold or livestock. This was much resented by them, and has been seen as the cause of a wave of revolts which swept Asante's southern tributaries in c.1820.[95] However, D. J. E. Maier argues that, at least for the Fante states, the rebellions were not prompted by the tribute conversion, since most of them already paid in gold, but rather by the imposition of an additional levy, a war tax, after the Gyaman campaign.[96] In any case, as has been seen, it became clear over the following years that the internal demand for slaves in Asante was sufficient to make it worthwhile for the government to continue to accept slaves on its menu of tribute. Meanwhile the diminution of income from slave-exporting was offset by the revenues deriving, directly and indirectly, from the expansion of the production and trading of kola and gold. Rates of tax and rent do not appear to have risen between 1807 and 1874, nor is there evidence of new taxes being imposed. While in the 1840s the Asantehene Kwaku Dua Panin exploited the judicial system to confiscate the property of wealthy individuals,[97] the relatively late date of this fiscal purge makes it hard to see it as a response to the ending of maritime slave exports. Overall, it may be concluded that the success of the state and economy in adapting to the implications of the abolition in respect of foreign trade and of the utilization of the continuing supply of slaves also enabled the state to cope with the fiscal challenge.

The one major query about the fiscal success of the Asante adaptation to the ending of the maritime slave trade is prompted by the military failure of 1874, when a British army fought its way through fierce resistance and proceeded to burn the Asante capital. It might be asked whether Asante could have averted this defeat had the government had more revenue. But this would over-extend the issue of response to the abolition of the Atlantic slave trade. Asante would have required a fundamentally more developed economy to have been able to afford the means, whether in imported weaponry and skills or otherwise, to offset the effects of the progressive reduction in the general cost of imperial coercion in Africa which the European industrial economies were experiencing through advances in medical and military technology.

The dialectic of Asante adaptation and British economic imperialism

Until the 1873–4 war, the response of the Asante state and economy to the adaptive challenges flowing from the closure of Asante's Atlantic market for slaves seems to have been overwhelmingly successful. External trade was re-oriented, apparently to the accompaniment of growth rather than decline; the continuing supply of imported slaves was re-deployed within Asante, particularly in the production of exportable goods; and the loss of government revenue from the Atlantic slave trade was offset by income from the growth of gold and kola exports. This success was undermined decisively by the British incursion of 1874. The invading army stayed only one day in Kumasi, but the political and economic consequences within Asante were enduring and profound. More important than the terms of the dictated treaty was the scale of the military defeat, which inspired a wave of secessions by most of the old tributaries. One of the major provincial chieftaincies, Dwaben, rebelled in 1874–5. Though it was suppressed, this action prefigured further attempts at secession during the next two decades by original components of the Asante state. Suddenly the government no longer possessed much of an empire, and was embarked upon a prolonged struggle to maintain the integrity of the kingdom itself. Commercially, Asante's monopolistic position in the transit trade between the savanna and the coast was weakened by the secessions, and the government seems to have allowed at least some Muslim traders from the savanna (probably Hausa) to pass through its territory to trade directly on the coast.[98] Meanwhile, the control exerted by Asante masters over their slaves was threatened because it became easier for the latter to escape: the British authorities, having extended their own empire to the river Pra, found themselves obliged by pressure at home and on the coast to abolish slavery in their new territories.[99] To summarize, these changes undermined the foundations of Asante's hitherto successful adaptation to the ending of the Atlantic slave trade: the state's capacity to create monopoly profits for Asante traders; the increased use of slave labour; and the continued availability to the state of lucrative tribute as well as revenue derived, directly and indirectly, from trade.

The decisiveness of the British raid of 1874, coupled with the eventual colonial occupation in 1896, raises the question of whether the British invasions were entirely exogenous to the Asante adaptation to the abolition of the Atlantic slave trade; or whether the very success of the initial adaptations, or the means by which that success was achieved, helped to induce these specific colonial interventions. It may be suggested that the answer hinges upon the balance of influence in British policy-making of two contrasting perceptions of the implications of the continued existence of the Asante state for Britain's commercial interests. One view was that a strong Asante polity was the key to prosperity for British trade on the Gold Coast, both because of the potential of the Asante economy itself and because the Asante state guaranteed the security of the trade routes to its hinterland, thus maximizing the savanna-coast trade at no cost to the British government. On this assumption, Britain's priority should be to smooth the path of Anglo-Asante trade by eliminating any bandits, tolls and embargoes along the route between the coast and the river Pra, the southern border of Asante proper, or even to permit Asante to secure its own access to the sea.[100] The other view was that the major commercial value of the Gold Coast lay inland of Asante, and that the Asante state obstructed rather than facilitated British access to that market. From this perspective British policy should be to weaken the central government of Asante, by encouraging the secession of tributaries and even provinces, and/or imposing colonial overrule.[101] Neither view demanded free trade in terms of cost: the abandonment of tolls and taxes on commerce. Both sought free trade in a physical sense: the removal of what, in their respective views, were the obstacles to the free movement of trade goods and traders. The difference between their policy implications may be summar-ized as free movement of trade *with* Asante, versus free movement of trade *through* Asante. As the century went on, Western advances in the technology of communications, medicine and warfare reduced the likely cost of both coercing and administering Asante. Other things being equal, it became increasingly likely that, first, the 'with Asante' policy would be imposed in full and, second, that the 'through Asante' option would eventually be adopted by British decision-makers.

Under the 1831 treaty Britain did indeed obtain free movement of trade goods and traders with Asante.[102] During the 1873–4 war, the government in London instructed the commander in the field to go further. While he was to have 'a large discretion' about the terms of the inevitable peace treaty, 'The King [of Asante] should . . . engage to keep the paths open through his domains, to promote lawful commerce to and through the Ashantee country, and to protect all peaceful traders passing through his dominions to the Coast'.[103] When the treaty was made, however, the general settled for the restoration of full free movement between the coast and Kumasi:[104] the 'with Asante' rather than 'through

Asante' policy. This back-tracking seems to have been overlooked by historians, and the reasons for it remain to be explored. Following the treaty, the British administration on the Gold Coast sought, in effect, to compensate for the missed opportunity by sending a series of missions to the north encouraging Asante's former or present tributaries to develop trade routes to the coast that bypassed Asante.[105] In 1881 a British officer, Captain Lonsdale, was sent to Kumasi itself to urge the Asante government to open the trade routes from the north, to bring about a free flow of through traffic with the coast. This request achieved little in practice.[106] In the words of a later British official and historian, Lonsdale

was detained in COOMASSIE for several weeks, as the ASHANTIS were particularly anxious that he should not open up new roads. They foresaw that if the trade roads were opened, it would be difficult, if not impossible, to refuse to the up-country and Coast traders equal rights with themselves to trade, and once these rights were granted they would be deprived of the profits as 'middlemen' between the Coast and the north.

When he was eventually allowed to proceed to Salaga he found that the Asantehene had transferred the market to Kintampo. He returned to the coast by an eastern route, having failed to open the roads through Kumasi-controlled country.[107]

The British government sought to avoid the relatively expensive task of administering and policing Asante.[108] Given the damage that the 1873–4 war had done to the political cohesion of the Asante state, however, it was perhaps not surprising that the attempts of Asantehene Mensa Bonsu (1874–83) to restore the material foundations of central authority through punitive fines and taxes resulted in his downfall, which in turn led to civil war (1884–8). The result of the British policy of long-distance intervention was that British officials and merchants had to watch while trade routes through Asante were repeatedly cut by internal political and military conflicts.[109] From the mid-1880s onwards, the British government came under considerable pressure to establish some sort of colonial administration of Asante, from British merchants on the Gold Coast and from the Manchester, Liverpool, London and Glasgow chambers of commerce.[110] The combination of such demands and government policy-makers' own perception of Britain's commercial interests seem to have contributed to the decision to occupy Asante in 1896.[111]

The analysis above supports Hopkins' general proposition of a causal link between the European partition of West Africa and the transition of West Africa's maritime trade from slaves to 'legitimate' commodities. The specific argument, however, is different. While the reaction of British merchants to political instability and the resultant blocking of trade routes may have owed much to a general trade depression, the underlying trend of their trade with Asante was promising. The price of gold was on an upward trend, and if less gold was being offered for sale this was apparently because it was being displaced by a new and apparently more mutually profitable trade in rubber.[112]

Asante's adaptation to the ending of the Atlantic slave trade had been based, partly but crucially, upon the ability of the state to protect the monopolistic middleman position of the economy in the savanna-forest-maritime trade. Ultimately, this condition made the adaptation self-defeating as far as the independent Asante state was concerned, because in the long term that position was unacceptable to the British. For the Asante economy, on the other hand, the opportunity presented after 1900 by high cocoa prices plus the colonial government's construction of a railway enabled Asantes to intensify their involvement in the new Atlantic commerce.[113]

Conclusions

I would highlight four aspects of this story of temporarily successful adaptation. The first is the fact that the redirection of Asante's foreign trade after 1807 was achieved with crucial contributions from both the state and the private sector. This essay has sought to revive and develop LaTorre's argument that a relatively autonomous private sector was an important force in the nineteenth-century economy. Equally, the state's coercive power secured what in several respects was a monopolistic position for Asante in its international trade.

The second point arises from the further expansion of the use of slave labour within Asante. It is reasonable to assume that the growth of internal demand for slaves explains much of the apparent revival of slave prices within Asante from c.1820, after the initial dip that followed the British withdrawal from slave buying. In turn, as Wilks hinted, the rise in the present value of slaves may account for the apparent decline in the frequency with which slaves were dispatched to serve the ancestors by or in the 1840s, in contrast to the apparent rise in such oblations in the years immediately following 1807.

The third point is a further implication of the growth of slavery. That the expansion of exports of kola nuts and gold (and, in the 1880s and 1890s, of rubber) should be in part attributable to the use of increased numbers of slaves within the Asante economy,[114] provides an interesting perspective on the use of 'vent-for-surplus' models to account for the much larger and more rapid growth of 'legitimate' exports that took place during the early colonial period in Asante and what is now southern Ghana generally, and in other parts of West Africa.[115] While the 'vent-for-surplus' proposition that such growth was made possible by the prior existence of 'surplus productive capacity'[116] may be at least partly true in relation to land, the models' complimentary prediction of the existence of a substantial reserve of leisure in the late pre-colonial economies is hard to reconcile with the readiness of producers to pay substantial sums to buy slaves and take pawns.

The final point is that between 1804 and 1873 the pattern of Asante economic history was influenced as much by events in the savanna, especially the emergence of the largest of the jihadist states, as by events on the coast.[117] This evidence of the dynamism of the interior economy of the region challenges Hopkins' assessment of the economic impact of the jihads as 'conservative'.[118] But it does so in a way which reinforces his general emphasis upon the dynamism of pre-colonial economies in West Africa. Asante's connections with the savanna helped it to achieve initial success in adapting to the economy of 'legitimate commerce': supplying slaves who assisted the growth of Asante production of kola and gold and generally contributing to the balance and sustenance of Asante's foreign trade. Ultimately, however, there was a contradiction between the continued independence of a powerful Asante and the establishment of the free trade sought by the British in the hinterland of the Gold Coast Colony. In the long term, Asante's conflictual relations with industrial Europe proved more influential than its cooperative links   ·
with the preindustrial savanna.

NOTES

My thanks to the participants in the Stirling conference in April 1993 for many useful comments on the first draft of this paper; and also to Tony Hopkins, Robin Law, Paul Lovejoy and Larry Yarak for additional comments. The paper draws partly on my doctoral and post-doctoral research in Ghana, which was funded by the UK Economic and Social Research Council.
  1 This traditional interpretation of the motivation of Asante attempts to establish political domination over the coast still seems reasonable, as long as it is recognized that political and ideological motives were also probably involved. See Kwame Arhin, 'The structure of Greater Ashanti (1700–1824)', *JAH*, 8 (1967), 65–85, and 'The financing of the Ashanti expansion (1700–1820)', *Africa*, 37 (1967), 283–91; J. K. Fynn, *Asante and its Neighbours* (London, 1971), pp. 124, 139–40, 142, 154; R. A. Kea, 'Trade, state formation and warfare on the Gold Coast, 1600–1826', PhD thesis, University of London, School of Oriental and African Studies, 1974, pp. 360–422.
  2 For overviews of slave exporting from the Gold Coast after 1803, see

Edward Reynolds, *Trade and Economic Change on the Gold Coast 1807–1874* (Harlow, 1974), pp. 37–45; Joseph Raymond LaTorre, 'Wealth surpasses everything: an economic history of Asante, 1750–1874', PhD thesis, University of California, Berkeley, 1978, pp. 435–7; Mary McCarthy, *Social Change and the Growth of British Power in the Gold Coast: The Fante States 1807–1874* (Lanham, Maryland, 1983), pp. 72–7. These accounts differ on the post-1830 period: the summary here is an attempt to reconcile the evidence they provide. On Asante participation see, in addition, T. Edward Bowdich, *A Mission from Cape Coast Castle to Ashantee* (London, 1819), pp. 337–40, 392, 413; Brodie Cruickshank, *Eighteen Years on the Gold Coast of Africa* (London, 1853), I, pp. 127–8; Margaret Priestley, *West African Trade and Coast Society: A Family Study* (London, 1969), pp. 132–8; Ivor Wilks, *Asante in the Nineteenth Century* (London, 1975), p. 147.

3 The first figure is from A. Norman Klein, 'Inequality in Asante: a study of the forms and meanings of slavery and social servitude in pre- and early colonial Akan-Asante society and culture', PhD thesis, University of Michigan, 1980, I, p. 125; the second from LaTorre, 'Wealth', pp. 427–35.

4 To use A. G. Hopkins' phrase: *An Economic History of West Africa* (London, 1973), p. 139.

5 On values, see Emmanuel Terray, 'Nature et fonctions de la guerre dans le monde Akan (XVIIe-XIXe siècles)', in J. Bazin and E. Terray (eds.), *Guerres de lignages et guerres d'état en Afrique* (Paris, 1982), pp. 387–9; Kwame Arhin, 'The Asante praise poems: the ideology of patrimonialism', *Paideuma*, 32 (1986), 163–97.

6 Hopkins, *Economic History*, pp. 125–7, 142–7.

7 '"No elders were present": commoners and private ownership in Asante, 1507–1896', *JAH*, forthcoming.

8 Ivor Wilks, 'Asante policy towards the Hausa trade in the nineteenth century', in Claude Meillassoux (ed.), *The Development of Indigenous Trade and Markets in West Africa* (London, 1971), p. 130; Wilks, *Asante*, p. 178.

9 Wilks, *Asante*, pp. 685, 689.

10 LaTorre, 'Wealth', pp. 443–5.

11 Paul E. Lovejoy, *Transformations in Slavery: A History of Slavery in Africa* (Cambridge, 1983), chs. 7–9 (quotation, p. 136); Patrick Manning, *Slavery and African Life: Occidental, Oriental, and African Slave Trades* (Cambridge, 1990), pp. 140, 142–8.

12 Hopkins, *Economic History*, p.126.

13 For an overview, see John E. Flint and E. Ann McDougall, 'Economic change in West Africa in the nineteenth century', in J. F. A. Ajayi and M. Crowder (eds.), *History of West Africa*, II (2nd edn, Harlow, 1987), pp. 379–402.

14 See especially Paul E. Lovejoy, 'Plantations in the economy of the Sokoto Caliphate', *JAH*, 19 (1978), 341–68. Also Lovejoy, 'Interregional monetary flows in the precolonial trade of Nigeria', *JAH*, 15 (1974), 563–85; Philip J. Shea, 'The development of an export oriented dyed cloth industry in Kano emirate in the nineteenth century', PhD thesis, University of Wisconsin, 1975; A. Mahdi and J. Inikori, 'Population and capitalist development in

precolonial West Africa: Kasar Kano in the nineteenth century', in D. Cordell and J. Gregory (eds.), *African Population and Capitalism: Historical Perspectives* (Boulder, CO, 1987), pp. 62–73.

15   Hopkins, *Economic History*, ch. 4.

16   Calculated from the figures in Reynolds, *Trade*, p. 61.

17   LaTorre, 'Wealth', pp. 439, 446.

18   Cruickshank, *Eighteen Years*, II, p. 244.

19   Cruickshank, *Eighteen Years*, II, p. 280; Reynolds, *Trade*; LaTorre, 'Wealth', pp. 381–2; Marion Johnson, 'Ivory and the nineteenth century transformation in West Africa', in G. Liesegang, H. Pasch and A. Jones (eds.), *Figuring African Trade* (Berlin, 1986), pp. 100–3, 130–1.

20   Paul E. Lovejoy, *Caravans of Kola: The Hausa Kola Trade 1700–1900* (Zaria, 1980), pp. 14–17.

21   The Akan are the cultural group to which the Asante belong, defined by common possession of the Akan or Twi language. Other Akan populations were and are to be found to the west and east of Asante, and especially to the south, where Fante, Akyem and other southern Akan states occupied the bulk of the territory between Asante and the sea.

22   LaTorre, 'Wealth', p. 380.

23   Cruickshank, *Eighteen Years*, II, p. 278.

24   Wilks, 'Asante policy', pp. 126, 129–30.

25   Lovejoy, 'Interregional monetary flows', p. 571; cf. 'Plantations', p. 367.

26   Lovejoy, *Caravans*, pp. 11, 114–16.

27   LaTorre, 'Wealth', p. 365.

28   David Carl Tambo, 'The Sokoto Caliphate slave trade in the nineteenth century', *IJAHS*, 9 (1976), 205; LaTorre, 'Wealth', pp. 417, 420; Lovejoy, *Caravans*, pp. 125, 134.

29   Bowdich, *Mission*, pp. 271, 324–5, 331–4; LaTorre, 'Wealth', pp. 383–4, 401; Lovejoy, *Caravans*, pp. 124–5, 133; Paul E. Lovejoy, *Salt of the Desert Sun* (Cambridge, 1986), pp. 26–7, 76, 194, 207, 211, 214–15, 243.

30   Bowdich, *Mission*, p. 332; Shea, 'Development', p. 21; Lovejoy, *Caravans*, p. 124.

31   Lovejoy, *Caravans*, p. 124: cf. Bowdich, *Mission*, p. 332.

32   Bowdich, *Mission*, pp. 334–5.

33   Shea, 'Development', pp. 75, 157–8.

34   George Metcalf, 'A microcosm of why Africans sold slaves: Akan consumption patterns in the 1770s', *JAH*, 28 (1987), 377–94 (quotation, p.379).

35   Selena Axelrod Winsnes (trans. & ed.), *Letters on West Africa and the Slave Trade: Paul Erdmann Isert's 'Journey to Guinea and the Caribbean Islands in Columbia' (1788)* (Oxford, 1992), p. 83 (letter dated 1784).

36   See, for example, D.J.E. Maier, 'Military acquisition of slaves in Asante', in D. Henige and T.C. McCaskie (eds.), *West African Economic and Social History: Studies in Memory of Marion Johnson* (Madison, 1990), p. 130.

37   Bowdich, *Mission*, p. 334n.

38   Bowdich, *Mission*, p. 334.

39   See M.J. Bonnat, extract translated in Marion Johnson (ed.), *Salaga Papers* (Legon, 1966), I, acc. no. SAL/34/1. A British attempt to do the same before their 1863 war with Asante was foiled by the refusal of the Dutch to

participate (Wilks, *Asante*, p. 220). For a longer perspective see LaTorre, 'Wealth', pp. 391–4.

40   On the former point see LaTorre, 'Wealth', pp. 387, 392, 468; on the latter see, e.g., Cruickshank, *Eighteen Years*, II, p. 41.

41   Colin Newbury, 'Prices and profitability in early nineteenth-century West African trade', in Meillassoux (ed.), *Development of Indigenous Trade*, pp. 93–4.

42   On the relative inelasticity of demand for firearms on the Gold Coast, upwards as well as downwards, see LaTorre, 'Wealth', pp. 391–2.

43   LaTorre, 'Wealth', pp. 262–3. I discuss the issue of state monopoly in more detail in 'No elders were present', the relevant part of which is summarized here.

44   LaTorre, 'Wealth', pp. 262–3. Wilks's source is Joseph Dupuis, *Journal of a Residence in Ashantee* (London, 1824), p. 167; but see ibid., pp. ix-x, 124.

45   Bowdich, *Mission*, p. 257.

46   R. S. Rattray, *Ashanti Law and Constitution* (Oxford, 1929), p. 110.

47   See LaTorre, 'Wealth', pp. 409–13; Larry Yarak, *Asante and the Dutch 1744–1873* (Oxford, 1990), esp. pp. 106–11.

48   LaTorre, 'Wealth', p. 414.

49   Cf. LaTorre, 'Wealth', p. 408. Larry Yarak is engaged in further work on the Dutch 'recruitment' in Asante, which, among other things, may test this conclusion.

50   Wilks, 'Asante policy', pp. 125, 128. For an illustration of the problem of banditry, albeit for a later period, see Krause manuscript in Jack Goody and T.M. Mustapha, 'The caravan trade from Kano to Salaga', *JHSN*, 3/4 (1967), 611–16.

51   Wilks, 'Asante policy', pp. 135–6.

52   Lovejoy, *Caravans*, pp. 11–12, 19; and 'Polanyi's "ports of trade": Salaga and Kano in the nineteenth century', *CJAS*, 16 (1982), 253–5, 258.

53   As Bowdich found at first hand: see, especially, Bowdich, *Mission*, pp. 119–20; also Wilks's comments in *Asante*, pp. 706–9.

54   Garrard, *Akan Weights*, pp. 158–66.

55   See, for example, K.Y. Daaku (ed.), *Oral Traditions of Adanse* (Institute of African Studies, University of Ghana, Legon, 1969).

56   Kwame Arhin, 'Market settlements in Northwestern Ashanti: Kintampo', *Research Review* (Institute of African Studies, University of Ghana), Supplement 1, *Ashanti and the Northwest*, ed. J. Goody and K. Arhin (1965), p. 143.

57   Marion Johnson, review of Lovejoy's *Caravans*, *African Economic History*, 11 (1982), 203.

58   Wilks, *Asante*, pp. 420–1.

59   LaTorre, 'Wealth', p. 249; Daaku, *Oral Traditions of Adanse*.

60   Maier, 'Military acquisition', pp. 119–32.

61   T.E. Bowdich, 'Remarks on Civilization in Africa', in his *The British and French Expeditions to Teembo with Remarks on Civilization in Africa* (Paris, 1821), p. 18.

62   Rattray, *Ashanti Law*, p. 92.

63   Bowdich, *Mission*, p. 333.

64 Klein, 'Inequality', I, pp. 99, 127.
65 Ivor Wilks, 'Land, labour, capital and the forest kingdom of Asante: a model of early change', in J. Friedman and M. Rowlands (eds.), *The Evolution of Social Systems* (London, 1978), p. 500, reprinted with revisions in Wilks, *Forests*; Kwame Arhin, 'Trade, accumulation and the state in Asante in the nineteenth century', *Africa*, 60 (1990), 525–7.
66 Lovejoy, *Caravans*, pp. 16, 22.
67 Emmanuel Terray, 'Long-distance exchange and the formation of the state: the case of the Abron kingdom of Gyaman', *Economy & Society*, 3 (1974), 315–45; 'Gold production, slave labor, and state intervention in precolonial Akan societies: a reply to Raymond Dumett', *Research in Economic Anthropology*, 5 (1983), 95–129.
68 Raymond E. Dumett, 'Precolonial gold mining and the state in the Akan region: with a critique of the Terray hypothesis', *Research in Economic Anthropology*, 2 (1979), 27–68; 'Traditional slavery in the Akan region in the nineteenth century: sources, issues, and interpretations', in Henige and McCaskie (eds.), *West African Economic and Social History*, pp. 17–18. See also Kwame Arhin, 'The political economy of the expansionist state', *Revue française d'historie d'Outre-Mer*, 68 (1981), 17, 24.
69 For discussion of the significance of funerary killings in pre-colonial Asante see, in particular, R. S. Rattray, *Religion and Art in Ashanti* (Oxford, 1927), pp. 105–9; Clifford Williams, 'Asante: human sacrifice or capital punishment?', *IJAHS*, 21 (1988), 433–41; Ivor Wilks, 'Space, time, and "human sacrifice"', in Wilks, *Forests*, pp. 215–40; and a forthcoming book by T. C. McCaskie.
70 School of Oriental and African Studies, University of London, Methodist Missionary Society Archive, Box 597, Thomas Birch Freeman papers, manuscript of unpublished book by Freeman entitled 'Reminiscences and Incidents of Travels and Historical and Political Sketches in the Countries Bordering on the Gold and Slave Coasts and in Ashantee, Dahomey, etc.' (c.1860), p. 38b (Freeman's emphasis).
71 Wilks, *Asante*, pp. 65–8, 164, 170, 177–8; Maier, 'Military acquisition', pp. 128–9.
72 LaTorre, 'Wealth', pp. 440–1. For a broader perspective see Lovejoy and Richardson's chapter in this volume.
73 Wilks, 'Space, time, and "human sacrifice"', p. 228. See also Robin Law, 'Human sacrifice in pre-colonial West Africa', *African Affairs*, 84 (1985), 77–8.
74 Wilks, 'Space, time, and "human sacrifice"', pp. 222–3.
75 Wilks, 'Space, time and "human sacrifice"', p. 229.
76 Ivor Wilks, 'Asante: human sacrifice or capital punishment? a rejoinder', *IJAHS*, 21 (1988), 452; 'Space, time, and "human sacrifice"', pp. 227–9.
77 Here I disagree with LaTorre, who argued that 'in general, slave-owning was the perogative of the upper stratum of Asante society': 'Wealth', pp. 117–19, 408–9; quotation, p. 117. He identified the 'upper stratum' as 'stoolholders and specified members of their families' (p. 94).
78 Klein, 'Inequality', esp. I, chs. 4 and 5. See, further, Austin 'No elders were present'.

79 Kwasi Boaten, 'Trade among the Asante of Ghana up to the end of the eighteenth Century', *Research Review*, 7, 1 (1970), 36.

80 Bowdich, *Mission*, pp. 332–3.

81 H. Pel, *Aanteekeningen gehouden op eene Reis van S. George d'Elmina naar Coomassie* (Leiden, 1842?), p. 24, quoted by LaTorre, 'Wealth', p. 407.

82 LaTorre, 'Wealth', p. 414.

83 Detailed in Austin, 'No elders were present'. For Adubease, see Daaku, *Oral Traditions of Adanse*, p. 45.

84 I have suggested elsewhere that pawns were particularly important within the labour portfolios of commoners as opposed to chiefs: Gareth Austin, 'Human pawning in Asante c.1820–c.1950: markets and coercion, gender and cocoa', in T. Falola and P. Lovejoy (eds.), *Pawnship in Africa* (Boulder, 1994), pp. 126, 133–4).

85 Arhin, 'Market settlements', pp. 144–5.

86 Dumett, 'Precolonial gold mining', pp. 45–6; 'Traditional slavery', pp. 17–18.

87 Garrard, *Akan Weights*, pp. 145–8; cf. Philip D. Curtin's analysis, for a Malian case, in 'The lure of Bambuk gold', *JAH*, 14 (1973), 623–31.

88 Manuscript Collection of the Royal Anthropological Institute, housed in the Museum of Mankind, London: R. S. Rattray papers, MS 106, 2033, quoted by Terray, 'Gold production', p. 117.

89 Wilks, *Asante*, pp. 106–9; LaTorre, 'Wealth', pp. 129–31; T. C. McCaskie, '*Ahyiamu* – "a place of meeting": an essay on process and event in the history of the Asante state', *JAH*, 25 (1984), 169–78; Gareth Austin, 'Rural capitalism and the growth of cocoa-farming in South Ashanti, to 1914', PhD thesis, University of Birmingham, 1984, pp. 165–9.

90 Austin, 'Rural capitalism', ch. 3.

91 Arhin, 'Market settlements', pp. 143–5, and as notes 67–8 above.

92 Hopkins, *Economic History*, p. 26.

93 Cf. Austin, 'Human pawning', p. 132.

94 For details see Rattray, *Ashanti Law*, pp. 107–19; Arhin, 'Financing'; Wilks, *Asante*, pp. 64–71, 431–45; LaTorre, 'Wealth', pp. 216–97.

95 Wilks, *Asante*, pp. 66, 164, 170, 178.

96 Maier, 'Military acquisition', pp. 127–8.

97 Thomas C. McCaskie, 'The paramountcy of the Asantehene Kwaku Dua (1834–1867): a study in Asante political culture', PhD thesis, University of Cambridge, 1974, pp. 106f.

98 C. S. Salmon, 'British policy in West Africa', *The Contemporary Review*, 42 (1882), 891.

99 Raymond E. Dumett, 'Pressure group, bureaucracy, and the decision-making process: the case of slavery abolition and colonial expansion in the Gold Coast, 1874', *JICH*, 9 (1981), 193–215.

100 See, for example, Thomas Gibson Bowles,'The Ashantee War unnecessary and unjust', *Fraser's Magazine*, 9 (Feb. 1874), 124–34; Salmon, 'British Policy', pp. 890–1; John D. Hargreaves, *Prelude to the Partition of West Africa* (London, 1963), pp. 63, 67; Agnes A. Aidoo, 'Political crisis and social change in the Asante kingdom, 1867–1901', PhD thesis, University of California, Los Angeles, 1975, I, pp. 132–3. This view was reasserted after

the British occupation, in a derisive polemic against recent British policy, by Richard Austin Freeman, *Travels and Life in Ashanti and Jaman* (London, 1898), ch. 16.

101 See comment by Sir Samuel Rowe, former governor of the Gold Coast, on paper by Captain Brandon Kirby, published in Kirby, 'A journey to the interior of Ashanti', *Proceedings of the Royal Geographical Society*, 6 (1884), 450–1; Major C. Barter, 'Notes on Ashanti', *Scottish Geographical Magazine*, 12 (1896), 455; LaTorre, 'Wealth', pp. 329–30; William G. Hynes, *The Economics of Empire: Britain, Africa and the New Imperialism 1870–95* (London, 1979), p. 122.

102 According to Wilks and LaTorre, in 1835 the Kumasi government obtained the agreement of British and other European merchants that the entry and residence of traders from the coast in Asante should again be greatly restricted, leaving the carriage of coast goods within most of Asante as an Asante monopoly: Wilks, *Asante*, p. 196; LaTorre, 'Wealth', pp. 327–8. Larry Yarak informs me, however, that from his research in the Dutch archives it appears likely that the initiative for the agreement came from big coastal merchants rather than from the Asantehene, who may not even have been party to it; but that in any case it had only a short-term effect.

103 Earl of Kimberley to Sir G. Wolseley, 10 Sept. 1873, reprinted in, e.g., J. J. Crooks (ed.), *Records Relating to the Gold Coast Settlements from 1750 to 1874* (Dublin, 1923), p. 467.

104 The text of the treaty is reprinted in, e.g., ibid., pp. 521–4.

105 Rowe's comment on Kirby, 'Journey', p. 451; Hargreaves, *Prelude*, p. 172; Wilks, *Asante*, pp. 281–2; Arhin, *West African Traders*, pp. 31–2; Donna Maier, 'Competition for power and profits in Kete-Krachi, West Africa, 1875–1900', *IJAHS*, 13 (1980), 39–40.

106 Parliamentary Papers, C.3386, *Further Correspondence Regarding Affairs of the Gold Coast* (London, 1882), pp. 66–7: Captain Rupert LaTrobe Lonsdale's report on his mission of 1881–82.

107 Sir Francis Fuller, *A Vanished Dynasty: Ashanti* (London, 1921), p. 156.

108 William Tordoff, *Ashanti Under the Prempehs, 1888–1935* (London, 1965), pp. 19–20.

109 See, for example, W. Scott Dalgleish, 'Ashanti and the Gold Coast', *Scottish Geographical Magazine*, 12 (1896), 11; Hynes, *Economics of Empire*, pp. 96–7.

110 Hynes, *Economics of Empire*, pp. 75–6, 96–7, 122.

111 Hynes, *Economics of Empire*, p. 122.

112 I lack local data on gold prices but see Pierre Vilar, *A History of Gold and Money 1450–1920* (London, 1976), p. 311. For declining gold output in Asante – to judge from the general Akan trend – see Garrard, *Akan Weights*, pp. 159, 162–6. The rubber trade was well under way in southern Asante by 1884 (Parliamentary Papers, C.4477, *Further Correspondence Regarding the Affairs of the Gold Coast* [London, 1885], p. 91: Captain Brandon Kirby's report on his mission to Kumasi, Accra, 15 April 1884).

113 Austin, 'Rural capitalism'.

114 On the use of slaves in rubber production see, especially, Kwame Arhin,

'The economic and social significance of rubber production and exchange on the Gold and Ivory Coasts, 1880–1900', *CEA*, 77–8 (1980), 56–60.

115 For example: Hla Myint, 'The "classical" theory of international trade and the underdeveloped countries', *Economic Journal* 68 (1958), 317–37; Robert Szeresewski, *Structural Changes in the Economy of Ghana, 1891–1911* (London, 1965); Barbara Ingham, *Tropical Exports and Economic Development* (London, 1981); Francis J. Teal, 'Growth, comparative advantage and the economic effects of government: a case study of Ghana', PhD thesis, University of London, 1984. For an alternative view, see Austin, 'Rural capitalism', ch. 3.

116 Myint, 'Classical theory', p. 321.

117 Lovejoy, *Caravans*, pp. 12, 15, 17.

118 Hopkins, *Economic History*, p. 134.

5 Plantations and labour in the south-east Gold Coast from the late eighteenth to the mid nineteenth century

Ray A. Kea

Trade cannot flourish without colonization and the cultivation of colonial produce.[1]

That there was a complex historical relationship between the abolition of the trans-Atlantic slave trade and legitimate commerce has been widely and lengthily debated among Africanists and others. The debate is virtually contemporaneous with the abolition of the external slave trade itself. A fundamental issue has been to determine the precise nature of the impact of abolition on West African social and political formations. According to Tony Hopkins, the European powers' decision to abolish the external slave trade created for West Africa 'the problem of developing alternative exports'. He continues: 'The outcome was a period of transition and experimentation, which is customarily referred to as the era of "legitimate commerce" in order to distinguish it from the illegal trade in slaves'. Hopkins argued that 'the structure of legitimate trade marked an important break with the past and signified a new phase in the growth of the market, a phase which can be seen as the start of the modern economic history of West Africa', and constituted a 'crisis of adaptation'.[2] Others have interpreted the commercial transition in less sweeping terms, suggesting that there was no decisive rupture with the past, and hence by implication no 'crisis of adaptation'.[3]

Immanuel Wallerstein, too, sees a continuity. His historical context is an expanding capitalist world-system and the (structural) incorporation of West Africa into it. In his view, it was not the shift from the slave trade to legitimate trade which brought about the incorporation of West Africa into this system. 'The initial impetus [for incorporation]', he maintains, 'was the expansion of the slave trade itself', and with this expansion slave-raiding became 'a veritable productive enterprise that entered into the ongoing division of labor of the capitalist world-economy'. Incorporation occurred in the second half of the eighteenth century with the steady rise in slave prices. In Wallerstein's view the pattern of exports from West Africa to the world-economy went through

119

three phases during the period of incorporation: 1) 'an increase in and continued concentration on slave exports, in absolute and probably in relative terms, from circa 1750 to 1793'; 2) 'a maintenance of significant slave export along with a steady increase in so-called legitimate trade, from the 1790s to the 1840s'; 3) 'the virtual elimination of the Atlantic slave trade and a steady expansion of primary products (particularly palm oil and peanuts), from the 1840s to the beginning of the full-scale colonial era in the 1880s'.[4] While this periodization raises certain questions, it nevertheless provides a useful frame of reference with respect to the Gold Coast's transition from the export slave trade to the export of primary products.

Covering the period from the late 1780s to the 1840s, the present essay offers an initial interpretation of the 'transition' from the export of slaves to the export of produce by considering certain aspects of the material and social organization of commercial agriculture in south-eastern Ghana, specifically the inland Akuapem polity and the hinterland of the coastal Accra and Adanme towns. Until 1826 these places were political dependencies of the Asante state.

Wallerstein has made the pertinent point that 'the link between cash-crop production and the expansion of market-oriented food production has been largely neglected, especially in the process we have been calling incorporation'.[5] The historical relationship between the two is the central issue addressed here. During the period under investigation there were two identifiable forms of commercial agricultural production in the south-east Gold Coast: food production for local urban markets (including the European coastal trading establishments and shipping); and cash crop production for overseas markets (principally European and West Indian). This production engaged various forms of social labour: slaves purchased in local markets; pawns; debtors; slaves hired out by their owners; and free wage labourers.

Denmark was the first European state to prohibit its subjects from participating in the trans-Atlantic slave trade. In 1792 a royal edict decreed that the Danish slave trade was to be abolished in 1803. Great Britain and the Netherlands abolished the slave trade for their subjects in 1807 and 1814 respectively. To replace the slave trade and to place its West African trading stations on a firm economic basis, the Danish government made a strong commitment to the establishment of plantations in the hinterlands of these stations during the first four decades of the nineteenth century. The plantations were to produce tropical plants (indigo, coffee, sugar cane, cotton and tobacco) for the Danish market.[6] In 1850 the Danish government sold its Gold Coast possessions to the British government.

In the course of the first half of the nineteenth century British and Dutch authorities, too, envisioned the Gold Coast as an exporter of cash crops, and the Basel and Wesleyan Methodist mission organizations were also strongly supportive of plantation development and the export of agricultural commodities.[7] However, it was Denmark which took the lead in promoting a commercial agricultural sector organized for export. The main Danish trading stations on the Guinea Coast included the following forts: Christiansborg, the headquarters and administrative seat, at Osu; Fredensborg at Great Ningo; Kongensten at Ada; and Prinsensten at Keta. These were the nodal points in what the Danish authorities called 'Danish Guinea', a territory comprising eleven 'provinces' according to an early nineteenth-century Danish report.[8] The move from a trade in slaves to a trade in agricultural commodities signalled a shift in Danish state interests in 'Danish Guinea', a shift from the mercantile – the administration of trade – to the territorial – the administration of export production; a shift from the operations of a chartered company which managed the external trade in slaves to the operations of a royal administrative department (The General Customs Chamber) which was responsible for plantation development and management. The profits derived from the sale of agricultural commodities were to be used, in part, to maintain the Danish Guinea establishments.

For a period of more than fifty years, from the 1780s through the 1830s, the Danish government sought to establish a plantation complex in the south-east Gold Coast, either directly with state subsidies and under state management (thus, the royal or state plantations) or indirectly by supporting and encouraging Danish and Afro-Danish merchants to engage in cash crop production (thus, the private plantations). One can identify three phases in the plantation project: (1) from the late 1780s until about 1811 the plantations were organized primarily for export production to Denmark; (2) from the early 1820s to the 1830s the Danish West Indies was the market for the plantations; (3) from the late 1830s to 1850 (the year Denmark gave up its West African possessions) plantation production was geared solely to local urban and rural markets. Employing a dependent labour force of men, women and children, both non-waged and waged labourers, the Danish plantation project was a labour-intensive, capitalist agrarian enterprise.

If the Danish and Afro-Danish planters represented one 'direction' or 'component' in the agricultural history of the south-east Gold Coast, the Accra, Adanme (namely Krobo and Shai) and Akuapem landed proprietors (pl. *awuranom* in Akuapem-Twi; sing. *nyontsho* or *owulali* in Ga) represented another. The term 'plantation' (*Plantage* in Danish; *Pflanzung* in German) was used by Europeans to refer to the farms, 'planted fields' or 'cultivated places' (*Rosahr-pladser/Rosarre Plads* in Danish) in the rural hinterlands. The proprietors pursued three different production (and wealth accumulation) strategies: (1) producing subsistence for their own labourers and urban households; (2) producing provisions and supplies for local urban markets; and (3) producing cash crops for overseas markets. Various kinds of dependent labour, including dispossessed sectors of the social order, were employed. The proprietors included merchants and/or brokers, office-holders and 'gentry' (i.e. 'those of the middle class who ... own a certain amount of estate, money [and slaves], and through their affluence are themselves above the rank of slaves'), many of whom had been directly involved in the selling of slaves to the Danish and other European factors.[9] The agricultural strategies of these dominant strata were oriented around their conditions of consumption and their 'regimes' of wealth accumulation.

From the 1790s to the mid-1810s the plantations of the Accra proprietors followed, in the main, strategies (1) and (2); from the mid-1810s through the 1830s the third production strategy assumed considerable importance; in the 1840s and thereafter there was an almost exclusive reliance on the first two production strategies. From the 1790s until the 1830s the plantations of Akuapem and Adanme (i.e. Shai and Krobo) proprietors followed the first and second production strategies almost exclusively; from the 1830s export production for European markets assumed overwhelming importance.[10] For the period under study agricultural practices in the area can be characterized as heterogeneous and multi-levelled, and thus not reducible to a single, linear development.

Export-oriented agriculture and legitimate trade demonstrated a particular set of patterns and variations of economic, social and cultural activity, changing power relations, and new authority structures; they generated, too, new contradictions, conflicts and struggles. The establishment of new organizational forms in the political and commercial centres during the course of the first half of the nineteenth century was no chance event. New technologies of power and new disciplinary apparatuses with their specific organizing and socializing practices 'framed' the development of legitimate trade. Schools, churches, prisons, hospitals and police-militia barracks were set up in various towns where they functioned as 'organs' of control and surveillance; schooling, 'medicalization', missionary evangelizing and judicial incarceration emerged as normative procedures in the new social and moral economy. Like the plantation projects, such phenomena can be interpreted as the effects and the conditions of the complex re-positioning of the Gold Coast's political economy within the world-economy's elaborate system of functional relations and division of labour.[11]

Origins

The late eighteenth-century work of C. B. Waldstrom refers to a Danish agrarian project on the southern frontier of the Asante imperium:

The Danish government, convinced ... of [the Atlantic slave trade's] impolicy and barbarity, determined that their part of it should be abolished in the year 1802; and, preparatory to this measure, they resolved forthwith to open their African ports [on the Gold and Slave Coasts] to all nations, and to establish a colony in some eligible part of that country.[12]

Waldstrom is referring to a concerted political effort by Denmark to establish an agricultural colony, a projected alternative to the external slave trade. The colony was to become a source of 'colonial products' – grains (chiefly maize), coffee, ginger, tobacco and sugar cane, crops associated with processing and mass consumption, and cotton and indigo associated with industrial manufacturing.

Plantations and the 'free' trade in 'colonial products' were to service the Danish kingdom's wealth at a time when the Danish economy as a whole and the urban sector in particular were experiencing significant growth. By the end of the eighteenth century 'a grand bourgeoisie milieu' had developed in Copenhagen. It was based on 'commercial and financial circles, the leading officials of the strong Danish absolutist state and some of the large landowners who had links with the political centre and a residence in Copenhagen'. The rate of real growth within the urban sector, and in Copenhagen in particular, was significant:

This urban growth enabled Copenhagen and ultimately the provincial towns to cease merely being an appendage to the agrarian sector and to develop on their own terms in constant interaction with, on the one hand, the agrarian sector and, on the other, foreign industry and the world market.

The Gold Coast plantations can be viewed as part – a territorial extension, as it were – of the Danish/Copenhagen urban sector and as one of the effects of the agrarian reforms.[13]

Private Danish and Afro-Danish traders resident in Osu, Labade and other coastal towns assumed the mercantile role formerly enjoyed by salaried agents of the Danish chartered companies of earlier years. From about 1794 onwards they set up warehouses and 'shops' and/or factories in different towns. Salaried state administrators at Christiansborg and other forts provided the traders with legal and military protection as well as, on occasion, credit and warehousing facilities.

The Danish government, however, wished to expand the economic role of private traders living in the vicinity of the Danish forts and factories and, at the same time, to encourage Accra, Adanme and Akuapem notables to actively support export agricultural production. Thus, a royal resolution of 1796 decreed:

Private persons who propose to cultivate land in the neighbourhood of the forts shall enjoy protection, encouragement, and assistance ... and if the state is to receive and profit from its establishments on the coast, it must be from agriculture [*Colonie Anlaeg*], from urging the Blacks to cultivate the earth, and from trading in their produce; in this regard, the two forts [Fredensborg and Kongensten] are the most suitable, as they lie closest to Aqvapim and the islands in the River Volta, which are the most fertile districts[14]

But 'Blacks' were already 'cultivating the earth'. In 1795 the Danish commissioner H. Moe wrote to Waldstrom about one Osu resident's expansive farming activities:

In the neighbourhood of Christiansborg at Acra, an old, respectable negro, a native of Dunco, at a considerable distance up in the interior part, has established himself on a solitary spot, and has planted large fields with cotton, maize and various kinds of provisions and garden stuffs. By his intelligence and laborious cultivation, he has distinguished himself so much, that he is now come into great repute. He raises such quantities of provisions, that he supplies not only Christiansborg, but also most of the neighbouring negro villages.[15]

Unfortunately, the 'Dunco'[16] proprietor is not identified by name, but we may see his enterprise as part of a strategy of Accra traders and brokers and political notables to expand agricultural production in the 1790s. His farms produced for local markets, Christiansborg Castle and, no doubt, the shipping which anchored off the Castle. Presumably, a portion of the cotton he grew was sold to the Danes.

Setting up plantations presupposes access to land and labour. In the first decade of the nineteenth century the Danish priest H. C. Monrad (who was on the Gold Coast from 1805 to 1809) remarked that nothing was easier than to purchase a sizeable stretch of land in the hinterlands of Accra towns and in the foothills of the Akuapem mountains. He indicates that a person with the means could purchase a substantial quantity of land for several ankers of spirits. Presumably, he meant the usufruct could be bought and not absolute ownership of the land itself.[17] A Danish report of 1803 suggests that this was, in fact, the case, for, it relates, 'the Blacks will not sell the land, but will allow the Danes to live on it, lay out plantations, and build fortifications against the payment of gratuities and regular stipends'.[18] In other words, continued use of the land necessitated the regular payment of 'rent'.

In the first decade of the century there were evidently many residents in the Accra towns who were acquiring farming rights and, perhaps in some instances, land as well. The 'Donco' referred to by Moe was, perhaps, an earlier instance of this phenomenon. Monrad noted that Danes and 'many Mulattoes and Blacks' had begun to lay out plantations, or 'cultivation-places', beginning about two miles from the littoral and extending up to the Akuapem foothills. The plantations were, generally, worked by servile labourers. The Danes were primarily engaged in export production; the others, for the most part, in market-oriented food production.[19] Interestingly, Monrad wrote that an Accra man who owned a 'palm-forest', in whose shadow cottages are raised for his labourers, is esteemed 'a rich man'.[20] Evidently, large-scale farming efforts carried social prestige. One supposes that wealthy traders and brokers in various Accra towns were purchasing land or the rights to it in the Akuapem foothills for the purpose of producing palm oil and other palm products, but not, at this time, for export but for local consumption.

How is this particular development to be accounted for? The historian the Rev. Carl Christian Reindorf wrote that from the 1730s to the 1820s the Accra ruling elite enjoyed peace and prosperity:

As traders and brokers to European merchants in the slave traffic, and also by several affinities to them, they acquired riches and popularity and improvement in their social life ... [Their] country was well peopled ... Their political and military administrations were in good order. They were mostly blessed with good, powerful, brave, and patriotic kings, chiefs, captains, and rich men.[21]

Reindorf locates the prosperity of this political order in commercial activity and mercantile accumulation. Here we may identify one major source of the wealth required for expanded agricultural production in the early nineteenth century.

With regard to Danish export agricultural efforts between 1794 and 1810, Reindorf observed:

[The Danes'] chief object was not only to instruct the natives in better cultivation of the soil, but to improve cultivation so far as to supply European markets with produce from Africa like that obtained from the West Indies. After the abolition of the slave trade, the Danish Government encouraged the cultivation of the vegetable productions gained in the West Indies. Plantations of coffee, cotton etc. were made on the Kuku and Legong hills. Further on they bought several lands from the Akuapems and founded their own villages: Sesemi, Bebiase, Kponkpo, Abokobi, Akropong, Togbloku, etc. Besides coffee they introduced vegetables unknown to the natives.[22]

Reindorf viewed this activity in terms of a 'civilizing mission' and, given his own educational background, was naturally supportive of it. A propos the farming 'improvements' of the Danes, he writes: 'Some

Danish colonists, as Messieurs Schoenning, Truelsen, Meyer, Groenberg and others, had established villages of their own at Sesemi, Dwaben, Bebiase and Kponkpo. A fine fort was built by Schoenning in his village and armed with cannon.'[23] Danish state funds and Danish merchant capital were responsible for the development of an export-oriented agricultural sector, just as Accra merchant capital was responsible for the parallel extension of commercial food production.

Early Danish plantations

The first concerted effort to set up a Danish plantation in the south-east Gold Coast occurred in 1788. On 28 February in that year Captain P. E. Isert (1756–89) concluded a treaty with Obuobi Atiemo, the ruler of Akuapem (died 17 May 1790). The treaty granted Isert the use of land on a mountain called Amanopa (rendered 'Amannopa' or 'Annanopasso' in Danish documents) for the establishment of a royal agricultural colony. He called the plantation Frederiksnopel ('Frederichsnopel'). It was located only a short distance from Akurupon, the state capital, on land under the king's direct authority, and was part of the *Gyaase-Koman* political division of the state. Initial payment for the use of the land was made in cowries and merchandise; henceforth, the Akuapem ruler and his 'grandees' were to receive monthly and annual stipends.[24]

In 1787 Isert had come to the conclusion 'that the creation of plantations on the west coast of Africa similar to those in the West Indies would reduce, if not completely eliminate, the traffic in slaves, while at the same time enrich and strengthen the African establishments'.[25] And the royal plantation was to be, in the words of one historian, Isert's 'utopia', where the 'demands of humanity and commerce' were harmonized.[26] Isert's intention was to have Frederiksnopel produce food crops, partly for local markets and partly for its own subsistence needs, and cash crops (cotton, indigo and tobacco) for export to Denmark; in addition the plantation was to raise livestock. To construct the necessary dwellings and to lay out a road six to seven miles long to Akurupon, Isert hired between 100 and 200 Akuapem labourers who worked daily for a period of three weeks. Other workers were employed to construct a road to the coast. Atiemo was to be responsible for maintaining the plantation's buildings and the roads by providing the necessary labourers.[27]

Akuapem had a vibrant agricultural economy when Frederiksnopel was laid out. Market-oriented food crop production had been a mainstay of the Akuapem economy since the founding of the polity in the early 1730s. One Danish factor related that Akuapem was a 'blessed land with an abundance of maize and produce', and in Isert's eyes it was an agricultural 'paradise'. A wide variety of crops were grown and sold in the Accra and Adanme urban markets. Akuapem served, in effect, as their 'granary'.[28]

What was Obuobi Atiemo's vision when he concluded his treaty with Isert which led to the establishment of the Amanopa *akuraa* ('plantation')? This is nowhere explicitly documented. In 1776 he had formed a political-military alliance with the Danish governor of Christiansborg, and he had known Isert since 1783. Was it his purpose to develop an export agriculture sector to complement town-oriented food crop production? Was the treaty part of his policy 'to win the love of his people' in order to emulate the esteem and popularity of Sa Ofori, the first ruler of Akuapem, and thus resolve the bitter legacy of civil war that plagued Akuapem in the mid-1770s?[29] One can easily imagine Atiemo's ambition was to increase the property-holdings of the *Gyaase-Koman* officialdom by means of export agricultural production as well as the stipends and gratuities in cash and merchandise of the Amanopa *akuraa*. Frederiksnopel provided the Akuapem royal court and central administration with a new revenue-producing and commercially viable agricultural complex.[30] At the same time, it was a 'link' between the Copenhagen and Akuropon urban economies, both of which were part of the same world-system.

After Isert's death in January 1789 his assistant, J. N. Flindt, continued to manage Frederiksnopel until 1792. Nevertheless, the plantation declined and by 1801 it consisted of just a few houses, a small piece of cleared land on which cotton was grown, and a work force of only seven people.[31] There is no indication in the Christiansborg records at least that cotton or any other crop was ever exported to Denmark. Nor did the plantation achieve self-sufficiency with respect to food production. In December 1789, for example, ten desperately hungry plantation workers fled Frederiksnopel with the intention of finding employment in Akuapem towns or villages so they could earn wherewithal to purchase food.[32]

In 1792 Flindt received Danish government funds to set up new plantations. The first to be established was called Frederikssted. It was near the Akuapem town of Dodowa, which, like Frederiksnopel, was part of the *Gyaase-Koman* political division. Flindt had reached an accord with Atiemo's successor, Ohempanyin Awukufrene, about setting up this new *akuraa*. Awukufrene was a staunch supporter of the Danish plantation project in Akuapem. A sawmill, three dwelling houses, a granary for corn, a stable and a large mansion-like dwelling (*Vaanings-huus*) were built within the course of several weeks. Cotton was the main crop and by 1795 Flindt expected to harvest between 4,000 and 5,000 pounds. The workers included 'ten elderly and infirm men', five women, and two Danish carpenters, both of whom were dead by July 1793. A small quantity of cotton, between 100 and 200 lbs, was exported from the plantation in 1796. Frederikssted continued to be worked until 1802, after which it was abandoned.[33]

In 1800 Flindt became the commandant of Fort Kongensten at Ada and with government funding he immediately set up a cotton plantation with over 4,000 plants next to the fort. Three other plantations devoted to maize cultivation were laid out in 1801 and 1802. In 1803 he established a plantation, named Eiboe, on one of the islands near the mouth of the Volta river. There he cultivated coffee, cotton, sugar cane, maize, yams and beans, as well as other crops. He also built a house for himself at Eiboe.[34]

Another state-funded plantation was set up in 1797 by governor J. P. Wrisberg. It was called Frederiksborg (or Frederiksberg) and was located about a mile north of Osu. A report of 1798 indicates that the plantation was largely devoted to the production of white and yellow cotton. In addition, it had a large garden for the cultivation of European vegetables. Wrisberg's plans included setting up a cotton plantation in the vicinity of Fort Prinsensten at Keta. The report concludes: 'With these plantations he hopes to convey to the Blacks a desire to work, and has, therefore, made known in the neighbouring towns that he will buy their produce. Some have already brought him some cotton which they themselves have cultivated.'[35] In 1796 Frederiksborg exported a small quantity of cotton to Denmark. By 1798 it had a couple of 'cotton machines' and a 'Black who knows how to operate them'. While cotton was the principal crop, coffee, lemon, cherry and tamarind trees were also grown. A road, 12 to 16 feet wide, was built between the plantation and Christiansborg, called Frederiksborg Allee. In 1804 Wrisberg planted 2,000 coffee trees and hoped to plant another 4–5,000 in spite of the absence of state funding. In 1808 the plantation had a total workforce of 48 men, women and children.[36]

In 1803 Frederiksborg Allee was extended northward to the Akuapem town of Bibiase, where, in 1802, a plantation had been set up by C. Schioenning, a Danish official and trader. Coffee, cotton and different kinds of fruit trees were grown. A man from the Danish West Indies was appointed to manage the plantation, but by 1809 it was in a neglected state.[37] Another state, or royal, plantation was laid out near Legon hill around 1804, but, as Monrad reported, it was never properly developed as an exporter of colonial produce.[38]

Perhaps the royal resolution of 1796 (see above) inspired the Danish trader Peter Meyer, who had been on the Gold Coast since about 1779, to embark on intensive farming projects. Monrad stated that among the Danish traders Meyer was the most deeply committed to farming and that traces of his cultivation efforts could be found from Little Popo on the Slave Coast to the Akuapem foothills. Before 1792 he had laid out plantations at Little Popo, Keta and Togbloku. Between 1794 and 1809 he set up plantations at Osu, Legon and near the Akuapem village of 'Ajeadufa'. At the latter he grew mainly coffee; on his other plantations he cultivated coffee, cotton, ginger, indigo, rice, sugar cane, plantain and fruit trees. All of the plantations were laid out at his own expense. In spite of requests for financial assistance, he never received loans from the Danish government.[39] In 1809 Meyer was living on the Bibiase plantation, which he had bought from Schioenning a few years earlier. According to Monrad, he neglected his other plantations while bringing Bibiase up to production. By 1809 he had lost interest in Bibiase and was beginning to clear other sites at the foot of the Akuapem mountains for cultivation, including one that was to be the location of a distillery.[40]

The largest of the early nineteenth-century Danish plantations was named 'Daccubie' (Dakobi). It was located in the *Adonten* political division of the Akuapem state and was laid out by Schioenning in 1807–8. He used his own private wealth and state monetary support to fund it. In October 1807 he acquired from a Berekuso man named Kwaku the usufruct for about 320 acres of land. He left a detailed account of the transaction, including a list of the Akuapem political notables involved in the transaction. Among them were senior office-holders who belonged to the *Adonten* and *Gyaase-Koman* organizations as well as members of the royal family. The Akuapem ruler Kwaw Safrotwe is said to have paid frequent visits to the Daccubie *akuraa*.[41] Describing his farming efforts Schioenning states that

In October 1808, I put some coffee-berries in the ground; and in the following June, I transplanted about 16,000 trees; I have every year added to this stock; and in November [1809], I had growing 36,500 healthy coffee-trees of different ages. Last year [1810] I had a nice crop; and I am sure, that I should have from 16,000 to 20,000 pounds weight of coffee this year [1811], had not the Ashantee war put a stop to my exertions.[42]

In 1811 the plantation had more than 50,000 coffee trees and a nursery with 100,000 coffee plants. Plantain and cassava were also grown on a large scale. Schioenning maintained a 'solid and attractive stone house' for himself and 30–35 cottages for the plantation workers. In 1808 the latter included 23 men and women who were Schioenning's own slaves. He also employed, on an occasional basis, 40 to 50 men who were part of the Christiansborg bonded labour force, as well as an unspecified number of hired wage labourers. With respect to his labour needs he is quoted as saying: 'To keep my plantation in good order, one person is necessary to one thousand trees'.[43]

The establishment of the various Danish-run plantations meant that another kind of order was being imposed on the countryside, different from the forms of domination and exploitation exercised by the possessors of plantation-villages. Relevant to an understanding of this new order is Raymond Williams' observation about the eighteenth-century English countryside: 'In the one case the land is being organised for production where tenants and labourers will work, while in the other it is being organised for consumption – the view, the ordered proprietory repose, the prospect.'[44] The Danish plantations set up in the Accra and Akuapem 'provinces' were, indeed, organized for export agricultural production, but they were organized for consumption as well: the tree-lined roadway, the stone house with gallery, hall and billiard room, the orchards, the workers' cottages, and the encompassing view.[45] Monrad could enjoy the 'grand prospect over the valley' from Dakobi and in the 1840s governor Carstensen could 'estheticize' the Akuapem landscape, admiring the cultivated fields of the plantations – signifiers of 'civilization' – and disdaining the 'darkness' generated by the 'close, tower-high trees' of the rain forest – signifiers of barbarism. His contemporary, the Danish military officer Svedstrup, had a 'fine' view of the landscape between Legon and the Akuapem mountains with its 'extensive plain with towns, oil palm forests, and tilled fields'. And the Basel missionary George Thompson wrote in 1843 that the road to the 'Royal Plantation', known as Frederiksgave, was 'agreeable to the eye', for one had 'a magnificent view of more than seventy miles up to the seacoast'. Generally, rural labour was unseen; it was 'dissolved' into an 'estheticized' landscape. The 'inscription' of Danish capital in the land gave it a signification different from others inscribed in it.[46]

Maize exporting in the 1820s

Between 1811 and 1822 Danish efforts to sustain and expand export agricultural enterprise were curtailed because of rebellions in Akuapem and other southern dependencies against Asante overlordship. The Asante armies' suppression of these revolts (1811–12 and 1815–16) led to the total destruction of many plantations, for example Dakobi, and severe damage to others.[47] During these years neither Danish officials nor merchants made serious and sustained efforts to re-establish the old plantations or to set up new ones. In contrast to the lack of Danish

agricultural efforts, the expansion of food farming and the development
of an export trade in agricultural commodities (maize, coffee and cotton)
was a foremost concern among a number of Accra merchants. Between
1818 and 1822 several merchants of 'British' and 'Dutch' Accra encouraged the establishment of 'Indian corn' plantations to produce for export
markets. In these years, several of them exported a total of 150,000
bushels of maize to Madeira and the West Indies.[48] This development
marks a departure from the agricultural strategy remarked upon by
Monrad earlier in the century.

The success of the export maize trade was enough to inspire the
Danish Council (comprising the governor, the commandants of the
different forts and other functionaries) to seriously consider producing
maize for export. Two policies, each with its adherents, were formulated
by the Council. The first priority was to pursue vigorously maize
cultivation on the royal plantations; the second was to restore the
Akuapem plantations and begin the cultivation of coffee, sugar cane,
indigo and cotton. In 1821 the Council used an initial sum of 4 to 5,000
rigsdaler to launch the production of maize. In 1823 a large maize
plantation was laid out at Frederiksborg, and already by 1824 American
and British ships purchased the first maize harvest at Christiansborg, and
transported the produce to Madeira and the Caribbean. The Council
proposed to the Danish government that a windmill be set up at
Frederiksborg so that maize could be ground before shipment, and one
was installed by 1827. The Council also proposed that several 'expert
journey millers be sent out [from Denmark] as it will take some time
before the natives learn to operate a mill, and a European foreman will in
any case be necessary'.[49]

From the mid-1820s the main agricultural export from Christiansborg
was maize. With the profits from maize sold in the West Indies
manufactured goods were purchased in Denmark and rum in the
Caribbean and these were sold in 'Danish Guinea'. The Council
estimated that 50,000 *rigsdalers'* worth of ground maize could be
exported to the Danish West Indies annually. This investment in maize
production was based on the fact that subsistence costs on the Danish
Caribbean plantations had risen appreciably following the abolition of
the external slave trade.[50]

Using Danish state funds, governor Steffens bought abandoned or
neglected plantations situated in the Akuapem foothills in the early
1820s. Danish or Afro-Danish merchants resident in Osu also made
purchases. In addition, the governor provided loans to planters whose
plantations had suffered damage during the Asante military campaigns.
With this support the planters were expected to lay out new ones.[51] Some

of the Akuapem plantations still had 'many coffee trees', and these were expected to form the basis of a lucrative export trade in coffee already in 1823. Major Richelieu, who became governor of Christiansborg in 1823, acquired a plantation near Bibiase in 1824. It had 3,000 fruit-bearing coffee trees, and the governor intended to plant an additional 20,000. In 1826 he bought the Dakobi plantation for 57 *cabes* 5 *damma* in cowries (i.e. nearly 4 ounces in gold). At the same time a new road was laid out between Osu and Bibiase, and was expected to be put into full operation as soon as pack animals were sent to Christiansborg from Denmark. In 1827 and 1828 British accounts considered the Danish coffee and cotton plantations to 'have been attended with success'. In 1828, some 3,000 lbs of coffee were exported to Denmark. In the view of some Danish Guinea officials the export of maize should have taken a subsidiary role to the cultivation and export of cotton, coffee, tobacco and sugar. Danish authorities in Copenhagen thought that the economic basis of the Danish Guinea establishments should be the production of maize for export to the Danish West Indies; the cultivation of coffee, cotton etc. was expected to be merely supplementary.[52]

The situation in the 1830s and 1840s

Writing in 1831, the Danish official B. Christensen stated that there were only about twelve plantations which formed the basis of the Danish state's plantation endeavour. Two belonged to Danes; the rest to Afro-Danes. In addition to yams, maize, millet, plantain, 'baco', palm (-oil) trees and other crops, the plantation owners had begun to cultivate coffee. Christensen commented that in 1828 there was hardly a total of 4,000 coffee trees on all of the plantations combined. By 1831 there were as many as 20,000 young trees, and the expectation was that shortly they would produce enough coffee for export. There were, also, plans to raise sugar cane, indigo, cotton and rice. He goes on to say that in the vicinity of the Danish/Afro-Danish agricultural establishments there were 'many, and in some cases considerable, plantations belonging to several of the more high standing free mulattoe families in Danish Akkra, however, just as in the single, neighbouring Blacks' plantation, they only cultivate the common cereals of the land.'[53] Some of the Danish/Afro-Danish plantations cultivated food crops for local markets and shipping and cash crops for export; other plantations produced for local markets. According to the Danish historian O. Justesen, Danish and Afro-Danish merchants were 'disinclined to put their own money into the production of [export cash crops]'. It was more profitable for them to 'invest their capital in trading in other locally-produced commodities [such as gold and palm-oil] and in the production of the established provisions which could be sold locally'.[54]

A Basel missionary report of 1832 confirms the evidence of dense agricultural settlement in the Akuapem foothills, referring to the 'many important plantations [*Negerpflanzungen*]' at the foot of the Akuapem mountains, with a small village by each. The plantation owners included Europeans, Afro-Europeans and 'wealthy Blacks' from the coast. The impression gained from Christensen's description and the various Basel Mission reports is that commercial agricultural activity along the base of the Akuapem mountains was intense and concentrated and that the area was heavily populated.[55] The 1790s and the first decade of the nineteenth century saw the early development of this agricultural and demographical phenomenon.

In his 1835 description of the royal and private Danish plantations, P. Thonning relates that the Danish state owned one working plantation of 100 *toender* (163.3 acres) and that the Osu merchants and Christiansborg officials owned together a total of 695 *toender* (947.285 acres). From information given by Christensen it would seem that these plantations occupied an area extending 16–17 miles along the Akuapem foothills and occupying nearly thirty-six square miles of land.[56]

The two officials provide fairly detailed accounts of these plantations and the history of their development. A summarized description of the plantations based on Thonning's and Christensen's accounts and other sources is given below:[57]

(1) The plantation Frederiksgave near Bibiase occupied 100 *toender* (136.3 acres) of land. This was the main royal plantation. It had a stone and clay house, consisting of a hall, a bedroom, a warehouse and an upper room or loft, and a labour force of 41 men, women and children who lived in an adjoining village of 20 houses. The labourers consisted of slaves and persons who had been pawned. According to an 1844 description, the plantation had 2–3,000 coffee trees and orange, lemon, banana, plantain, tamarind and guava trees. The overseer was a pensioned non-commissioned officer.

(2) Most of the other royal plantations were less successful: Frederiskborg plantation, set up by Wrisberg in 1796, was devoted mainly to the cultivation of cotton and was fairly prosperous in the 1820s and '30s. Isert's Frederiksnopel had been abandoned since about 1802. Frederikssted at Dodowa, which had been laid out by Flindt in 1792, was purchased by a Danish officer in the 1820s(?), but he never cultivated it and in the 1830s it was not in production.

(3) *Forsynet* plantation, near Bibiase, occupied 130 *toender* (177.19 acres). The Afro-Danish merchant-official Richter, one of the wealthiest

men on the Gold Coast, owned it; he bought it for 130 piasters from the estate of a Danish official in 1830. Earlier in the century it had been owned by the merchant Meyer. In 1831 the labour force numbered 35, excluding women and children; in 1835 it consisted of 31 men, 14 women and six children. The labourers are referred to as 'serfs' (*livegne*) by Thonning; their dwellings were on the plantation. It produced maize, plantain and other vegetables and fruits, and coffee. In 1835 the coffee trees numbered 4,000, and these produced, on average, 350 lbs of coffee a year. Five years earlier, they numbered 2,000 and in 1831 he planned to plant 3,000 more.

(4) *De Tvende Broedre* (also known as *De Forenede Broeder*) plantation was located west of Richter's and had about the same acreage; its owner was G. A. Lutterodt, a Danish merchant and administrator who had been on the Gold Coast since about 1805. It was laid out in 1830 or 1831. Its work force included 16 men, 14 women and 8 children; they were all Lutterodt's property (*eidendom*). Their village community had 20 houses. Maize, yams, pineapple, plantain and other food crops were grown, as well as orange and lemon trees and palm trees which produced palm wine. The plantation had 2,000 coffee trees, 100 of which were expected to provide 24 lbs of coffee in 1835. Lutterodt maintained a large thatch-roofed stone house on his land, in contrast to Richter who had no house for himself on his plantation.

(5) *Anonebi* plantation was owned by the Afro-Danish merchant Christian Balck; he came to Osu in about 1805 from the Danish West Indies where he was born. The plantation's land amounted to 100 *toender* (136.3 acres). The workers included 13 men, women and children, who lived in 12 cottages. The plantation had only 200–250 coffee trees and yielded 40 lbs of coffee yearly.

(6) *Den Nye Proeve* plantation was owned by the Afro-Danish merchant Svanekjaer; it was established by Schioenning in 1807 and was then known as Dakobi. It amounted to 40 *toender* (54.52 acres) of land, with a workforce of 13 slaves. Svanekjaer paid 400 piasters for it. He grew European vegetables as well as local fruits and vegetables.

(7) *Bikuben* plantation was purchased in 1828 by governor Lind and developed by him; in 1831 it was bought with public funds by governor Hein. It had 7,000 young coffee trees and a workforce of 15 adult male slaves, 9 women and 6 children. There was a government house on the plantation.

(8) *Myreturen* plantation was owned by a Danish official named Brock. It had 75 *toender* (102,225 acres) of land. No information was provided about its workforce and crop production.

(9) *Adancee* plantation was the property of the merchant Molm, and

was the same size as Richter's and Lutteroldt's plantations. Nothing was said about its labour force or crops.

(10) *Boy* plantation was owned by the Afro-Danish merchant Aarestrup; it had 110 *toender* (149.93 acres) of land. The size of its workforce is not given, nor is there any information about its crops.

(11) *Valdemars Hvile* plantation was owned by a Danish(?) official named Magnussen, but there is no information about it.

(12) The Afro-Danish merchant Holms owned a plantation, but there are no particulars relating to it.

The plantations were the site of subsistence (non-commodity) and commercial (commodity) production, and were linked to local and over-seas markets. They were, as well, residential/work sites for the labourers and leisure sites for the plantation owners. Control over the production process emanated from the proprietor's rural mansion or urban villa. Each plantation had its overseer. The slaves were responsible for transporting provisions to the coastal towns and conveying salt, fish and trade goods to the plantations.[58]

In the 1840s the Danish-affiliated plantations were engaged primarily in producing provisions for the coastal towns. They grew coffee and other 'colonial produce', but these were for local consumption and not for export to Denmark or the West Indies. In 1843 governor Carstensen recorded that only Frederiksgave produced coffee; Lutterodt's plantation raised just a little, Svanekjaer's even less and Richter's none at all.[59] Export production, even of maize, had been abandoned. Thonning opined that the plantation owners used their plantations only to support those slaves whom they did not require on the coast as their personal assistants, trading agents, construction workers, artisans, boatmen and so on. In Carstensen's view the central problem was the annual illness of the plantation workers, which compelled their owners to employ waged labour to harvest the crops.[60]

Export agricultural production in the 1830s and '40s was carried out in the plantation-villages of Akuapem and Krobo. From the late 1820s palm oil was a major export from the Accra towns and over the next 20 years production increased as new plantation-villages were set up in the Krobo and Akuapem 'provinces'. Akuapem, Krobo and Shai farmers were the leading producers of palm oil in the south-east Gold Coast and their plantation-villages were the sites of large-scale export agricultural production. In the era of the external slave trade Akuapem and Krobo were suppliers of provisions to trading caravans and the coastal Accra and Adanme towns; Shai was the principal supplier of pottery to towns and villages throughout the south-east Gold Coast. In the era of legitimate trade all three areas became deeply involved in production for overseas markets.[61] The plantation owner and merchant Richter purchased his palm oil from these places and sold it from his factory at Kpone.[62]

Labour

Bulk export trade was labour-intensive and as this trade began to take off in the 1830s there was a rapidly growing demand for slave labour in areas of expanding agricultural production, whether for local or overseas markets. Christensen stated that without slaves plantation agriculture in the Akuapem foothills was virtually impossible, and in 1848 a Danish official stated that all work in the houses and in the fields was carried out by slaves.[63]

According to Monrad,, the greatest number of slaves sold on the coast, for example at Osu, came from Asante, Fante, Agotime ('Acotim'), Krepe ('Crepee') and Donko ('Duncan'). The three Accra towns (Kinka, Ga and Osu) formed together a major trade centre for slaves throughout the first half of the century.[64] In 1819 it was said of this centre that 'from its extensive trade with the interior [it] is of considerable commercial importance'; in the 1830s and 40s it was a leading slave market for the internal slave trade.[65]

Christensen offers one account of how a merchant or official could become a plantation owner:

One buys from some Black, who because of a 'palaver' or gambling has fallen into debt, which regrettably happens all too often, a piece of land, whose price up till now ... has been 50–60 *pjastre* for 20–25 *toender* [27–35 acres] of land, and whose quality is excellent, for without manure and only a short fallow it can be harvested twice a year and, yet, yield maize 7–900 fold. Now one acquires a couple of slaves or more ... and sends them into the interior, and there in a twinkling they build for themselves, without a whit of expense to the owner, their cottages of clay, battened in wood and thatched with grass.[66]

The owner provides his slave with a wife as well as tools, household goods, a flintlock musket etc. Christensen continues: 'The slave works a lot and certainly mostly for himself; indeed, he works at the most only four days a week for his owner, and, besides that, he shall pay a predetermined rent [*Afgifter*] in kind.'[67] With respect to the Bikube plantation he relates that its 30 unfree workers had to smoke-dry the plantation's coffee beans and hand over to the owner a 'rent' of yams, maize and other produce. In the early 1830s an adult male slave bought at Accra cost 150 *rigsdaler* and his annual subsistence amounted to 30 *rigsdaler*.[68]

For the Danish planters there were several sources of labour: first, the

'Inventory slaves' who were employed at the forts as artisans, boatmen, soldiers, labourers and servants; second, slaves purchased on the market; third, pawns; and fourth, hired (free and unfree) labourers. Writing in 1796, Wrisberg recommended to Danish state authorities in Copenhagen as necessary for setting up a cotton plantation: 'capable people from the West Indies and, what is absolutely essential, Blacks of the nation which is called "Dunco" must be bought at Accra, for they are hard-working and loyal'. In 1800 Flindt proposed three ways of getting the requisite plantation labour: to employ slaves awaiting shipment to the Danish Caribbean, 'Inventory slaves' and black artisans brought from the West Indies.[69]

According to the official journal of the Frederiksnopel plantation, two forms of labour were employed. The majority of labourers were known as 'colony slaves' (*Colonister*); they had been bought locally and included 'Donko', 'Crepee' and 'Adampe' men and women. The second category were hired men, seldom women, from Akuapem and Osu and other Accra towns, who received wages. The mortality rate among the 'colony slaves' was horrendous and, for plantation management, there was also the 'problem' of slave resistance – in the form of running away.[70]

In 1808 Frederiksborg's labour force of 'inventory slaves' and pawns consisted of 48 men, women and children, and in that year they received a total subsistence allowance of $84\frac{1}{2}$ *rigsdaler* a month. In 1807 seven of the men and women workers at the Bibiase plantation were listed as debtors in the Christiansborg debt-book. In 1816 this plantation's labour force consisted almost solely of purchased slaves and pawns. In the early 1830s over 600 unfree labourers worked on the 12 plantations described by Thonning and Christensen.[71]

From Frederiksnopel in 1788 to Frederiksgave in the 1840s the general practice was for the labour force to feed itself on the land it was alloted. The reproduction costs of the slave or pawn household lay on the shoulders of the slaves and pawns themselves. They, and not their owners, were responsible for their own subsistence, although, as Christensen noted, the owners supplied the slaves with 'simple clothing' every year. While in all cases they had to work for the proprietor three or four days a week, only in some cases were they obliged to hand over a part of the harvest from their own allocated plots of land as 'rent'.

To eliminate slave-holding on the royal plantations Christensen proposed that their land be divided up among the slaves' families. For a period of three years each family would grow coffee and other produce, after which its members would be emancipated and the land would become the family's property. They would continue to cultivate 'colonial produce', of which one-tenth would be taken as annual rent. Efforts to carry this out in the 1840s met with limited success.[72]

In the late eighteenth and early nineteenth century only a very few persons were brought from the Caribbean to manage the plantations. This idea was again put forward in 1828, but was deemed unsuitable.[73] Instead, there were proposals that youths from Osu be sent to Denmark to be trained as millers or artisans, or to the West Indies to be instructed in plantation cultivation. In 1828 another submission advised that four sons of the richest Osu families be sent to St Croix where they could learn plantation management, after which they could return to the Gold Coast to manage the Danish plantations. Of these proposals the only one implemented was to send youths to Denmark. Still another plan was presented in 1829: '[O]ne should let the school children from the mulatto school cultivate the land on the Frederiksborg [cotton] plantation: the boys plant and the girls clean and spin; this is to be done in order to make this useful plant better known.' However, this project was never seriously carried out.[74]

Conclusion

What was the specificity of the Danish agricultural enterprise on the Gold Coast? With respect to the Danish kingdom itself two particular and related developments can be proposed: the agrarian reforms of the late eighteenth and nineteenth centuries and urban growth in Denmark in the same period. The debates and social and political struggles that gave rise to the agrarian reforms led to the transforming of the Danish agrarian structure, on the one hand, and the relative strengthening of the absolute monarchy, on the other. The reforms entailed the 'liberation' of manorial tenants from feudal ties, land reallocation and consolidation (including the break-up of the great manorial estates and the creation of a peasant-farmer class of freeholders), and the promotion of capitalist relations in the countryside. The policy of establishing royal and merchant estates on the Gold Coast under the aegis of the absolute monarchy was a type of 'late mercantilism' practiced by the Danish government in social-political 'alliance' with the Copenhagen bourgeoisie, the peasant-farmers and the great landowners.

The ultimate failure of the Danish effort has been attributed to various causes. The destruction of plantations during the Asante wars was a severe blow. Perhaps of even greater import to the plantation-building effort was the dominant role of British trade in the commercial practices of Danish merchants and trading establishments. After 1828 the value of the gold and palm oil trade increased substantially owing to British trade, and Danish and Afro-Danish merchants began to show less interest in plantations for export production than in greater opportunities for trade in gold (from Asante and Akyem) and palm oil (from Akuapem and Krobo).[75] The plantations they owned were intended to support their trading endeavours.

NOTES

1 B. Christensen, 'Bemaerkninger om de danske Besiddelser i Guinea, 1831', 121–2, Den Guineiske Komission II (1788) 1820–1847, Rigsarkivet, Copenhagen [RA], Generaltodkammerets Archiv [GKA].

2 A. G. Hopkins, *An Economic History of West Africa* (London, 1973), p. 124.

3 See Robin Law, 'The historiography of the commercial transition in nineteenth-century West Africa', in Toyin Falola (ed.), *African Historiography* (Harlow, 1993), pp. 91–115.

4 Immanuel Wallerstein, *The Modern World-System: The Second Era of Great Expansion of the Capitalist World-Economy, 1730–1840s* (San Diego, 1989), pp. 142–3 and n73, 147.

5 Wallerstein, *The Modern World-System*, p. 148.

6 Georg Noerregaard, *Danish Settlements in West Africa 1658–1850* (Boston, 1966), ch. 19; Ole Justesen, 'Danish settlements on the Gold Coast in the nineteenth century', *Scandinavian Journal of History*, 14 (1979), 12ff. See also Peter Thonning, 'Indberetning om det danske Territorium i Guinea fornemmelig med Hensyn til naervarrende Kultur af indiske kolonial Produkter eller Beqvemhed for samme' (in RA: GKA, Sager til den Guineiske Journaler [SGJ], 1803), 16–17, 67ff, 75ff.

7 See e.g. Edward Reynolds, *Trade and Economic Change on the Gold Coast 1807–1874* (London, 1974), pp. 63–9 and ch.2; J. A. de Maree, *Reizen op en Beschrijving van de Goudkust van Guinea* (The Hague and Amsterdam, 1817–18), I, pp. 6–7, 54–6, 193–200; Basel Mission Archives [BM], D-1.2, J. G. Widmann et al., 21 March 1848; Methodist Missionary Society Archives, London [MMS], 259, William Allen, Cape Coast, to General Secretaries, 20 Feb. 1843.

8 Thonning, 'Indberretning', pp. 30–40; RA: Privatarkiver, Kortsamlingen Nr 227, P. Thonning, 'Kort over de danske Etablissementer og allierde Nation i Guinea, 1802'.

9 The Danish and German terms were also used to refer to villages of labourers attached to the plantations, hence the term 'plantation-village'. For a description of the social structure, with particular reference to Akuapem, see Oheneba Sakyi Dan, *The 'Sunlight' Reference Almanac of the Gold Coast and its Dependencies* (Aburi, n.d.), p. 114.

10 For an overview of the area's early nineteenth-century structure, see Reynolds, *Trade*, ch.1; also Marion Johnson, 'Migrants' progress', *Bulletin of the Ghana Geographical Association*, 9/2 (1964), *passim*.

11 For one Danish official's discussion of these 'apparatuses' with respect to the town of Osu and 'Danish Guinea', see Christensen, 'Bemaerkninger', pp. 29, 31–7, 107–15. For discussions and analyses of these (Foucauldian) appara-

tuses, see Hubert L. Dreyfus and Paul Rabinow, *Michel Foucault: Beyond Structuralism and Hermeneutics* (Brighton, 1992); Giles Deleuze, *Foucault* (Minneapolis, 1988).

12 C. B. Waldstrom, *An Essay on Colonization, particularly applied to the Western Coast of Africa* (London, 1794), p. 175.

13 See Thonning, 'Indberetning', pp. 16–17, 63–8; H. Arnold Barton, 'The Danish agrarian reforms and the historians, 1784–1814', *Scandinavian Economic History review*, 36/1 (1988); Vagn Waahlin, 'The growth of bourgeois and popular movements in Denmark ca. 1830–1870', *Scandinavian Journal of History*, 5/5 (1980), 133–4, 153–6.

14 RA: GKA, Guineiske Journaler, No. 218, 1796.

15 Waldstrom, *Essay*, p. 317.

16 I.e. *Donko* in the Ga language. According to the Basel missionary J. Zimmerman this word is the 'name of the mostly mohamedan countries in the plains at the upper Volta [river], in the interior of Ashanti, Akyem, Akwamu and Ayigbe ... Most of the slaves come thence': *A Grammatical Sketch and Vocabulary of the Akra- or Ga-Language, with an Appendix on the Adanme Dialect* (1858; repr. Westmead, 1972), p. 45.

17 H. C. Monrad, *Bidrag Til en Skildring af Guinea-Kystem og Dens Indbyggere* (Copenhagen, 1822), p. 327.

18 RA: GKA, Guineiske Journaler, No. 502, 1803.

19 Monrad, *Bidrag*, pp. 326, 327 & note.

20 Monrad, *Bidrag*, p. 200.

21 C. C. Reindorf, *History of the Gold Coast and Asante* (Basel, 1895), p. 178.

22 Reindorf, *History*, pp. 268–9.

23 Reindorf, *History*, p. 245.

24 'Dokumenter angaaende de af P.E. Isert foreslaaede Kolonienlaeg ven Rio-Volta'. in *Archiv for Statistik, Politik og Huusholdnings Videnskaber* (ed. F. Thaarup, Copenhagen, 1797–9), III, pp. 248–51; 'Journal for Colonien Fridrichs Nopel' (in RA: Finanskolligiet 1784–1816, Papirer og Docukemnter vedr. Kolonien Friedrichsnopel 1792, 1794). Also Selena A. Winsnes (ed.), *Letters on West Africa and the Slave Trade: Paul Erdmann Isert's Journey to Guinea and the Caribbean Islands in Columbia (1788)* (Oxford, 1992), pp. 227–45.

25 C. D. Adams, 'Activities of Danish botanists in Guinea 1783–1850', *Transactions of the Historical Society of Ghana*, 3/1 (1957), 36. Also Christian Degn, *Die Schimmelmans im Atlantischen Dreieckshandel: Gewinn und Gewissen* (Neumuenster, 1974), pp. 223, 232–5.

26 Degn, *Die Schimmelmanns*, p. 230. See also Thorkild Hansen, *Slavernes Kyts* (Haslev, 1967), pp. 130–9.

27 'Dokumenter aangaaende', pp. 244–5, 255–64; 'P. Thonning's report on the Guinea plantations, *c*.1835' (in RA: GKA, Den Guineiske Komission II (1788) 1820–1847), pp. 30–7; Degn, *Die Schimmelmanns*, pp. 232–5.

28 'Bioerns Beretning 1788 om de danske Forter og Negerier', in *Archiv for Statistik*, pp. 204–5; Thonning, 'Indberetning', pp. 37–9; [P.] Isert, *Reize van Koppenhagen naar Guinea og van daar naar de Westindien en de Caribische Eilanden in Amerika* (Amsterdam, 1797), p. 257.

29 Isert, *Reize*, p. 249; Mader, 'Akuapem und seiner Bewohner, Akropon, May

1859', pp. 14–15; M. A. Kwamena-Poh, *Government and Politics in the Akwuapem State 1730–1850* (Evanston, 1973), pp. 60–1.

30 See 'Journal for kolonien', *passim*; Monrad, *Bidrag*, p. 317.

31 RA: GKA, Guineiske Journaler, No. 225, 1796; No. 179, 1801; 'Thonning's report', pp. 31–40; Hendrik Jeppesen, 'Danish plantations on the Gold Coast 1788–1850', *Geografisk Tidsskrift*, 65/1 (1966), 74–5.

32 'Journal for colonien', entry for 20 Dec. 1789.

33 'Thonning's report', pp. 40–4; RA: GKA, Guineiske Journaler, No. 415, 1797; Jeppesen, 'Danish plantations', pp. 78–9.

34 RA: GKA, Guineiske Journaler, No. 101, 1799; No. 9, 1800; No. 13, 1800; No. 524, 1803; Thonning, 'Indberetning', pp. 44–7; Monrad, *Bidrag*, pp. 319–20; Jeppesen, 'Danish plantations', pp. 78–9.

35 'Thonning's report', pp. 47–8; RA: GKA, Guineiske Journaler, No. 216, 1796; No. 415, 1797; No. 365, 1798; Monrad, *Bidrag*, pp. 321–2; Jeppesen, 'Danish plantations', pp. 77–8. The Keta cotton plantation was not a success.

36 'Thonning's report', pp. 47–9; RA: GKA, Guineiske Journaler, No. 415, 1798; No. 75, 1799; No. 179, 1801; No. 466, 1803; No. 671, 1805; RA: GKA, Inventarienegrenes Gageboeger 1801–8, entries under 'Friderichsbergs Negerne'; Christensen, 'Bemaerkninger', pp. 15–17, 50–1; Monrad, *Bidrag*, p. 320.

37 RA: GKA, Guineiske Journaler, No. 466, 1803; Monrad, *Bidrag*, pp. 320–1; Jeppesen, 'Danish plantations', p. 80.

38 Monrad, *Bidrag*, p. 321.

39 'Thonning's report', pp. 9–51; RA: GKA, Guineiske Journaler, No. 415, 1798; No. 466, 1804; No. 491, 1804; No. 502, 1804; No. 864, 1805; Monrad, *Bidrag*, pp. 323–4; Jeppesen, 'Danish plantations', pp. 80–3.

40 Monrad, *Bidrag*, p. 324; Noerregaard, *Danish Settlements*, p. 182.

41 'Thonning's report', pp. 51–5; RA: GKA, SGJ, letter from C. Schioenning, Bibease, 2 Oct. 1805; Reindorf, *History*, p. 145.

42 C. Schioenning, quoted in H. Meredith, *An Account of the Gold Coast of Africa* (London, 1812), p. 219n. See also RA: GKA, Guineiske Journaler, No. 1208, 1811; No. 1314, 1814; No. 1348, 1814.

43 'Thonning's report', pp. 51–4; RA: GKA, Guineisker Journaler, No. 1124, 1809; RA: GKA, Kopibog for udgaaende breve til Generaltoldkammeret 1807–15, letter from C. Schioenning to Count Schimmelmann, 24 Jan. 1808; RA: GKA, Inventarienegrenes Gageboeger 1801–8, entry under 'Gouverneur Schioennings Negere'; Jeppesen, 'Danish plantations', p. 81.

44 Raymond Williams, *The Country and the City* (New York, 1973), p. 124.

45 Cf. Monrad, *Bidrag*, pp. 324–5, on the 'prospect' of Dakobi. For archaeological studies of some of the Danish plantation sites, see Jeppesen, 'Danish plantations', pp. 78, 81–2; Christopher R. Decorse, 'Historical archaeological research in Ghana 1986–87', *Nyame Akuma*, 29 (1987), 28–30. See also Christensen, 'Bemaerkninger', pp. 141–7; Hansen, *Slavernes Kyst*, pp. 187–9.

46 Monrad, *Bidrag*, p. 325; *Guvernoer Edward Carstensens Indberetninger fra Guinea 1842–1850* (ed. G. Noerregaard, Copenhagen, 1964), pp. 152 and 158 [entry for 19 Sept. 1845]; RA: Privatarkiver, Loeitnant Johan Vilhelm

Svedstrups arkiv (1819–55), 'Kort Fremstilling af Johan Vilhelm Svedstrups tilvaerelse her paa Jorden', entry for 7 Oct. 1844; BM: D-1.2, letter from G. Thompson, Akropong, to the Inspector, 12 Sept. 1843.

47 For a detailed account of these conflicts and their aftermath, see Ivor Wilks, *Asante in the Nineteenth Century* (Cambridge, 1975), chs 4–5.

48 RA: GKA, Guineiske Journaler, No. 26, 1821.

49 RA: GKA, Guineiske Journaler, No. 384, 1824; Christensen, 'Bemaerkninger', pp. 31, 33–4; PRO: CO 267/117, B.F. Murphy, 'Memoir on the Gold Coast', 1831 (My thanks to Larry Yarak for drawing my attention to this source); PRO: CO 267/117, J. Bannerman, Accra, to Major Rowan, 3 Nov. 1826.

50 RA: GKA, Guineiske Journaler, No. 384, 1824. For subsistence costs on the Danish Caribbean plantations, see Hans C. Johansen, 'Slave demography of the Danish West Indian Islands', *Scandivanian Economic History Review*, 29/1 (1981), 9; Jeppesen, 'Danish plantations', pp. 83–4.

51 Justesen, 'Danish settlements', pp. 19–20. Some plantations were bought from the Accra or Adanme widows of Danish planters. Thus, in 1816 Meyer's widow inherited the Bibease plantation together with its labour force of slaves and pawns: RA: GKA, Brevbog for Kongensten 1810–16, J. N.Flindt, Kongensten, to Governor Schioenning, 22 Feb. 1816. For private traders, both Danish and Afro-Danish, from the 1820s to 1840s, see Christensen, 'Bemaerkninger', pp. 22–3; Justesen, 'Danish settlements', pp. 22–3, 25–8.

52 RA: GKA, Guineiske Journaler, No. 512, 1824; No.807, 1826; No. 827, 1827; No. 917, 1827; No. 925, 1827; No. 33, 1828; No. 35, 1828; No. 93, 1828; No. 100, 1828; No. 149, 1828; Nos. 150–1, 1828; No. 149, 1829; No. 264, 1829; Nos. 308–9, 1829; Nos. 361–2, 1829; PRO: CO 267/93, J. Bannerman, Accra, to Major Rowan, 3 Nov. 1828; Jeppesen, 'Danish plantations', pp. 83–4; Justesen, 'Danish settlements', p. 20.

53 [Balthar Christensen], 'Breve fr og om Guinea, Christiansborg, 1 April 1831', *Valkyrien*, 2 (1831), 271–4.

54 Christensen, 'Bemaerkninger', pp. 45–6, 60; Jeppesen, 'Danish plantations', p. 84; Justesen, 'Danish settlements', p. 21.

55 'Aus einem Briefe der Missionarien Jaeger und Riis, Ussus, bei Christiansborg, den 20 June 1832', *Der Evangelische Heidenbote*, 23 (1832), 94; 'Reise der Brueder Riis und Muerdter in die Umgegenden von Akropong', ibid., unnumbered vol. (1839), 53–6. Also Johnson, 'Migrants' progress', p. 15.

56 'Thonning's report', pp. 59, 63–8; [Christensen], 'Breve', p. 271; 'Bemaerkninger', p. 53.

57 'Thonning's report', pp. 59, 63–8; [Christensen], 'Breve', pp. 270–1, 273–4; 'Bemaerkninger', pp. 59–60, 61–3.

58 Carstensen, *Indberetninger fra Guinea*, p. 44 [10 Feb. 1843].

59 Carstensen, *Indberetninger*, pp. 22–3 [6 Sept. 1842]; p. 46 [10 Feb. 1843].

60 'Thonning's report', pp. 8–9' Carstensen, *Indberetninger*, p. 46 [10 Feb. 1843].

61 Johnson, 'Migrants' progress', pp. 14, 15, 17; Reynolds, *Trade*, chs. 1–3; Louis E. Wilson, *The Krobo People of Ghana to 1892* (Athens, OH, 1991), pp. 72–3, 77, 86–7.

62   Christensen, 'Bemaerkninger', 46.
63   RA: Privatarchiv, Balth. Christensen Nr 5262, Bundle C. Sager vedr. Balth. Christensens ophold in Guinea, 1830–1, Christensens Dagbog, 17 Nov. 1830; RA: DAG, Brevkopibog 1846–50, R. E. Schmidt, [Christiansborg], 7 Aug. 1848.
64   Monrad, *Bidrag*, p. 294.
65   G. A. Robertson, *Notes on Africa* (london, 1819), p. 218; Justesen, 'Danish settlements', p. 17. For the internal slave trade of the area, see Carstensen, *Indberetninger*, 37, [entry for 26 Oct. 1842]; 141 [13 May 1845], 172 [20 Nov. 1845]; BM: D-12, Letter from Widmann, Akropong, 16 June 1848; Abstracts from correspondence in the Basel Mission Archives 1828–51, by Dr Hans Delbrunner (1956); 'Der Sklavenhandel in Afrika (Bericht von Schiedt), Friedrichsgave, 20 August 1849', *Der Evangelische Heidenbote*, 5 (1849), 37–40.
66   [Christensen], 'Breve', pp. 274–5.
67   [Christensen], 'Breve', p. 275.
68   'Thonning's report', p. 73.
69   RA: GKA, Guineiske Journalier, No. 255, 1796; No. 13, 1800.
70   'Journal for colonien', *passim*.
71   RA: DAG, Inventarienegrenes Gageboeger 1801–08, Entry 'Friendrichsbergs Negerene'; Gaeldboeger 1798–1808, entry 'Debet liste over arbeiderne ven Bibase', 11 Oct. 1807; Christensen, 'Bemaerkninger', p. 59; 'Thonning's report', *passim*.
72   Christensen, 'Bemaerkninger', pp. 134–5. Also 'Thonning's report', p. 88; RA: DAG, Brevkopibog 1846–50, R. E. Schmidt, [Christiansborg], 7 Aug. 1848.
73   RA: GKA, Guineiske Journaler, No. 150, 1828.
74   RA: GKA, Guineiske Journaler, No. 93, 1828, and No. 622, 1829. Also Christensen, 'Bemaerkninger', pp. 107–8. For references to Osu youths educated in Denmark, see RA: GKA, Guineiske Journaler, No. 873, 1827; Carstensen, *Indberetninger*, pp. 55, n1; 370 [5 July 1849], & n1.
75   Justesen, 'Danish settlements', pp. 19–33 *passim*.

6   Owners, slaves and the struggle for labour in the commercial transition at Lagos

Kristin Mann

The degree to which slaves could participate in the palm produce trade in their own behalf remains a key question in the debate over the impact of the transition from the slave trade to the vegetable products trade in nineteenth-century West Africa. Did the new 'legitimate' commerce create opportunities for slaves to trade for themselves, and through their efforts to accumulate resources, as many contemporary Europeans believed it would? Could slaves, on the basis of greater wealth, redefine their relationship with their owners, rising even to challenge the authority of the established rulers? Or did the old slave-trading oligarchies dominate the trade in palm produce, as they had that in slaves, retain control of the labour of their slaves, and maintain their political authority? Alternatively, could new, large-scale entrepreneurs capture the labour of slaves, harness it in trade, and challenge the pre-eminence of the old oligarchies?[1] This essay provides a new perspective on these problems not by looking at trade and politics, the usual approach, but rather by probing the owner–slave relationship during the era of the transition. The data come from Lagos, a leading centre of the palm produce trade, whose late nineteenth-century sobriquet, the 'Liverpool of Africa', captures its commercial importance.

Lagos emerged as a centre of the slave trade late in the history of the commerce, between roughly 1780 and 1860.[2] During these years, slavery became a dominant means of organizing labour in the town, although the contribution of wives, children and different types of clients to production and trade was also important. The local rulers, the *Oba* (king) and chiefs, and important traders enriched themselves through their role as middlemen in the international slave trade. They invested their new wealth in people – wives, children, clients and above all slaves – as well as in canoes, guns, gunpowder and consumer goods, used to arm and reward their large followings.[3] The slave trade exacerbated deep-seated political conflict between rivals for the Obaship, most famously Kosoko and Akitoye, by enlarging and militarizing their factions. During the era of the slave trade, the rulers of Lagos used their slaves not only in trade and production, but also in politics and warfare.[4]

By the time the Atlantic slave trade reached its height in Lagos, the abolition movement had begun achieving success first in Britain and then internationally. European industrialization was simultaneously creating a growing demand for African vegetable products such as palm oil, which was produced in the interior of Lagos. In the mid nineteenth century, key reformers and policy-makers in Britain believed that ending the African slave trade would require replacing it with commerce in other commodities.[5] In 1851 Britain bombarded Lagos and deposed the Oba Kosoko, whom Foreign Secretary Palmerston had come to see as an incorrigible slave-trader. Her Majesty's forces installed in Kosoko's place his arch-rival Akitoye, who had been courting British opinion by posing as an opponent of the slave trade while exiled in the nearby town of Badagry. This flurry of gunboat diplomacy failed to secure British interests, and in 1861 Britain annexed Lagos to abolish the slave trade and promote 'legitimate' commerce.[6] Historians of the event have dichotomized these goals and argued about their relative weight, but most mid-Victorians understood them as inextricably connected parts of a single process of reform.[7]

Following the annexation, the international slave trade died quickly in Lagos and trade grew rapidly first in palm oil and later, more dramatically, in palm kernels. Between 1866 and 1870, Lagos exported an average of 5,697 tons of palm oil annually, while between 1876 and 1880 it sold onto the world market an average of 29,305 tons of palm kernels annually.[8] The growth of the overseas trade in palm produce increased the demand for labour in Lagos, as it did elsewhere in Africa. Manning has estimated that in Dahomey, where the production process was much the same as in the interior of Lagos, the manufacture of one ton of palm oil required the equivalent of 315 days of labour.[9] Palm kernels had then to be picked by hand from the residue of oil production. Trade in palm produce, more important in the economy of urban Lagos than its production, also required extensive labour. Palm oil and kernels were both bulky commodities. Until the opening of the railroad in the 1890s, Lagos or interior traders had to organize their transport from the hinterland to the coast by canoe or, more labour-intensive still, on the heads of porters.[10] Once these goods reached the port they had to be unloaded, bulked, stored and transported to the point of embarkation for shipment.

The capacity of Lagosians to engage in the palm produce trade depended on their ability to mobilize labour, first their own and then that of others. Slaves performed much of the labour in trade, although the work of family members, clients and pawns was also significant.[11] The new export trade further expanded demand for labour by stimulating local production of food crops. Many of the important chiefs and traders of Lagos in the second half of the nineteenth century established farms in rural areas where their slaves, clients and other dependants grew food for consumption by their vast households and for sale in local markets.[12] In Lagos, as in other parts of West Africa, the growth of the external trade in vegetable products increased the domestic demand for slave labour just as the foreign slave trade was ending.[13]

Given the centrality of labour in general and the labour of slaves in particular to the organization of the palm produce trade, a better understanding of the owner–slave relationship during the era of transition should shed new light on the ability of different kinds of Lagosians to benefit from commercial change. Focusing on slavery has the added value of directing attention to the wider issue of labour, a pivotal yet under-studied problem in the growth of the vegetable products trade. The picture that emerges is one of competition for the labour and support of slaves between their owners and new entrepreneurs; and also of on-going struggle between the slaves and either their owners or others to whom they attached themselves over terms of labour and access to resources, especially land and housing. In Lagos, the slave trade ended and the palm produce trade developed simultaneously with the imposition of British colonial rule. The impact of the commercial transition on owners and slaves needs, therefore, to be understood in the context of British policy regarding domestic slavery and of specific changes in trade, land tenure and legal authority that accompanied colonialism.

Data for the study come from British official correspondence and from oral history, standard sources for the study of the African past. They come also from the records of cases involving owners and slaves or their descendants that were heard by the British Supreme Court in Lagos. Court records proved valuable in this research because they contain data of unparalleled richness about the daily struggle between owners and slaves to alter the demands being made on the slaves and the rights and privileges they enjoyed.[14] The court records employed here date not from the 1850s and 60s, the first two decades of the transition in the external trade of Lagos. Although the litigants and witnesses in the cases sometimes told stories that illuminate these early years, the cases came before the court between 1876, the year it was founded, and 1900. The practical reason for using late nineteenth-century data is that the records of the tribunals that sat in Lagos

earlier do not survive. Information of the kind cited in the final two
sections of this essay is not available for the period before 1876. There
are substantive advantages, however, to using late nineteenth-century
data. They show decisively that the owner–slave relationship changed
gradually. Slavery died a slow death in Lagos. Indeed, a number of
the conflicts analysed here occurred not between persons who themselves had been owners and slaves at mid-century, but between their
children twenty to thirty years later. The transformation in labour
relations which followed the abolition of the international slave trade
and the transition to that in vegetable products spanned the second
half of the nineteenth century.

Changes in trade, land tenure and legal authority

Immediately after the British bombardment in 1851, European and
Sierra Leonean merchants interested in legitimate commerce exclusively
began arriving to open businesses in Lagos. Their number increased in
the 1860s and 70s.[15] The merchants expanded the volume of their
businesses beyond what local capital would have supported by extending
the 'trust' or credit system that had underpinned the slave trade to the
palm produce trade.[16] Merchants established contacts with Lagos traders
of indigenous and Sierra Leonean and Brazilian repatriated slave origin
and sold them, on credit, imported goods and cowries, the local currency.
The traders broke bulk and used the goods and money to buy palm
produce or other exports at regional markets or from interior or lesser
Lagos traders. With the exports, the traders were supposed to repay their
debts to the import–export merchants.[17] Lagos traders also conducted
much of their business on credit, owing to a shortage of capital
throughout the economy.[18] Debt fuelled the growth of the new legitimate
commerce, forming in the words of the first governor of Lagos, H. S.
Freeman, 'the genius of African trade'.[19]

Large-scale traders had dominated the slave trade. Significant participation in it required substantial capital in the form of canoes to
transport the slaves, guns to control them, barracoons to house them,
and provisions to feed them while they awaited export.[20] Only persons
of substance could meet these requirements. Large-scale traders continued to play a prominent role in the palm produce trade, as middle-
persons between the import–export merchants and both interior and
lesser Lagos traders.[21] Indeed, some slave-traders, such as Kosoko and
his war-chief Oshodi Tapa, adapted successfully to the palm produce
trade.[22] But the new trade also created opportunities for small-scale
traders in the vast network of collection and distribution needed to

move many thousands of tons of exports and imports between the interior and the coast.[23] Although large-scale traders enjoyed certain advantages, entering the palm produce on a small scale required but little capital and labour. Small-scale traders could expand their businesses if they were able to accumulate capital or obtain credit and if they could mobilize labour.[24]

Beginning in the 1850s and 60s, population growth and commercial development increased the demand for land in Lagos on which to build residences and storehouses. Immigrants from the interior obtained use-rights to land from local families who owned it communally.[25] Many Europeans and Brazilian and Sierra Leonean repatriates, however, turned to the Oba for land.[26] They treated his grants as giving them individual rights of absolute ownership in property, although local land tenure recognised no such thing. The repatriates started buying and selling land soon after their arrival. A market for real estate developed and land prices rose. For the first time land began to be alienated and individually owned, and it acquired commercial value.[27] The new land rights did not supplant communal tenure, but rather coexisted with it.[28] The old land-owning families, however, lost control of much of the most valuable commercial and residential property in the town before they realized its value.[29]

From the beginning, European and Sierra Leonean merchants experienced difficulties collecting trade debts. To provide themselves a modicum of protection, they began demanding that local traders pledge landed property as security for loans. Soon many Lagos traders adopted the practice. Local culture offered mechanisms for organizing credit, and these continued to operate.[30] But by the 1860s and 70s mortgaging land to secure commercial credit had become widespread.[31] Land-ownership provided a new means of obtaining access to credit, and hence of mobilizing capital.

Changes in legal authority as well as in trade and land tenure shaped the impact of abolition on the local community. A. G. Hopkins has shown that policy-makers in Britain identified the development of the palm oil trade with the security of debts and private property rights. A desire to promote the spread of new property rights helped motivate the annexation.[32] In the 1860s, the colonial state moved quickly to establish colonial courts with jurisdiction over debts and property.[33] It also appointed commissioners to ascertain 'the true and rightful owners of land' and issue crown grants to it. These documents were frequently treated as giving the holder rights of individual ownership in the property.[34]

In 1876, the colonial government reformed the legal system by abolishing the earlier courts and creating a Supreme Court and Magistrates' Courts. British officials presided over these tribunals, but they were supposed to apply local law to conflicts between 'natives'. To determine the content of local law in cases where it was in doubt, Supreme Court judges called local big men to advise them. The treaty of cession had left the Oba authority 'to decide disputes between natives of Lagos with their consent, subject to appeal to British laws', and the king and chiefs continued to hear many non-criminal disputes. Ultimate authority had passed to the British, however, and although persons of property were over-represented among litigants, Lagosians of all classes took cases to the Supreme Court.[35] The colonial legal system created new authorities to whom locals, including slaves, could turn in their conflicts with one another.

The growth of the palm produce trade created new economic opportunities for some slaves. Robin Law's contribution to this volume cites evidence in consular correspondence from the 1850s which shows that male and female slaves could trade palm oil on their own account.[36] In the early 1860s, two slaves who returned with their owner Kosoko from exile began independent trade as soon as they reached the colony.[37] The development of Lagos's external trade, moreover, triggered a broader commercial expansion, which introduced trading opportunities for slaves in foodstuffs and local manufactures, as well as in imports such as cloth, tobacco, spirits, salt and hardware.[38] Some slaves obtained access to land or palm trees in the rural areas surrounding Lagos and began growing crops or making palm oil for sale.[39] With the income derived from these activities, slaves sometimes managed to redeem themselves, their children or their compatriots.[40] A few slaves such as Jacob Ogunbiyi and Oluyode Layeni expanded their businesses, invested in land and dependants, and became large-scale traders.[41] Those who enjoyed such success, however, normally rose with the support of their owners, as did Ogunbiyi and Layeni. Most slaves who managed to begin trading for themselves remained small-scale operators. Some, such as the two who had returned with Kosoko, soon gave up trying to make it on their own and began working for a patron.[42]

A free market for wage labour developed more slowly in Lagos than did markets for land and capital. Slaves and clients performed most of the non-family labour in trade and production throughout the second half of the nineteenth century. Yet in the 1850s, 60s and 70s limited opportunities to work for wages existed within the colonial government, expatriate firms and missionary societies. A few slaves escaped slavery by finding paid employment as policemen, domestics, porters or other manual labourers.[43]

Britain and domestic slavery

If economic change created new opportunities for some slaves, the arrival of Christian missionaries and British officials introduced allies to whom others could turn for help when trying to escape their owners.[44] Appeals for assistance did not always succeed, however, because neither missionaries nor officials consistently supported slaves. Sentiments regarding slavery and attitudes towards individual owners shaped the responses of Europeans to slaves' pleas for help. In 1853, Consul Campbell insisted that Oba Akitoye free a female slave whom Campbell's nemesis, the powerful Madam Tinubu, had given to a European merchant and subsequently reclaimed.[45] But a few months later he returned to the recently installed Oba Dosunmu a number of female slaves who had sought refuge in the consulate fearing that they would be sacrificed during the funeral services for his predecessor Akitoye.[46]

Assistance to slaves seeking manumission picked up at the end of the 1850s. The British consuls freed a few slaves and issued them 'emancipation papers', but the numbers were tiny compared to Lagos' vast slave population: three in 1857, five in 1858, seventeen in 1859, thirty-three in 1860.[47] Escape to their homelands proved impossible for most slaves, because it required traversing vast territories inhabited by slave-raiding and periodically warring peoples. Facial scarification, or its absence, set runaways off as strangers, vulnerable to recapture. Opportunities to return home did not improve markedly until after the British penetration of the Yoruba interior in the 1890s. In the late 1850s, British consuls gave a few emancipated northern slaves 'Arabic passports' stating that they were free, but it is difficult to believe that these documents provided their holders much security on their journey home.[48] In 1859, Dr W. B. Baikie and Lieutenant J. H. Glover, of Britain's Niger Expedition, recruited porters for a journey to the Niger River from among northern slaves in Lagos and promised them safe passage to the river. Slave-owners in Abeokuta, north of Lagos, attacked the party unsuccessfully in an effort to recapture the slaves and avoid a dangerous precedent.[49]

A further development affected Lagos slaves from the 1850s on. The abolition of the international and, more slowly, the domestic slave trades in the vicinity of Lagos diminished the threat of sale as a means of disciplining slaves. Removal of this means of control widened the social space within which slaves could act and increased the possibility of redefining the owner-slave relationship. The combination of greater economic opportunity, new political support and weaker social control may have emboldened slaves to wider-spread resistance at the moment of the British annexation in 1861. William McCoskry, the colony's first acting Governor, made the tantalizing remark in September 1861 that questions arising out of domestic slavery were giving him 'more trouble than all the rest of the [colony's] business together'.[50]

No matter what slaves hoped, the British annexation did not bring immediate emancipation. Despite the centrality of the abolition of the slave trade to contemporary discourse about the annexation of Lagos, neither the Foreign Office nor the Colonial Office discussed what to do about domestic slavery in the town prior to colonization. The Colonial Secretary wrote in 1862 that the British government had not yet considered 'the status of the domestic slaves in Lagos ... and the mode in which we are to deal with them'.[51] By 1861, Britain had had more than two decades of experience trying to re-educate former slaves in her West Indian colonies to make them disciplined wage-labourers. Optimism had waned about the ability of the state to instil in former slaves the virtues of work for their former masters and respect for political authority.[52] Fearing that to end slavery would create labour shortages and political disorder, early colonial administrators did not free domestic slaves in Lagos.[53] Instead, they adopted a number of *ad hoc* measures that enabled a few slaves to leave their owners, while upholding labour relations and the social order.[54]

In 1862, Governor Freeman submitted to the Colonial Office the first in a series of proposals to deal gradually with the emancipation of Lagos's slaves by apprenticing them to their owners, as had been done in the British West Indies.[55] The Colonial Office favoured the idea, but the Law Lords disallowed it on the grounds that the 1833 Abolition of Slavery Act had 'utterly and forever' abolished slavery throughout the British empire.[56] Unable to recognise slavery and unwilling to end it, the Colonial Office responded by pressing local administrators to minimize the problem at Lagos by restricting the territory over which Britain exercised sovereign rights and maintained British law, as on the Gold Coast.[57] Local administrators reacted by flatly denying that domestic slavery presented a problem, because they opposed a solution that would reduce the colony's territory and, they feared, its revenue. In what became from then on the official position of local administrators on the issue, Governor-in-Chief Blackall stated that Lagos offered no difficulty with regard to slavery, because 'it is sparsely inhabited and the people fully understand they are free'.[58] In future British officials occasionally intervened to help individual slaves obtain manumission. But the government would do nothing to free slaves as a body. It fell to the slaves themselves to redefine their relationship with their owners.

Economic changes in the 1870s and 80s made trading independently and making money from it more difficult for slaves than it had been in the 1850s and early 60s. As the demand for labour increased with the growth of trade and agricultural production, some owners sought tighter control over the labour of their slaves. Once it became clear, moreover, that the annexation would not bring emancipation, owners may have felt more confident than before about resisting slaves' efforts to achieve autonomy. To compound matters, palm oil prices began a long decline in the late 1850s, bottoming locally in 1890 at less than a third of what they had been at their height.[59] The expansion of trade in general and of palm kernels in particular cushioned the effects for a time, but palm kernel prices also began to fall in the late 1860s. Declining prices cut into traders' profits, and, to exacerbate the situation, the cost of credit soared locally in the 1870s and 80s.[60] A depression struck in the 1880s, making it harder for prosperous Lagosians, much less slaves, to earn income from commerce.[61] Some slave-owners tried to sustain their businesses in the face of falling profits by squeezing more labour out of their dependants.[62]

Opportunities to work for wages expanded in the 1880s and 90s, but they were still not good. The government, the largest employer of wage labour, refused to pay enough to attract many Africans, slaves included.[63] Moreover, most Lagosians preferred trading, fishing and farming to working for wages, even when obtaining the resources necessary to engage in these activities meant remaining in relationships of subordination. The experience of a slave who tried to improve his lot by contracting to work in the Congo Free State, where labour conditions were so bad that they eventually provoked a scandal in Britain, underscores the grim choices facing many slaves.[64]

Despite adverse conditions, the European commercial and political expansion into Lagos created opportunities for some slaves to earn money, acquire land, and begin living and working on their own. But if the economic and legal changes of the early colonial period enabled some slaves to claim their freedom, court records reveal that many others remained with their owners, either because they believed they had no choice or because they thought this was the best option. The owners provided the slaves limited resources and assistance in return for labour and support. The slaves struggled over time to redefine their relationship with their owners, either through absorption into the owners' families as kin or by gradually accumulating the resources and connections they needed to live on their own and then leaving their owners.

Studies of emancipation in New World cultures have shown that in places where governments publicly liberated slaves, freedom had limited meaning so long as former slaves depended on their former owners for the resources they needed to establish viable units of production.[65] In the

African context, where persons obtained assistance and protection as well as access to resources based on their social identities, slaves could not easily alter the owner–slave relationship simply because the British Law Lords maintained they were free. Court records illuminate the experiences of slaves and slave descndants who remained with owners or their kin after 1861.

Contesting the owner–slave relationship

At the time of the annexation, most slaves lived on their owners' land and some resided in houses built by their owners. In the final forty years of the nineteenth century, many owners and their descendants allowed slaves and their offspring to retain access to landed property. Intense competition for labour and political support existed in Lagos. As will be seen, slaves could obtain access to land, housing and assistance by leaving their owners and entering patron–client relationships with others of wealth and influence. If owners wanted to retain the labour and support of slaves, they had no alternative but to permit them continued access to landed property. This arrangement, however, did not work to the complete advantage of the slaves. So long as they depended on their owners for land and housing, the owners retained a mechanism of control over them.

By the end of the nineteenth century, influential chiefs and public opinion had defined as customary the right of slaves and their offspring to use the land on which the slaves had been placed by their owners, so long as they were well-behaved. This strengthened the access of slaves and their children to a valuable resource. Brimah Akilogun told the Lagos Supreme Court in 1894 that Faliyi, the son of one of his father's slaves, 'should have the right to live' in his deceased father's compound 'so long as he behaves himself well'.[66] The Court upheld this rule. Seeking to eject a woman from a house following a quarrel, three descendants of Kosoko argued that their ancestor had put his slaves in the dwelling and that the woman occupied it as the descendant of one of the slaves. They asserted that they, not the woman, were entitled to the house as the direct descendants of Kosoko. The British judge declared the plaintiffs non-suited, or without a case to make, and the woman kept the house.[67] If owners wanted the support of the chiefly authorities and colonial state in forcing slaves or their children off land or out of houses, they needed to sustain charges of misconduct. When Brimah Akilogun sought to eject Faliyi from his father's compound, he accused him of eating cats, ravishing girls and entertaining thieves. Had the descendants of Kosoko focused their case on the woman's conduct rather than her origins, they might have succeeded in obtaining a decision for ejection.

Although the colonial state sought to maintain labour relations and to avoid widespread desertion by slaves, its courts could not uphold owners' rights to the labour of their slaves if conflicts were presented in those terms. Owners seeking to control slaves and their descendants, however, in time translated their rights to landed property occupied by such persons into rights to the labour and support of the occupants. Land-owners asserted the customary legitimacy of 'service' tenure, which they invoked in relation to clients as well as to slaves and their descendants. The Supreme Court recognised and upheld this relationship. Because the records of the early colonial courts do not survive, it is impossible to trace the development of service tenure. Two inter-related 1885 cases, however, nicely illustrate this method of disciplining slaves.

In November of that year, Oladega Asogbon, an Abagbon chief and formerly a big slave-trader, went to the Supreme Court to recover possession of land and houses occupied by two slaves, Jinadu Somade and Yesufu Okin. The British judge saw the connection between the two cases and decided them together. Asogbon testified that he was 'dissatisfied' with the men's 'conduct' and wanted them out of his property.[68] He said that he had placed them in the service of his powerful client and former slave Jacob Ogunbiyi, who had put them in houses of Asogbon's that he was using. The chief said of Somade: 'You go about abusing me, and you refuse to obey Ogunbiyi. It is native law that the chiefs would turn him out for behaving so'. Ogunbiyi testified: 'Service is the condition under which the house is occupied. It is the law among the natives that boys living in a compound should give service to their chiefs as they pay no rent. If a boy gives no service he must pay rent. Six months ago he refused service'. Lest we imagine that service did not involve labour, Ogunbiyi went on to describe what Somade had done for him in the past: 'You superintended the building of my house. You were my groom.' Asogbon complained of Yesufu Okin: '[He] has given up the service of his master ... When I went to go out [he] never came with me as was his duty. The defendant does no service to me nor does he stay in my quarter so I want his house.'[69] The British judge ruled that Chief Asogbon should recover possession of the houses in question and that the defendants should pay costs, but not back rent. As the heads of the families that owned much Lagos land, the Idejo chiefs took a keen interest in the cases. Six of them were present in the courtroom when the decision was handed down. The judge asked them whether, according to native law, Chief Asogbon should recover possession of houses held in service if that service was refused. Quick to uphold their interest, they replied unanimously that it was native law.

Service was required of both slaves and clients in return for access to land and housing, and failure to perform it satisfactorily was grounds for ejection in the eyes of the colonial courts and chiefly authorities. Service consisted of both labour and political support. Control of access to land and housing gave slave-owners and patrons a means of disciplining their slaves and clients and controlling their labour and support. The statements made by Jinadu Somade and Yesufu Okin in court illustrate the power of big men over their dependants. Chastened by Asogbon's anger as well as by the threat of eviction, Somade pleaded: 'I was with Asogbon from a child. I have always done what Ogunbiyi and Asogbon said ... I am willing to do what Asogbon says now.' Okin cried: 'I have done wrong!'[70]

These cases between Asogbon and his slaves occurred in the context of a wider conflict between Oba Dosunmu, supported by Chief Asogbon and other members of their faction, and Taiwo Olowo, a new entrepreneur and rising power in the community. The issue was further complicated by the fact that while Taiwo may once have served Asogbon, he had subsequently become identified with Kosoko and Tapa, archenemies of Dosunumu and his father Akitoye. Of humble origin in Lagos, Taiwo made a fortune in the 1850s and '60s trading palm oil and imported goods, assisted at different points in his early career by both Asogbon and Tapa. Taiwo had used his wealth to build a huge retinue and establish a political power-base in the community.[71] Shortly before the cases between Asogbon and his slaves came to trial, Taiwo had quarrelled with the Oba and his supporters (including Asogbon), and subsequently he refused to accept their authority.[72] In Asogbon's testimony against Somade, he accused him not only of failing to serve himself and Ogunbiyi but also of transferring his service to Taiwo. The conflict between Taiwo and the Oba may have created an opening for Somade and Okin to shift their labour and support from one big man to another in hopes of improving their circumstances. In the heated and factionalized climate of the day, Taiwo must have been only too glad to welcome new dependants, especially ones drawn from his opponents. Conversely, Asogbon must have felt the need to deal decisively with slaves transferring their labour and support to a rival such as Taiwo.

A third case, which revolved around marriage rather than service, further illustrates how owners and their descendants used control of landed property to discipline slaves and their offspring. In the 1890s, a man tried to pressure Ramatu, the daughter of one of his father's slaves, into marrying his son. She refused and, perhaps in an effort to end the matter, began a sexual relationship with another man. The owner's son retaliated by trying to drive Ramatu out of the house where she lived, which had belonged to his father.[73] The marriage itself offered the owner's son a method of securing a wife for his son and of capturing for the family the labour and reproductive power of the daughter of one of his father's slaves.

In the early colonial period, owners bound slaves to them by means in addition to allowing them access to land and houses. Owners often promised, for example, that if male slaves served them faithfully, they would one day help them marry. This might involve contributing to bridewealth and performing the roles of kin in marriage rituals.[74] Owners sometimes attempted to tie female slaves to them by making them wives or by arranging marriages between them and male relatives.[75] Beyond this, owners led slaves to believe that they would one day help them begin trading, fishing or farming on their own, if they remained faithful servants.[76] Owners frequently failed to live up to their promises, but betrayal sometimes became clear only after years of broken or half-kept commitments. They delivered often enough to keep slaves hoping for more. A sufficient number of slaves benefited from continued association with their owners to sustain the belief that faithful service offered a road to upward social mobility. It was, after all, often in the owner's best interest to help loyal slaves accumulate wealth and followers, even if the price was greater autonomy, for the resources of a loyal ex-slave could be harnessed in support of the former owner; Ogunbiyi, for example, began his association with the Asogbon family as a slave. An ideology of mutual benefit encapsulated the owner-slave relationship, and served as a powerful mechanism of control.

Slaves sometimes succeeded in redefining their relationship with their owners. If they were lucky, this happened during their lifetime. More commonly, it occurred in the generation of their children or grand-children. Some slaves managed to obtain access to land and capital, establish residences of their own and gain control of their labour. Occasionally, such slaves rose to positions of wealth and power, as in the cases of Jacob Ogunbiyi and Oluyode Layeni. More often slaves who left their owners to live on their own remained persons of modest means struggling to survive in petty trade or some other small-scale activity. Many such slaves retained ties to their owners or owners' descendants and in return for deference and support received protection and assis-tance.[77] But some broke definitively with their owners. A case analysed in the next section involved three slaves who redeemed themselves and left their Brazilian owner. They apparently neither had nor wanted any further contact with him.

When slaves remained in their owners' households, their descendants were sometimes absorbed into their families as kin, albeit ones who rarely enjoyed the same status as descendants of freeborn members of the family. Absorption of slave offspring occurred through a number of means. They could assert their position as kin by contributing to family affairs, especially ceremonies surrounding birth, marriage and death, of which funerals were the most important.[78] Care of a family member during illness, particularly a final illness, could also prove decisive.[79] Women won a place for themselves in families by mastering the *oríkì* (praise-poems) of the lineage and its members and reciting them on ritual occasions.[80] Having behaved as kin, slave descendants could consolidate their new identity by successfully making the same claim as kin to a family-owned resource, such as land, a house or a title. Female slaves sometimes constructed marriages or sexual relationships with owners or their relatives to secure the identity of children of the union as kin.[81] Owners occasionally gave trusted male slaves their daughters as wives. Sunmonu Animasaun, for example, married a daughter Menumatu to his slave Idrisu. While this gave the slave's offspring a connection to the owner's family through their mother, it did not necessarily make them members of it.[82]

The relationship between owners and slaves was rarely redefined in a single, decisive moment. Whether through assertion of independence or absorption as kin, the process took place over time and often involved struggle and negotiation. If there were few definitive moments on the road to freedom, there were none the less critical junctures. The contests that occurred on these occasions revolved around the interpretation of those events or control of those resources that figured centrally in the process of redefinition itself. It is impossible here to investigate all of these junctures in detail. To further explore the phenomenon, however, this essay examines the experiences of descendants of slaves seeking separation not absorption and probes the struggles between them and descendants of their ancestors' owners over control of landed property.

If slaves or their offspring wanted to minimize the demands of others on them for labour and support and to maximize control over their own time and work, they needed land and a house of their own. So long as they depended on the slave-owning family for these resources, its members could make claims on them. Land and houses were important not only for their use-value and because they could free persons from the demands of others, but also because they could be pledged as collateral to secure credit for trade and other purposes. If one owned land and a house, moreover, one could begin attracting dependants of one's own.[83]

Owners sometimes checked slaves' efforts to redefine their relationship by blocking ownership of land or a house.

The emergence of private property rights in land and the establishment of a colonial land office where one could obtain crown grants to land created opportunities for slaves to redefine their rights to landed property on which they had been placed by their owners. If slaves could obtain crown grants to the land they occupied, they could often assert private ownership rights to it.[84] But to apply for a crown grant required having the land measured, a visible public act that tipped the occupant's hand. The land commissioner, moreover, was supposed to investigate the applicant's claim.[85] Owners or their kin often intervened during this process to block the use of the grant and halt the redefinition of land rights. In 1881, for example, Zafungbo, the son of a slave named Zadugba, called a surveyor to measure a plot of land on which nine years earlier his father had been given permission to build a hut by elders of his deceased owner. Shortly before, the owner's son, Zaderow, had left Lagos for the interior, and Zafungbo's father had died. This conjunction of events may have led Zafungbo to act when he did. Soon after the owner's son returned to Lagos, he petitioned the Supreme Court to have Zafungbo ejected from the land. He stated at the trial: 'I returned from the interior three months ago to find that in my absence Zadugba had died and the defendant his son had been measuring the land through the engineer. I therefore brought this action and want to have the defendant ejected. I want this because he had the land measured.'[86]

Slaves or their descendants could also redefine rights to landed property by occupying it for a long time, often over more than one generation, and then successfully defending their claim to the property when it was challenged. In the early 1890s, Oluyode Layeni, the wealthy trader and former slave, died leaving two sons. Layeni had allowed his own slaves and their offspring to occupy some of his houses. After his death, his sons sought to recover possession of as many of the properties as possible, perhaps because they feared that if they did not the family would eventually lose all claim to them. Unable to get a group of occupants out of one house, the Layeni brothers sold it to a female trader named Phoebe Adjayi, making the problem of obtaining possession hers not theirs. Soon poor Phoebe found herself the reluctant plaintiff in a complex court case, full of much conflicting testimony about who enjoyed what rights to the house and why. The judge concluded that it was 'not at all easy to disentangle the evidence', but that the balance appeared to favour the current occupants of the house, who were permitted to retain possession. The slaves and their descendants kept the house and, equally important, they could in future point to the court's decision as proof that it belonged to them, thus consolidating their hold on a valuable asset.[87]

Efforts to redefine rights to land through litigation worked, however, only when the slave-owning family could not establish clear rights to it. When the woman Ramatu went to court in an effort to establish title to the land and house she occupied, the judge ruled that as the descendant of a slave who had been put there by his owner, she could occupy the property but not alienate it. He did not construe her refusal to marry the grandson of her father's owner as misconduct warranting ejection, but made clear that she did not own the land and house.[88]

Wanting cash more than landed property itself, or believing that they had little hope of redefining their land rights, some slaves or their descendants sought to benefit from the property they occupied by selling it.[89] Given the informality of many land sales and the difficulty of verifying most titles, they sometimes succeeded in this strategy. The colonial courts and chiefly authorities, however, regarded attempts to sell land or to redefine rights to it as misconduct worthy of ejection. In the case between Zaderow and Zafungbo, the judge called to advise him Chief Kakawa and wealthy traders Sunmonu Animasaun and Oluyode Layeni, whom he asked if Zaderow was entitled to eject Zafungbo. They answered 'yes', and the court ordered Zafungbo out of the house his father had built.[90] Numerous owners went to the Supreme Court to have slaves and their descendants ejected for such offences. Others got rid of troublesome dependants simply by running them off the land. Owners vigilantly upheld their claim to landed property not only to protect a valuable resource, but also to prevent their slaves from acquiring one, thereby moving a giant step closer to freedom.

From slaves to clients

If in the years following the annexation many slaves and their descendants remained with owners or their kin, others fled and obtained the resources, assistance and protection necessary to live in the community by entering the service of patrons. Different types of patron–client relationships existed in nineteenth-century Lagos. Persons who found themselves in the town without resources or kin could enter one type by approaching men and women of wealth and influence, usually through an intermediary, and asking to serve them. In return for regular labour and support, the dependants received clothing, food, housing, protection and assistance. Homeless and 'like dependent children', clients of this kind, known locally as *asáforigę*, enjoyed rights to occupy their patrons' property.[91] Patrons often promised, that if such clients served them faithfully they would one day help them marry and provide them the resources to begin working on their own. A contemporary described this type of relationship as follows:

The native law and custom with our boys in relation to us is for them to live with us in the house or compound and we feed them, clothe them, treat them as if they were our own family, but pay them no wages, as should they require money we dash them some. If they conduct themselves well we get them wives and give them money to start for themselves. If they behave badly we send them away without anything. In return for this they do our work and go to market or where we wish them to go.[92]

After the annexation, slaves in Lagos who wanted to leave their owners but did not have the resources to live on their own could become *asáforígẹ* of rich and powerful patrons. The big and growing demand in the town for labour and political support, coupled with the existence in local culture of a type of patron–client relationship that enabled persons of wealth and power to harness the labour and support of freeborn dependants, provided slaves an alternative to remaining with their owners. The relationship gave new entrepreneurs seeking to take advantage of opportunities in the palm produce trade a means of mobilizing labour at a time when slavery as it had once existed was coming to an end.

A pair of cases that came before the Supreme Court in the 1870s illuminates clientage as a means of organizing labour. It opens a window, moreover, onto the experiences of slaves who left their owners by entering the service of patrons. Three men, Oso, Opeluja and Ogudula, were living in Ile-Ife when they were enslaved and subsequently sold to a Brazilian repatriate residing in Lagos. Around 1874 the three slaves left their owner. In the eyes of the state, an 1862 proclamation had transformed slaves belonging to Brazilians and Sierra Leoneans into apprentices who were to serve their owners for from two to seven years and then become free. This act apparently had little effect on the three slaves' relationship with their owner or their sense of identity. Briamah Apatira, a successful Muslim trader, appeared as the plaintiff in the case. Speaking first, he testified that the slaves had run away from the Brazilian. The former slaves said that they had redeemed themselves 'by paying [their] master' and had been 'told to go wherever [they] liked'.[93] The court records unfortunately tell us nothing more about the circumstances in which the slaves left the Brazilian, and we have no way of knowing who was telling the truth. By 1874 the slaves ought not, according to British policy, have had to pay redemption. They may not have known this, however, or they may have believed that despite colonial policy redemption was the only sure way to terminate their owner's claims to them. It is possible that Apatira testified that the slaves had run away, knowing that they had redeemed themselves, in order to cast his relationship with them in the most favourable light. Alternatively, the slaves may in fact have run away and claimed to have redeemed themselves when dragged into court some years later, because they were uncertain about their legal status.

In court both Apatira and the former slaves stated that when the men left their master they had some cowries. Either they possessed insufficient funds to establish a household of their own, or they believed they would be better off living in the household of a patron. Whatever the reason, they approached Apatira and 'told him [they would] like to stay with him'.[94] Apatira said of the relationship:

I bought the land twelve years ago. The house required repairing, so I got my boys to do it. They added three rooms to the house, making it four not one. The defendants are my boys. I put them in the house as tenants whom I could turn out at any time. In return the boys gave me their services when I required them. I promised to support them if they accepted my terms. By that I mean if any one of them got a wife I would share the expenses according to country custom. They stayed with me some time when Oso bought a house and Opeluja bought another. After they had done this I told them to leave my house or pay rent. Oso had been in my house for two years before he bought the new house of his own. The boys gave me their services as labourers when I required them, and in return I paid them no money but allowed them to live in my house rent free.[95]

At the trial Apatira produced a crown grant to the land in question. He also introduced a paper purporting to be an agreement between the defendants and himself allowing them to live in his house rent-free in consideration for services as labourers. Court records unfortunately rarely include supporting documents, and it is impossible in this instance to recover the content of the written agreement.

When Apatira had finished speaking, Oso, whom Apatira called 'the headman of the defendants', testified:

We went to the plaintiff and told him we'd like to stay with him. He agreed promising to be as a father to us and help us in any difficulty. We were to be his sons and do what he wished us to do. He put us in a house near to his own. We repaired it and gave it to the plaintiff. The plaintiff took us to the land in question, and we paid him for it. We promised to pay him rent later, and he refused to accept it. We worked for him. He helped one of us take a wife. The plaintiff helped a brother of another to get goods to trade. The plaintiff got annoyed and told us to leave when we did not spend all of our time working for him. We went to the plaintiff because we heard he was a good man.[96]

These statements make clear that when Oso, Opeluja and Ogudula left their Brazilian owner, they became Apatira's *asáforígę*. Moreover, the testimony enables us to see how the parties constructed their relationship. Both sides agreed that the men first approached Apatira and told him they would 'like to stay with him'. Apatira then put them in a one-room house of his rent-free. They repaired it and enlarged it, and worked for him in other ways as well. Apatira paid his clients no wages, but in addition to allowing them to live in his house without paying rent he shared the expenses of one man's marriage. Apatira said that he helped the brother of another to get goods to redeem himself, perhaps because he knew that this would make a favourable impression on the judge; the defendants claimed that he helped the brother get goods to trade.

Open conflict emerged between Apatira and what were referred to in English as his 'boys' when they sought to redefine their labour relationship with him. Apatira stated: 'About three years ago [the men] ceased to work for me.'[97] Oso testified: 'The plaintiff got annoyed ... because we did not spend all our time working for him'. The trouble began soon after two of the men bought houses of their own, when they must have felt more able than before to resist their patron's labour demands because they no longer depended upon him for housing. Apatira evidently feared that home-ownership would weaken his control over the men's labour. He testified that soon after the two men bought their houses, he told them to leave his house or pay rent. The third man, who had acquired land but not a house, was to be permitted to remain in Apatira's dwelling, along with another boy. Ordered to quit, the clients got 'people', including a Muslim priest, to beg Apatira to allow them to stay, rent-free. Apatira testified that he relented for six months but then insisted that the men vacate. When they refused, he initiated a suit against them in the Supreme Court.

The court treated the conflict between Apatira and Oso, Opeluja and Ogudula as a dispute over landed property. The registrar entered Apatira's claim as a request to recover possession of the house, establish title to it, and recover back rent. Perhaps Apatira formulated the claims in this way; more likely the registrar imposed this formulation on his more open-ended complaints. The three ex-slaves played into this definition of the conflict when they defended themselves by arguing that they were in fact buying the house in question from Apatira. Oso maintained that they had given Apatira cowries when they entered the house and that these were partial payment for it. Apatira countered that the men had given him cowries for safe-keeping, a common practice between clients and patrons, and that he had spent the money on the marriage of one of them and the brother of another. The clients asserted that Apatira had contributed to these causes in his capacity as patron.

While the court narrowed the focus of the dispute to a case involving landed property, the conflict was not only over that but also over the terms of the relationship between patrons and *asáforígę*, particularly over the labour obligations of the latter. Apatira presented the relationship as a straight exchange of labour for housing and assistance. In an effort perhaps to retain control over the labour power of men who no longer depended on him for housing, he sought to commoditize the relationship by calling them tenants and demanding a cash equivalent, rent, when they stopped paying for the use of his house by working to his satisfaction. While two of the men had succeeded in acquiring houses of their own and the third could doubtless have lived with one of them, they may not have had the capital to pay back rent. Apatira culminated his argument by asserting that the relationship between him and his boys was rooted in contract, a modern arrangement associated with the penetration of commercial capitalism and advent of British colonialism. He produced a written document, which the men acknowledged signing, purporting to be such a contract.

Oso presented the boys' case in the language of kinship not contract. Despite his ineffective attempt to prove that the three men were buying Apatira's house, he stressed Apatira's promise 'to be as a father to us and to help us in any difficulty ... We were to be his sons and do what he wished us to'. By implication, fathers could not turn sons out 'at any time'. The relationship between them was not based on an exchange of labour for housing and assistance, which could be commoditized and given a cash equivalent. Oso also introduced morality into the argument. Before the dispute came to trial, the three men had enlisted public opinion and Islamic authority on their side by getting 'people', including a Muslim priest, to 'beg' Apatira to let them stay. In court Oso concluded by stating that he and his associates had approached Apatira originally because they had heard he was a 'good man'. By this remark, Oso suggested that norms of patronage existed in local culture to which a 'good man' should conform. These norms, likened to the relationship between fathers and sons, were rooted in custom not contract. If Oso could accomplish nothing else, he could throw Apatira's virtue into question by pointing out his failure to abide by these norms. In a community where upwardly mobile traders depended heavily on the labour of clients and where great competition existed for labour and political support, Oso's argument was not without force. It could affect Apatira's ability to attract and hold clients.

The judge ruled that Apatira had established title to the land and house and that the clients had not proved subsequent sale. Apatira recovered possession of the property. Unlike the slaves whom Chief Asogbon succeeded in having ejected, Oso, Opeluja and Ogudula were ordered to pay ten shillings back rent. Apatira had successfully used the court to uphold his right to the property; but this was not all he had accomplished. He had successfully disciplined his clients and upheld his claim to their labour. If they refused to work to his satisfaction, they had not only to leave his house but also to pay him back rent.

A second brief case involving Apatira and Oso came before the court about three weeks after the first. Ordered to vacate and pay rent, Oso, perhaps with the help of the other two men, tore doors, ceilings and other improvements out of Apatira's house.[98] This may have been an act of rebellion. In some West African cultures, however, clients who improved a patron's house were entitled when they left to take doors and ceilings that they had added.[99] Oso may have believed that he was within his rights to remove such things. Once again Apatira turned to the Supreme Court not only to enforce his property rights but also to uphold his authority. Threatened with damages, Oso pleaded that he had removed the doors through ignorance, expressed regret for what he had done and promised to repair all the damage. Oso then 'begged' Apatira to drop the proceedings against him. Apatira's second case, in effect, compelled Oso, the leader of the men and clearly the strongest among them, to submit to his authority.

Conclusion

The commercial transition in Lagos during the second half of the nineteenth century expanded opportunities for small-scale traders, including slaves. Through their efforts, a few slaves rose, normally with the support of their masters, to become substantial traders. These slaves accumulated the resources necesssary to live and work on their own, especially access to credit and individually-owned land and houses. In time, they redefined the daily demands that owners made on their time and labour, although many continued to express deference through periodic service and ritual giving and to receive protection and assistance. But if a few slaves rose to become wealthy and powerful, the vast majority remained economically marginal small-scale traders, farmers, fishers or artisans, tied to their owners or others of wealth and influence for housing, land and other resources, as well as for help and protection. New commercial entrepreneurs did rise in the community, but they were drawn disproportionately from among Sierra Leonean and Brazilian repatriated slaves, not from domestic slaves.[100] While some slaves clearly benefited from the commercial transition, it did not have the widespread liberating effect that contemporary European reformers and officials prophesied.

A full explanation of the reasons for the failure of the commercial transition to emancipate slaves in Lagos lies beyond the scope of this essay. A more extensive discussion of the organization of trade than was possible here is needed to make sense of the phenomenon. But the data presented here highlight three central elements in the continued subordination of slaves. First, British policy with respect to domestic slavery was ambivalent, at best. The colonial state could not recognize and uphold the obligations of slaves to work for their owners. This weakened owners' control over their slaves and widened the social space within which slaves could manoeuvre. At the same time, the government refused to free slaves and sought to check widespread desertion by slaves of their owners. Second, privatization of land occurred, and some slaves managed to acquire individually owned landed property. But most slaves remained dependent on owners or others to whom they attached themselves for access to land and housing. The state, through its courts, recognised the right of slaves to remain on land or in houses that belonged to their owners, but upheld the owners' title to the property. Control of land and housing enabled owners to continue to make demands on their slaves for labour and support. This restricted slaves' ability to work for themselves. Finally, the data point to the continued importance of membership in communal groups defined by kinship and patronage. Through such memberships, individuals obtained not only access to land and housing, but also protection and other necessary forms of assistance. There was little place in Lagos for outsiders. Unless persons enjoyed sufficient wealth and power to establish communal groups of their own, they needed to belong to a kin group or patron. Even if they could establish groups of their own, the support of patrons and kin remained important to them. British policy regarding domestic slavery and local land tenure coupled with the continuing relevance of communal identities helped the Lagos Oba and chiefs retain their slaves following annexation. This helped sustain this group's economic and political power, weakened by British annexation and abolition of the international slave trade.

When slaves remained with their owners following the annexation, neither they nor their offspring passively accepted subordination. Court records enable us to glimpse some of the ways such persons endeavoured both to limit the demands being made on their time and labour and to extend their rights, especially in relation to land and housing. Through their struggle slaves and their offspring sought over time to redefine the owner-slave relationship by either absorption into the slave-owning family or separation from it. The tense interplay between owners, slaves and their descendants in the early colonial period unfolded to shape the meaning of freedom in Lagos.

The existence in the town of a type of patron-client relationship that enabled outsiders to attach themselves to big men and women and receive housing, food, clothing, protection and assistance in return for labour and support provided many slaves their only alternative to slavery. In the years following the annexation, when owners could not hold slaves by force, numerous slaves fled their owners by entering the service of patrons. This type of patron–client relationship allowed new entrepreneurs such as Taiwo Olowo and Briamah Apatira to mobilize workers for trade, in an era when slavery was slowly ending but a free market for wage labour had not yet developed. The most ambitious among the new entrepreneurs, such as Taiwo Olowo, by attracting runaway slaves and other means built large retinues which they used to establish political power-bases in the community. This brought them into conflict with the Oba and chiefs, when they refused to accept their authority.

The cases between Apatira and Oso, Opeluja and Ogudula show that having left their owners by entering the service of patrons, ex-slaves could soon find themselves engaged in struggles to redefine the relationship with their patrons similar to those undertaken by slaves who stayed with their owners. Economic, political and legal changes in the early colonial period gave slaves the mobility to transform themselves into clients. But these same changes also gave patrons mechanisms for enforcing the labour relationship with their clients. The demands on slaves and *asáforígę* for labour did not differ dramatically in the second half of the century. Indeed, *asáforígę* may have been more vulnerable than slaves, because they normally had weaker rights to their patrons' resources than slaves did to their owners'.[101] By leaving owners to serve patrons slaves were not gaining freedom, they were simply exchanging one type of subordination for another.

NOTES

1 Cf. Robin Law, 'The historiography of the commercial transition in nine-teenth-century West Africa', in Toyin Falola (ed.), *West African Historiography* (Harlow, 1993), pp. 91–115.
2 C. W. Newbury, *The Western Slave Coast and its Rulers* (Oxford, 1961), pp. 17–32; Robin Law, 'Trade and politics behind the Slave Coast: the lagoon traffic and the rise of Lagos, 1500–1800', *JAH*, 24 (1983), 343–7; Ade Adefuye, 'Oba Akinsemoyin and the emergence of modern Lagos', in

A. Adefuye, B. Agiri and J. Osuntokun (eds.), *History of the Peoples of Lagos State* (Lagos, 1987), pp. 39–43.

3 Interviews in Lagos with A. W. A. Akibayo, 5 Feb. 1985; D. O. Oshodi, 10 Jan. 1974; M. O. Oshodi, 12 Jan. & 25 Feb. 1985.

4 A. B. Aderibigbe, 'Early history of Lagos to about 1850', in A. B. Aderibigbe (ed.), *Lagos: The Development of an African City* (Ikeja, 1975), pp. 11–18; Adefuye, 'Oba Akinsemoyin', 41–2; Robin Law, 'The career of Adele at Lagos and Badagry. c.1807—c.1837', *JHSN*, 9/2 (1978), 35–9; Robert S. Smith, *The Lagos Consulate 1851–1861* (London, 1979), pp. 2–17.

5 J. Gallagher, 'Fowell Buxton and the new African policy, 1838–42', *Cambridge Historical Review*, 10 (1950), 36–58; Robert Gavin, 'Nigeria and Lord Palmerston', *Ibadan*, 12 (1961), 24–7; Howard Temperley, *White Dreams, Black Africa: The Antislavery Expedition to the Niger* (New Haven, 1991), pp. 20–39.

6 Smith, *Lagos Consulate*, pp. 16–17.

7 On the debate over the causes of the annexation, see Smith, *Lagos Consulate*, pp. 18–33; A. G. Hopkins, 'Property rights and empire building: Britain's annexation of Lagos, 1861', *JEH*, 40 (1980), 781–2. Thomas Fowell Buxton's influential *The African Slave Trade and its Remedy* (London, 1840) shaped and exemplifies the mid-Victorian view.

8 Figures derived from data in Sara S. Berry, *Cocoa, Custom and Socio-Economic Change in Rural Western Nigeria* (Oxford, 1975), p. 23.

9 Patrick Manning, *Slavery, Colonialism and Economic Growth in Dahomey 1640–1960* (Cambridge, 1982), p. 99.

10 See e.g. descriptions in W. H. Clarke, *Travels and Explorations in Yorubaland (1854–1858)* (Ibadan, 1972), pp. 5, 10–13, 264–5; M. R. Delany and Robert Campbell, *Search for a Place: Black Separatism and Africa, 1860* (Ann Arbor, 1969), pp. 112–13. Also Archivio de Stato Sezione Prima, Turin [hereafter, ASSPT]: Materie Politiche Relative al Estero: Consolato Nazionali, 1. Lagos, 1856–57, G.B. Scala, Lagos, 10 March 1856. My thanks to Sandra Barnes for translations of Scala's correspondence.

11 Public Record Office, London [hereafter, PRO]: CO.147/4, Chiefs and traders of Lagos to Glover, 8 Sept. 1863, encl. in Glover, Lagos, 10 Oct. 1863; Sir John Pope-Hennessy, 'British settlements in West Africa', *Journal of the Royal Society Arts* (1873), 443. My thanks to A. G. Hopkins for the latter reference. Also *Jinadu Somade v. Seidu Ebite*, Lagos State High Court, Judge's Notebooks in Civil Cases [hereafter, JNCC], Vol. 2, pp. 101–7, 17 April 1879; and interviews with A. W. Animasaun, 20 Feb. 1974; G. B. Animasaun, 15 Feb. 1985; T. Y. Akilaja, 18 Dec. 1984.

12 Interviews with G. B. Animasaun, D. O. Oshodi, M. O. Oshodi; and N. A. Olukolu, 25 July 1974 & 23 Jan. 1985. Also Jean Herskovits Kopytoff, *A Preface to Modern Nigeria: The 'Sierra Leonians' in Yoruba, 1830–1890* (Madison, 1965), p. 287; Kristin Mann, 'The rise of Taiwo Olowo: law, accumulation and mobility in early colonial Lagos', in Kristin Mann and Richard Roberts (eds.), *Law in Colonial Africa* (Portsmouth NH, 1991), p. 94.

13 Cf. Martin Klein, 'Slavery, the slave trade and legitimate commerce in late nineteenth-century Africa', *Etudes d'Histoire Africaine*, 2 (1971), 5–28; Law, 'Historiography', pp. 98, 104–7.

14 For a fuller discussion of the Lagos Supreme Court records, see Mann, 'Taiwo Olowo', pp. 90–2.

15 Newbury, *Western Slave Coast*, pp. 46, 66, 77–95; A. G. Hopkins, 'An economic history of Lagos, 1880–1914' PhD thesis, University of London, 1964, pp. 15–19; Smith, *Lagos Consulate*, pp. 35–40, 73–80; Martin Lynn, 'From sail to steam: the impact of the steamship services on the British palm oil trade with West Africa, 1850–1890', *JAH*, 30 (1989), 227–45; 'Technology, trade and "a race of native capitalists": the Krio diaspora of West Africa and the steamship, 1852–95', *JAH*, 33 (1992), 421–40.

16 C. W. Newbury, 'Credit in early nineteenth-century West African trade', *JAH*, 13 (1972), 86; Kristin Mann, 'Trade, credit and the commercialization of land in early colonial Lagos', unpublished paper, African Studies Center, University of Illinois, 1987.

17 ASSPT: Materie Politiche Relative al Estero: Consolati Nazionali, 1. Lagos, 1856–7, Scala, Lagos, March 1857; PRO: FO.84/976, Campbell, Lagos, 12 Feb. 1855; *Halliday, trustee for J. P. L. Davies v. Johnson & Shamuse*, JNCC, Vol. 3, p. 364, Jan. 1882; *R. B. Blaize v Moses Johnson*, JNCC, Vol. 2, p. 175, 7 Oct. 1879.

18 PRO: FO.84/976, Campbell, Lagos, 30 Aug. 1855; CO.147/9, Glover, Lagos, 7 Oct. 1865; *Jose & Edmund Davidson George, administrators of Eshubi's estate v. Ondowoh*, JNCC, Vol. 4, p. 260, 1882.

19 PRO: CO.147/6, Freeman, Lagos, 9 March 1864.

20 Parliamentary Papers: Correspondence relating to the Slave Trade 1854–5, II, no. 7: Campbell, Lagos, 1 June 1854. Also interviews with A. W. A. Akibayo, D. O. Oshodi & M. O. Oshodi.

21 Smith, *Lagos Consulate*, pp. 46–57; Oladipo Yemitan, *Madame Tinubu, Merchant and Kingmaker* (Ibadan, 1987), pp. 11–29, 54–64. Also PRO: FO.84/920, Fraser, Lagos, 30 May 1853; FO.84/950, Campbell, Lagos, 1 May 1854.

22 PRO: FO.84/950, Campbell, Lagos, 18 May 1854; FO.84/976, Campbell, Lagos,, 2 June 1855; FO.84/1002, Campbell, Lagos, 1 Oct. 1856; CO.147/1, Freeman, Lagos, 7 June 1862; CO.147/2, McCoskry, Lagos, 4 Oct. 1861 & 5 Dec. 1861. Also John B. O. Losi, *History of Lagos* (Lagos, 1914), pp. 80–2.

23 PRO: FO.84/1002, Campbell, Lagos, 14 June 1856; CO.147/5, Freeman, Lagos, 20 Nov. 1862, encl. in Foreign Office to Rogers, London, 21 Feb. 1863; CO.147/6, Freeman, Lagos, 4 July 1864. Also T. J. Bowen, *Central Africa: Adventures and Missionary Labours in Several Countries in the Interior of Africa* (Charleston, 1857), p. 103; Delany & Campbell, *Search for a Place*, p. 208.

24 Mann, 'Taiwo Olowo', pp. 85–107. Also interviews with A. W. Animasaun and G. B. Animasaun.

25 Interviews with A. L. A. Ojora, 15 Oct. & 5 Nov. 1984, & 31 Jan. 1985; S. B. A. Oluwa, 23 Jan. 1985.

26 PRO: CO.147/1, Freeman, Lagos, 7 Oct. 1862; CO.147/6, Freeman, Lagos, 4 July 1864; CO.147/7, Lewis, Lagos, 12 Sept. 1863, encl. in Fenn to Cardewell, London, 20 June 1864. A list of Dosunmu's land grants survives at the Lagos Land Registry.

27 Hopkins, 'Property rights', pp. 790–2; Mann, 'Trade, credit'.

28 G. B. A. Coker, *Family Property among the Yoruba* (London, 1958), pp. 190–204.
29 PRO: CO.147/5, Freeman, Lagos, 29 June 1863; CO.147/86, Smith, Lagos, 12 Aug. 1892.
30 *Dorishawa v. Obalorisha*, JNCC, Vol. 7, p. 280, 14 Nov. 1887; University of Ibadan Library: Minutes of Central Native Council, 17 April 1902. Also A. K. Ajisafe, *Laws and Customs of the Yoruba People* (Lagos, 1946), pp. 63–6; Adebesin Folarin, *The Laws and Customs of Egbaland* (Abeokuta, 1939), pp. 8–10, 57–9, 80–1; N. A. Fadipe, *The Sociology of the Yoruba* (Ibadan, 1971), pp. 163–5, 189–93.
31 Mortgages recorded at the Lagos Land Registry document this phenomenon.
32 Hopkins, 'Property rights', pp. 782–9.
33 T. Olawale Elias, *The Nigerian Legal System* (London, 1963), pp. 40–66; Omoniyi Adewoye, *The Judicial System in Southern Nigeria, 1854–1954* (London, 1977), pp. 45–52; Mann, 'Taiwo Olowo', pp. 87–8.
34 PRO: CO.147/3, 'Extracts of the minutes of the council', 24 June 1862–30 June 1863; Glover, Lagos, 10 July 1863; CO.147/5, Emigration Office to Elliot, London, 24 July 1863; Freeman, Lagos, 29 June 1863.
35 This conclusion is based upon a reading of cases in JNCC, 1876–1900.
36 See PRO: FO.84/976, Campbell, Lagos, 2 June 1855; FO.84/1002, Campbell, Lagos, 27 May 1856.
37 *Jinadu Somade v. Seidu Ebite*, pp. 101–7.
38 Interviews with N. A. Olukolu; D. A. Ogunbiyi, May 1974; A. Alli Balogun, 25 Feb. 1985. Also *Fadipe v. Brimah*, JNCC, Vol.?, p.283, 13 Nov. 1895. Many of the bound volumes containing court records have been torn apart, making it sometimes impossible to cite volume number.
39 *Baya Aku & Awojo v. Senlele, Awudu & Ioao*, JNCC, Vol.?, pp. 131–9, 144–52, 15 April 1876.
40 See Law, in this volume. Also PRO: CO.147/27, Pope-Hennessy, Lagos, 6 Feb. 1873; *Awa v. Disu*, JNCC, Vol. 6, p. 2, 5 March 1885; *Abasi Opere v. Robert Johnson*, JNCC, Vol. 3, pp. 107–8, 20 July 1894.
41 Interviews with D. A. Ogunbiyi; A. W. A. Akibayo.
42 *Jinadu Somade v. Seidu Ebite*, pp. 101–7.
43 E. Adeniyi Oroge, 'The fugitive slave question in Anglo-Egba relations, 1861–1886', *JHSN*, 8/1 (1975), 65–7; PRO: CO.147/6, Freeman, Lagos, 6 May 1864.
44 Bowen, *Central Africa*, p. 151.
45 PRO: FO.84/920, Fraser, Lagos, 20 Feb. 1853; Campbell, Lagos, 19 Sept. 1853.
46 PRO: FO.84/920, Campbell, Lagos, Oct. 1853.
47 PRO: FO.84/1115, Brand, Lagos, 18 Jan. 1860; Hand, Lagos, 31 Dec. 1860, cited in Smith, *Lagos Consulate*, p. 161.
48 PRO: FO.2/28, Campbell, Lagos, 4 Feb. 1859, cited in Smith, *Lagos Consulate*, pp. 73, 161.
49 Smith, *Lagos Consulate*, p. 107; Lady Glover, *Life of Sir John Hawley Glover* (London, 1897), pp. 78–80.
50 PRO: CO.147/2, McCoskry, Lagos, 3 Sept. 1861.
51 PRO: CO.147/1, Colonial Office minute attached to Freeman, Lagos, 4 June 1862.

52 Thomas C. Holt, *The Problem of Freedom: Race, Labour and Politics in Jamaica and Britain, 1832–1938* (Baltimore, 1992), pp. 115–76; Robin Blackburn, *The Overthrow of Colonial Slavery, 1776–1848* (London, 1988), pp. 419–72.

53 PRO: CO.147/7, Rogers to Law Officers, London, 13 Feb. 1864, encl. in Russell to Rogers, London, 6 Feb. 1864.

54 Kristin Mann, 'The emancipation of female slaves in early colonial Lagos', unpublished paper, Annual Meeting of the African Studies Association, St Louis, 1991.

55 PRO: CO.147/1, Freeman, Lagos, 9 Oct. 1862.

56 PRO: CO.147/7, Rogers to Law Officers, London, 13 Feb. 1864, encl. in Russell to Rogers, London, 6 Feb. 1864; Law Officers to Newcastle, London, 20 Feb. 1864.

57 PRO: CO.147/7, Glover, Lagos, 10 Nov. 1863; CO.147/11, 'Proceedings in relation to slavery at Lagos', encl. in Cardwell to Blackall, London, 23 Feb. 1866.

58 PRO: CO.147/11, Cardwell to Blackall, London, 23 Feb. 1866.

59 Berry, *Cocoa*, p. 23; Newbury, *Western Slave Coast*, pp. 46, 86–7; Hopkins, 'Economic history of Lagos', pp. 49–59, 250, 299–300.

60 Mortgages on file at the Lagos Land Registry often cite interest rates.

61 A. G. Hopkins, 'Economic imperialism in West Africa: Lagos, 1880–92', *EHR*, 21 (1968), 584–6; Kristin Mann, *Marrying Well: Marriage, Status and Social Change among the Educated Elite in Colonial Lagos* (Cambridge, 1985), pp. 21, 70.

62 *Jinadu Somade v. Seidu Ebite*, p. 104.

63 A. G. Hopkins, 'The Lagos strike of 1897', *Past & Present*, 35 (1968), 133–55.

64 *Salawura v. Captain Harper*, JNCC, Vol. 6, p. 99, 21 Sept. 1885.

65 James L. Roark, *Masters without Slaves: Southern Planters in the Civil War and Reconstruction* (New York, 1977), pp. 68–155; Jonathan M. Wiener, *The Social Origins of the New South: Alabama, 1860–1885* (Baton Rouge, 1978), pp. 35–73; Eric Foner, *Nothing but Freedom* (Baton Rouge, 1983); Rebecca J. Scott, *Slave Emancipation in Cuba, 1860–1899* (Princeton, 1985), pp. 201–78; Holt, *Problem of Freedom*, pp. 143–76, 345–79.

66 *Brimah Akilogun v. Faliyi*, JNCC, pp. 113–14, 116–18, 19 Jan. 1894.

67 *Kasunmu Fansonya, Sasi Momonau & Ige Abisaye v. Gbanbose Osisi*, JNCC, Vol.?, pp. 287–9, 5 April 1894.

68 *Asogbon v. Jinadu Somade*, JNCC, Vol. 6, p. 127, 9 Nov. 1885.

69 *Asogbon v. Yesufu Okin*, JNCC, Vol. 6, p. 137, 16 Nov. 1885.

70 *Asogbon v. Jinadu Somade*, p. 136; *Asogbon v. Yesufu Okin*, p. 137.

71 Mann, 'Taiwo Olowo', pp. 99–102.

72 For the background, see Losi, *History*, pp. 50–4, 80–5; Patrick D. Cole, *Modern and Traditional Elites in the Politics of Lagos, 1884–1938* (Cambridge, 1975), pp. 32–44; Takiu Folami, *A History of Lagos, Nigeria: The Shaping of an African City* (Smithtown NY, 1982), p. 34.

73 *Ramatu v. Abuduranu*, JNCC, Vol. 18, pp. 207–14, 11 Nov. 1896.

74 Interviews with D. O. Oshodi, A. L. A. Ojora; and C. B. Thomas, 15 Oct. & 5 Nov. 1984.

75 Mann, 'Emancipation'.

76 Interviews with D. O. Oshodi, A. W. A. Akibayo and T. Y. Akilaja.
77 Interviews with A. W. A. Akibayo; and R. S. A. Animasaun, 12 Dec. 1983.
78 Interviews with D. O. Oshodi; A. L. A. Ojora; C. B. Thomas.
79 *Egunleti & Saye v. Ayifemi*, JNCC, Vol.?, pp. 309–11, 21 Nov. 1894.
80 Interview with Mrs Kofo Pratt, 18 Sept. 1984.
81 Mann, 'Emancipation'.
82 Interview with A. W. Animasaun.
83 On the relationship among land, labour, wealth and power in Lagos, see Mann, 'Taiwo Olowo'; and 'Women, landed property, and the accumulation of wealth in early colonial Lagos', *Signs*, 16 (1991), 682–706. Also Sandra T. Barnes, *Patrons and Power: Creating a Political Community in Metropolitan Lagos* (Bloomington, 1986), pp. 47–69; 'Women, property and power', in Peggy Reeves Sandy and Ruth Goodenough (eds.), *Beyond the Second Sex* (Philadelphia, 1990), pp. 255–80.
84 Mann, 'Taiwo Olowo', p. 94; PRO: CO.147/86, Smith, Lagos, 12 Aug. 1892; 'Commemoration: Benjamin Fagbemi Mabinuori Daowdu', *Lagos Guardian*, 6 Feb. 1991. My thanks to T. G. Forrester for the last reference.
85 PRO: CO/147/3, Glover, Lagos, 10 July 1863; CO.147/5, Emigration Office to Elliot, London, 24 July 1863.
86 *Zaderow v. Zafungbo*, JNCC, Vol. 4, p. 20, 24 Feb. 1882.
87 *Phoebe Adjayi v. Momo Dangana & Titi (alias Asatu)*, JNCC, Vol.?, pp. 283–9, 316–28, 411–14, 25 May 1896.
88 *Ramatu v. Abuduranu*, pp. 207–14.
89 *Amuleye v. Thomas*, JNCC, Vol. 2, p. 70, 19 Feb. 1879.
90 *Zaderow v. Zafungbo*, p. 2.
91 Sandra T. Barnes, personal communication, 7 May 1991; A. G. Hopkins, 'A report on the Yoruba, 1910', *JHSN*, 5/1 (1969), 77–8; and interview with A. L. A. Ojora.
92 *Omotoso v. Seidu Olowu*, JNCC, Vol. 3, p. 298, July 1881.
93 *Eshuby, alias Brimoh Apatira v. Oso, Opeluja & Ogudula*, JNCC, Vol. 2, p. 129, 14 July 1879.
94 *Apatira v. Oso*, p. 129.
95 *Apatira v. Oso*, pp. 126–7.
96 *Apatira v. Oso*, p. 129.
97 *Apatira v. Oso*, p. 127.
98 *Eshuby, alias Brimoh Apatira v. Oso*, JNCC, Vol. 2, p. 141, 6 Aug. 1879.
99 V. R. Dorjahn and Christopher Fyfe, 'Landlord and stranger: change in tenancy relations in Sierra Leone', *JAH*, 3 (1962), 391–7.
100 Hopkins, 'Economic history of Lagos'; Mann, *Marrying Well*, pp. 25–34; Kopytoff, *Preface*.
101 Hopkins, 'Report', pp. 77–8; Barnes, personal communication.

7 Slaves, Igbo women and palm oil in the nineteenth century

Susan Martin

Like many of the other papers in the present collection, this one engages with the arguments of Tony Hopkins. Indeed, it was inspired by the experience of sitting in his Masters' class some fifteen years ago and hearing him lament the shortage of research on smallholders. In his view 'the modern economic history of West Africa' is in large part the history of their efforts in developing agricultural export production, efforts which were truly heroic given their limited access to capital, the 'traditional tools' and family labour on which they relied, and the long-standing local dominance of slave-using warriors and merchants, who continued to threaten both their peace and their profits. Given the well-documented importance of smallholders in twentieth-century West Africa, it seemed a pity that so little was known about them in the nineteenth. In particular, it was difficult to test two of Hopkins' assumptions: that free smallholder, as opposed to large-scale, slave-based, export production was significant from the start; and that the smallholder households of the nineteenth century were similar in their production techniques and social structure to their 'modern', mid twentieth-century counterparts. Did no scars result from their heroic nineteenth-century struggles? And was none left from the era of the Atlantic slave trade; none from the process of its ending?[1]

This paper will address these questions through a case study of the Ngwa-Igbo region, through which the caravans supplying the Atlantic slave trade passed from the seventeenth to the nineteenth centuries, and which became a major centre of palm oil export production towards the end of this period. Although evidence on nineteenth-century conditions is scanty, it will be argued that small-scale household production was important within the Ngwa oil palm industry from the outset. The study will focus on social relations within the household, especially on the extent and limitations of domestic slavery and on the role of women, who did most of the work in palm oil production. It will be shown that relationships within the household were changing, in a way which fits uneasily with Hopkins' model of modernity.

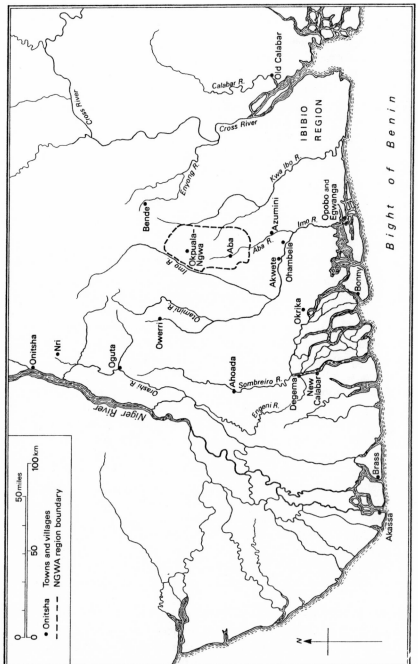

Map 2   The Ngwa region, major rivers and nineteenth-century ports.

The relationship between farmers and long-distance traders will also be examined, addressing a central question within the well-known 'crisis of adaptation' debate: whether traders were able to move painlessly from dominating the Atlantic slave trade routes to dominating the hinterland palm oil producers. Finally, the competitive strengths and weaknesses of smallholders will be compared with those of large-scale, slave-using palm oil producers, addressing a second key issue within the wider debate. In contrast to the research summarized by Lovejoy in 1983, which suggested that the importance of slave-based production systems was growing right up to the moment of their destruction by colonial rule, it will be argued that, having expanded alongside slave-based systems in the Ngwa-Igbo region during the early nineteenth century, household producers then proved better able both to sustain expansion and to weather the storm of the late nineteenth-century slump.[2]

Hinterland Igbo societies and the Atlantic slave trade

The Ngwa-Igbo region lies some sixty miles north of the ports of Bonny and Opobo, about sixty-five miles to the south-east of Onitsha and a similar distance to the north-west of Calabar. In other words, its location placed it well away from all the direct points of contact between Africans and Europeans in nineteenth-century south-eastern Nigeria. It was a quintessential hinterland region, something of a backwater in commercial terms but a well-populated centre of agricultural production. Many Agbaja slaves from the region to the north-east of Onitsha passed through in the nineteenth century, destined for Bonny and the Atlantic trade. Ngwa farmers developed a profitable trade in food to supply these slaves and their accompanying traders, and to sustain the specialized coastal trading communities of Bonny and Okrika. Slaves were also exported in smaller numbers from the Ngwa region itself.[3]

Any attempt to study social trends within the Ngwa and neighbouring Igbo societies before 1900 is greatly handicapped by the absence of European visitors or of any other source of documentary evidence. There is an abundance of oral evidence indicating a continuity of basic social structures like the patrilineal family, but such evidence is clearly open to doubt because of its role in legitimating the social structures in place when the traditions were recorded. Nevertheless, it is possible to balance the view found in recorded traditions with external evidence on trading and settlement patterns, and so at least to establish whether any obvious pressures for social change had arisen from such sources. Evidence on the relationships between hinterland Igbo farmers and coastal slave-traders can also shed light on who were the most powerful members of hinterland societies, which groups of people were best able to make contact with outsiders, and to what extent hinterland societies were dominated by the traders who linked them to the world economy. Such evidence can provide a useful benchmark for assessing the changes which took place as the palm oil trade grew up alongside the slave trade and finally displaced it.[4]

Within the constraints just outlined for hinterland Igbo history, the Ngwa case is relatively well documented. Local oral traditions were studied in some detail by colonial officials, as were twentieth-century social structures, following the Igbo Women's War of 1929 in which the Ngwa played a prominent part. Further collections of traditions bearing directly on nineteenth-century economic and social life were made by Ukegbu and Oriji in the 1970s. Oriji has already drawn out the implications of his evidence for the 'crisis of adaptation' debate, focusing on the fortunes of lineage and village heads and their wives, who in his view benefited most from the nineteenth-century palm oil trade, and members of the *Okonko* secret society, which had cooperated with the long-distance Aro traders in supplying slaves for the Atlantic trade. His argument was well integrated with Dike, Jones, Latham and Northrup's pioneering studies of coastal trading societies and of the Igbo peoples' Niger Delta and Ibibio neighbours. However, it will be argued below that Oriji over-emphasized the importance of slaves within the lineage-based production system, and under-estimated the difficulties faced by *Okonko* members once the Atlantic slave trade had finally ended, especially during the long period of coastal warfare and external trade depression after 1870.[5]

At the height of the Atlantic slave trade the Ngwa were a people on the move, and their social structures were extremely fluid. They belong to the southern or Owerri branch of Igbo culture, which differs from the northern branch centred on Nri in having no *Ozo* or similar title to celebrate and reinforce individual eminence. In direct contrast to the ethos of *Ozo*, Ngwa traditions of origin celebrate the cooperation of junior men in breaking free from their seniors' control, and identify the Ngwa as an exceptionally quick-witted and fast-moving group by comparison with their Igbo kin and neighbours. Their founding settlement at Okpuala-Ngwa was made at some time before the eighteenth century, and when the Atlantic slave trade was at its height they were engaged in a process of peaceful migration southwards and eastwards through thinly-populated territory.[6]

Ngwa traditions reinforce the well-known paradox that the Atlantic slave trade in the Bight of Biafra did not appear to lead to endemic warfare or depopulation. By the early twentieth century south-eastern

Nigeria had one of the highest population densities in tropical Africa, yet it had also suffered heavy losses through the slave trade. From its origins on a small scale in the seventeenth century, the Biafran trade grew to a volume of 2,300 slaves per year in the first decade of the eighteenth century and 10,600 per year in the 1750s, by which time the region had overtaken the Bight of Benin as the single most important source of slaves from West Africa. The Biafran trade peaked at a volume of 22,500 per annum in the 1780s, and still stood at the relatively high annual level of 12,300 in the first decade of the nineteenth century. Over 220,000 slaves were exported during the twenty-two-year period 1821–43, and it was only after the British Naval Squadron began actively intervening in the mid-1830s that the trade finally petered out. Even so, 12,200 slaves are recorded as having been transported from the Bight between 1844 and the formal ending of the trade in 1867.[7]

Ngwa traditions also confirm David Northrup's explanation of the paradox, in that judicial enslavement and kidnapping are held to have been the main sources of slaves sold overseas. Northrup has emphasized that such means of enslavement had far fewer destructive side-effects than those associated with warfare and armed slave raids elsewhere. This had important implications not only for population and economic life, but also for local social structures. People were able to live in dispersed settlements and to conduct their affairs with very little reference to central authorities. In the Ngwa region by the early twentieth century people typically lived in compounds (*Onu Ovu*), consisting of a small number of closely related men (for example, a father and his sons) and their respective households. The household, consisting of one senior man, his wives, children, slaves, and clients, formed the basic unit of agricultural production. Each household head acknowledged allegiance to the *Ezi*, a minimal patrilineage which was often synonymous with the *Onu Ovu*, and to the *Mba*, or village. Yet in practice there was little village-wide cooperation except in warfare and in path clearance, and by the early twentieth century the village head was often impoverished. During the eighteenth and early nineteenth centuries, when the Ngwa region was still thinly settled and when ambitious junior men had ample opportunity to break away and found new villages, his position must have been weaker still.[8]

Against this background, Oriji has argued that during the period of the Atlantic slave trade, power rested mainly in the hands of the *ofo*-holders, or *Ezi* heads, and of the members of the new *Okonko* secret society. The family *ofo*, or staff of authority, is central to Ngwa cultural identity. A key stage in the founding of each new settlement was the making of a shrine at which the *ofo*-holder would then make regular sacrifices. His office carried with it the right to allocate the family farmland among adult males at the start of each farming season, and to receive in return gifts of palm wine, gin and yams, and a share of any animals killed. *Ezi* members had to work on their *ofo*-holder's personal farm on every *Orie* day (that is, on one day in every four). However, the *ofo*-holder had no judicial authority, and village-level systems of justice were weak. Hence, Oriji has argued that kidnapping was more important than justice as a source of the slaves exported from the Ngwa region.[9]

In Oriji's view, the key actors in the slave trade from the Ngwa region were the members of a new and exclusively male secret society, the *Okonko* society, which colonial observers had thought to be of recent origin but which he believed to have been founded by the Aro slave-traders. The first recruits to the society were local traders who accompanied pilgrims to the Aro oracle, the Long Juju, which was a renowned source of arbitration in inter-lineage disputes. Drawing its identity and authority from links with the world outside the village, and recruiting its members from those with ruthless entrepreneurial spirit rather than seniority, the society was an attractive route to power for those who were junior within their lineages, but did not wish to migrate and found fresh settlements. Oriji argued that *ofo*-holders may even have found themselves eclipsed by *Okonko* members as the society and the slave trade grew, and that the rise of the palm oil trade in the nineteenth century provided them with a welcome opportunity to regain lost ground.[10]

While Oriji's argument about the origins of *Okonko* ties in well both with the traditions widely known within the Ngwa region today and with the work of other authors on the Aro, his views on its later history have two main weaknesses. One is that, like the traditions themselves, Oriji's version of developments between the abolition of the slave trade and the imposition of colonial rule has a certain timeless quality. In the following sections of this paper it will be shown that it is possible to develop a chronology of this period, and in so doing to reach a fuller understanding of the impact of abolition upon *Okonko* members. The second weakness is more difficult to remedy. It is the omission of women from the argument. Both the traditions and the sources on external trade are largely silent on the role played by hinterland Igbo women in the period of the slave trade. However, export statistics and twentieth-century archaeological and anthropological data on farming systems can go some way towards filling the gap.

The Atlantic slave trade brought radical changes to hinterland Igbo farming systems. Imported iron tools made it easier for the Ngwa and others to clear tracts of virgin forest, and a wide range of new crops was introduced. Many of the new crops, in particular the cocoyam, became known as 'women's crops', meaning that women harvested them as well as performing their routine work of planting and weeding. Women's workloads probably increased as a result. Previously the local diet had been heavily dependent on the yam, which men harvested in addition to their main task of land clearance. The view that women's workloads, and hence their economic value locally, were rising is supported by the fact that the proportion of women in the Atlantic slavers' cargoes was falling. During the seventeenth and eighteenth centuries men barely outnumbered women as victims of the slave trade from the Bight of Biafra. By the early nineteenth century the proportion of men in the Biafran slavers' cargoes was rising, and between 1810 and 1867 it averaged 65 per cent.[11] It will be argued below that women's economic value continued to increase as oil palm exports grew. Ngwa *ofo*-holders, who had firm control of the local marriage system, found their power enhanced as a result. Yet, in contrast to Oriji's view, this development will be seen as a continuation of previous trends rather than a reversal of them.

The rise of the palm oil export trade

The oil palm is indigenous to the Southern Igbo region, and palm oil has long been a staple of the local diet. Together with the yam, it was an early item in the provisioning trade supplying the slave caravans and ships. However, its commercial importance was limited until the rise of an export trade to Britain, where it was used in candle-making and as a lubricant for industrial machinery from the late eighteenth century onwards.[12] Exports grew steadily until the mid-1850s, but international trading fluctuations and local coastal warfare produced several swings of fortune thereafter. It will be argued in the following section that the fates of women producers, *ofo*-holders and *Okonko* members were influenced as much by these swings as by the underlying trend of expansion. In the severe depression which began in 1885, *ofo*-holders and the smaller households within their compounds appear to have fared better than the *Okonko* members, prompting changes in the character of the *Okonko* society itself.

Palm oil exports from Old Calabar grew from the very low levels of the 1780s to reach 1,000 tons per year in the 1810s, and over 4,000 during the 1830s. Bonny, the main port linked to the Ngwa region, entered the trade more cautiously with exports of just 200 tons a year in the 1810s, but drew level with Old Calabar in the 1830s and by 1847 had overtaken it with exports of nearly 8,000 as compared with 5,000 tons per annum. Between then and 1870 Old Calabar's trade fluctuated around the 4,000-ton level while Bonny's grew, averaging almost 10,000 tons a year in

1850–51, and (together with New Calabar, which played a lesser role in the trade) 16,000 from 1855 to 1864. Like Old Calabar, Bonny and New Calabar were some distance from the main centres of palm oil production. In 1869 the trade of all three came under threat through the foundation of Opobo, at the mouth of the Imo River which led directly to the Ngwa region. A series of wars soon began between New Calabar, Bonny and Opobo, and the hinterland trade routes shifted eastwards to avoid the embattled zones. In the early 1880s, the combined exports of Bonny and Opobo came to just 12,000 tons a year, while those of Old Calabar averaged 7,000. The total volume of palm oil exported from the region now known to British traders as the Niger Delta (rather than the Bight of Biafra) thus remained constant at about 20,000 tons per annum from the mid-1850s to the mid-1880s.[13]

Meanwhile the terms of trade for palm oil exports, which had risen sharply from the 1810s to the 1850s, began to fluctuate and from 1885 dropped decisively. During the first half of the century both slave and palm oil exporters had benefited from falling import prices. After 1850 little is known about import price trends, but the details available on British palm oil prices, ocean transport cost savings and reduced profit margins among shippers following the introduction of the steamer, suggest a levelling off in the real prices available to palm oil sellers in West Africa. After 1878, Latham's research on London palm oil prices shows growing instability followed by a dramatic collapse in 1885, when prices fell sharply from £30–40 to £20–24 per ton. Liverpool prices fluctuated around the level of £25 per ton throughout the 1890s, recovering only in 1906. Meanwhile, West African import prices followed a varied set of trends. Cotton piece goods and trade spirits became cheaper in the 1880s, but this trend was reversed for trade spirits in the decade which followed. Salt became steadily more expensive throughout the 1880s and 1890s, but tobacco prices stagnated. Overall, it is therefore unlikely that import price trends either offset or worsened the impact of the disastrous fall in palm oil prices.[14]

One bright spot in the gloom of the late nineteenth century was provided by the rise of the palm kernel export trade. Palm nuts, a by-product of oil processing, were a women's perquisite which previously had no cash value in the Ngwa and neighbouring Igbo regions. Following William Lever's pioneering work on a 'self-washing' soap made from kernel oil and coconut oil, aimed at working-class consumers in hard-water areas, an export trade in kernels began from Old Calabar, rising in volume from 1,000 tons in 1869 to 10,000 in 1887. The flat prices of the 1890s stunted the growth of the new trade but did not kill it. After 1900 a rapid revival began, not only in palm kernel but also in palm oil exports. By this time the restoration of peace had also restored the fortunes of Opobo, which in 1906 exported 13,000 tons of palm kernels and 14,000 of oil. The whole region between twentieth-century Degema and Calabar, which had been exporting a regular 20,000 tons of oil a year during the thirty years before 1885, was now supplying 33,000 tons of kernels and 29,000 of oil to the world market.[15]

These trading figures imply that the palm oil trade from the Ngwa region began to flourish just before the British Naval Squadron began its active campaign against the slave trade in the mid-1830s. The trade continued to grow until the mid-1850s, when it levelled off in volume terms. During the 1870s and early 1880s it was disrupted by instability along the coast, but was probably diverted rather than destroyed. Living on the edge of the Ibibio region, Ngwa farmers were well placed to use the overland trade routes running through it to Old Calabar, although transport along these routes would have been more expensive than along the Imo River. During the period 1885–1906, hinterland transport costs probably fell again as the fortunes of Opobo revived, softening the impact of low and stagnant British palm oil prices.

Certainly, Ngwa farmers decided to stick with the palm oil industry throughout the late nineteenth-century slump. Their decision was probably prompted by demographic and ecological factors as well as by the rise of the kernel trade. Palm producers elsewhere in West Africa began shifting into the wild rubber and cocoa industries after 1885, but the advantages of this strategy were weaker in the Igbo region than elsewhere. The oil content of fruit from palms grown in eastern Nigeria was exceptionally high by West African standards, while the dense population of the Ngwa and neighbouring Igbo regions meant there was a scarcity of virgin forest, the natural habitat of wild rubber vines and the site of the best cocoa soils once cleared. These facts, combined with the final point that relatively dense populations also meant relatively high concentrations of oil palms on fallowed farmland, help to explain both the early entry of hinterland Igbo farmers into the world palm oil trade, and their loyalty to it once the barter terms of trade stopped improving after 1850, once the trade routes were disrupted after 1869, and once the depression took hold in 1885.[16]

Smallholders and slave-users in the palm oil industry

There is widespread agreement that the vast bulk of Niger Delta palm oil in the nineteenth century was processed on a small scale, whether by family or slave-based producers. The few large plantations established by erstwhile long-distance slave traders were designed mainly to provide food for their own coastal towns, and even in this they were hampered by the low fertility of coastal soils. Within the more productive hinterland Igbo region, smallholders were dominant.[17]

Like other southern Igbo farmers, the Ngwa worked on a small scale and used 'traditional tools', thus conforming to Hopkins' famous type. However, in three other ways they differed significantly from the household producers described by Hopkins, whose entry into the agricultural export sector in the nineteenth century heralded 'the start of the modern economic history of West Africa'. Firstly, as Northrup has argued, they could well have supplied the provisioning trade for centuries, so that 'modernity' would have begun for them somewhat earlier than Hopkins thought. Secondly, not all of them lacked access to capital. Social differentiation existed within the lineage, creating the possibility of wealth accumulation by lineage heads. This raises the interesting question of how wealth was used, if not to improve on 'traditional tools'. Oriji's answer suggests a third contrast with the Hopkins model. He argued that lineage heads were also extensive slave-users, and that they gained a far greater share of the palm produce trade than did Hopkins' 'modern' households using only family labour. This argument supports Lovejoy's thesis that slavery was becoming stronger within commercialized West African farming systems in the nineteenth century, so that households involved in export production were becoming less, rather than more 'modern' from Hopkins' point of view. However, the slave-using suggestion is presented only tentatively by Oriji, and it runs counter to his more confident statement that, for *Okonko* members, the sale of slaves to lineage heads was an inadequate replacement for the Atlantic slave trade, so that tolls levied by the society on the palm oil trade routes became an increasingly important source of income.[18]

An alternative view of the fortunes of household and lineage heads will be presented below, using additional evidence on the hinterland slave trade and sexual division of labour and incorporating the chronology of trading fluctuations outlined above. In essence, it will be argued that opportunities for accumulating wealth existed both before and during the palm oil export boom, but that there is little sign of this wealth being converted into large holdings of slaves. The factors limiting the extent of slavery will be explored, and Oriji's argument about the difficulties faced by *Okonko* members will be developed further. Finally, attention will be paid to the range of social and economic changes, other than the growth of slavery, which occurred in the Ngwa region as the oil palm industry grew.

Within most hinterland Igbo societies, the key to a man's success in commercial palm production lay in control of women's labour. Women did most of the work in palm processing as in yam cultivation, but their male household heads were able to claim ownership of the product. Women's work involved planting, weeding and carrying home all the crops grown on the household's farm. They were also responsible for many other time-consuming daily tasks, ranging from the collection of water, firewood and nutritious forest leaves through cooking and child-care to petty trade. Yet they were not allowed to perform certain tasks like climbing palm trees, clearing the bush prior to farming or harvesting yams. As farming systems changed through the introduction of new crops, tools or working methods, there was some scope for change through the allocation of new or transformed tasks to either men or women. Once a task had been given a gender association, however, the link rarely changed, and so the overall sexual division of labour acquired a timeless quality. To some extent this division reflected practical considerations like the need for society's valuable mothers to avoid highly dangerous work such as palm-climbing, or the greater effectiveness of men at the exceptionally tough work of clearing the primary forest. Yet by the end of the nineteenth century it had also acquired an ideological significance which strongly favoured men. The authority of *ofo*-holders was founded ultimately on their ancestors' role in clearing the forest, while the task of harvesting conferred ownership rights over the end product. Women were allowed to harvest new and subsidiary crops like cocoyams, but men retained firm control over the indigenous staples.[19]

Two main palm oil processing methods were used in the Niger Delta and hinterland Igbo region in the nineteenth century. In the Niger Delta and in some regions north and east of Bende, which were thinly populated and where there were heavy alternative demands on local labour for canoe transportation and highly commercialized yam-growing, a labour-saving method was used. Capitalizing on the abundance of local creeks and streams within these areas, men placed palm fruit in large canoes by the waterside, left it to ferment and then trod it to a pulp. The oil could then be washed out with cold river water. Because of the long period of fermentation it was a semi-solid or 'hard' oil, full of fatty acids and unsuitable for eating. Hence, it is reasonable to assume that this production method was designed specifically to meet the new export demand from nineteenth-century industrialists. The oral evidence collected by B. N. Ukegbu bears out this view, and suggests that the method used in the Ngwa and neighbouring regions, although yielding a superior 'soft' oil, also represented a change from the early domestic norm.[20]

Ukegbu suggests that palm oil for cooking had originally been a 'female' product. Women collected windfall fruit from trees which were seen as part of the secondary forest, in the same way as they collected okazie leaves and other semi-wild ingredients for soup. They boiled and pounded the fruit in small quantities and squeezed out the oil by hand. When a market developed for palm oil, which on Northrup's evidence may have begun on a small scale with the growth of the provisioning trade, men began to take more care to preserve oil palms when clearing land for farming. However, their care stopped short of planting fresh palms, which indeed would hardly have been necessary. In 1907 a colonial survey found that only 40 per cent of the palms growing naturally in symbiosis with long-fallow food farming in the southern Ngwa region were being harvested regularly. By this time men were climbing the trees to harvest the fruit, and pounding large quantities of it in hollowed-out tree stumps. Their contribution took relatively little time but gave them vital property rights. Although women carried the fruit bunches from the palm to the compound for processing, separated the individual fruits from the spiky bunch and continued to boil them and squeeze out the oil, men now claimed the right to the saleable product.[21]

Given this sexual division of labour and property rights, the opportunity clearly existed for Ngwa household and lineage heads to acquire wealth by organizing yam and palm oil production to serve the nineteenth-century provisioning and palm oil export trades. Little pressure was put on their male labour resources by the palm oil industry in particular, since palms were harvested throughout the year and men's contribution to processing, though vigorous, was brief. However, women's work in palm oil extraction was both laborious and time-consuming. The more women a household head could have to work for him, the more benefit he could derive from the male labour available. The emphasis laid by Oriji's sources on investment in people as a key use of wealth is therefore understandable, but it is likely that such investment was overwhelmingly in women rather than men.

Although domestic slavery existed in the Ngwa region in the early twentieth century, and the ownership of slaves along with many wives and clients was a well-known sign of wealth, documentary sources suggest that slavery was by no means extensive. In this respect, the Ngwa-Igbo case presents a sharp contrast to that of the Ahoada and Degema regions and the middle reaches of the Cross River, where labour scarcity was acute, as noted in the discussion of 'hard' oil production above. The latter regions imported large numbers of slaves in the late nineteenth century and continued to import children until the mid-1930s. As in the case of the Atlantic slave trade, the Ngwa region was not a key source of slaves for this internal trade. Most came from the region stretching to the north-west towards Onitsha, where in 1911 recorded population densities were at least 50 per cent greater than in the Ngwa region.[22]

When interviewing people in the Ngwa region in the early 1980s, I was struck by their unanimity in saying that wealthy men had many wives to work for them. Most people did not speak of slavery, which I was inclined to ascribe to natural reticence until uncovering the documentary evidence cited above. Of the three men who did mention the subject, two emphasized that the slaves bought by Ngwa farmers were male, and that their labour was considered sufficiently dispensable that they were the first to be sent to school. Chief I. W. Ebere of Nbawsi added that they were responsible for tasks like the care of domestic animals, which were subsidiary to the main work of Ngwa farmers. Finally, the family historian Augustine Amaeze Nwogu told the story of one of the early colonial Warrant Chiefs, Nwogu, who had been a noted warrior and slave-trader in the late nineteenth century. Nwogu used to buy slaves from the Aro, who travelled by night and brought them directly to his compound. He took them down to the Ndokis of Akwete, Ohambele and Azumini, and never kept any, preferring to rely on the labour of his eleven wives and many children. The Aro Expedition of 1901–2 put paid to his trading expeditions, but he and his brother Osundu made the best of the new situation. Osundu was made one of the first Warrant Chiefs at Amiri, and when he died Nwogu succeeded him. Echoes of the past were heard when prisoners awaiting trial were brought to the Chief's compound by the Court messengers.[23]

Nwogu's story illustrates how a man could be both a slave-trader in the classic *Okonko* mould, and a successful yam and palm oil producer in his role as household head. It also confirms the other informants' view that to have many wives, rather than many slaves, was the key to success in farming. Wives were obtained publicly, through the payment of brideprice to their parents, rather than clandestinely, through visits to the compounds of slave-traders. Wives could also be obtained locally, rather than through exchanges with the Ngwas' western neighbours beyond the Imo River or through purchases from the Aro and their *Okonko* partners. Wives could even have been cheaper to obtain than slaves who had been transported expensively from further north, and who could find more desperate buyers in the thinly-populated areas further to the south and north-east. Wives could return to their parents, but in such cases a refund of brideprice could be demanded, if not always obtained. Meanwhile, most of the cultural features which have been associated with high levels of female slavery elsewhere in nineteenth-century Africa were absent in the Ngwa case. Ngwa society was not matrilineal, so that Ngwa fathers were able to have power over their children without resorting to kinless 'wives'. The general status of Ngwa women was not high, and their access to wealth was extremely limited until the rise of the palm kernel export trade, so that they had little prospect of buying female slaves and using them to free themselves from work. Finally, Ngwa society was not highly militarized, so that no premium was placed on female slaves' docility as rendering them less liable to revolt. Indeed, as compared with free wives who felt some personal stake in the fortunes of their household, slave women might even have been more prone to passive resistance when asked to put in extra hours handling spiky palm bunches or squeezing bristly pulp.[24]

If most of the wives of wealthy Ngwa men were indeed women of local origin, rather than slaves brought in from elsewhere, then demographic factors could well have reinforced the control of senior and wealthy men over junior men and clients. The abundance of wives for the few implied a scarcity for the many, and could well have forced many young men to delay marriage, especially if they came from poor families which found it hard to accumulate the brideprice. In other words, the control of many wives implied the prolonged control of unmarried junior men, providing yet another reason for senior and wealthy men to take little interest in buying male slaves.[25]

This logic supports the evidence that no large-scale demand for slaves developed among the Ngwa to counteract the ebbing of demand from the Atlantic after 1830. It is not known to what extent the gap was filled by a rise in demand for slaves from other buyers, in particular the Niger Delta canoe houses and Cross River yam farmers. Clearly Nwogu at least was still able to benefit from the transit trade through the Ngwa region, but it is unlikely that he saw slave-trading as a growth area even before colonial rule, since he was keen to build up an alternative source of income from agriculture. This strategy of adaptation was both practical and sensible, but evidence from other sources suggests that it was unlikely to lead to conspicuous economic success for the bulk of Ngwa slave-traders and *Okonko* members. In the competition with *ofo*-holders for labour resources, their access to slave-trading networks, which might on the face of it have seemed a key asset, now appears irrelevant. Their wealth would have helped them win wives, but in this they were competing on level terms with the more prosperous of the yam-farming lineage and village heads. Meanwhile, further evidence on oil palm property rights, which will be surveyed below, indicates that *ofo*-holders were using their ideological link with the land to steal a march on their upstart slave-dealing rivals. *Okonko* members who were also *ofo*-holders had the best of both worlds; but membership of *Okonko* alone was becoming an increasingly rocky route to prosperity.

As Ngwa population densities grew and junior men saw fewer opportunities to establish new settlements and shrines towards the end of the nineteenth century, the land rights held by existing *ofo*-holders gave them increasing power. Ukegbu has argued, using oral evidence collected in the Ngwa and neighbouring regions, that this power was simultaneously being used to extend senior men's property rights. Oil palms had originally been considered a wild communal resource, but once men began harvesting them and preserving them on farmland, they became the subject of ownership claims. *Ofo*-holders successfully established a title to palms growing on the land they were currently cultivating, on compound land and on the site of previous lineage settlements. They also began to dictate the intervals at which wild 'bush' palms could be harvested. Like their rights over land, the new oil palm rights enabled *ofo*-holders to control access to natural resources and to use them more extensively than their junior kin. Yet they did not include the power to sell resources or transfer their use to people outside the lineage, unless all the men within the lineage consented to the deal. Hence an *Okonko* member who was not also an *ofo*-holder had little prospect of using his wealth to build up an extensive agricultural enterprise.[26]

Both *Okonko* members and *ofo*-holders suffered from a further difficulty, which was that an extensive agricultural enterprise was not necessarily a more productive one, able to generate wealth more quickly through its competitive edge over smaller rivals. Hopkins' classic statement that there were few economies of scale within West African export agriculture needs some qualification for the palm oil industry, but its social implications still hold firm. Two main caveats need to be made, both of which relate to the work of palm oil processing rather than the more strictly agricultural work of fruit supply. Firstly, as argued above, significant economies of scale were obtained by moving the site of pounding from the cooking pot to the canoe or tree stump. Secondly, twentieth-century experience has shown that, following the introduction of factory production in the Belgian Congo and South-East Asia from the 1920s, further economies of scale could be made within the new system of production. However, the early factories and hand-operated machinery probably offered few cost savings over the classic manual methods, and even this machinery was not available to hinterland Igbo palm oil producers in the nineteenth century. Meanwhile, the work of fruit supply was even less susceptible to economies of scale. In the absence of factories, whose effective operation has usually depended on a regular supply of fruit from plantations, large-scale cultivation had no economic advantage. Indeed, to have cultivated oil palms in the Ngwa region, with its abundant supply of semi-wild trees, would probably have put the grower at a distinct disadvantage by loading his oil-processing operations with extra overhead costs. In other words, once Ngwa men had moved into the palm oil industry in the early nineteenth century, they had no further opportunity to gain a competitive edge from economies of scale, whether by employing machinery or by using more people to plant palms. Access to more land, palms and people could enable a wealthy man to extend his enterprise, but not to construct a new one which would be different in kind from that of the junior male household head.[27]

Ambitious *Okonko* members would thus have found export agriculture a poor route to economic dominance. Like any other male household head, an *Okonko* member could easily have entered the palm oil industry, but would have found his growth prospects limited by the *ofo*-holders' strengthening grip on land and palms, and his ability to eliminate small competitors limited by his own lack of distinctive economic strengths. In the face of this dilemma an obvious alternative strategy would have been for *Okonko* members to seek dominance of the palm oil trade, in which their previous experience as slave-traders might well have been expected to give them a competitive edge. Northrup and Oriji have argued that this strategy too was fruitless, but it will be suggested below that their arguments exaggerate the case. During the first two-thirds of the nineteenth century the trading networks established to serve the Atlantic slave trade may well have carried palm oil too. The real threat to the trading dominance of *Okonko* came not from the early palm oil trade, but rather from the rise of the palm kernel trade and the shift in trade routes prompted by warfare after 1860.[28]

Northrup has argued that because palm oil was so heavy and bulky the new trade was largely confined to creeks and rivers rather than the overland routes favoured by the Aro. Along the Cross River in particular, Efik traders from Old Calabar began to venture up subsidiary creeks in search of direct contact with hinterland Ibibio middlemen. Northrup suggested that these middlemen may have been different from the groups who served the Aro. The new middlemen visited produce markets in daylight and bargained publicly for the oil. Similarly, in the case of the Ngwa and neighbouring Igbo groups, it is known that Bonny traders established new settlements in the Ndoki area during the 1820s to promote the palm oil trade and establish more direct contact with producers. Yet Northrup conceded that the Aro remained a powerful and wealthy group, and that they continued to dominate long-distance trade in many areas, including the Ngwa region. Northrup did not explain the exceptions to his rule, beyond stating that each Aro settlement was free to choose its own trading tactics. However, it is likely that during the first third of the nineteenth century, while the Atlantic slave trade was still heavy and the palm oil trade was relatively light, slaves were used to transport not only themselves but also palm oil from the drier hinterland regions towards the creeks and rivers. In the middle third of the century Hargreaves has shown that many slaves were imported to Bonny itself to man the new canoes of the creek-based palm oil trade, so that the Aro and their hinterland allies like the *Okonko* members could still have combined the two trades. Only in the 1860s did the established trade networks begin to disintegrate, firstly through warfare in the Ndoki region between Akwete and Ohambele, and then through the coastal wars between Bonny, Opobo and New Calabar.[29]

The eastward shift of hinterland trade routes towards Old Calabar after 1870 coincided with the slow rise of Ngwa women's incomes following the growth of the palm kernel export trade. At last women, who had long dominated the small-scale produce trade of the periodic markets, had the opportunity to sell valuable exports on their own account. They could begin to accumulate capital to finance palm oil as well as palm kernel trading operations. Some women may well have been aided financially by *ofo*-holding husbands, who were also able to order junior men to accompany them on their travels. Male help was vital in carrying the oil and in protecting travelling women traders, though the drawback of accepting family help rather than hiring male servants independently was that the female trader would almost certainly have had to pay a large share of her trading profits to her husband. Be that as it may, oral sources indicate that women played a prominent role in the palm oil trade of the Ndoki region by the end of the nineteenth century. Free Ngwa and Ndoki women were joined by slave women from Bonny, released from an earlier ban on travel away from the coast.[30]

The rise of female palm oil traders was quickly reversed following the colonial transport innovations of the early twentieth century, but meanwhile it posed a severe challenge to the wealth and status of *Okonko* members, reinforcing the damaging effects of the late nineteenth-century world trade depression. Oriji has suggested that they made up for lost trading income by taxing the established trade routes, but this is unlikely for two reasons. Firstly, by the time the *Okonko* trading system began to weaken the established trade routes were also disintegrating, as shown above. Secondly, Oriji's main source of evidence on the taxing of trade is highly suspect. The first European to travel through the Ngwa region, Major A. G. Leonard, saw three *Okonko* houses along his route to Bende in 1896. He guessed that they could be toll booths; but his guess was unsupported by any evidence from subsequent forays into the region, or from the economic surveys made by early colonial administrators. Northrup noted that no toll demands were made of Leonard's party, and it may be added that throughout his journey he seemed more under threat from his own fears than from the Ngwa. He assumed that an African visitor who failed to remove his hat had intended to insult him, and he saw swords, rifles, bows and arrows everywhere; but in sober fact no attempt was made to harm him.[31]

Three of the main strategies of adaptation as defined by Hopkins – continuing to trade in slaves; using slaves in agriculture and the produce trade; and exacting tribute by force from their small-scale rivals – had thus proved of limited value to *Okonko* members by the end of the nineteenth century. One final option remained: the reform of their own secret society so as to give the new export producers an increased stake in it. By the early twentieth century the *Okonko* society was becoming increasingly involved in village-level politics, taking upon itself the authority to recover debts and opening its membership to all men who were willing to pay for the privilege. It gained the reputation of being a good investment, as existing members shared in the fees paid by new recruits. Each new member also provided a feast for the rest. In this way, the erstwhile slave-traders became able to share in the new wealth of the *ofo*-holders; and the village judicial system was enriched by the *Okonko* members' links with Aro justice and experience of commercial disputes. As in the Hopkins model, this fourth strategy of adaptation was greatly hindered by the imposition of colonial rule. The colonial courts provided an alternative arena for settling debt claims and the more forceful displays of *Okonko*'s power were driven underground by administrators and missionaries. Yet the society survived and, as an association of title-takers, remains a respectable and prosperous bulwark of Ngwa society.[32]

Conclusion

The Ngwa-Igbo case provides a classic illustration of Hopkins' analysis of the 'crisis of adaptation'. Members of the *Okonko* society tried out the full range of strategies he identified, and found themselves under especially acute pressure during the late nineteenth-century world trade depression, as he would have expected. However, the history of the *ofo*-holders and their families fits far less neatly into Hopkins' blueprint. Ngwa lineage heads were certainly smallholders by comparison with the factory and plantation owners who now dominate the palm oil industry worldwide, but their society was both more fluid and more differentiated than in Hopkins' model. The rise of the palm oil industry brought changes in Ngwa agricultural operations, in the workloads of men and women, and in the balance of power between the sexes and the generations, but these were not unprecedented. Instead, they formed part of a series of incremental changes, driven by local demographic and ecological factors as well as by commercial contacts, which had already begun during the period of the Atlantic slave trade, and which were to continue in the twentieth century. There was no dramatic break with the past and no start of a distinctively 'modern' Ngwa economic history in the nineteenth century.[33]

The most important way in which nineteenth-century Ngwa palm oil producers differed from Hopkins' blueprint for 'modernity' was through the incorporation of households whose members had little access to capital, into lineages whose heads were comparatively wealthy. The transport innovations and fresh educational opportunities of the early twentieth century were to prompt a renewed struggle for independence on the part of junior men, but during the nineteenth century the growing shortage of virgin forest strengthened the hand of their seniors. In this way the tide of 'modernity' was held back by factors quite different from the commercial impulses transmitted from the Atlantic. However, this paper has strongly contested Oriji's contention that the tide had been not merely held, but actually turned back through the rise of domestic slavery in palm oil production.

Two main factors limited the usefulness of slaves in palm oil production. Firstly, the increasingly dense population of both people and palms in the Ngwa region rendered plantations redundant, and lifted the pressure on labour supplies which was closely associated with slave imports to other regions within eastern Nigeria. Secondly, the structure of social relations within the lineage gave lineage heads, the *ofo*-holders, strong property rights over the palm oil produced by their wives and daughters. Marriage remained an attractive alternative to the purchase of slaves. One implication of this was that most female producers of palm oil remained free to accumulate wealth on their own account when the palm kernel trade developed in the late nineteenth century, and a few women even emerged as prominent oil traders on the eve of colonial rule.

Many more case studies of nineteenth-century cash-cropping are needed before the Ngwa-Igbo case can be pronounced to be either an interesting oddity or a universal model. However, one general conclusion can be drawn even at this early stage. Models of smallholder-based export expansion can no longer assume that smallholder societies are undifferentiated or that commerce is the main force driving economic and social change within them. Future studies will need to focus on gender and generational differences as well as slavery, and on ecological and demographic pressures as well as trading incentives, in order to make sense of the transformations taking place at village level.

NOTES

1   A. G. Hopkins, *An Economic History of West Africa* (London, 1973), pp. 6, 124–5, 142, 226–9; the continuing scarcity of research on smallholders may be seen in the Appendix to the present volume. The further questions of how far West African smallholder societies have changed since the mid twentieth century, and hence of how far the 'modern' type as defined by Hopkins may still be accepted as 'modern', are tackled for the Ngwa-Igbo in S. M. Martin, *Palm Oil and Protest: An Economic History of the Ngwa Region, South-Eastern Nigeria, 1800–1980* (Cambridge, 1988), ch. 10.

2   P. E. Lovejoy, *Transformations in Slavery: A History of Slavery in Africa* (Cambridge, 1983), pp. 160, 183, 276; see also the Introduction and Martin Lynn's paper in this collection for fuller discussions of the 'crisis of adaptation' debate.

3   D. Northrup, *Trade Without Rulers: Pre-Colonial Economic Development in South-Eastern Nigeria* (Oxford, 1978), pp. 62–3, 120, 171–81.

4   This approach to hinterland Igbo social and economic history is discussed more fully in Northrup, *Trade Without Rulers*, pp. 7–10; Martin, *Palm Oil and Protest*, pp. 14–17.

5   Colonial Intelligence Reports on the Ngwa Clan, by J. Jackson, 1931, and by J. G. C. Allen, 1933, National Archives, Ibadan [hereafter, NAI]: CSO 26/29033, Vols. I and II; B. N. Ukegbu, 'Production in the Nigerian oil palm industry, 1900–1954' PhD thesis, University of London, 1974; J. N. Oriji, 'A History of the Ngwa people: social and economic developments in an Igbo clan from the thirteenth to the twentieth centuries', PhD thesis, State University of New Jersey, New Brunswick, 1977; and 'A re-assessment of the organization and benefits of the slave and palm produce trade among the Ngwa-Igbo', *CJAS*, 16 (1982), 523–48; and 'A study of the slave and palm produce trade amongst the Ngwa-Igbo of Southeastern Nigeria', *CEA*, 91, 23–3 (1983), 311–28; K. O. Dike, *Trade and Politics in the Niger Delta, 1830–1885* (Oxford, 1956); G. I. Jones, *Trading States of the Oil Rivers* (London, 1963); A.J.H. Latham, *Old Calabar, 1600–1891* (Oxford, 1973); Northrup, *Trade Without Rulers*. Oriji's interpretation has been incorporated into overviews of the 'crisis of adaptation' debate by, e.g., Lovejoy, *Transformations*, pp. 176–7; P. Manning, 'Slave trade, "legitimate" trade, and imperialism revisited: the control of wealth in the Bights of Benin and Biafra', in P. E. Lovejoy (ed.), *Africans in Bondage: Studies in Slavery and the Slave Trade* (Wisconsin, 1986), pp. 224–5.

6   Northrup, *Trade Without Rulers*, pp. 31–34, 164–71; Martin, *Palm Oil and Protest*, pp. 22–3; Allen, 'First Ngwa Report', NAI: CSO 26/29033, Vol. I, p. 14; Oriji, 'History of the Ngwa', pp. 40–8, 50–87, 130–6.

7   Sources – for the period 1450–1700, Northrup, *Trade Without Rulers*, pp. 50–4; for 1700–1810, D. Richardson, 'Slave exports from West and

West-Central Africa, 1700–1810: new estimates of volume and distribution', *JAH*, 30 (1989), 17, cited approvingly by P. E. Lovejoy, 'The impact of the Atlantic slave trade on Africa: a review of the literature', *JAH*, 30 (1989), 373–4; for 1821–67, research by D. Eltis cited in Lovejoy, 'The volume of the Atlantic slave trade: a synthesis', *JAH*, 23 (1982), 490–2; on the British Naval Squadron, D. Northrup, 'The compatibility of the slave and palm oil trades in the Bight of Biafra', *JAH*, 17 (1976), 357; for the early twentieth century, 'Report on the Southern Nigeria Census', 1911, Public Record Office, London [hereafter, PRO]: CO.592/9, f. 634.

8   Northrup, *Trade Without Rulers*, pp. 13, 65–84, 164–81; Martin, *Palm Oil and Protest*, pp. 26–7.

9   Oriji, 'History of the Ngwa', pp. 50–3, 130–6, 189–206.

10   Oriji, ibid., 189–206; 'Study of the slave and palm produce trade', pp. 313–7.

11   Sources – on crops, tools and gender roles: Martin, *Palm Oil and Protest*, p. 23; S. M. Martin, 'Gender and innovation: farming, cooking and palm processing in the Ngwa Region, South-Eastern Nigeria, 1900–1930', *JAH*, 25 (1984), 411–27; on slave exports, Northrup, *Trade Without Rulers*, pp. 77–8; D. Eltis, 'The volume, age/sex ratios, and African impact of the slave trade: some refinements of Paul Lovejoy's review of the literature', *JAH*, 31 (1990), 489.

12   Northrup, *Trade Without Rulers*, pp. 178, 184–92.

13   Northrup, *Trade Without Rulers*, pp. 183, 191–4; Latham, *Old Calabar*, Appendix I; S. M. Hargreaves, 'The political economy of nineteenth-century Bonny: a study of power, authority, legitimacy and ideology in a Delta community from 1790 to 1914', PhD thesis, University of Birmingham, 1987, pp. 183–4, 197–8, 284–309; M. Lynn, 'From sail to steam: the impact of the steamship services on the British palm oil trade with West Africa, 1850–1890', *JAH*, 30 (1989), 241.

14   Latham, *Old Calabar*, pp. 70–5; Northrup, *Trade Without Rulers*, pp. 208–14; C. W. Newbury, 'Prices and profitability in early nineteenth-century West African trade', in C. Meillassoux (ed.), *The Development of Indigenous Trade and Markets in West Africa* (Oxford, 1971), pp. 93–4; A. J. H. Latham, 'Price fluctuations in the early palm oil trade', *JAH*, 19 (1978), 213–4; Lynn, 'Sail to steam', pp. 227–231; Martin, *Palm Oil and Protest*, pp. 45–6, 144–5.

15   Latham, *Old Calabar*, Appendix 2; Martin, *Palm Oil and Protest*, pp. 45–8, 152–3.

16   Martin, *Palm Oil and Protest*, pp. 46–7; A. G. Hopkins, 'Innovation in a colonial context: African origins of the Nigerian cocoa-farming industry, 1880–1920', in C. Dewey and A. G. Hopkins (eds.), *The Imperial Impact* (London, 1978), pp. 83–96; K. Arhin, 'The economic and social significance of rubber production and exchange on the Gold and Ivory Coasts, 1880–1900', *CEA*, 20 (1980), 49–62.

17   Latham, *Old Calabar*, pp. 92, 116 ; Hargreaves, 'Political economy of Bonny', pp. 95–7.

18   Hopkins, *Economic History*, p. 125; Lovejoy, *Transformations*, pp. 160, 183, 276; Oriji, 'Study of the slave and palm produce trade', pp. 318–23.

19   Martin, *Palm Oil and Protest*, pp. 23–6.

20   Ukegbu, 'Production in the Nigerian Oil Palm Industry', pp. 25–55; J. H. J. Farquhar, *The Oil Palm and Its Varieties* (ed. and revised by H. N. Thompson, London, 1913), pp. 13–14, 24–6.

21   Sources as previous note, and 'Annual Report on the Eastern Province, Southern Nigeria, 1907', PRO: CO.592/3, p. 32; 'Report on the Cultivation of Oil Palms', 1908, National Archives, Enugu [hereafter, NAE]: Calprof 14/3/807, E 2760/8.

22   Oriji, 'Study of the slave and palm produce trade', pp. 323; D. Northrup, 'Nineteenth-century patterns of slavery and economic growth in South-Eastern Nigeria', *IJAHS*, 12 (1979), 1–16; Granville, 'Report on the Ozoakoli Slave Market', 10 June 1902, NAI: Calprof 10/3, Vol. III; Allen, 'First Ngwa Report', NAI: CSO 26/29033, Vol. I, p. 70; Miller, 'Report on Slave Dealing and Child Stealing, Southern Provinces', 14 June 1934, NAI: CSO 26/28994.

23   Interviews conducted in the Ngwa region with Patrick Ikonne Ndubisi, Chief I. W. Ebere and Augustine Amaeze Nwogu, Jan.–Feb. 1981. A full list of other interviews may be found in Martin, *Palm Oil and Protest*, p. 191.

24   For comparative case studies, see C. C. Robertson and M. A. Klein (eds.), *Women and Slavery in Africa* (Madison, 1983).

25   Martin, *Palm Oil and Protest*, ch. 8, examines the ways in which junior men sought to improve their marriage prospects in the early twentieth century.

26   Ukegbu, 'Production in the Nigerian Oil Palm Industry', pp. 30–6, 42–44; H. S. Burrough, 'Report on Land Tenure in Aba District', 31 Oct. 1912, enclosure in Lugard to Harcourt, 19 Feb. 1913, PRO: CO.520/122; Allen, 'First Ngwa Report', NAI: CSO 26/29033, Vol. I, pp. 33–4. Oriji, 'Study of the slave and palm produce trade', p. 321, noted this pattern of oil palm property rights but asserted that it has always existed.

27   Hopkins, *Economic History*, p. 125; J. H. Maycock, 'The developments in palm oil factory design since the early 1900s', *The Planter*, 51 (1975), 335ff.; 'The African palm oil industry – III, Machinery', *Bulletin of the Imperial Institute*, 15 (1917), 57–78; W. K. Hancock, *A Survey of British Commonwealth Affairs*, Vol. II, Part 2 (London, 1942), pp. 188–200.

28   Oriji, 'Study of the slave and palm produce trade', pp. 322–5; Northrup, 'Compatibility', pp. 361–2.

29   Northrup, *Trade Without Rulers*, pp. 199–207; Dike, *Trade and Politics*, pp. 69, 99; Hargreaves, 'Political Economy of Bonny', pp. 47, 268, 299.

30   Interview with Chief J. Isaac Wabara and Dr A. Epelle of Ohambele, 18 Jan. 1981; Oriji, 'Study of the slave and palm produce trade', pp. 323–4; Hargreaves, 'Political Economy of Bonny', p. 97.

31   H. S. Burrough, 'Commercial Notes on Aba District', June 1912, NAE: Rivprof 3/5/104, file E 3031/11; interviews with Chief Wabara and in the Ngwa region with Oji Akpuka, Dec. 1980–Jan. 1981; Oriji, 'Study of the slave and palm produce trade', p. 319; Northrup, *Trade Without Rulers*, pp. 155–6; A. G. Leonard, 'Notes of a journey to Bende', *Journal of the Manchester Geographical Society*, 14 (1898), 190–207.

32   Hopkins, *Economic History*, pp. 142–5; Oriji, 'Study of the slave and palm produce trade', p. 316. Oriji does not put a date to the transformation of

Okonko, but a detailed account of late nineteenth- and early twentieth-century changes is provided by Allen, 'First Ngwa Report', NAI: CSO 26/29033, Vol. I, pp. 76–8, and Allen to D.O. Aba, 17 July 1933, NAE: Abadist 1/26/278, file 529.

33 Hopkins, *Economic History*, pp. 124–5, 142–5, 154; twentieth-century Ngwa history is surveyed in Martin, *Palm Oil and Protest*, chs. 3–10.

8 'Legitimate' trade and gender relations in Yorubaland and Dahomey

Robin Law

Although there has been much interest of late in the history of gender relations in Africa, relatively little has been done in studying these issues specifically in the pre-colonial period.[1] In part, this may reflect a perception that there are insufficient detailed and reliable data to permit the reconstruction of the earlier history of gender relations in Africa; but one may also suspect the persisting influence of an assumption of effective social stasis in the pre-colonial period, implicit in the still common use of extrapolation from twentieth-century ethnography to provide an imputed cultural background for pre-colonial history. In fact, there is quite a bit of relevant evidence for the pre-colonial period, in contemporary European accounts of African societies. In particular, it seems possible to consider the implications for gender relations of the two great transformations in the character of West Africa's overseas commerce, the rise of the Atlantic slave trade in the seventeenth century and its replacement by 'legitimate' trade in the nineteenth. This essay considers the implications of the ending of the slave trade and the expansion of 'legitimate' trade (principally in palm oil and kernels) for gender relations in one specific region of West Africa, the neighbouring areas of Yorubaland and Dahomey (south-western Nigeria/southern Bénin). In intention it is exploratory and to some degree speculative rather than definitive or conclusive, raising questions rather than pro-posing clear answers to them.[2]

The slave trade impacted on gender roles in two ways. First, both raiding for and trading in slaves were predominantly male enterprises: although there were some female slave-traders, such as (in Yorubaland) the famous Tinubu of mid nineteenth century Lagos and Abeokuta, these were clearly exceptional.[3] Secondly, a majority of the slaves exported were men – though the ratio of men to women appears to have been lower among slaves exported from Dahomey and Yorubaland than elsewhere in West Africa.[4] Tony Hopkins in his pioneering study of West African economic history published in 1973 raised the issue of whether the export of males for the Atlantic slave trade may have affected the sexual division of labour within West Africa, but noted cautiously that 'generalisation on this issue is difficult, partly because of lack of information, and partly because the division of labour between the sexes was by no means the same in all West African societies'.[5] It may be noted here that evidence from the Dahomey area, although fragmentary, tends to support the proposition of a shift in sexual roles. At any rate, in the coastal kingdom of Whydah in the 1690s (prior to its conquest by Dahomey) it was noted that, unlike on the Gold Coast to the west, 'men as well as women ... are ... vigorously industrious and laborious', and in particular that males undertook agricultural work, from which 'the King and a few great men only are exempted'.[6] In Dahomey itself, in contrast, the English trader Robert Norris in the 1780s reported that 'the men sleep and smoke', leaving 'the whole task of agriculture' to fall upon the women.[7]

The ending of the Atlantic slave trade and its replacement by 'legitimate' trade in agricultural produce such as palm oil might be expected to have had an equal if not greater significance for gender questions, not only because more enslaved males were now being retained within West Africa but also because, unlike the slave trade, agricultural production generally and the making of palm oil in particular were, at least in many West African societies, predominantly female occupations. Hopkins himself, although noting the preponderance of female labour in production for 'legitimate' trade, did not pursue the implications of this, merely recommending the topic as one which 'merits further research'.[8] The question seems, however, to have attracted little attention in subsequent literature. At any rate, a recent survey of the historiography of the commercial transition of the nineteenth century fails almost entirely to mention gender issues, and I would like to believe (since it was I who wrote it) that this reflects the lack of published research on the issue rather than the limitations of the author's perspective.[9]

The only previously published account which addresses the gender aspect of 'legitimate' commerce is the study of the palm produce trade in the Ngwa area of Igboland by Susan Martin.[10] Palm oil production there was originally a female occupation, but Martin argued that with the development of an export trade in the oil men entered directly into the production process; although women's labour was still required, the men now appropriated most of the product (though women retained control of the palm kernels, which were also exported). Although Martin's analysis was essentially concerned with developments in the twentieth century, in her contribution to the present volume she has elaborated her argument with more extended reference to the pre-colonial period. The cases of Yorubaland and Dahomey studied here present both similarities

(in terms of the critical role played by female labour in palm oil
production and trading) and contrasts (in terms of the relative autonomy
of female oil producers and traders) with that of the Igbo.

Large-scale and small-scale enterprise

Part of the context in which the issue of the impact of 'legitimate' trade
on gender relations has to be considered is the debate over the relative
importance of small-scale and large-scale production in it. Hopkins
argued that, whereas the slave trade had been dominated by a small
number of large entrepreneurs, the production and trading of agricultural produce could be carried out on a small scale, enabling the mass of
the population to enter the export trade; but this has been contested by
others, such as Ralph Austen, who maintain that existing chiefs and
large-scale merchants were generally able to dominate the new trade as
they had the old.[11]

Hopkins' analysis, although subsequently generalized to the whole of
coastal West Africa, was originally worked out with reference to the
specific case of Yorubaland. While acknowledging that 'a considerable
proportion' of the palm produce exported from Yorubaland was produced by 'a relatively small group of large producers' employing slave
labour, he argued that there was also 'a large number of small producers'.[12] In a critique of Hopkins, Julian Clarke maintained that palm oil
production in nineteenth-century Yorubaland continued to be dominated
by the large households of the major war-chiefs, and that independent
small-scale farmers did not emerge until the colonial period – though
not, it must be said, on the basis of very much concrete data, and more
especially without any detailed confrontation with the available contemporary evidence for the nineteenth century.[13]

Some of the contemporary evidence for Yorubaland in the nineteenth
century does support an emphasis on large-scale production of palm oil.
The American Baptist missionary William Clarke, who travelled widely
in Yorubaland in the 1850s, for example, observed that 'The extracting
of the ... oil in the palm districts employs a large number of labourers
and presents more the appearance of a manufactory than any other
department of labour. I have seen establishments of this kind where
perhaps fifty persons or more were engaged in labour.'[14] Another
American Baptist missionary, R. H. Stone, who lived at Ijaye in 1859–62,
also describes palm oil production in terms which imply large-scale
enterprise, involving an elaborated division of labour: 'One set of women
separates the nuts from their integuments, another boils them in large
earthen pots and still another crushes off the fibre from the kernel nut in

large mortars', prior to actual treading and further boiling.[15] The predominance of large-scale establishments in the export trade in Yorubaland is also suggested by the observations of the British Consul William Baikie in the 1860s (though with regard to cotton rather than palm oil). Baikie reported that in Nupe, north-east of Yorubaland across the Niger, as many as three-quarters of the farming population, including slaves as well as freemen, were 'at liberty to have their own farms and sell the bulk of their own crops', and that such 'small farmers' would be the principal beneficiaries of any growth in cotton exports; he even speculated that the profits they derived from selling cotton would enable many slaves in Nupe to purchase their freedom. But he interestingly contrasted this situation with that in Yorubaland, where 'more is produced by large traders' and where in consequence the growth of the cotton trade had reinforced rather than undermined slavery, causing 'an increased demand and price for slaves'.[16]

Such evidence, however, is by no means in contradiction to Hopkins' analysis, which explicitly acknowledged the importance of large-scale production. Other contemporary reports, in fact, make clear that there was small-scale enterprise in the oil trade in Yorubaland also. At the coastal port of Lagos, the British Consul Benjamin Campbell in 1854, for example, noted that whereas the slave trade had been 'confined to the King, his Chiefs and principal people', who had therefore had to provide for the maintenance of their slaves, now the latter could maintain themselves by trading independently in palm oil and other articles.[17] Likewise in the interior, the missionary David Hinderer, resident at Ibadan, in 1860 reported that the development of the oil trade had enabled 'numbers of young men' there to enrich themselves, 'simply from at first carrying palm oil from the interior, and ultimately trading in it and other things up and down the country'.[18]

In the case of Dahomey, a study by Catherine Coquery-Vidrovitch, although stressing the prominence of palm oil production by the 'caboceers' or chiefs, on 'vast plantations' employing slave labour, also acknowledged the involvement of 'a mass of small traders', who by implication were mainly women.[19] The main evidence she cited for the coexistence of large- and small-scale suppliers was that of the British naval officer Frederick Forbes, on a mission to Dahomey in 1850, who reported seeing palm oil traders arriving at the factory of the Brazilian merchant José Francisco dos Santos at the coastal port of Whydah, 'some with only a gallon, others having slaves loaded with large calabashes of oil'.[20] More explicitly, the French missionary Laffitte, who resided at Whydah in 1861–4, while noting the existence of 'immense plantations of palms' owned by the king and chiefs, also observed that 'every free black possesses a few feet of them', and indeed that even slaves 'pilfer a little everywhere'.[21] The French trader Chaudoin, who was at Whydah in 1890 (and taken captive on the outbreak of hostilities between Dahomey and France in that year) likewise distinguished three categories of merchants in Dahomey: the 'great traders', the king's agents, and 'the small merchant [petit marchand]' – the last of whom 'provides for his subsistence by exchanging a few pots of oil in the factories against goods, which he will sell piecemeal, in the markets'.[22]

Contemporary accounts of Dahomey are less clear than those relating to Yorubaland as to whether references to large 'plantations' are to be understood as implying the large-scale cooperative organization of labour (and the appropriation of the entire product by the owner), or merely large concentrations of slaves, who operated as independent producers (while paying a rent or duty to their master). The British official Archibald Ridgway, however, visiting a 'palm-oil manufactory' near Whydah in 1847, did describe a team of workers treading out the oil in a coordinated manner: in a pit measuring 12 by 6 feet, he saw 'as many men as could stand abreast .... keeping time to the measured cadence of a song by a kind of overseer, who stood outside and regulated their movements'.[23]

While the coexistence of large-scale and small-scale production in both Yorubaland and Dahomey seems clearly established, it may be suggested that the importance of the latter is indirectly attested by the role of cowry shells, used locally as currency, among the goods imported in exchange for palm oil. The connection between oil exports and cowry imports was explicitly noted, with regard to the eastern Gold Coast, by the British official Brodie Cruickshank, who argued that the take-off of palm oil exports from that region in the 1830s had been made possible by the introduction there of the cowry currency, which was 'capable of great sub-division' and therefore adapted for payment to small-scale producers.[24] The link between cowry imports and the palm oil trade was also noted in Yorubaland, where traders bringing palm oil from Abeokuta to Lagos in 1855 were reported to 'insist on being paid for their oil in great part with the cowrie shell, which is the currency of the country, instead of taking manufactured goods in payment'.[25] Cowries had, of course, been imported into Yorubaland and Dahomey in exchange for slaves earlier, but whereas in the slave trade cowries were usually paid out in bulk (by weight or measure), in the oil trade they were commonly *counted* out, implying smaller-scale transactions. Several accounts of the oil trade in Dahomey observed that the counting out of cowries was a prominently visible feature of it. Ridgway in 1847, for example, visiting the British factory at Whydah, saw 'a number of women who were occupied in counting out a cask of cowries'; and Forbes in 1850, in dos Santos's factory, observed that 'dozens of his own slaves were counting out cowries to pay for the produce'.[26]

Slave and free

The gender dimension of 'legitimate' trade has also to be considered in the light of the relationship between slavery and free labour. Here it should be stressed that the distinction between slavery and free labour is not necessarily co-extensive with that between large-scale and small-scale production, as is sometimes implicitly assumed. Baikie's evidence, cited above, shows that in Nupe many slaves were able to operate as independent producers, paying a duty to their owners but otherwise retaining control of the product and profits of their labour. Although Baikie himself contrasted this arrangement with the large-scale production which he said was more characteristic of Yorubaland, other evidence shows that in at least some contexts slaves could operate as independent petty entrepreneurs there also. In Lagos, for example, the slaves engaged in palm oil commerce, noted by Consul Campbell in the report of 1854 quoted earlier, were clearly trading on their own account. Indeed, in another report a few years later, Campbell stated that the wealth so derived could be used by these slaves to purchase their freedom: 'The acquisition of property, earned by their own labour and industry, has naturally led to the desire, on the part of many domestic slaves, to purchase their own freedom from their masters'.[27]

In Dahomey, a report by Brodie Cruickshank, on a mission there in 1848, although not referring specifically to trade in palm oil, attests the existence of a similar system: 'It appears to be a general practice, with the masters of slaves, to permit them to prosecute their own affairs, and to receive in exchange for this concession, a stipulated monthly sum derived from their labour'. As in Lagos also, Cruickshank asserts that a slave in Dahomey was 'sometimes' able to redeem himself with the profits of his work, by paying the value of two slaves as the price of redemption.[28] Likewise Chaudoin in 1890 noted that the petty trader in Dahomey was sometimes a slave, who worked on his own account, while paying a duty to his master.[29]

It should be noted further, in the case of those slaves who were employed in classic 'plantations' rather than as autonomous producers, that even though the system theoretically prevented such independent accumulation, slaves might in practice be able to engage in illicit enterprise. Laffitte's reference in Dahomey in the 1860s to the stealing of oil by slaves was quoted earlier. As Laffitte observed, efforts by owners to repress such thefts were ineffective: 'The owner's cane lashes their shoulders from time to time to impress upon them the distinction between yours and mine; but they only wait for their shoulders to heal to resume the robbery'.[30] Chaudoin also states that those slaves who operated as 'small merchants' had 'generally' obtained their original capital by stealing from their masters.[31]

Male and female

The sexual division of labour

The differential roles of the sexes in the production and export of palm oil have to be related to the more general (and, insofar as the evidence permits its reconstruction, pre-existing) sexual division of labour. This can conveniently be considered under the separate headings of agriculture, trade and transport.

First, as regards agricultural production – in the case of Yorubaland, the first European explorer in the area, Hugh Clapperton, travelling through the Oyo kingdom in 1825/6, observed that 'all the labour of the land' devolved upon women.[32] This is, however, contradicted by subsequent evidence. The American Baptist missionary Thomas Bowen, who travelled widely in Yorubaland in the 1850s, for example, observed that 'women never cultivate the soil as they do in [Upper] Guinea'.[33] His fellow Baptist missionary William Clarke was even more emphatic: 'The females ... are never known to cultivate the farms ... The males are the only class on whom this duty devolves.' Although he did note that women assisted in the harvest and in carrying produce home from the farm, 'so strong is the aversion of the native mind to this kind of female servitude that I have yet to see the first instance of a woman engaged, hoe in hand, in cultivating the earth'.[34] The Yoruba Christian clergyman (and pioneer local historian) Samuel Johnson, later in the nineteenth century, likewise presents farming as primarily men's work, although he too notes that 'women and children assist in reaping and bringing the harvest home'.[35]

The contradiction between Clapperton and later accounts on this issue is not easy to explain. It is conceivable that it reflects a real change during the course of the nineteenth century, women having originally undertaken a greater share of agricultural labour but being largely withdrawn from it with the rise of the export trade in palm oil, since the manufacture of palm oil was a predominantly female occupation. It is possible, however, that Clapperton was misled by the time of his journey through Yorubaland (in December/January), which coincided with the second (lesser) harvest season, since women (as noted by Clarke and Johnson) did take some part in harvesting. Although women in Yoruba-land may have played little role in farming, however, it is clear that they handled the processing of crops, including (as will be seen below) the manufacture of palm oil.

In Dahomey, in contrast to Yorubaland, most agricultural labour appears to have been undertaken by women. Robert Norris in the 1780s, as quoted earlier, claimed that 'the whole task of agriculture' fell upon women; and he also alludes to the fact that the king's plantations were cultivated by women.[36] Later evidence shows that this was something of an oversimplification, but confirms the preponderant role of women. Vallon, leader of a French mission to Dahomey in 1856, for example, noted that the man undertook the initial clearing and planting, but 'thereafter he rests or goes to war', implying that the subsequent tending and harvesting was done by the women.[37] Vallon's account is, in turn, consistent with twentieth-century ethnographic evidence, which likewise reports that the land was cleared and planted by the men, but the crops then tended and harvested by women.[38]

In the area around the Dahomian capital Abomey, in the interior, where water was scarce and had to be brought from sources at some distance from the city, the situation was somewhat different. According to Frederick Forbes in 1849–50, much of women's labour here was taken up in fetching water, and consequently 'unlike the rest of Africa, men labour in the fields'.[39] The diversion of women's labour into the supply of water here, it may be noted, may possibly have reflected in part the expansion of the export trade in palm oil, since (as noted by Susan Martin in the Ngwa case) great quantities of water were required for the processing of the oil, especially for the initial boiling of the fruits.

Secondly, as regards trade – petty trade, and especially trade in foodstuffs (including palm oil) for the domestic market, was even more clearly a predominantly female occupation. In Yorubaland, the earliest European explorer, Clapperton in 1826, visiting the market at Kulfo, in Nupe north-east of Oyo, noted that the 'small traders' (also distinguished as 'those who sell their goods for cowries', i.e. retail, as opposed to wholesale) there, who came from Oyo (and also from Borgu, north-west of Oyo) were 'nine out of ten women'.[40] Likewise Richard and John Lander in 1830, at Igan, in northern Egbado, observed that 'women here are the chief, if not the only traders'.[41] The American missionary Bowen in the 1850s, similarly asserted that trade was pursued by 'a good many men, and still more women', and that 'the women ... buy and sell most of the provisions which pass through the market'.[42]

Petty trade was similarly a predominantly female occupation in

Dahomey. A visitor to the coastal port of Whydah in the 1780s noted that 'except for the slave trade which is the province of the men, trading of all kinds is left to women'.[43] This is consistently corroborated by nineteenth-century evidence. Forbes in 1849, for example, noted of the markets at Abomey that all the stalls 'are owned and are generally attended, by women, the wives of all classes and orders, from the miegans [i.e. the Migan, the highest-ranking chief in Dahomey after the king] to the blacksmiths'.[44] The French officer Bouet, on a mission to Dahomey in 1851, similarly reported that 'the women alone do the trade in the markets'.[45] The British Consul (and pioneer anthropologist) Richard Burton, visiting the market of Whydah in 1863 also observed that those attending it were 'especially women'.[46] Likewise Chaudoin in 1890 confirms that it was the woman who 'in the markets monopolizes all the petty trade'.[47] The same picture is given also in twentieth-century ethnography, which reports that traders were 'principally women, for there are few Dahomean men who engage in traffic'.[48]

This dominance of women in petty trade in both Yorubaland and Dahomey has a bearing on the export trade in oil, inasmuch as if the latter did indeed involve (as Hopkins suggested) a multiplicity of small producers, and therefore required a large number of small-scale intermediaries to market their produce, it was women traders who would naturally have filled this role.

Thirdly, transport. In Yorubaland and Dahomey, except where canoe transport along the rivers and coastal lagoons was available, goods (including palm produce) were normally moved by human porters, carried on the head. Women clearly played a major role in such head porterage.[49] In Yorubaland, Clapperton in 1825, on the road north from Badagry, observed that those carrying cloth, plantains and akasan (maize cakes) to market were 'principally women'.[50] Bowen, travelling from Badagry to Abeokuta in 1850, recorded meeting 'numbers of men, women and children' carrying palm oil, foodstuffs and firewood to the Badagry market; and Stone, on his way from Abeokuta to Ijaye in 1859, likewise met 'hundreds of carriers of both sexes', carrying palm oil and ivory to the coast.[51] Their colleague Clarke observed more generally that in Yorubaland 'females ... are the principal bearers of burdens'.[52]

These accounts do not make clear whether the women carrying burdens referred to were petty traders working on their own account, or slaves or hired porters working for larger-scale traders. Some evidence suggests that professional porters in Yorubaland may have been mainly male. Clapperton in 1825 and the Landers in 1830, for their journeys from Badagry to Oyo, and Bowen in 1850, from Badagry to Abeokuta, for example, all note explicitly that the porters they hired were men.[53]

However, Stone on his way from Abeokuta to Ijaye in 1859 hired both female and male porters.[54]

While the evidence for Yorubaland is too fragmentary to sustain an inference that the use of female labour for porterage was increasing, in Dahomey this suggestion is perhaps somewhat stronger. Eighteenth-century accounts of the hiring of porters by European traders in the Dahomian port of Whydah do not specify their sex, which can perhaps reasonably be interpreted to imply that they were male.[55] Ridgway in 1847, however, for his journey from Whydah to the capital Abomey, recorded engaging 40 women among his bearers, observing that women 'it must be remembered, are in this country as much, if not more, accustomed to hard labour than men'.[56] Forbes in 1849 likewise hired 16 men and 20 women to carry his baggage, and in 1850 20 men and 40 women carriers.[57]

This apparent increase in the use of women as porters by the mid nineteenth century may possibly reflect the demands of the expanding oil trade. The physical quantities involved in the nineteenth-century palm produce trade were very great, a ton of palm oil representing over 300 gallons, which would have required around 60 porters to move. The expanded demand for porterage arising from this may have necessitated an increasing resort to the employment of females for the purpose.

The palm produce trade

Given the important role played generally by women in the areas of agriculture, trade and transport (despite differences between the two areas) in both Yorubaland and Dahomey, it should be unsurprising that the weight of the available contemporary evidence demonstrates clearly that the manufacture and export of palm oil was, to a large degree, a female business.

In Yorubaland, Clarke in the 1850s observed that women undertook 'all household duties and many other departments of labour that require confinement within the walls', including 'the making and extracting of oil'.[58] Likewise his colleague Stone in the 1860s: 'The women ... make .. palm-oil'; although it was the men who climbed the trees to harvest the fruits, 'the oil is extracted by women'.[59] Samuel Johnson in the late nineteenth century still observes that the making of palm oil (and also of palm kernel oil and shea-butter) were 'exclusively female industries'.[60] When palm kernels began to be exported (from the 1860s), the work of shelling the palm nuts to extract the kernels was probably also done mainly by women, though the evidence on this is less clear-cut. The British trader John Whitford, active at Lagos in the 1860s and 70s, states that the shelling of nuts was done by the young and old of both sexes – 'girls and boys and old men and women'; but Johnson asserts that it was done more specifically by the 'aged women'.[61]

It is also clear that women were prominent in the trading of palm produce to the coast, as well as its initial production. As Consul Campbell noted of Lagos in 1858, for example, 'it is the women that trade at the oil markets'.[62] Likewise John Whitford, on a voyage through the lagoons in 1865, observed that the passengers on the canoes carrying palm oil, kernels and foodstuffs to Lagos were 'chiefly women traders'.[63]

The identification of palm oil as women's work was, indeed, so strong in Yorubaland as to constitute an ideological obstacle to it as an alternative to the slave trade. Traders from Abeokuta, complaining about the low prices paid for palm oil at Lagos in 1855, thus recalled that when they had originally been asked by the British to give up the slave trade (i.e. in the 1840s),

Shodeke [the chief of Abeokuta] called all the Egbas [people of Abeokuta], told them that the Queen say that they must not sell slaves any more; so they asked Shodeke what work they are to do when they leave off selling slaves. Then Shodeke asked the white man what to do after [they] leave off from selling slaves. The white man told them to trade palm oil; so they ask how is that – is not a woman to sell palm oil, how can a man sell oil like a woman?[64]

The situation in Dahomey is less clear-cut, but there too women appear to have played the predominant role in oil production and exporting. Vallon in the 1850s was categorical on this point:

The woman alone is charged with gathering the fruits, preparing the oil and bringing it to the factories ... It is very rare to see a man come to Whydah for this purpose, unless he is accompanying his wife to carry off the sack of cowries or the cloths which she receives in exchange.[65]

Other evidence confirms the predominance of women in the delivery of oil to the coast. Ridgway in 1847, for example, at the British factory at Whydah, reported seeing 'a constant influx into the fort of women, bearing large pots of palm oil on their heads'; the context implies that these were petty traders selling on their own account, rather than hired or slave porters working for a male trader.[66] The king of Dahomey's palm oil, according to the British explorer J. A. Skertchly in 1871, was carried to the coast by 'Amazon gangs of oil carriers', referring probably to female slaves attached to the royal palace rather than to 'Amazons' in the strict sense of the king's contingent of female soldiers.[67]

The situation as regards the production of palm oil is less clear-cut. The implication in Vallon's account that women undertook the harvesting of fruits, as well as the extraction of oil, is supported by the report of the British explorer John Duncan, referring to Sierra Leonean repatriates settled at Whydah in the 1840s, that their men were supported by the work of the females, including laundry and 'collecting palm-nuts for making oil' (though this may not have been representative of the indigenous Dahomean population).[68] Nowadays, however, the climbing of trees to cut down the fruits is normally done in Dahomey, as in Yorubaland, by men. It may be that the nineteenth-century accounts refer only to the collection of windfalls.

In the extraction of oil from the fruits, a second member of the French mission of 1856, Dr Repin, supports the view that female labour was used exclusively, sneering that 'while their lord drinks, sleeps or smokes, [his women] make the palm oil'. Another French official, in the 1880s, likewise observes that the treading out of the oil was done by 'the women, all naked'. Chaudoin in 1890, more ambiguously, reported that treading was done by a man's 'wives and slaves', which may imply that male as well as female slaves were involved; but he also says that the shelling of kernels was 'very often' done by the wives.[69]

Other evidence, however, points to a significant role for male labour in the production of palm oil in Dahomey. Ridgway in 1847 (as cited earlier) explicitly noted that those treading out oil in the 'palm-oil manufactory' which he visited were men. Burton in 1864 stated that the treading of palm oil was done 'by both sexes'; while Skertchly in 1871 said that the treading was done by a 'workman or workwoman'.[70] It seems possible that in Dahomey males, and perhaps especially male slaves, played a bigger role in the production of oil when increased output for export was demanded, creating a shortage of labour (especially as women here took a larger part than in Yorubaland in general agricultural labour). This is, indeed, implied in the observation of a French naval officer in 1844, in the early days of the export trade in palm oil from Dahomey, that local merchants were using slaves to produce palm oil, instead of exporting them; as most of the slaves exported earlier had been men, this implies that male slaves were now being used to produce palm oil.[71]

That male labour played an important role in oil production in Dahomey is also implied by European complaints that mobilization for war under King Glele (1858–89), who reasserted Dahomey's traditional militarism, was undermining the oil trade. The French trader (and Vice-Consul) Béraud in 1866, for example, complained that military mobilization left only 'the women and a few more or less healthy men' to collect the fruits, prepare the oil and deliver it to the factories.[72] This seems strictly to imply that men (and indeed, more specifically free men, since slaves were not normally conscripted into the Dahomian army) would otherwise have been available for oil production. However, it may be that military mobilization interfered more particularly with the initial harvesting of the palm fruits, which, as suggested earlier, was probably done mainly by men. Moreover, it should be noted that military mobilization in Dahomey diverted female as well as male labour away from other activities: as a British observer noted in 1862, not only were some women as well as men recruited into the army (as the king's 'Amazons' or female soldiers), but in addition 'the rest of the [women]' were conscripted to carry provisions for the army.[73]

Social implications

While the predominant importance of female labour in the palm oil trade in Yorubaland and Dahomey seems clear enough, the implications of this for gender relations are difficult to determine. For this question, it is of course necessary to distinguish between the conditions of large-scale and small-scale production. In those cases where men organized large-scale enterprises, using the labour of their wives and female slaves, they presumably also appropriated the profits, and their womenfolk thereby suffered an intensified exploitation and subordination. Not all large-scale enterprise in the oil trade was controlled by men: the prominent female merchant Tinubu of mid nineteenth-century Lagos, for example, traded in palm oil as well as slaves, and at the time of her expulsion from Lagos in 1856 was reported to owe oil to the value of over £5,000 – equivalent, at current prices, to 250 tons – to traders there.[74] But in general, the implications of large-scale production for women were probably negative.

In those cases, however, where women were able to operate as independent producers and traders, potentially at least, their ability to earn money in the oil trade strengthened their economic position, and increased their independence *vis-à-vis* their menfolk. According to Consul Campbell in 1858, this was indeed precisely the effect of the palm oil trade at Lagos. Noting the tendency there of slaves to operate independently and aspire to freedom, he observed specifically that 'this desire is strongly evinced by women who are in the unfortunate position of slaves, more strongly so if they are mothers and have children living'. Because of the dominance of such female slaves in the palm oil trade, he noted further, 'many of them by care or frugality soon amass sufficient cowries to pay a heavy sum for the redemption of themselves and their children'. However, Campbell also noted that, while masters were generally ready to allow male slaves to redeem themselves, they were less willing to emancipate their female slaves: 'It is the unfortunate female slave who meets with difficulty in obtaining the redemption of herself and her children, particularly if they happen to be daughters ... the masters often show great unwillingness to part with them.' Although Campbell himself in his capacity as British Consul interceded in their support, such women now had to pay 'an exorbitant rate compared to the price formerly paid'. According to Campbell, the differential treatment of male and female slaves was due to the calculation that males, if not granted manumission, would simply abscond.[75] An additional factor, however, may have been that female labour, with the rise of the oil trade, was more valuable.

If women slaves through the oil trade acquired new opportunities for independent accumulation, one would *a fortiori* expect this to be true also of free wives. Clapperton and Richard Lander in the 1820s understood that the wives of the king of Oyo who engaged in petty trade did so on his behalf, and paid over their profits to him.[76] If this was correct, however, it must be supposed either that these royal women were treated differently from the generality of wives, or that conditions subsequently changed in women's favour (perhaps in consequence of the development of the palm oil trade?). Bowen in the 1850s noted explicitly that in Yorubaland 'every woman is a free dealer, who labors for herself and supports herself'. Although the husband could reclaim the brideprice in case of divorce, 'further than this he has no claim on her property ... The woman is the sole owner of her property and her earnings'. Bowen saw this as an advantage for the husband: 'the man escapes the burden of supporting his wives and children'. But it must clearly also have increased women's effective autonomy.[77]

The situation in Dahomey is less clear, or at least there is a lack of comparable evidence for the nineteenth century. Twentieth-century evidence suggests, however, that there also wives themselves appropriated the proceeds of their commercial activities: 'a woman retains the right to all her personal earnings in the market-place, or to the proceeds of whatever she produces by her own efforts'; 'commercial gains are a woman's own property and she spends her money free of all controls'.[78]

The general implication, therefore, is that the transition from the slave trade to 'legitimate' trade would have tended to enrich and empower women, at the expense of men, in Yorubaland and Dahomey. It should not be supposed, however, that the liberating tendencies of the oil trade were necessarily fully realized. Just as male slave-owners, as reported by Campbell in Lagos, might seek to refuse manumission to their female slaves, so it may be supposed that men sought ways of countering the growing independence of their free wives. In this context, it may be suggested (if only very speculatively, as being based at best on ambiguous hints in fragmentary evidence) that attention might be directed to the role of male masquerade societies in maintaining men's control over their wives, in the face of the enhancement of the latter's economic position.[79]

In Yorubaland, the principal male masquerade societies were Oro and Egungun. The former was concerned especially with the punishment of criminals, but was clearly directed also against women, who were forbidden to go out of their houses during Oro's appearances. One consequence of this, as nineteenth-century European witnesses explicitly observed, was to close down the markets in which women traders predominated. Bowen noted of an Oro masquerade which he witnessed in Abeokuta in 1851: 'There was no market, no going out to the farms, all business was suspended ... The absence of busy women from the streets and markets, gave the whole town a peculiar sort of aspect, as if something was wanted.' Likewise his colleague Clarke, speaking of Oro appearances more generally: 'no female is allowed to leave the compound under the severest penalty. At this time the streets present a desolate appearance, the markets are closed'. Clarke also observed explicitly that Oro was utilized by men to 'keep [women] in a subordinate position'.[80]

Likewise of Egungun, a masquerade representing the spirits of deceased persons, Clarke spells out its employment by men to keep women in their place:

by this means the female population is kept in subjection. If a man's wife becomes uncontrollable, or offers any resistance to her husband, he has but to call to his assistance one of these women terrifiers and his success forthwith becomes complete. If she dares resist, Egungun gives her a drubbing not to be forgotten and takes his exit with the thanks of the victorious husband.

More concretely, Clarke suggests that Egungun was used 'to secure money from the poor deluded women'.[81] This is, indeed, corroborated by later accounts. Samuel Johnson thus observes that Egungun festivals were 'a lucky time for men', since women were obliged to pay for the feasts, but the food was consumed by the men.[82] Another account, based on observations at Abeokuta in the 1890s, records that the male Egungun exploited their status to despoil female market traders, driving the women from their stalls and 'help[ing] themselves (in their own persons, or through their followers) to the commodities exposed for sale'.[83] Egungun thus operated as a mechanism whereby men were able to appropriate a share of women's commercial wealth.

It should also be noted that one of Egungun's principal functions was the execution of witches, who in Yorubaland were presumed to be mainly women.[84] As Lorand Matory has recently observed, there is a conceptual association in Yoruba thought between witchcraft and markets; not only are witches believed to hold their nocturnal meetings in marketplaces, but also marketwomen are seen as the 'daytime counterparts' of witches, being 'known for hoarding money [and] circumventing husbandly authority'.[85] A study of witchcraft beliefs and accusations in the nineteenth century might shed light on the gender tensions arising from women's expanding commercial role.

Although no comparable male masquerades seem to have existed in Dahomey itself, there is a close parallel among the culturally related Gun people of Porto-Novo, called Zangbeto, which was likewise drawn exclusively from males, and during whose appearances women had to stay indoors.[86] Although Zangbeto is generally described as having police functions directed principally against thieves, it appears that they also played a role in maintaining control over women produce-traders. One modern account notes that Zangbeto was charged with enforcing price controls on the (mainly female) traders in the markets: 'Zangbeto watches the merchants and if they find that a woman trespasses the law, the members of the association will walk through the village for seven nights, cursing the woman who disregarded the custom.' The offending woman trader was then obliged to pay a fine to Zangbeto, if she failed to discharge which it was believed that she would die.[87] The contradiction of interest between consumers and sellers was thus expressed here in terms of gender.

NOTES

1   See, for the case of Yorubaland, LaRay Denzer, 'Yoruba women: a historiographical study', *IJAHS*, 27 (1994), 1–39.
2   Postgraduate research currently in progress by Francine Shields, at the University of Stirling, on the position of women in Yorubaland in the nineteenth century, will hopefully clarify some of these issues.
3   Oladipo Yemitan, *Madame Tinubu: Merchant and King-Maker* (Ibadan, 1987). A wealthy woman trader is documented in the Dahomian port of Whydah in the 1780s also, though it is not specified that she was trading in slaves: Archibald Dalzel, *The History of Dahomy* (London, 1793), p. 208. Dahomey in the nineteenth century also made considerable use of female soldiers, so that here women were involved even in slave 'production': Robin Law, 'The "Amazons" of Dahomey', *Paideuma*, 39 (1993), 245–60.
4   David Geggus, 'Sex ratio, age and ethnicity in the Atlantic slave trade: data from French shipping and plantation records', *JAH*, 30 (1989), 23–44.
5   A. G. Hopkins, *An Economic History of West Africa* (London, 1973), p. 122.
6   William Bosman, *A New and Accurate Description of the Coast of Guinea* (London, 1705), p. 342. This passage might be read to imply that only men did agricultural work, but Bosman later (pp. 343–4) refers explicitly to farming by women.

7 Robert Norris, *Memoirs of the Reign of Bossa Ahadee, King of Dahomy* (London, 1789), p. 147.

8 Hopkins, *Economic History*, p. 126, n. 5.

9 Robin Law, 'The historiography of the commercial transition in nineteenth-century West Africa', in Toyin Falola (ed.), *African Historiography: Essays in Honour of Jacob Ade Ajayi* (London, 1993), pp. 91–115.

10 Susan Martin, 'Gender and innovation: farming, cooking and palm processing in the Ngwa region, South-Eastern Nigeria, 1900–1930', *JAH*, 25 (1984), 411–27.

11 Hopkins, *Economic History*, esp. pp. 104–6, 125–6; Ralph A. Austen, 'The abolition of the overseas slave trade: a distorted theme in West African history', *JHSN*, 5/2 (1970), 257–74.

12 A. G. Hopkins, 'Economic imperialism in West Africa: Lagos, 1880–92', *EHR*, 21 (1968), 580–606.

13 Julian Clarke, 'Households and the political economy of small-scale cash crop production in south-western Nigeria', *Africa*, 51 (1981), 807–23.

14 W. H. Clarke, *Travels and Explorations in Yorubaland (1854–1858)* (ed. J. A. Atanda, Ibadan, 1972), p. 274.

15 R. H. Stone, *In Africa's Forest and Jungle, or Six Years among the Yorubans* (Edinburgh, 1900), p. 24.

16 Parliamentary Papers [hereafter, PP]: Correspondence relating to the Slave Trade 1862, II, no.65: Consul Baikie, Bida, 26 Feb. 1862. For slave villages (*tungazi*) in nineteenth-century Nupe, including their participation in agricultural exports (principally shea-butter) from the 1860s, cf. Michael Mason, 'Captive and client labour and the economy of the Bida Emirate, 1857–1901', *JAH*, 14 (1973), 453–71: this tends to confirm that slaves operated as independent producers, while making payments in cash or kind to their owners.

17 PP: Correspondence relating to the Slave Trade 1854–5, II, no.7: Consul Campbell, Lagos, 1 June 1854.

18 Public Record Office, London [hereafter, PRO]: FO.84/1115, Rev. D. Hinderer, Ibadan, 8 Sept. 1860.

19 Catherine Coquery-Vidrovitch, 'De la traite des esclaves à l'exportation de l'huile de palme et des palmistes au Dahomey', in Claude Meillassoux (ed.), *The Development of Indigenous Trade and Markets in West Africa* (London, 1971), pp. 107–23.

20 Frederick E. Forbes, *Dahomey and the Dahomans* (London, 1851), I, p. 114.

21 Abbé Laffitte, *Le Dahomé* (Tours, 1874), p. 170.

22 E. Chaudoin, *Trois mois de captivité au Dahomey* (Paris, 1891), pp. 302–3.

23 Archibald Ridgway, 'Journal of a visit to Dahomey', *New Monthly Review*, 81 (1847), 412–3.

24 Brodie Cruickshank, *Eighteen Years on the Gold Coast of Africa* (London, 1853), II, p. 43.

25 PP: Correspondence relating to the Slave Trade 1855–6, II, no. 10: Consul Campbell, Lagos, 30 Aug. 1855. This report implicitly contrasts the Abeokuta traders, in this respect, with those from Ijebu, Porto-Novo and elsewhere; this may suggest a greater degree of central control over the oil trade in these other places.

212   Robin Law

26 Ridgway, 'Journal', p. 196; Forbes, *Dahomey*, I, p. 114. The French factory at Whydah in the 1850s also employed numerous people to count out cowries: Dr Repin, 'Voyage au Dahomey', *Le Tour du Monde*, 1/1 (1863), 69.

27 PP: Correspondence relating to the Slave Trade 1858–9, II, no. 11: Consul Campbell, Lagos, 28 March 1858. Cf. also the observation of a Sierra Leonean resident in Lagos at this period, that 'Nearly all the slaves here are working for themselves, and give only occasional helps to their masters': Correspondence relating to the Slave Trade 1857–8, II, inclosure in no. 14: John Davis, Lagos, 18 May 1857.

28 PP: Missions to the King of Ashantee and Dahomey, 1849, Report by B. Cruickshank, 18 Nov. 1848.

29 Chaudoin, *Trois mois de captivité*, p. 302.

30 Laffitte, *Le Dahomé*, p. 170.

31 Chaudoin, *Trois mois de captivité*, p. 302.

32 Hugh Clapperton, *Journal of a Second Expedition into the Interior of Africa* (London, 1829), p. 58.

33 T. J. Bowen, *Central Africa: Adventures and Missionary Labours in Several Countries of the Interior of Africa* (Charleston, 1857), p. 308.

34 Clarke, *Travels*, pp. 245, 260.

35 Samuel Johnson, *The History of the Yorubas* (London, 1921), p. 118.

36 Norris, *Memoirs*, p. 86.

37 F. Vallon, 'Le royaume de Dahomey' (Part 1), *Revue maritime et coloniale*, 1 (1960), 357.

38 Melville J. Hersvovits, *Dahomey: An Ancient West African Kingdom* (New York, 1938), I, pp. 30–5.

39 Forbes, *Dahomey*, I, p. 31.

40 Clapperton, *Journal*, p. 135.

41 Robin Hallett (ed.), *The Niger Journal of Richard and John Lander* (London, 1965), p. 71.

42 Bowen, *Central Africa*, pp. 307–8.

43 Selena Winsnes (ed.), *Letters on West Africa and the Slave Trade: Paul Erdman Isert's Journey to Guinea and the Caribbean Islands in Columbia (1788)* (Oxford, 1992), p. 109.

44 Forbes, *Dahomey*, I, p. 70.

45 Auguste Bouet, 'Le royaume de Dahomey', *L'Illustration*, 20 (1852), 40.

46 Richard Burton, *A Mission to Gelele, King of Dahome* (London, 1864), I, p. 77.

47 Chaudoin, *Trois mois de captivité*, p. 310.

48 Herskovits, *Dahomey*, I, p. 86. Herskovits also states that 'almost half of all Dahomean women sell in the markets': *Dahomey*, I, p. 57.

49 As noted, for the Nigerian area generally, by 'Deji Ogunremi, 'Human porterage in Nigeria in the nineteenth century: a pillar in the indigenous economy', *JHSN*, 8/1 (1975), 37–59. For Dahomey, cf. Patrick Manning, 'Merchants, porters and canoemen in the Bight of Benin', in Catherine Coquery-Vidrovitch and Paul Lovejoy (eds.), *The Workers of African Trade* (London, 1985), pp. 53–9.

50 Clapperton, *Journal*, p. 6.

51 Bowen, *Central Africa*, p. 100; Stone, *In Africa's Forest*, p. 46.

52 Clarke, *Travels*, p. 245.

53 PRO: CO.2/15, Journal of Hugh Clapperton, 3 Dec. 1825; Hallett (ed.), *Niger Journal*, p. 58; Bowen, *Central Africa*, p. 100.

54 Stone, *In Afric's Forest*, p. 45.

55 e.g. Norris, *Memoirs*, pp. 62–3.

56 Ridgway, 'Journal', p. 196.

57 Forbes, *Dahomey*, I, pp. 51–2; II, p. 80.

58 Clarke, *Travels*, p. 245.

59 Stone, *In Afric's Forest*, pp. 23–4.

60 Johnson, *History*, p. 124. Palm kernel oil was manufactured for the domestic market (for use as lamp oil), rather than for export.

61 John Whitford, *Trading Life in Western and Central Africa* (Liverpool, 1877), p. 94; Johnson, *History*, p. 124.

62 PP: Correspondence relating to the Slave Trade 1858–9, II, no. 11: Consul Campbell, Lagos, 28 March 1858.

63 Whitford, *Trading Life*, p. 105.

64 PP: Correspondence relating to the Slave Trade 1855–6, II, inclosure in no. 17: S. B. Williams, Report of meeting on 17–18 Sept. 1855.

65 Vallon, 'Le royaume de Dahomey', p. 358.

66 Ridgway, 'Journal', p. 196.

67 J. A. Skertchly, *Dahomey As It Is* (London, 1874), p. 51.

68 John Duncan, *Travels in Western Africa* (London, 1847), I, p. 187.

69 Repin, 'Voyage au Dahomey', p. 99; A. d'Albéca, *Les établissements français du Golfe de Bénin* (Paris, 1889), 75; Chaudoin, *Trois mois de captivité*, p. 65.

70 Burton, *Mission*, I, p. 129n.; Skertchly, *Dahomey*, p. 33. (But Skertchly may be here, as often, merely echoing Burton.)

71 F. de Monleon, 'Le Cap de Palmes, le Dahomey, Fernando-Po et l'Ile du Prince en 1844', *Revue maritime et coloniale*, 6 (1845), 72.

72 Xavier Béraud, 'Note sur le Dahomé', *Bulletin de la Société de la Géographie*, 5ème série, 12 (1866), 384.

73 PP: Correspondence relating to the Slave Trade 1862, II, no. 21: Consul Freeman, Lagos, 1 July 1862.

74 PP: Correspondence relating to the Slave Trade 1856–7, II, no. 16: Consul Campbell, Lagos, 26 May 1856. Likewise on the lower Niger, the British expedition of 1832 met a women at Aboh who claimed to be 'the mistress of more than two hundred slaves, whom she employed in collecting palm-oil, cultivating yams, & c.': MacGregor Laird and R. A. K. Oldfield, *Narrative of an Expedition into the Interior of Africa* (London, 1837), I, p. 100.

75 PP: Correspondence relating to the Slave Trade 1858–9, II, no. 11: Consul Campbell, Lagos, 18 March 1858.

76 Clapperton, *Journal*, p. 21; Richard Lander, *Records of Captain Clapperton's Last Expedition to Africa* (London, 1830), II, p. 197.

77 Bowen, *Central Africa*, p. 304.

78 Herskovits, *Dahomey*, I, p. 86; Claudine Tardits and Claude Tardits, 'Traditional market economy in southern Dahomey', in Paul Bohannan and George Dalton (eds.), *Markets in Africa* (Evanston, 1962), p. 102.

79 It is not, of course, suggested that these masquerade societies were created in

the nineteenth century, in response to the rise of the palm oil trade, only that they may have been exploited by men to cope with changes in gender relations arising from the commercial developments of that period. In Yorubaland, the Oro masquerade is already attested (though not named) in 1826, in a context (in the north of the Oyo kingdom) where palm oil exports cannot have been a factor: Clapperton, *Journal*, p. 22.

80 Bowen, *Central Africa*, p. 138; Clarke, *Travels*, pp. 282–3.

81 Clarke, *Travels*, p. 284.

82 Johnson, *History*, p. 30.

83 Stephen S. Farrow, *Faith, Fancies and Fetish, or Yoruba Paganism* (London, 1926), p. 78.

84 J. Omosade Awolalu, *Yoruba Beliefs and Sacrificial Rights* (London, 1979), p. 84; for nineteenth-century corroboration, cf. e.g. Johnson, *History*, p. 30.

85 J. Lorand Matory, *Sex and the Empire that is No More: Gender and the Politics of Metaphor in Oyo Yoruba Religion* (Minneapolis, 1994), p. 54.

86 A. Akindélé and C. Aguessy, *Contribution à l'étude de l'histoire de l'ancien royaume de Porto-Novo* (Dakar, 1953), pp. 128–30. Zangbeto also existed in Badagry, but few details are given of its operation there: T. O. Avoseh, *A Short History of Badagry* (Lagos, 1938), p. 40. Zangbeto is also attested in this century in Whydah, though since it is not mentioned there in any nineteenth-century source, it may be a recent importation: Herskovits, *Dahomey*, I, p. 249.

87 Tardits and Tardits, 'Traditional market economy', p. 101.

9   In search of a desert-edge perspective: the Sahara-Sahel and the Atlantic trade, c. 1815–1890

E. Ann McDougall

During the Atlantic slave trade, the desert-edge functioned as an interface not only between the Sahara and Sudan, but also between their economic systems and those of the Senegambian coast. It influenced the slave trade's operation, its price structure, and its impact on the far interior.[1] When abolition came, its impact also was refracted through this desert-edge prism. This essay studies the nature of this impact as measured in the social, political and economic changes which followed in its wake.

The essay is divided into four sections. The first sketches existing perspectives on the ending of the slave trade in West Africa, and situates those specific to the 'interior' in historiographical context. Key to this is the work of Claude Meillassoux. His arguments frame the analysis in the second section, which questions established interpretations of price behaviour and gender preference in the slave trade. In the third section, revisionist interpretations are suggested, based largely on work by Martin Klein, Richard Roberts, James Webb, John Hanson, Paul Lovejoy and David Richardson, and myself. In the fourth and final section, I return to the larger picture of the impact of abolition, and offer some observations of what this revisionist analysis means for this ongoing debate, especially with regard to A. G. Hopkins' influential concept of a 'crisis of adaptation'.[2]

Historiography

In thirty years of debate over the impact of the ending of the Atlantic slave trade on West Africa, the theme of continuity or change has remained central.[3] Despite the volume of detailed research generated, the debate can still be reduced to a handful of key questions. As 'legitimate' commerce replaced the slave trade, did old political structures and warrior elites continue to control and benefit, or did the former suffer disintegrative and destabilizing effects and the latter lose out to new merchant elites? Was the rise of new producers and merchants really a

215

consequence of the ending of the slave trade, or merely contemporaneous with it? Was change a question of degree rather than kind? Most recently attention has centred on domestic slavery. To what extent did the ending of the overseas slave trade and the growth of 'legitimate' commerce stimulate a domestic trade in and use of slaves? To what extent did the domestic demand for slaves affect slave prices in the post-abolition era? In his recent historiographical survey, Law concludes that this topic has produced the most consensus, with 'the growth of domestic slavery ... seemingly documented throughout the West African region in this period'; he argues that 'this growth of domestic slavery tended to cushion the effects of the loss of the overseas markets for West African slave suppliers, although widespread evidence for falling slave prices shows that it did not fully compensate for it'.[4]

Law's survey limited itself to the coast and its immediate hinterland, and did not discuss developments in the interior. This neglect is common to other general works, which tend to give brief, undeveloped analyses when they give any at all.[5] Regional studies tend to treat the question in passing, but even these are few in number.[6] The limitations of Law's historiography to a large extent reflect the present state of research; historians of the interior have yet to give the question the systematic attention it deserves.

In so far as the question has been addressed, there is disagreement over whether the Atlantic slave trade (and therefore its abolition) had any significant impact on the interior at all. My own overview of economic change in the nineteenth century treats the 'continental' and 'coastal' economies independently, thereby implying that the Islamic states emerging in the interior and the slave trade ending on the coast were parallel, but not related, influences.[7] Paul Lovejoy is more explicit:

In many places ... there was a growth in the internal market [for slaves] without any strong links with the external market and its collapse. The *jihad* states of the northern savanna had little direct association with the foreign trade in slaves, although some slaves were in fact exported from these states. The growth of slavery there was more related to internal factors.[8]

Equally categorical, but in an opposite sense, is Catherine Coquery-Vidrovitch, in arguing that the spread of Islamic theocracies was an outcome of the malaise created by the Atlantic trade, a causal relationship which continued after abolition:

These political upheavals [the savanna *jihads*] were accompanied by profound social changes based on a consolidation within the countries of a mode of production based on slavery, reinforced by the abundance of slave labour available. This glut increased throughout the nineteenth century as the Atlantic trade ... [was] gradually eliminated.[9]

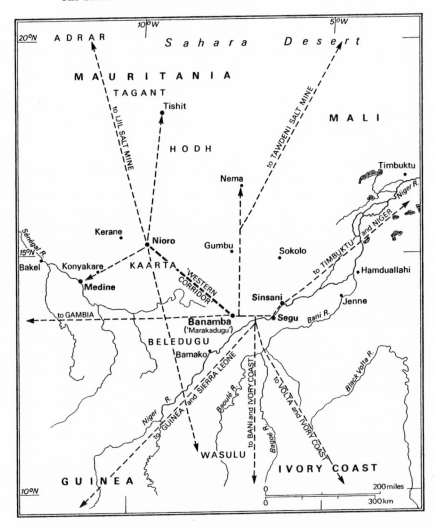

Map 3 The desert edge commercial interface, nineteenth century

Most recently, Arhin and Ki-Zerbo argue for an immediate and profound impact, drawing us back into the debate about a 'slave-gun cycle' in the Atlantic trade:

The abolition of the slave trade ... introduced an element of structural imbalance ... During the second half of the nineteenth century slavery expanded very substantially, especially in the Niger bend. This was because the cost of weapons increased steadily, so that progressively greater numbers of slaves had to be offered in exchange.[10]

More specialized works yield variation in emphasis but not in issues. Emmanuel Terray, for example, has looked at the formation of slave prices, arguing that there was an internal and an external slave market, each operating independently.[11] In contrast, Martin Klein's corpus of works repeatedly emphasizes linkages between the slave trade, slavery and Islam.[12]

To date, the only attempt at a comprehensive analysis of the impact of the international slave trades and their demise has come from Claude Meillassoux. The key to his understanding of the nineteenth century is a gendered analysis of the domestic slave market.[13] He argues that the male-dominated composition of the eighteenth-century Atlantic trade can be explained by the fact that the African market wanted primarily women and children. When the Atlantic trade ended, the principal market for men was lost. In effect, Meillassoux argues, it became so unprofitable to enslave men that warriors began killing them on the battlefield. This meant a reduction of income from any given battle, as so much of the human booty was now almost worthless. War escalated in an attempt to compensate for the lost revenue, and with this increased supply of slaves the market became saturated. Prices fell further. More people bought slaves and expanded production. During the second half of the century, slavery and slave sales increased, and slave-based production expanded. But the revenues of slaving states continued to diminish. With warfare carried out on such a scale, Muslim warriors found themselves increasingly enslaving not 'Bambara' pagans, but fellow-Muslims – a practice prohibited by Islamic law. Warfare and enslavement, therefore, needed new justification: the concept of 'good' and 'bad' Muslims accordingly acquired new significance, as the former launched yet more *jihads* against the latter.

Collectively, Meillassoux's depiction of the supposed 'repercussions' of abolition gives a description of late nineteenth-century reality with which few historians would disagree. But Meillassoux's concept of the 'interior' marginalizes the southern Sahara. For an extension of his analysis into the desert, we need to look at the work of Constant Hamès.[14] He links the demise of the Atlantic slave trade, increased warfare and falling profits in the Sudan to the changing relations between Saharan *hassani* (warriors) and *zawaya* (clerics).[15] Although his analysis is not gender-specific, he shares the assumption that the closure of the Atlantic markers caused prices to drop and trade into the desert to increase. He also posits a causal link between Islamic ideology and warfare. However, he does not see slave use within the desert developing to the extent that it did in the Sudan, because labour requirements in a pastoral economy, even among the more economically active *zawaya*, were limited. Client-ship and dependency continued to privilege social relations.

Meillassoux's arguments, and Hamès' extension of them, suggest that the ending of the Atlantic slave trade had a dramatic effect on the southern Sahara and Sahel. By implication, they challenge views such as Terray's which hypothesize 'independent development', and support those which integrate the history of the interior with that of the coast. They also tend to support Hopkins' concept of a 'crisis of adaptation'. But at present, their interpretations lack a sustainable basis of historical research. They depend upon assumptions about gender preferences in the domestic trade, universal price differentiations based on sex, downward price trends following abolition, and the significance of killing male prisoners, which are as yet unproven. Also, we need at least to question the applicability of Meillassoux's analysis to the desert, and the degree to which more distinction should be made between developments in the Sahel and the Sahara.

Criticism

Meillassoux's assertion that it was the strong preference for women in the domestic market that shaped the male profile of the export trade is developed in several articles.[16] Generally, he reasons that in addition to household labour, most agricultural work in the Sahel was women's domain. Moreover, the production of one of the Sahel's most important commodities, cotton, depended on women dyers and spinners. One male weaver needed eight to ten women spinning to keep him supplied with thread. Indeed, so significant was the role of female labour that Meillas-soux argues that it alone explains West African preferences for female slaves.[17] Martin Klein has also looked extensively at the same issues and challenges Meillassoux on several of them.[18] Klein points out, for example, that when slaves were allowed to farm for themselves, men owed twice as much grain as women in payments to their masters: 'Clearly, men could produce more grain, or at least, that is what the slave masters believed'.[19] He goes on to explore the real reasons he feels women were preferred: their ability to have children (a reason Meillas-soux expressly rejects), their relative docility, their ability to help integrate male slaves, and their service as food preparers, especially for warriors. Differences in reasoning aside, however, Klein's work fully supports the notion of a strong gender preference in domestic markets.

Price data, scattered and incomplete as they are, generally support the argument as well. Travellers' accounts from the late seventeenth century and the turn of the nineteenth century cite female slaves as costing twice as much as males.[20] Klein's nineteenth-century figures for the Sudan show price differentials ranging from as little as 10 to as much as 100 per cent.[21] Consistently, the figures presented by Lovejoy and Richardson in this volume show price preferences for women in the range of two to three.[22] As for the question of killing males on the battlefield, this practice has been attested to by everyone working on the nineteenth-century interior, Klein in Senegambia, Roberts in the Middle Niger, Hanson in the Tukolor Empire, and McDougall in the southern Sahara.[23]

None the less, the evidence is not incontrovertible. In the Banamba and Sinsani region, for example, male slaves were used extensively in long-distance trade, weaving, construction, building maintenance and agriculture. In the latter part of the nineteenth century, 'Marakadougou' was populated with slave villages comprising men, women and children engaged in growing grain, cotton and indigo. Oral and archival evidence argues strongly for the exploitation of slaves of both sexes. 'Our slaves did everything', I was told in Banamba, 'the master and his family did not work'.[24] In Sinsani, Roberts' informants maintained that young women were consistently at the upper end of the price range but that Maraka planters paid virtually the same for healthy females and males. 'Slaves', Roberts was told, 'had become indispensable' – slaves of both sexes.[25]

Census information from the turn of the century on male–female slave percentages is less illuminating that one might hope.[26] It varies according to cercle, and even within cercles. Klein's overview based on the 1904 survey in the French Sudan finds regions like Jenne with twice as many female as male slaves, others like Sokolo with one-third more men than women, and still others like Segu with more or less even numbers. Indeed, Segu is particularly instructive as Roberts reports that in 1894 there had been 4.5 females to each male there. Even taking into account differences in the counting procedure, as well as who was counted, this suggests that significant change could take place in only a decade.[27] This means that census data are of limited use with respect to the question of gender preference and related price behaviour.

But what of the practice of killing males on the battlefield?[28] It is certainly a widely cited 'proof' of the preference for women, and Klein argues that it increased with the decline of the Atlantic slave trade.[29] But are we correct to attribute it to the lack of a domestic market for slaves? This is more problematic. According to Klein, such killings only increased in the early nineteenth century; they had taken place previously, presumably for other reasons. Moreover, several of the examples from the nineteenth century involve revolts against the state or refusal to accept Muslim authority, suggesting reasons more 'political' than gender-orientated.[30] John Hanson has recently approached this question with reference to Umarian practice. His textual analysis of Arabic documents reveals 'derogatory terminology and unabashed representations of killing ... [which] convey a clear and unshakable moral certitude that death befitted Umar's opponents'. He argues that this had nothing to do with the declining profitability of enslaving men but, rather, was ideological.[31] In summary, while there would seem to have been a market preference for female slaves, it was by no means exclusive of males. Moreover, it varied with region and, in all likelihood, with era. Neither price nor census data are conclusive, and the killing of male prisoners seems to have taken place for many different reasons.

Meillassoux also argues that the Saharan trade's preference for women accentuated the market bias for females. The female profile of the desert trade has been fairly well explored.[32] But trans-Saharan demand, aimed at North African and Middle Eastern markets, should not be confused with demand within the Sahara itself. We know much less about Saharan use of slaves than Sahelian. Mungo Park's familiar account emphasizes the arduousness of women's and girls' domestic labour in the camp where he was imprisoned.[33] But he saw only a dry-season camp populated largely by women and children; he did not witness work done in date-palm oases, in irrigated cultivation of grains and vegetables, in camel, sheep and goat herding, in warfare or in long-distance caravan travel. While some maintenance and palm-grove gardening involved women, and sheep, goat and cattle herding was often assigned to children, most work associated with irrigation systems, date harvesting, salt mining, camel herding, trade and war was normally performed by males.[34] In the latter part of the century, evidence suggests that it was women and children who were most often carried off in raids, and who were most frequently found in caravans stopped by French authorities. But it can also be argued that this particular sex/age ratio reflected the fact that slaves taken in raids had to be quickly and easily carried off and it was easier to transport women and children than young men.[35] In the Timbuktu region in 1894, male and female slaves sold for close to the same price, averaging 125 FF and 150 FF respectively.[36] As will be seen below, in the late nineteenth century Saharan slaves were being settled in the Sahel, where both men and women cultivated and traded.[37] In summary, although work generally was delineated in terms of gender and age, the wide range of tasks performed by men, women and children allowed for considerable purchasing flexibility. Moreover, we must remember that as market conditions changed, slaves absorbed in the desert could be sold out of it to North Africa or back into the Sahel.

The second pillar of Meillassoux's hypothesis is the behaviour of slave prices. He argues that prices dropped as the male slaves who would previously have fed the Atlantic glutted the domestic market. This situation continued to pertain even later in the century because of increased warfare. Whereas prices should have evened out as domestic demand responded to cheaper labour, the gender preference remained, precluding this 'normal' economic development.[38] This downward trend in prices is generally accepted and has recently been incorporated into a continent-wide theory of slavery.[39] Yet, Klein comments that prices 'do not seem to have dropped as much as might have been expected',[40] and Roberts and Hanson, in their work on the Middle Niger and Karta respectively, actually saw an increase in slave prices in the latter part of the century.[41] Although they assume that their own cases are exceptions,[42] two prices from proximate regions on the Senegal suggest they may not be. In 1818 Mollien reported chiefs in Futa Tooro saying that 'Moors' bought slaves on the river at half the price Europeans had paid, namely 300 FF; in 1878/9 Étienne Péroz observed 'Moors' in Kitta purchasing slaves for 400 FF. Along the eastern desert-edge, in the Timbuktu-Jenne region, Daumas reported slaves selling for as low as 25–30 FF in 1841; even allowing that this was an exceptionally low price, those given in the 1894 report noted above, namely 125–150 FF, indicate some rise occurring.[43]

Lovejoy and Richardson's contribution to this volume, together with a forthcoming article on prices in the interior, are the first attempts to look systematically at the impact of ending the slave trade on prices. They produce similar findings. In the interior 'the level of prices seems after 1820 to have been at or about the level of the 1780s when the trans-Atlantic trade was at its peak'. Indeed, they address Meillassoux's argument directly: 'Contrary to [Meillassoux] ... therefore, abolition of slaving by Britain and the USA did not precipitate a general collapse in slave prices in the interior.' They conclude that the Saharan slave trades, both into and across the desert, expanded sufficiently to buoy up prices.[44] Males spilling onto the market in the immediate wake of abolition did not affect the sex-price ratios, which reinforces the argument that a sizeable market for them already existed. While it is possible that prices were behaving differently in the Sahara than in the Sahel, we currently lack data to pursue the point, and must assume that they followed the same trend as prices paid by Saharans in the Sahel and along the river.

It remains to consider the issues of domestic slavery and Islam. On neither topic can we develop a full critique. The former is too large a subject with too extensive a literature for this limited study; the latter is too complex, with too little material available for a comprehensive review. Meillassoux's influential arguments about the expansion of slavery in the Sahel in the wake of increased commodity production have found fertile ground in the work of others. Klein's extensive research across the Sudan, as well as regional studies by Roberts, McDougall and Hanson, for example, confirm a growing use of slaves in grain, gum, groundnut and cotton production.[45] Meillassoux's approach is reflected in work on the Sahara also. As has been seen, Hamès argues for a growing retention of slaves as a consequence of more and cheaper slaves entering desert commercial networks.[46] But if the slaves were not significantly cheaper, as may have been the case, does the same conclusion hold? I have argued elsewhere that it does.[47] Hamès takes insufficient account of the growth and diversification of the Saharan economy, in large part an outgrowth of the increasing commoditization occurring in the Sahel (as will be seen below). As for the numbers of slaves involved, it may well be true that simple pastoral economies have a limited capacity to absorb labour, but the Saharan economy of the nineteenth century was no longer simple or exclusively pastoral. It provided many opportunities for slavery to take root.

To what degree were Islam and theological warfare becoming little more than justifications for enslavement? This is a more problematic issue. Klein, for example, has implied as much in his works linking the slave trade and *jihads* in the Sudan.[48] But for such a generalization to hold, it would have to be applicable to most instances across the Sahel and the Sahara; and as yet the question has not been asked systematically of al-Hajj Umar, Uthman dan Fodio or the charismatic *shaikhs* of the southern Sahara, among others.[49] However, if Hanson's argument that Meillassoux's emphasis on profitability and slaving is misplaced in the case of al-Hajj Umar, then the whole hypothesis is going to need some careful rethinking before it is applied generally.[50]

Reinterpretation

So far, there is no reason to disagree with Meillassoux that domestic slavery grew in the wake of the abolition of the Atlantic slave trade, though there is reason to disagree with his explanation of this, as well as to insist that more attention be given to the Sahara. I propose beginning where Lovejoy and Richardson leave off in their study of the interior. While arguing that interior markets were largely independent, they also acknowledge that the trans-Saharan trade was influential. This needs further refinement. The role of an 'intra'-Saharan trade rooted along the desert edge needs to be distinguished. Then, given that Meillassoux's argument that falling prices stimulated demand for slaves has been called into question, a return to Law's observation that domestic demand for slaves served as a 'cushion' with respect to prices is in order. I will argue, however, that it should be extended in time and space: that the 'cushion' was operative for most of the century, and that the demand extended well into the interior.

First, however, a brief note about the organization and significance of the Atlantic trade for the states and merchants of the interior. In spite of the importance of 'Bambara' slaves to the overall trade, merchants from the central supply region, the Middle Niger, rarely dealt directly with European agents.[51] In the south and west, they sold to *juula*; in the Sahel, in places like Sinsani, Nioro and Gumbu, the intermediaries were Saharans. Just as *juula* transported slaves to the Gambia and Senegal Rivers, and incorporated them into agricultural and commercial activities,[52] desert-edge merchants sold slaves into the North African trade, the Senegal system (through Galam)[53] and the Sahara itself, where they harvested gum, cultivated dates and grain, and tended animals.[54] Niger valley merchants received a range of exchanged goods, including *guinée* cloth from across the Sahara, and salt from the desert itself. Saharans left salt in the Sahel at the end of the dry season for an agreed price to be paid the following year. Meanwhile, Maraka merchants sold it, usually for more than the pre-arranged price. In effect, the 'off-season' commercial activities were financed by Saharan salt.[55]

A second facet of the slave trade which we need to understand was its role in channelling arms and ammunition into the Segu-Bambara state. Roberts argues that in spite of attempts by the state to monopolize the arms trade, merchants and warriors found ways to obtain weapons privately. The extension of the Middle Niger system to the south and west was based largely on the Maraka-*juula* slaves-for-arms trade, a trade which ended soon after abolition.[56] The Segu-Bambara political economy became dependent on the firearms, gunpowder and other European manufactures supplied through the Atlantic trade system. And yet, Roberts concludes:

The Atlantic trade remained tangential to the ecozonal character of Maraka commerce. Because commercial ties with the desert and forest regions remained strong, the economy of the Middle Niger valley was resistant to the dramatic swings in the coastal export economy. To some extent, trans-Saharan trade competed with Atlantic imports. With the exception of war material, most consumer goods available through the Atlantic trade could be supplied more cheaply through trans-Saharan routes. Manufactured goods occasionally arrived via trade routes along the desert edge from Senegambia.[57]

But there is a contradiction implicit here. If the Middle Niger political economy was dependent on firearms and gunpowder, how could the trans-Saharan trade, which did not supply war materials, have provided any competition at all? The answer is, it did not. The Saharan salt trade supplied the Maraka with the finance they needed for other commercial activities, including the Atlantic trade, and the desert-edge network gave the merchants (and through them, the warriors and states) of the interior access to both the import–export systems, Atlantic and trans-Saharan. It was the desert-edge, not the trans-Saharan trade which was the real competition. And in the wake of abolition, it expanded. Roberts' work chronicles the growth of Maraka trading networks in this era. Prior to 1816,[58] their long-distance trading activities had focused on the Niger-Kankan axis, and from there into Wassulu and Buré; they had been delineated in the east by Jenne's control of the Niger–Bani axis to Bobo Juulasso and Kong. By the 1830s, Maraka from the Middle Niger controlled both networks.[59] Access to the gold and kola fields of the Volta river systems meant an expansion of well-established trading relations with *juula* and Saharans. Indeed, it clearly necessitated increasing supplies of exchange goods. Slaves no longer moved south,[60] so commerce consisted primarily of desert salt, grain and indigo-dyed cloth. More salt required more trade with Saharans; more grain and cloth required more labour to produce it. No longer valued principally as commodities, slaves acquired an increasing worth as labourers. The effects of this dynamic were felt throughout the Middle Niger, including the newly established Islamic theocracy centred in Hamdullahi.[61]

The establishment of al-Hajj Umar's empire from the 1850s introduced important new dynamics to the situation. State policy built on the desert-edge system to develop commercial networks which would allow it access to foodstuffs (including salt) and imports (including arms). From the mid-1860s, Umarian soldiers with grants of land and slaves in Karta produced surpluses of grain. At the same time, state officials negotiated with Saharans and merchants in the Senegal valley to open routes for the gum trade through Karta to Medine. As Hanson points out, 'gum arabic, ... was the primary commodity desired by the merchants who had access to French firearms ... [The state] escorted caravans through Karta, and collected tolls from desert-side caravans and customs from Medine gun merchants'.[62] This expanding commerce provided Umarians with arms, and Karta colonists with new grain markets. Saharans bringing gum, and Senegalese merchants with arms and *guinées*, bought grain in return. By the 1880s, demand for slaves by producers in the new 'grain colony' had raised slave prices to twice those paid in the nearby Senegal valley.[63]

The other staple was salt. Al-Hajj Umar chose to develop Nioro as Karta's capital by encouraging salt merchants from Tishit to settle there. Desert salt was stockpiled and sold when prices rose; then grain, slaves and *guinées* were purchased. According to Hanson,

Skaykh Umar's initial contact with Tishiti salt merchants involved the exchange of slaves for salt, and the slave/salt exchange remained the primary basis of the trade throughout the late nineteenth century. The wars and raids which the Futanke conducted in the name of Islam provided a large share of the slaves exchanged for salt in Nioro. The Futanke military did not meet the demand for slaves, however, and Soninke merchants who travelled from Nioro to the major slave markets of the southern savanna provided the bulk of the slaves which entered the desert-side from Nioro. The creation of a warrior state south of Karta by Samori Turé made its commercial center of Wassulu the largest slave market in the Western Sudan. Consequently, the Nioro-Wassulu trade route was quite active during the late nineteenth century.[64]

By the 1880s the Karta regional economy was centred on Nioro, fed by exchanges which tapped into the slaves of Wassulu and the gum of Medine. It channelled slaves into the desert and the Sahel, salt into the Sudan and Wassulu, gum towards the coast, and grain into the Senegal valley and desert. It also sent salt and arms to the state's capital on the Niger, Segu. A commercial corridor which paralleled the Karta system in its development, complete with road tolls and protective caravan escorts, passed by the town of Banamba.[65] Bambara rebellions frequently closed the corridor and attempts to ensure imperial control over its traffic failed by 1880. None the less, as the route remained crucial for funnelling salt and arms to Segu, concerns over this trade shaped a good deal of Umarian policy.[66] Banamba grew like Nioro. A small village in 1864 when seen by Eugène Mage, by 1894 it was one of the 'great towns' of the *cercle* of Bamako,

populated by Saracolets [Maraka], transient Juula and slaves who cultivate immense areas of field. All the commerce of the area is carried on in Banamba, the assembly point for caravans coming from Medine, Gumbu, Nioro, Segu and different states from the right bank. The commerce of this village is comprised primarily of salt brought by the Moors from Nioro and Gumbu, kola and slaves (the last all from the right bank) and cloth (*pièces de guinée*) from Medine.[67]

In many ways, Banamba replicated earlier Maraka activity in Sinsani.[68] The 'immense areas of field' cultivated by slaves grew grain and cotton, and slave villages populated the region. Banamba's Maraka 'cultivator-merchants' tapped into the *guinée* trade with Medine, the salt trade with Nioro, and the slave and kola trade with southern *juula*. They also dealt in grain, locally produced indigo-dyed cotton, horses and donkeys. The key to Banamba's prominence was the success with which Maraka integrated plantation and commercial economies, each rooted deeply in desert-side relations with Saharans. Although Banamba's Maraka continued to think of themselves as 'cultivators', in 1899 they were described by Émile Baillaud as a 'wealthy class of merchants such as one finds in Bamako, Nyamina and Segu', whose trading activities took them and their slave agents everywhere in the French Sudan.[69]

Like Nioro, Banamba and the surrounding region attracted Tishiti salt merchants, as well as their clients and slaves. One of the best known families was the Haidara, whose slaves both farmed and conducted business in Banamba. Their salt caravans were found in all the major trading centres, epitomizing the 'sedentary Moorish merchants' Binger described in 1889, 'whose slaves traded for them while they remained sedentary and lived a life of luxury'.[70] Another was Sidi Muhammad Sibi wuld ab-Allay, who first accepted Umar's invitation to Nioro, then sent a son to Segu who ultimately settled in Bamako and established a village in his name nearby. Other family members developed slave-worked date-palm groves in Nema, engaged in exporting dates to the Sudan and then, in the 1890s, migrated to Banamba where they became salt merchants. Other Tishiti and their slaves installed themselves in villages around Banamba, as well is in the *cercle* of Gumbu, where they grew grain, manufactured cotton and traded salt. Their activities came to resemble those of the Maraka.[71]

The political economy of the emergent Umarian state was shaped in large part by its development of desert-side trade. By drawing Tishit salt merchants and their slaves into Nioro, Banamba, Segu and surrounding areas, Umarians linked their own economic fortunes with those of the southern Sahara. Their own ability to feed and arm themselves depended on Saharans providing salt and gum, and increasingly, this 'dependence' took on a political profile, as military alliances with Saharan confederations became state policy.

For the southern Sahara, these developments offered tremendous potential. The 'Tishit diaspora' was one response; Hanson's study of the gum trade on the Upper Senegal, dating from the founding of Bakel, chronicles another.[72] The Ida Aish, ruling *hassani* lineage in the Tagant, allied with the French and received payments proportional to the amount of gum they could assure safe delivery of to Bakel. The opening of Medine, some distance downstream, encouraged the Ahl Sidi Mahmud (also from the Tagant) to do the same.[73] In return, they wanted grain, *guinées* and arms. Grain had long been a standard exchange good. Earlier French forts on the river had difficulty feeding themselves because the 'Moors' exchanged their salt first for any surplus grain available.[74] By the late 1860s, Saharan demand for grain in Medine was sufficient to encourage Senegalese *traitants* to go in search of more; the Karta colony of Jomboxo responded eagerly. *Traitants* who could offer Saharans both grain and *guinées* soon had a decided advantage on the market.[75] Saharan preferences were also a factor in the French *guinée* trade. In the 1780s, when Rouen *guinées* were first imported to Senegal, their market share *vis-à-vis* the Indian variety remained small because the 'Moors' would not accept them. According to Roberts, the role of *guinées* in the Senegal economy did not change following the ending of the Atlantic slave trade because it remained the base of the gum trade. And gum, according to all accounts, 'remained the most important commodity motivating the economy of Senegal'.[76] In the early decades of the century, freer trade led to better terms of exchange for Saharan suppliers and, gradually, to new forests being brought into production. The fact that production, transport and trade in the Tagant-Hodh involved totally different peoples from those exploiting the Lower Senegal forests, and that some time was needed to acquire and organize labour, meant that market response was relatively slow.[77] None the less, it marked a significant expansion and diversification of the economy.

Saharans also wanted arms. While there are few data available on the firearms trade,[78] other evidence implies that the trade was considerable. Arms so acquired played a key role in the Ida Aish victory over the Ahl Sidi Mahmud, the result of a long-term conflict which itself grew out of the competition over shares of the gum trade in Bakel and Medine. And in the Hodh, the Meshduf, a 'commoner' tribe who became involved with the trade in the early part of the century, purchased enough guns and gained enough support among Saharans to overthrow a powerful confederation who had controlled the region since the seventeenth century. 'As a result', Hanson writes, '*zawaya* groups who supported the Mashduff gained access to large tracts of acacia forests of the Hodh and increased the amount of gum arriving at the market at Medine.'[79]

The other aspect of Saharan economic involvement revolved around the salt–slave exchange.[80] The vitality of the desert edge affected all aspects of Saharan trade and production. Expanding gum production meant expanding labour supplies, and that meant acquiring more slaves. Similarly, as salt industries grew, they needed more labour. One of the most important, Ijil, used few slaves for mining,[81] but employed them in domestic labour, caravan transport and marketing. Tawdeni, operating mostly in the Niger Bend but contributing to Middle Niger supplies, made extensive use of slaves in the mines as elsewhere.[82] Increasing salt production allowed for the purchase of more slaves, an escalating series of exchanges with the Sahel and, ultimately, growth in other sectors of the economy. Oasis agriculture, for example, expanded in the Adrar; commerce and caravan travel increasingly employed slave workers; and both cultivation and trade were being carried out in the Sahel by slaves and freed slaves (haratin) belonging to Saharans. While the subject cannot be pursued here, the use of slaves on a permanent, rather than a seasonal, basis in the Sahel was a major nineteenth-century development, closely linked to slave availability.[83]

These developments also had political consequences for the Sahara.[84] French efforts to develop the gum trade, especially after 1815, contributed to the growing wealth and power of the Ida Aish hassani. The payments they received for facilitating trade to Bakel competed with 'traditional' income zawaya earned harvesting and marketing gum. On the other hand, the clerical Ahl Sidi Mahmud successfully cut into Ida Aish income by developing the parallel trade at Medine. This entrepreneurship was equivalent to a political challenge to the emiral Ida Aish and engendered decades of conflict.[85] Umarian efforts to ensure a continuing flow of arms and other imports via Medine and Nioro inextricably bound the politics of the southern Sahara to those of the Sahel. Saharan coalitions formed in response to these efforts. The Awlad M'Barak led a strong force in opposition, while the 'upstart' Meshduf coalesced a powerful group which fought to assist them. The latter's success in a major confrontation in 1865 immediately led to initiatives with respect to the Medine market. Hanson's reading of the evidence is that the Umarian leader in Karta had obtained southern Saharan support in his war precisely because he promised to open trade routes across Karta. Ida Aish resistance to these developments was ineffective. The Meshduf gained enough power to guarantee gum caravans safe passage between the Hodh and Karta, and their leader is believed to have invested personally in slave-based gum production. In addition, wars fought by the Umarian–Meshduf alliance contributed large numbers of slaves to the flourishing gum industry, thereby drawing Saharans further into the slave-producing, slave-using societies of the desert-edge.[86]

The 'Tishit' diaspora stimulated by the Umarian desire to promote the salt trade also acquired a political profile. With the successful French conquest of Nioro in 1891, Umarian forces withdrew to Tishit, where they planned a retaliatory jihad. The French replied with economic warfare: they levied a salt tax on all merchants from the Tishit region equivalent to 50 per cent of their supplies. That this took place during a period of famine in the Tagant-Hodh exaggerated the impact. Migrations into the Sahel accelerated during the next few years.[87]

To the degree that we can generalize from this evidence, it would appear that ending the Atlantic slave trade affected the Sahara in a number of interrelated ways. Most immediately, there was an influx of slaves, especially from the Senegambia region, who previously would have been shipped to the coast. Saharans increased dramatically their involvement in 'legitimate' trade, replacing slaves with gum. This new trade put a significantly larger number of firearms in the hands of Saharans, which in turn fed Saharan warfare and slave-raiding. Slaving and slavery both assumed a more critical role in the nineteenth century. The combined influence of increasing integration with the Sahelian economy, especially Umarian state-building, and the acquisition of arms may well have generated an even more profound change. In earlier times, wealth generated by trade was measured in slaves, food, cloth and animals, and it was controlled by *zawaya* lineages. Access to these commodities meant security, which, in turn, attracted students and clients. *Zawaya* groups' reputations grew in tandem with their follow-ings. In the nineteenth century, wealth apparently bought power more directly as *zawaya* added arms to their arsenals of religious and material 'security'. *Hassani* as well began to increase their economic base. These developments had the potential to alter *zawaya/hassani* relations in 'untraditional' ways.[88] Perhaps most important of all, ending the Atlantic trade focused economic and political attention on the desert-edge, and on the networks of markets and merchants who continued to supply the interior with the arms, foodstuffs, cloth and labour previously delivered via the Atlantic system. To the degree that the Sahara and Sahel had been distinct entities at the outset of the century, they had become integrated into a single political economy by its end.

Conclusions

This re-interpretation of nineteenth-century responses to the ending of the Atlantic slave trade is consistent with the evidence examined above, in the second section of this essay. Looking to the desert-edge allows us to see an alternative dynamic in the demand for slaves, one which explains why prices not only did not fall, but actually increased in some regions. It is not coincidental that where production became most commoditized, in Karta and the Middle Niger for example, there is evidence of prices rising. Moreover, as the desert and desert-edge economy grew, and as slaves were increasingly utilized, the preference for women probably became less pronounced relative to overall demand.[89] This would explain Maraka acknowledging that women were worth more, but nevertheless saying that they paid the same for healthy slaves of both sexes. Where and how merchants marketed goods within these parameters had a strong impact on which areas developed agriculturally, and consequently, which had the largest demand for slaves. Prices varied accordingly. Hamès underestimated Saharan potential in assuming that pastoralism precluded the significant growth of slavery. The same dynamic which shaped Sahelian economies took hold in the desert, with the same results.[90]

This revisiting of the evidence reinforces Meillassoux's argument that nineteenth-century domestic slavery and Islam were closely linked, but prompts different perspectives on the nature of that relationship. Meillassoux and Hamès argued that ideological concerns became subsumed to the profitability of slaving; it could as well be suggested, however, that it was the increasing use of slaves and the growing wealth generated by slave labour that freed Maraka and Saharan masters for the further study and teaching of Islam. It could also be argued that the economic and political integration centred on the desert-edge was accompanied by religious integration because Saharan *zawaya* like the Kunta and Tishit *shurfa* [91] included teachers who established Koranic schools as well as merchants who opened boutiques. It is also noteworthy that the Umarian-stimulated diaspora introduced a new theological influence into what was previously Qadiriyya territory, namely Tidjanism. Hanson's emphasis on the ideological aspects of nineteenth-century warfare may have implications for understanding economic change that we have not yet realized.

Returning to the broader debate, it is evident that a study of the interior has much to offer. It is also evident that the Sahel and the desert, although becoming increasingly integrated in historical reality, need some individual analytical consideration. The issue of 'legitimate commerce' is a case in point. In the Sahel/Sudan there was no measurable substitution of legitimate for slave commerce; the slave trade continued (and probably escalated) alongside the 'legitimate' grain and cloth trade. What differentiated the interior was that neither commerce was directed principally to Europeans. It was Saharan merchants who had long negotiated with Europeans and, not surprisingly, Saharan merchants who responded most immediately to commercial changes following abolition. The consequences of developing the gum trade for the southern Sahara were comparable to those experienced by coastal societies moving into cocoa or palm-oil production. But the question nags, to what degree were they really attributable to the ending of the trade in slaves? Like palm oil, gum had been exported alongside slaves for more than two centuries; its market was industrialized Europe. Demand for these products was independent of that for slaves, and its increase in the nineteenth century was not solely a function of abolition. In the case of gum, merchants operating along the Senegal had tried to shift French government support to the gum rather than the slave trade since the mid eighteenth century.[92] As with palm oil, new people and new regions were drawn into the increased *scale* of production and trade, but we must be cautious about attributing all the repercussions of that expansion to the ending of the slave trade. In the Sahara, significant political change accompanied involvement in the gum trade, but it is not evident that it was 'destabilizing', nor that it involved qualitative changes or is attributable to abolition. More realistic, I believe, is a view looking at adaptation to expanding opportunities not only with the Europeans and the high-profile gum trade, but also with the peoples of the Sahel/ Sudan through the intensification of more traditional relations.

The short-term effect of an influx of slave imports aside, where the decline of the Atlantic trade affected Saharans most was in the arms and *guinée* trade. Whereas previously slaves brought by *juula* were the main commodities for which Europeans exchanged firearms, in the nineteenth century it was gum brought by Saharans. This, in turn, fed networks serving the Maraka, the Umarian state and *juula*, especially from Wassulu. In response, domestic grain production expanded; towards the end of the century, Umarian grain bought French arms directly. These developments also altered the pattern of *guinée* imports. In the 1880s, the majority of *guinées* still came across the desert; by the 1890s, Medine's success had largely eliminated this import strategy.[93] Nevertheless, the new market continued to depend on the old desert-side salt exchange flourishing in Nioro and Konyakary under Umarian encouragement.[94]

These observations have several implications. First, the desert-edge economy reflected both change and continuity. New commodities and new networks were operating, but remained rooted in previous relationships. In both the desert and the Sahel the salt trade continued to finance much of the 'new' commercial activity. Secondly, is the issue of the exchange of slaves for guns, and its impact on the post-abolition era. Contrary to Arhin and Ki-Zerbo's assumption, cited earlier, guns continued to be imported, but for 'legitimate' commodities like gum and grain, not for slaves. The role arms came to play, especially in the Sahara, echoes earlier research by Klein in the Senegambia and deserves more attention.[95] Third, the findings here serve to complicate rather than resolve the debate about the degree to which the interior operated independently of the Atlantic market. The Lovejoy/Richardson thesis, echoing Terray and earlier Lovejoy works, is still attractive but would seen to overstate the case. It continues to formulate discussion in terms of the overdrawn dichotomy of trans-Atlantic 'versus' trans-Saharan trade. The notion of an independent interior colours the argument, but in essence it merely substitutes a trans-Saharan for a trans-Atlantic causality. The Meillassoux and Coquery-Vidrovitch arguments, on the other hand, hold abolition directly responsible for all major social and political change, thereby very much oversimplifying the case. What these perspectives do not take into account is the mediating role played by Saharans and the desert-edge economy, both during and after the hey-day of the Atlantic trade. While current research does not yet permit firm conclusions, it is likely that future work will show the ending of the slave trade to have reverberated as loudly in the desert as in the Sahel. Or, to paraphrase Hopkins' now famous 'crisis of adaptation', it is arguable that it was precisely because 'adaptation' took place in the Sahara that 'crisis' was avoided in the Sudan.

NOTES

The original version of this paper was presented in the names of E. A. McDougall and M. A. Klein. Conflicting time commitments meant that Martin Klein was unable to participate in the preparation of this revised version; I remain appreciative of his interest and willingness to comment on the final draft.

1 I hope to develop this point in a separate paper. See also E. A. McDougall, 'Salt, Saharans and the trans-Saharan slave trade: nineteenth-century developments', in Elizabeth Savage (ed.), *The Human Commodity: Perspectives on the Trans-Saharan Slave Trade* (London, 1992), pp. 61–88. The 'far interior' is defined here as the catchment basin for Senegambian slave exports lying between the Upper Senegal and the Middle Niger, including the bordering southern Sahara. Slaves from this area were identified as 'Bambara' and in the eighteenth century comprised the largest component of exports in the Senegambian trade: see Philip Curtin, *Economic Change in Pre-Colonial Africa: Senegambia in the era of the Slave Trade* (Madison, 1975), 178–82; Abdoulaye Bathily, 'La traite atlantique des esclaves et ses effets économiques et sociaux en Afrique: le cas du Galam, royaume de l'hinterland sénégambien au dix-huitième siècle', *JAH*, 27 (1986), 269–94.

2 See esp. A. G. Hopkins, *An Economic History of West Africa* (London, 1973), pp. 124—66.

3 For fuller discussion, see Robin Law, 'The historiography of the commercial transition in nineteenth-century West Africa', in Toyin Falola (ed.), *African Historiography: Essays in honour of Jacob Ade Ajayi* (London, 1993), pp. 91–115.

4 Law, 'Historiography', p. 109.

5 For example, Hopkins, *Economic History*, pp. 112–17, deals only with

coastal and hinterland regions; LaRay Denzer, 'Abolition and Reform', in J. F. Ade Ajayi and Michael Crowder (eds.), *History of West Africa*, II (3rd edn, London, 1987), pp. 66–8, lists several coastal regions as having been affected, but makes no reference to the interior other than a map which includes it as having been involved in the slave trade itself. Cf. also Ralph Austen, *African Economic History* (London, 1987).

6 See esp. Richard Roberts, *Warriors, Merchants and Slaves: The State and the Economy in the Middle Niger valley, 1700–1914* (Stanford, 1987); James Webb, *Desert Frontier: Ecological and Economic Change along the Western Sahel, 1600–1850* (Madison, forthcoming); John Hanson, 'Umarian Karta (Mali, West Africa) during the late nineteenth century: dissent and revolt among the Futanke after Umar Tal's Holy War', PhD thesis, Michigan State University, 1988; Abdel Wedoud ould Cheikh, 'Nomadisme, Islam et pouvoir politique dans la société maure précoloniale (XIème siècle–XIXème siècle): essai sur quelques aspects du tribalisme', Thèse de Doctorat d'État, Université de Paris V, 1985. Martin Klein is currently preparing a major work on the ending of slavery in the French Sudan; I am finishing a manuscript on the development of the southern Sahara, 1700–1900.

7 John E. Flint and E. Ann McDougall, 'Economic change in West Africa in the nineteenth century', in Ajayi and Crowder (eds.), *History*, II, pp. 379–402; my contribution to the revision of this chapter (by John Flint in the 1st edn) was the 'continental perspective'. On parallel influences, see pp. 401–2.

8 Paul E. Lovejoy, *Transformations in Slavery: A History of Slavery in Africa* (Cambridge, 1983), p. 154.

9 Catherine Coquery-Vidrovitch, *Africa: Endurance and Change South of the Sahara* (Berkeley, 1988), pp. 27–8.

10 K. Arhin and J. Ki-Zerbo, 'States and peoples of the Niger Bend and Volta', in J. F. Ade Ajayi (ed.), *UNESCO General History of Africa, VI: Africa in the Nineteenth Century until the 1880s* (Berkeley, 1989), p. 685.

11 Emmanuel Terray, 'Réflexions sur la formation du prix des esclaves à l'intérieur de l'Afrique de l'ouest précoloniale', *Journal des Africanistes*, 52 (1982), 119–44.

12 Martin A. Klein, *Islam and Imperialism in Senegal* (Edinburgh, 1968); 'Social and economic factors in the Muslim Revolution in Senegambia', *JAH*, 13 (1972), 419–41; 'The slave trade in the Western Sudan during the nineteenth century', in Savage, *Human Commodities*, pp. 39–60; 'Slavery and social order in the Muslim states of the Western Sudan', paper presented at the International Congress of Historical Sciences, Madrid, August 1990.

13 Claude Meillassoux, *The Anthropology of Slavery* (Chicago, 1991), Part I, ch. 1, esp. pp. 60–4; also Part III, esp. pp. 243–8, 263–7.

14 Constant Hamès, 'L'évolution des émirats maures sous l'effet du capitalisme marchand européen', in L'équipe écologie et anthropologie des sociétés pastorales, *Pastoral Production and Society* (Paris, 1977), pp. 375–98.

15 *hassani*: a social grouping, in theory descended from the Bani Hassan, which saw its main role in Mauritanian society as that of 'warriors'; *zawiya* (pl. *zawaya*): the theoretically pacific, usually religious component of the *hassani* in the social charter. In reality, many *hassani* took up arms, and *hassani* became *zawaya*.

16 See his 'État et condition des esclaves à Gumbu (Mali) au XIXème siècle', in
    Claude Meillassoux (ed.), *L'esclavage en Afrique précoloniale* (Paris, 1975),
    pp. 221–52; also 'Female slavery', in Claire C. Robertson and Martin A.
    Klein (eds.), *Women and Slavery in Africa* (Madison, 1983), esp. pp. 49–66;
    Anthropology of Slavery, Part 1, pp. 41–139, *passim*.

17 'Female slavery', pp. 51–9; *Anthropology of Slavery*, pp. 78–84.

18 See his 'Women and slavery in the Western Sudan', in Robertson and Klein,
    Slavery in Africa, pp. 67–92; also 'The demography of slavery in the Western
    Sudan: the late nineteenth century', in Dennis C. Cordell and Joel W.
    Gregory (eds.), *African Population and Capitalism: Historical Perspectives*
    (Boulder, 1987), esp. pp. 55–61.

19 'Demography of slavery', p. 59.

20 Cornelius Hodges reported women slaves as selling for 2 and men for 1 oz.
    of gold in the desert-edge market of 'Tarra' (1689–90); and Mungo Park was
    told that in Sinsani (1805) a man was worth 40,000 and a woman 80–100,000
    cowries: Thora G. Stone, 'The journey of Cornelius Hodges in Senegambia,
    1689–90', *English Historical Review*, 39 (1924), 92; Mungo Park, *The Journal
    of a Mission to the Interior of Africa in 1805* (London, 1815), pp. 161–2.

21 Klein, 'Women in slavery', p. 74. The averages run 20 per cent–30 per cent.

22 See also Paul Lovejoy and David Richardson, 'Competing markets for male
    and female slaves: slave prices in the interior of West Africa, 1780–1850',
    IJAHS, forthcoming.

23 Klein, 'Women in slavery', pp. 71–2; Roberts, *Warriors, Merchants and
    Slaves*, p. 116; John Hanson, 'Representations of warfare and enslavement
    in late nineteenth century narratives of Umar Tal's *jihad*', paper presented at
    the conference of the Canadian Association of African Studies, Toronto,
    May 1993; McDougall, 'Trans-Saharan slave trade', p. 67.

24 McDougall, '"We did not know how to work": the making of masters and
    slaves in Banamba, Mali', paper presented to the conference of the Canadian
    Association of African Studies, York University, Ontario, March 1984. See
    also 'The Ijil salt industry: its role in the pre-colonial economy of the western
    Sudan', PhD thesis, University of Birmingham, 1980, ch. 7, for more
    discussion of slavery and identification of informants.

25 Roberts, *Warriors*, pp. 112–18, on slavery and the Maraka economy;
    quotation, p. 117.

26 It is also flawed. See Lovejoy's critique in *Transformations*, ch. 9; Roberts,
    Warriors, pp. 116–21. The 1904 French census was taken following the
    exodus of thousands of slaves; men were more likely to leave than women,
    especially those with children. In Marakadougou, it is likely that many of
    the outlying slave hamlets, where healthy male slaves lived, were missed,
    leaving the impression of larger numbers of women and children represented
    in towns like Banamba and Sinsani. And there is the insurmountable
    problem that the censuses were administered by the French. Masters often
    undercounted in order to keep taxes low, while slaves gave what might have
    been inflated figures to convince the French of the extent of the problem.

27 Klein, 'Demography of slavery', p. 58; Roberts, *Warriors*, pp. 118–19.

28 Or, to be more precise, of killing *free* males; those already enslaved were
    taken prisoner along with women and children.

29   Klein, 'Women in slavery', p. 72.
30   This includes the Maraka revolt in 1864 cited by Meillassoux, *Anthropology*, pp. 264—5. Roberts makes the same argument: *Warriors*, p. 116. But surely refusal to acknowledge state authority would provide reason in itself to kill male warriors. Klein's examples are Ma Ba, who gave prisoners the choice of shaving their heads in token submission to Islam or death, and Samory, whose forces killed male captives on occasion, 'especially when resistance or revolt was implied'. Prices paid for male slaves do not seem to have been the issue here: Klein, *Islam and Imperialism*, pp. 73–4; 'Women in slavery', p. 72.
31   Hanson, 'Representations of warfare'.
32   See e.g. Patrick Manning, *Slavery and African Life: Occidental, Oriental and African Slave Trades* (Cambridge, 1990); Lovejoy, *Transformations*.
33   Mungo Park, *Travels in the Interior Districts of Africa* (London, 1799), p. 117.
34   See McDougall, 'Ijil Salt Industry', ch.7.
35   This was an additional reason why men were often killed. Archives Nationales de Sénégal [hereafter, ANS]: K 14, Rapport sur la captivitié, 1894, Goundam.
36   ANS: K 14, Rapport sur la captivité, 1894, Région de Tombouctou.
37   For references to travellers' accounts of desert slave labour, see McDougall, 'Trans-Saharan slave trade', pp. 72–6.
38   Meillassoux, *Anthropology of Slavery*, pp. 62–3.
39   Manning notes that 'One of the most remarkable aspects of nineteenth-century African slavery was the continued supply of large numbers of slaves even as the prices of slaves fell sharply'. Since economic logic would suggest that 'If the price of slaves falls, the incentive to capture and deliver the costliest slaves disappears, and the quantity supplied diminishes', he then devotes several pages to explaining why this did not happen: *Slavery and African Life*, pp. 105–9.
40   'Slave trade in the Western Sudan', pp. 39–41, with price chart, p. 40. One of the problems with the data as presented is that they are not in comparable currencies; consequently, it is difficult to assess the decline.
41   Roberts concludes that 'despite occasional dips over the nineteenth century as a whole, prices for slaves increased', referring to a price table with data still, unfortunately, unconverted to a single currency (he uses both French francs and African cowries): *Warriors*, p. 117. Hanson notes that prices in Konyakary were twice those paid in the middle Senegal valley in consequence of the demand by the Futanke immigrants for agricultural labour: 'Generational conflict in the Umarian movement after the *jihad*: perspectives from the Futanke grain trade at Medine', *JAH*, 31 (1990), 212.
42   Roberts says that Maraka willingness to pay the same for men and women 'suggests a significant departure from the slave price trends elsewhere on the continent'; Hanson that the increase in Konyakary occurred 'at a time when prices in other regions were declining'.
43   T. Mollien, *L'Afrique occidentale en 1818* (Paris, 1967), p. 76, cited in Hamès, 'L'évolution des émirats', p. 395; Étienne Péroz, *Du Soudan français: souvenirs de guerre et de mission* (Paris, 1891), pp. 195–6; E. Daumas, *Le Sahara algérien: études géographiques, établissements français* (Paris, 1845),

p. 302, cited in Lovejoy and Richardson, 'Competing markets'. Their prices are given in cowries; I have converted using 1 FF = 500 cowries.

44 Lovejoy and Richardson, 'Competing markets'.

45 See notes 11–12 above, esp. Klein, 'Women in slavery'. James Searing documents a similar development in the Lower Senegal in connection with the eighteenth-century slave trade itself, as slaves were employed to cultivate grain for the river commerce and Saint Louis: *West African Slavery and Atlantic Commerce: The Senegal River Valley, 1700–1860* (Cambridge, 1993).

46 On the slave trade into and absorption of slaves in the desert, see also ould Cheikh, 'Nomadisme, Islam et pouvoir politique', pp. 428–35.

47 McDougall, 'Ijil salt industry', ch. 7; also in part, 'Trans-Saharan slave trade', pp. 72–80.

48 Klein, 'Slave trade in the Western Sudan', pp. 40–2.

49 Hamès, 'L'évolution des émirats maures', refers to all of Mauritania, but really looks only at the riverine areas directly involved in the slave and gum trades. His conclusion reiterates Meillassoux: '[the clerics] fournissent l'idéologie justificatrice de l'esclavage' (p. 395).

50 Hanson, 'Representations of warfare'. He concludes: 'Islam ... was not merely a cover for the business of enslavement ... but rather intimately related to the process of *jihad*'.

51 This, in spite of the fact that Europeans sent delegations directly to Segu in 1828–9 and in 1848. Both expeditions failed: Roberts, *Warriors*, pp. 59–60.

52 On this southern trade, see Roberts, *Warriors*, pp. 58–68.

53 On the 'Senegal river system', see Searing, *West African Slavery*.

54 Roberts, *Warriors*, pp. 46–50; McDougall, 'Trans-Saharan slave trade', pp. 72–7.

55 Maraka not only sold locally, but took caravans south and south-west, where desert salt brought an even higher price: see Roberts, *Warriors*, pp. 66–7, 121–6; McDougall, 'Ijil salt industry', pp. 153–9.

56 Roberts, *Warriors*, pp. 38–9, 58–62.

57 Roberts, *Warriors*, p. 60.

58 Coincidentally, 1816–17 marked not only the ending of the French Atlantic slave trade, but also the *jihad* in Masina which established the caliphate of Hamdullahi.

59 Roberts, *Warriors*, pp. 60–1.

60 Indeed, as Roberts comments, it is ironic that by the latter part of the century slaves would move north by thousands, along routes from Wassulu which had a century earlier carried them south.

61 The seminal work on this Islamic theocracy remains the regrettably unpublished work of William Brown, 'The Caliphate of Hamdullahi, *c.*1818–1864: a study of African history and tradition', PhD thesis, University of Wisconsin, 1969; see also Marion Johnson, 'The economic foundations of an Islamic theocracy: the case of Masina', *JAH*, 17 (1976), 481–95. The state promoted both sedentarization of Fulani cattle-herders and large-scale use of slaves to expand agriculture.

62 Hanson, 'Generational conflict', p. 203.

63 Hanson, 'Generational conflict', p. 212.

64   Hanson, 'Umarian Karta', p. 111.
65   Roberts, *Warriors*, p. 102. Some *juula* were involved but much of the arms trade was in the hands of Futanke.
66   Hanson, 'Umarian Karta', pp. 110–14. Hanson points out that the Karta network, drawing on Wassulu and Medine to feed the Saharan traders, was largely independent of the Nioro-Segu commerce.
67   McDougall, 'Ijil salt industry', ch. 7; ANS: 1 G 189, Capt MacLeod, 'Rapport sur le Cercle de Bamako (Marcadougou)', Oct. 1894.
68   The Sinsani market was destroyed by the Umarian regime following the Maraka revolt in 1863–4; Banamba replaced it.
69   McDougall, 'Ijil salt industry', p. 156. It is notable that Maraka commerce, as well as cultivation, used slave labour. Slaves accompanied caravans and sometimes trusted ones (*sofa*) were responsible on behalf of their masters. See also Roberts, *Warriors*, pp. 66–7.
70   Louis Binger, *Du Niger au Golfe de Guinée par les pays du Kong et de Mossi, 1887–1889* (Paris, 1892), I, p. 32; for discussion, McDougall, 'Ijil salt industry', pp. 325–8.
71   McDougall, 'Ijil salt industry', pp. 324—34.
72   Hanson, 'Umarian Karta', pp. 104—7. The fortified French post which gave prominence to Bakel was built in 1818.
73   Hanson, 'Umarian Karta', p. 104.
74   Bathily, 'La traite atlantique', pp. 285–9. Webb argues that by the 1740s, Saharan traders effectively controlled the river grain trade: *Desert Frontier*.
75   Hanson, 'Umarian Karta', p. 123.
76   Richard Roberts, 'Guinée cloth: linked transformations within France's empire in the nineteenth century', *CEA*, 32 (1992), 607; see also James L. A. Webb, Jr., 'The trade in gum arabic: prelude to French conquest in Senegal', *JAH*, 26 (1985), 149–68.
77   Roberts, 'Guinée cloth', p. 609. He observes that the 'Moors were slow to respond, even to dramatic price increases'. This was not because of lack of entrepreneurship, rather because Bakkar wuld Sweid Ahmad had only just acceded to power after more than a decade of civil war.
78   Cf. Hanson, 'Umarian Karta', p. 109.
79   Hanson, 'Umarian Karta', p. 104. Their access to arms was aided by alliance with the Umarians (as seen below).
80   I have discussed this elsewhere, and will only summarize relevant points here: see 'Trans-Saharan slave trade'.
81   It employed a 'client' group known as Azazirs.
82   On the history of these and other desert mines, see McDougall, 'Salts of the Western Sahara: myths, mysteries and historical significance', *IJAHS*, 23 (1990), 231–57.
83   This argument is developed further in McDougall, 'Ijil salt industry', ch. 7.
84   While a full study of Saharan political evolution has yet to be written, some observations are evident from the limited material presented here. A more extensive analysis is attempted, McDougall, 'Ijil salt industry', ch. 8.
85   Hanson, 'Umarian Karta', p. 104.
86   Hanson, 'The Umarian role in the Upper Senegal valley economy during the

late nineteenth century: warfare and the gum trade' (paper presented at the conference of the African Studies Association, St Louis, Nov. 1991).

87 McDougall, 'Ijil salt industry', 326–7.

88 In this I do not disagree with Hamès' conclusions However, these shifting relations cannot be attributed solely to penetration of European merchant capital through the gum trade or, even more simply, to the ending of the slave trade; rather, there was a complex series of interrelated changes.

89 These ideas have been advanced somewhat more speculatively by Meillas-soux, 'Female slavery', pp. 58–9; Klein, 'Women in slavery', *passim*.

90 This is developed more fully in McDougall, 'Ijil salt industry', ch. 7.

91 *Shurfa*: descendants of the Prophet.

92 Recent studies have shown the role of the gum trade in the Senegambian economy to have been as important if not more important than slaves even in the eighteenth century: Webb, 'Trade in gum arabic'; Bathily, 'La traite atlantique'.

93 McDougall, 'Ijil salt industry', p. 157.

94 The travels of Suleyman Emina of Konyakary in the 1870s, recounted by Hanson, admirably illustrate this complex dynamic. 'Suleyman told [Paul] Soleillet [whom he accompanied to Segu] how, during a diplomatic mission to Bakel, he exchanged several donkey loads of grain for *guinée* cloth, the primary currency in the gum markets. Once back in Jomboxo, Suleyman traded the *guinée* cloth for Ijil salt bars from desert-side merchants who resided at Konyakary. Suleyman completed his transactions by exchanging salt bars for gold at Buré': 'Generational conflict', p. 211.

95 Klein, 'Economic and social factors', pp. 422–4.

A. G. Hopkins

That the definition of a problem has a strong, even a determining, influence on the solution proposed is a truism acknowledged by historians more often than it is acted upon. This is partly because the empirical tradition encourages scepticism towards 'abstract' thought, and partly because historical enquiry inevitably becomes distanced from the presuppositions that launch it. This is why the conceptual foundations of substantial historical controversies require periodic inspection, especially if they have been running for a generation or more, as is the case with the debate over the 'transition' in nineteenth-century West Africa. At this point, readers learned in the ways of academe may already fear that they are about to be lured into one of the many deep holes that specialists dig to trap their unwary colleagues. Certainly, this debate has produced case studies that can match those generated by other historical problems in their detail and, some might say, in their obscurity too. But the wider issues ought to command wide attention: they go to the heart of the problem of the long-run economic development of Africa; they can also be set in a much broader, international context, one that encompasses European imperialism in the late nineteenth century, as this essay will try to show.[1]

Two main kinds of conceptual reflection suggest themselves. The first consists of an inquiry into the language of the debate, the terms of trade, so to speak, and the way in which it has entered the evolving historiography of the subject and has helped, in turn, to shape the conclusions currently on offer. This is an exercise of fundamental importance that ideally requires an essay of matching weight and scope. The task will not be undertaken here, chiefly because Robin Law has recently completed an outline of the subject and is better qualified to fill it in,[2] though some brief comments on the economic aspects of the problem will be made in the next section as an introduction to the main theme of this paper. My chief concern is with the second type of reflection, that is the wider historical setting. The point I wish to argue in the central part of my text is obvious once stated but remains obscure because it has not been acted

240

upon: it is that the debate on West Africa needs now to be placed in a broader continental and international framework if it is to retain its vitality and hence fulfil its original purpose in seeking to unravel some of the most intricate problems in the history of the period. Specialists on other regions of Africa can gain from having a much greater awareness than they have shown so far of advances made on similar issues by historians of West Africa; West Africanists can benefit by pausing to reflect on the ways in which a comparative perspective might influence their underlying assumptions and their current conclusions.

Analytical and historical aspects of the debate

The central problem encapsulated in the concept of the nineteenth-century transition can be broken into two analytical parts: one deals with changes in economic structure; the other with changes in economic performance. Of course, these two types of change interact, and their conjuncture may prove on occasion to be a turning-point in the history of the economy and indeed of the country concerned. Nevertheless, it is essential to begin by considering the two separately to ensure that features pertaining to one are not used to draw conclusions about the other.

The concept of an economic structure involves some knotty problems of definition, but these have the merit of directing the attention of historians to what economists call the production function, that is the combination of factors required to produce a given output, and to the ways in which different combinations affect employment and the value added through linkages with the wider economy. I note this basic point here simply to underline two observations that are central to the debate. The first is that the technical, physical and capital inputs required to produce 'legitimate' exports in the nineteenth century enabled small African 'firms' to participate in international trade for the first time, in contrast to slaving activities, where economies of scale in gathering, purchasing, guarding and moving slaves favoured large 'producers'. This hypothesis was based initially on a mixture of historical evidence and logical deduction.[3] Any evaluation of it, however, first needs to bear in mind the relationship between the parts and the whole. To demonstrate that there were continuities in trade, especially in wholesaling (to take a prominent example) is not to show either that the transition as a whole was evolutionary rather than revolutionary or that West Africa escaped a crisis of adaptation in the nineteenth century. To the extent that the evidence bears out the proposition, it can be said that the economy underwent structural change, at least as far as the (Atlantic) export sector was concerned.

The second observation is that the significance of the transition should not be discounted or even underestimated merely because certain economic activities that came to prominence in the nineteenth century were not entirely new or because they were consistent, in a number of cases, with the maintenance of existing output. Alterations to the organization of production, involving larger numbers of small producers, to give the best known example, or shifts in the division of labour between men and women, to cite a more recent finding,[4] or changing work loads between old and young, to suggest a future possibility for research, could have a dramatic effect across the economy of a region, even if the item produced remained unchanged. Increases in the scale of output, from producing for local needs to producing for export, for instance, began within a given economic structure but could become sufficiently great to change the structure itself and, in addition, to have sizeable social and political consequences.[5] The fact that export production might still have accounted for a minor share of total output in Africa is irrelevant in this context, as is the fact that the value of exports placed West Africa at the foot of the international rankings.[6] Conclusions that are applicable to a region or sector can always be diluted by averaging them across a much larger area. However, this procedure should be resisted in the case under review because structural change characteristically begins from particular nodal points or growth poles, and identifying this development is central to the debate over transition. It is worth adding, since it was one of the main concerns of the original hypothesis, that the Scramble for Africa was launched from specific points, too, and that these coincided with regions that were experiencing some of the greatest strains of transition.

Changes in performance were also of two kinds and frequently interacted: those internal to the economic system itself, typically manifestations of the business cycle such as shifts in the terms of trade, and those that took the form of exogenous shocks, such as war, drought and disease. The evidence now available on West Africa generally confirms the hypothesis that the profitability of the export trade was indeed greatly reduced during the late nineteenth century;[7] the data for other parts of the continent, referred to later, are suggestive but still too fragmentary to permit a grand synthesis. Detailed evidence of exogenous shocks to the economy has begun to accumulate only recently, partly as a result of work inspired by the *Annales* school, and it is too early to say what effect it will have on existing general interpretations of the period. But it is undoubtedly a promising theme that should eventually be incorporated into analyses of the transition. However, the point to stress here concerns the statement of the argument, not its proof: scholars who deny that there was a 'crisis of legitimate commerce' in the late nineteenth century are sometimes addressing one aspect of the problem, performance, and not the totality. Accordingly, to accept this particular conclusion is not to disprove the proposition that the period witnessed a 'crisis of adaptation' arising from the changing structure of the economy.[8]

It follows from these considerations that judgements about whether the transition of the nineteenth century is to be placed towards the evolutionary or the revolutionary end of the spectrum of historical change can properly be made only after these analytical steps have been taken and evaluated by empirical research. To complete this counsel of perfection, it should be added that the results need also to be specified with respect to time and place: we now have enough studies, at least of West Africa, to begin to envisage different groups of conclusions, and these will be reinforced and extended once the rest of Africa is brought into the story. A magnificent book, synthesizing this work and involving, of necessity, a new interpretation of African history in the nineteenth century, now awaits a fresh and enthusiastic author. The historiographical ramifications are at least as wide-ranging as these analytical considerations, but the commentary here will be confined to the purpose in hand and to just two observations. The first concerns the circumstances in which the modern debate was formulated in the 1960s; the second refers to the specialization that has marked the progress of African studies since that time.

My own early interest in this subject lay in the relationship between commercial fluctuations and the Scramble for Africa, with special reference (as the titles of many PhD dissertations used to say) to the Robinson and Gallagher thesis. In the case of Lagos, one of the great distributive centres, it was apparent that legitimate commerce was associated both with a marked degree of continuity in wholesaling activities and with some striking innovations in the shape of new merchants and new forms of commercial organization.[9] This perception followed the pioneering work of Dike,[10] and was scarcely memorable in itself, though it may have helped to keep the question of the balance between continuity and change in the coastal entrepots on the agenda of historical enquiry. The theme was then taken up by John Latham in his excellent study of Old Calabar,[11] and has since engaged the attention of a number of scholars, the most recent being Martin Lynn, who is now the authority on this subject.[12]

At the start of the 1960s, when my own doctoral research was in progress, historical scholarship was inspired by the ambition of rewriting Africa's past to give weight to indigenous rather than to imperial developments. This priority carried a challenge for economic historians to move beyond trade to the study of production. Accordingly, though many elements of my particular criticism of Robinson and Gallagher were put in place in my PhD thesis, it seemed to me to be necessary to pause before publishing my own account to consider whether the analysis could be extended in a more Afro-centric direction, and in this way to link the question of imperialism with the problem of marking out the study of African economic history – a subject that was then, of course, still in the very early stages of its academic development. One contribution to these related questions, published in 1966, explored the shift from slave labour to free labour in Lagos and its hinterland and drew attention to the intensified use of unfree labour in the production of 'legitimate' exports in the second half of the nineteenth century.[13] Another article, which appeared two years later,[14] emphasized the rise, simultaneously, of small, household producers of palm produce, and suggested that their ability to compete in the overseas sector for the first time *en masse* constituted a fundamental change in the structure of export production.[15] This change, combined with a deterioration in the performance of the export sector, amounted to a 'crisis of adaptation' for the 'warrior entrepreneurs' who were trying to negotiate the transition from the era of slave exports to a new international order that recognized only 'legitimate' products. This interpretation was then generalized, but I hope also refined, and applied to West Africa as a whole.[16]

Whether these ideas have validity as well as interest is discussed elsewhere in this volume. The observation I wish to make at this juncture is simply that what then seemed to be the most important and moreover the most difficult problem, namely the history of agriculture (and gathering) in the pre-colonial period, has yet to be dealt with adequately, even for the nineteenth century. Until it is, we cannot be sure of resolving the debate about transition. Of course, advances in this direction have been made: Paul Lovejoy's work, for example, has been especially valuable in extending the debate to regions far removed from the coast, and in underlining the role of slavery on inland 'plantations'.[17] Yet we still cannot point to a series of monographs on export agriculture in the nineteenth century. It is also possible that the emphasis on slave labour, inspired partly by a concern in the USA in the 1970s with the history of slavery in the South and the attendant issue of human rights, has shifted historical attention away from the less controversial and seemingly less problematic issue of non-slave labour in nineteenth-century Africa.

It is a puzzle to know why the history of farming and of cultivation generally should have lagged behind so many other subjects. Of course, there remains the perennial problem of source material, but recent work has shown just how much can be done to overcome this obstacle, even in forest areas long thought to be impenetrable by historians.[18] Moreover, in the 1970s and early 1980s, when modes became fashions and markets went out of favour, the role of production as the fount of all value was approved and heavily emphasized in African studies. Yet the influence of Marxism did not produce the expected result. Indeed, in some respects the debate over the nineteenth-century transition languished: certainly it never took off, even though it was tailor-made for studies of coexisting and competing modes of production and bristling with potential for historians who had rapidly developed an eagle-eye for the emerging class struggle. This unexpected outcome was partly the result of a paradox whereby advocates of the role of materialist forces in history found themselves in the grip of an idealism of their own making that led them away from reality and into the more speculative (and at the time also more prestigious) business of building castles in the air. Marxist historians who were committed to serious empirical research tended to favour studies of the emerging 'working class', which meant urban wage-earners rather than small farmers, whose role in the contemporary revolutionary struggle lacked ideological purity, to say the least. In addition, from the mid-1970s onwards the frontier of historical research tended to move to East, Central and southern Africa, where the legacy of white settlement threw up a rather different set of problems. It was there that 'peasants' were discovered and their emergence and decline (and, later, re-emergence) were traced. Unfortunately, none of the contributors to this new literature related his or her research to work already published on the transition in West Africa, even by way of contrast; their successors in post-Marxist studies continue today to work within the boundaries laid down by the first academic partition of the continent in the 1960s. On the contrary, the trade was one way and in the other direction: specialists on West Africa imported the term 'peasant', which they had hitherto managed to do without, and it subsequently became part of the language of historical discussion. The appropriateness of the term was never clearly demonstrated but it enjoyed a certain *cachet* that enabled it to surmount humdrum (though also fundamental) problems of definition.

This brings us to what is now a particularly interesting moment in the historiography of the subject: on the one hand, the study of agricultural production in Africa is widely recognised by historians as being the biggest gap and the most pressing need; on the other hand, the demands of specialization have herded historians into regional groupings that remain in many respects more isolated from one another than the African societies they analyse. Detailed local studies will remain the foundation of all generalization, and at this level we now have research of a quality that was simply not envisaged thirty years ago. But we also need to begin to connect these studies not only to others within the region concerned, but to the wider world as well.

The world's first development plan

It has long been a commonplace that 'legitimate commerce' arose from European-inspired attempts to develop substitutes for slave exports from Africa. It is generally accepted, too, that the origins of this initiative lay in a mixture of material ambition stemming from industrialization and spiritual purpose impelled by a revitalized Christian mission. The exact proportions of the mix remain controversial, but this is a debate that specialists on Africa have wisely left others to stumble over, because their own enquiries have long become detached from their European starting-points. This being so, it might be useful to offer a brief statement of European, specifically British, policy towards Africa in the nineteenth century, both to emphasize the unity of purpose that linked different parts of the continent in the official mind and to suggest some lines of enquiry that might also raise points of comparison for regional specialists to consider.[19]

With the end of the French Wars in 1815, Britain turned her energies to the task of creating a lasting peace. This endeavour was not simply, or even predominantly, an initiative taken by new industrial forces but arose from a recognition by the established order, the landed interest and the 'moneyed men' who financed them, that far-reaching policy changes were needed both at home and abroad. At home, the intolerable burden of the national debt, the looming problem of population growth and food supply, the difficulties experienced by the new industries, which suffered from excess capacity and low profitability for much of the 1820s and 30s, and the attendant risk of political radicalism, compelled attention and demanded urgent action. Abroad, the need to ensure that neither republicanism nor secularism would again endanger the British way of life implied that policy-makers had to devise ways of putting in place a set of congenial allies, in Europe and overseas, who would help to make the world safe for the monarchical, propertied order that had survived, providentially, the revolutionary upheaval of the late eighteenth century. At home and abroad, the trick of policy, played for the highest stakes, was to install a programme of reform that would offer progress, or, in the language of the day, 'improvement', without also unleashing forces that would endanger property and civil order. New urban gentlemen were invented in Britain in the nineteenth century to be agents and beneficiaries of this programme; their counterparts abroad were identified or educated for the same task. International commerce, financed and managed by Britain, was to provide the material basis of the new world order. 'Likemindedness', which was essential if the rules of the game were to be understood and endorsed, was to emerge from cultural affinities, whether by harnessing local ambitions for achieving improvement and defending legitimate forms of property, or by implanting new values enshrined in the Anglican version of the Christian message, which opposed slavery and proclaimed the equality of all men in the eyes of God while also endorsing unequal property rights, social privilege and political discrimination among the free-born. In this way, so it was hoped, a new world order would emerge to claim the middle ground between what Canning called the old, 'worn out' monarchies of continental Europe, with their instinct for repressing change, and the 'youthful and stirring' nations of the New World, personified by the United States, with their alarming propensity for embracing 'the evils of democracy'.[20]

On the international front, the new policy found concrete expression in the moves towards free trade, beginning in the 1820s and culminating in the late 1840s with the repeal of the Corn Laws and the Navigation Acts, in revitalized missionary enterprise, and in early attempts at 'nation-building' – all of which suggest comparison with the policy adopted by the United States in 1945 at the close of a subsequent and even greater war. The programme was a truly global one in that it embraced both the empire and the world beyond Britain's formal control. The colonies of settlement in Canada and Australasia were allotted a central role in the design because they were regarded as being the most promising territories for reproducing, and hence strengthening, the social order at home, offering as they did openings for migrants as well as for capital and trade and providing seemingly congenial launching-points for the 'Anglicizing' mission.[21] India, too, had a prominent part to play in the experiment, as witness the attempts made in the first half of the nineteenth century to identify and promote a stable and progressive propertied order and to establish the principle that sound money, free markets and good government marched together.[22] Outside the formal empire, strenuous efforts were made to create compliant satellites in the newly independent republics of South America, where constitutions, commerce and capital were all on offer through banking agencies in London.[23] Britain's ambitious plans also found expression in attempts to 'open up' the Ottoman and Chinese empires from the 1830s by imposing free trade treaties and plans for internal reform. The experiment in establishing 'legitimate' commerce in Africa, though distinguished by its close connection with the abolitionist movement, was essentially part of this wider drive towards the creation of a new international order, and is therefore best seen in this context.

Viewed from the metropolitan perspective and in the long run, the main difference between tropical Africa and the rest of the world lay less in the presence of the slave trade than in the absence of the state structures needed to underwrite this innovative vision of cooperative international development. Just as there could be no sovereign debt without sovereignty, so there had to be state structures capable of promoting 'improvement', which in practice meant attracting foreign finance. Because foreign investors would not risk their capital without security, governments seeking to borrow money from abroad had to establish and police approved property rights, raise revenues to service loans (chiefly through exports) and generally manage their affairs in ways that met the approval of their creditors. Such was the nature of the virtuous circle that was supposed to characterize the history of modernizing states in the nineteenth century. Africa's problem in this regard was not the lack of organized states so much as the presence of rather too many of them, and the absence, correspondingly, of a few large centralized polities on the scale found elsewhere that foreign investors could readily identify as being suitable vehicles for development. Whatever else it was, the Partition of Africa was the prelude to a process of state-building that made public foreign borrowing possible for the first time – and with it the pattern of enlarged export development that was to characterize the colonial era.

Britain's vision of a new world order made slow progress during the first half of the nineteenth century. The colonies of settlement struggled to stand on their own feet, foreign investors burned their fingers in South America, India disappointed the unrealistic hopes of its first generation of paternal, imperial developers, the package of free trade and reforms pressed upon the Ottoman empire was recycled in Byzantine ways, and the Treaty Ports failed in their allotted task of 'opening up' China's vast hinterland. The history of Africa's overseas trade thus fits into an international pattern: the expectation that the external slave trade would wither away once it had been made illegal proved to be mistaken, slaves continued to be exported in large numbers, and the growth of 'legitimate' exports remained limited.[24] This gloomy record had specific local causes, which are well known to the specialists concerned, but the fact that the phenomenon was a global one suggests that a more general explanation is needed. The difficulty of expanding world trade in the era before the steamship, the railway and the submarine cable is a standard and still essential part of the story.[25] But economic policy restraints also need emphasizing: it was not until the end of 'Old Corruption' and the scaling down of the national debt that British capital became more readily available for investment overseas, and it was only when Britain moved decisively to install free trade that market conditions favouring the expansion of the international economy were fully established. Before then, Britain was knocking on the door but not opening it; there was an imperialism of intent but not yet of result.

It was in the second half of the century, broadly speaking, that this situation changed following the adoption of free trade, the transport revolution, and the rise of London to become the financial capital of the world. The colonies of settlement in Canada and Australasia experienced a rapid increase in population and trade, while South America, especially the leading republic, Argentina, entered a 'Golden Age' of export growth that remains the point of departure today for discussions of the continent's current development problems. India, being directly managed by Britain, fell into line too, becoming a vast receptacle for British capital as well as for British goods, and paying for both by exporting a rising volume of agricultural exports. The Middle East and China presented a rather different picture, one that lent credence to the view that it was necessary not only to show the light but also to lead the way if indigenous societies were to be drawn into the new international economic order. The Ottoman Empire's default on its foreign debt in 1876 was the culmination of a series of ungentlemanly actions; China's mandarins, on the other hand, frustrated foreign interests by refusing to engage in foreign borrowing;[26] neither region seemed capable of sustaining a profitable export trade. No wonder that Lord Salisbury hardened his heart as well as furrowed his brow in the 1870s: henceforth, 'oriental societies' were placed in a separate category created for those that needed firmer treatment if they were to enjoy the benefits of progress.

Africa fell into this category too. Half a century of endeavour had brought many false dawns, but, as far as the development experts of the time were concerned, the continent remained in darkness. If the planners came, conventionally, to blame the recipients rather than the plan, this was not, as we now know from modern research, because of a lack of response from African societies. It is true, of course, that international trade was still on a small scale, that the influence of Christian missions was confined largely to a few footholds on the coast, and barely that in the Muslim north and east of the continent, and that no state in tropical Africa was able to raise loans on foreign money markets, even if it had wanted to. Considering the evidence now available, it is very difficult to accept that Britain managed to establish an informal empire in any part of Africa: the argument is often repeated but the evidence still does not lie readily to hand.[27] Nevertheless, the pace of change undoubtedly quickened in the second half of the nineteenth century. The rate of growth of international trade was impressive if looked at from the perspective of particular regions and commodities, even if the totals were still trivial in relation to world trade as a whole.[28] Private credit lines were extended into and beyond the important entrepots, despite the continuing obstacles to public sector borrowing.[29] In the absence of the degree of cultural assimilation that made policing the rules of the game a generally agreeable feature of policy towards the colonies of white settlement, Britain prepared herself for a more rudimentary relationship with Africa as the century advanced. Palmerston's minimalist maxim, that local states should be 'well-kept' and 'always accessible', still held;[30] 'native customs and practices' could be tolerated provided that British priorities were not endangered. Circumstances dictated, however, that the border between the two was never easily defined and was therefore an area of potential dispute. The use of gunboat diplomacy, supported at times by military action, indicated that Britain stood ready to exercise the 'forbearing use of power' that Samuel Smiles regarded as being 'one of the surest attributes of the true gentleman'.[31] It is still legitimate to argue that Britain was 'reluctant to intervene' in the internal affairs of African states, but her reluctance has to be set against the need to safeguard British interests; it has to be recognized too that these were expanding, not declining, in the late nineteenth century. Britain not only dominated the foreign trade and finance of the continent as a whole but was also especially prominent in the two regions that accounted for the greater part of the total: Egypt and South Africa. In the eyes of contemporaries, both businessmen and policy-makers, these were the parts of the continent that really mattered.[32]

In Egypt, the transformation of production occurred much earlier than in other parts of Africa and was linked, additionally, to a programme of modernization that sought to promote local manufactures and a Western-style bureaucracy and army.[33] These developments began in the 1820s and centred on the intensive cultivation of cotton, which rested, in turn, on the taxable potential of the densely settled Nile delta.[34] The greater part of state revenues came from the land tax. Land (and crops) also formed security for the credit advances that fuelled export growth. About two-thirds of the cotton crop was grown by small farmers; the rest came from large estates which employed a mixture of free and forced labour (including some slaves).[35] As commodity exports expanded in the second half of the century, following the adoption of free trade, the arrival of the steamship and the establishment of modern banking facilities, so the potential for public-sector borrowing rose.[36] Foreign investment, especially from the City of London, grew rapidly from the 1860s onwards until Egypt became caught up, fatefully, in the global financial crisis that struck in 1873.

Egypt's attempt to join the new international economy can also be placed within the specific context of the rise of 'legitimate' commerce. Although the number of slaves held in Egypt appears to have been limited, trade in slaves remained active until the close of the nineteenth century. Muhammad Ali created an empire in the Sudan primarily to secure recruits for his army; as a result, the slave trade underwent a considerable expansion, especially in the 1830s. Following the Anglo-Ottoman free trade treaty of 1838, Egypt became increasingly oriented towards Europe: government-sponsored slaving expeditions were progressively reduced, and formal measures against the slave trade were initiated in 1854. Nevertheless, a sizeable private trade survived. The Anglo-Egyptian Convention of 1877 outlawed the slave trade, but in practice probably did more to offend slaving interests than to end the traffic; effective abolition occurred only after the British occupation in 1882 and the emergence of a free labour market.[37]

The precise effect of these measures in the period before the occupation remains unclear. But the moves towards abolition began at a time when the Egyptian economy was experiencing far-reaching structural change: agriculture, property rights and the land tax had all been profoundly altered,[38] entrepots had been developed, and foreign investment had flowed in, pumping up the Egyptian economy just as it had inflated the economies of countries outside Africa. There are indications, too, that these changes intersected with a developing 'crisis of adaptation' in the third quarter of the century. Competition among cotton-producers became intense in the 1870s, when the price on the world market dropped sharply, following the boom years of the previous decade. Egypt's large estates, which were not as efficient as its small family firms, survived only because they used forced labour and benefited from political influence. The abolition of forced labour on vice-regal lands in 1878 increased the pressure on estate-owners at a time when slave labour was ceasing to be an option with a future. At the same time, Egypt's growing external indebtedness added greatly to the burden of taxation, which the large farmers, who had influence in high places, tried, with some success, to shift to their smaller rivals. The state itself succumbed when bankruptcy was declared in 1876. Egypt had failed, comprehensively, one of Palmerston's tests: it was no longer 'well kept'. It was still, for the moment, 'always accessible', but in 1882, when the discontent engendered by high taxation and the squeeze on incomes fed into nationalist demands for greater control over government business, the bailiffs decided that the terms of 'conditionality' had been broken. It was then time to exercise 'the forbearing use of power'.[39]

At the other end of the continent, South Africa also experienced structural change and a crisis of adaptation arising from the performance of the economy, though the content of both differed from the Egyptian case. The difference was not simply that South Africa had minerals and Egypt did not, but rather that South Africa's problems arose first from the failure of the export drive, whereas Egypt's sprang from its success, which enabled her to engage in foreign borrowing. The expected frontier of settlement, populated by new gentry, was slow to establish itself and slower still to advance inland.[40] The attempt to base settler farms on free labour helped to push Afrikaners inland away from Anglicizing influences, stimulated competition from indigenous household producers and led to conflict over land rights with African societies, while the rising demand for cattle products encouraged raiding and heightened competition for pasture.[41] By mid-century, the settler community was still struggling to demonstrate the advantages of free labour (and resorting on occasion to coercion). Slave labour, among other forms of labour, remained in use in the vast areas that remained outside British control, and slave-raiding, like cattle-rustling, promoted military and expansionist elements among the Nguni kingdoms of the eastern Cape and Natal.

The growth of overseas trade in the second half of the century (following the shift to free trade and the arrival of the steamship and 'imperial' banks in the 1860s) gave fresh impetus to the Cape's leading export, wool, and held out the prospect of raising the sinking fortunes of the settler gentry, who in turn were supposed to underpin the success of the colony as a whole. Without prosperous exports, colonial revenues would remain meagre; without sizeable revenues the Cape's own viability was in doubt and it had no hope of carrying the mission of improvement into the far-flung interior. As Egypt was falling heavily into debt, the Cape remained a burden on Britain's defence budget and had scarcely begun to borrow money to prime the pump of development. However, the prosperity that sprang from the rising volume of exports and the high prices paid for them in the 1860s failed to secure the colony's future. As recent research has revealed, the expansion of agriculture and pastoralism in the second half of the nineteenth century further increased competition for land and labour, and generated disputes that quickly assumed a political form.[42] Worse was to follow. As the settlers battled to establish an economic structure that was both efficient and based on approved property rights, they were struck by fluctuations that seriously affected the performance of the fledgling export sector. Exposure to free trade hit the prices of agricultural exports from the 1870s onwards and stepped up the pressure from farmers for government action to cut labour costs. This turn of events became caught up with the natural disasters of drought and rinderpest that afflicted much of southern Africa after 1869 and intensified conflicts between rural communities.[43] These developments cut into the support that the Cape government had tried to nurture among the colonial gentry: depressed exports, rural indebtedness, and a credit squeeze to the point of foreclosures generated political disaffection in both the western Cape and Natal, and played a critical part in stimulating Afrikaner nationalism.[44]

Subsequent events in south Africa cannot be explored here. The important point to note in the context of the present discussion is that the Cape's economic and political problems stemmed from incomplete structural change combined with severe fluctuations in the performance of the economy. This aspect of the story needs to be put firmly in place before the familiar question of control over newly discovered minerals is considered. We can now see that expansion inland was closely related first to the attempt to restore the prosperity of the colonial gentry by establishing 'law and order' and supplies of cheap labour, and then to the realization that successive 'lucky strikes' of diamonds and especially of gold held out the prospect of repositioning the economic basis of the colony so that it rested on minerals rather than on agriculture. Thus it was that Britain annexed the diamond areas of Griqualand West in 1871, that Carnarvon launched his grand design for a South African Confederation after he became Colonial Secretary in 1874, and that, finally, and in an infinitely convoluted way, the road to the Anglo-South African war, paved with bad intentions, was laid. The Transvaal had ceased to be 'well kept' and 'always accessible', so it was claimed, because it stood in the way of the most efficient means of managing the gold mines and because it threatened to establish an independent route to the east coast, thus again leaving the Cape without a prosperous and dependent hinterland.

Tropical Africa will be dealt with here in composite fashion. This procedure will not do justice to the diversity of the region; on the other hand, it has the merit of ensuring that evidence from West and East Africa is considered together instead of, as is usual, separately by discrete sets of specialists. In the case of West Africa, there is already a framework of discussion and a sizeable literature;[45] for East Africa, by a curious historiographical divergence, there is a good deal of scattered research on the subject of commercial change and some considerable work on labour history, but no comparable general debate on transition, adaptation or crisis. The aim of the comments that follow is to encourage specialists to begin a dialogue that will eventually produce a clarification of the similarities and differences in both the economic structures and the performance of the two regions.

As far as the structures of export production are concerned, it is evident that 'legitimate' commerce involved both slave and free labour throughout tropical Africa, and that only a minority of exports can be attributed exclusively to one or other form of labour input. It appears that ivory was produced throughout the region by hunters, free-raiders so to speak, who did not employ slaves; cloves were grown on the east coast on estates manned exclusively by slave labour.[46] These extremes provide good illustrations of how the nature of a product can exert an almost determining influence on the production function. The majority of exports, however, were produced by both slave and free labour. This was true of leading commodities, such as palm oil and groundnuts, wherever they were found, though in the second half of the century the balance seems to have moved in favour of free producers.[47] Examples of other exports produced by both types of labour range from coffee (in Angola) to sugar (in Mozambique) – and the list could be greatly extended. However, the key question arising from the data is whether the two methods of producing a single commodity coexisted in peaceful competition or whether there was an inherent antagonism between them. The original formulation,[48] which postulated that small producers possessed advantages that large producers could not match in the absence of significant economies of scale, has strong logical appeal and a fair measure of empirical support. In West Africa, latent conflicts manifested themselves in some of the key groundnut and palm-produce exporting areas in the late nineteenth century under the pressure of market forces. In East Africa, the closure of slave markets in Zanzibar after 1873 demonstrated that the clove plantations were uneconomic without forced labour, and greatly increased competition to locate and control alternative exports, of which the most important (ivory and rubber) were supplied mainly by free hunters and gatherers. Nevertheless, it has to be acknowledged that we still lack, for reasons suggested earlier, enough case studies, especially of free households and of regions outside West Africa, to be confident that we have a sufficient understanding of either the economics or the history of export production in the era of 'legitimate' commerce.

Two additional comments may be worth inserting here on the course taken by this aspect of the debate in recent years. First, to show that slaves were used in the production of 'legitimate' exports undoubtedly establishes a line of continuity with the past,[49] but it in no way minimizes the economic significance of using slaves to export primary products from Africa, as opposed to exporting slaves to produce primary products in other parts of the world. Non-slave products had of course been shipped from Africa long before abolition, but in the nineteenth century new products, many of which were to become prominent in the twentieth century, joined the list. The volume of these exports greatly expanded, especially after 1850. This process involved structural change in the economies concerned, quite apart from the issue of how production was organized. The second comment refers to one of the more subtle findings of recent research. The original hypothesis about the transition was based on a distinction between large producers who used slaves, and small producers who used free labour – mainly their own. However, there is now evidence for parts of West Africa that, in the second half of the nineteenth century (and probably relating to the falling price of slaves), some small producers also acquired slaves. It might seem at first sight that this finding changes the nature of the problem, which can no longer be treated as a matter of slave versus free labour. On reflection, however, the conclusion becomes less compelling. Leaving aside the possibility (much debated elsewhere)[50] that the definition of a 'slave' in a predominantly non-slave household may not have been comparable to a slave on a centrally managed plantation, the basic question remains unchanged: as noted above, it concerns the relative advantages of large- and small-scale producers. The nature of the labour force is an element in understanding this problem, but it is not the problem itself.

Regarding marketing functions, it is widely agreed that there were strong continuities with the past in the coastal entrepots, where whole-salers were needed whatever product was exported. Evidence of these continuities stretches across the continent from Lagos to Zanzibar, from slaves to palm oil and cloves. Existing trade networks, also typically employing slaves, transported new export products to the coast, distrib-uted manufactured imports (the most important of which remained, as in the eighteenth century, textiles), and used the same currencies and methods of dealing with foreign merchants. The position lower down the commercial hierarchy, however, has attracted far less research and there-fore remains unclear. In the original formulation, the proliferation of export producers, spread over a wide area, implied a multiplicity of traders and a problem of controlling internal markets that suggested, in turn, a potential conflict between the 'centre' and the 'provinces' over the distribution of gains from new and expanded activities. Were the 'big men' successful in extending their reach to encompass numerous, scat-tered local markets, adapting by becoming rentiers rather than (or as well as) becoming large producers? Alternatively, was the taxable potential of 'legitimate' commerce realized more easily by authorities in the localities, or perhaps minimized by the ability of small producers to take the greater share of the value added in the form of private profit? The questions are rhetorical but they are worth posing because this aspect of the commercial side of the transition needs to be brought into focus before we can be sure that our judgements about continuity and change are accurate ones.

There is much greater agreement, however, that the entrepots themselves experienced substantial change in the second half of the century. The steamship not only enabled trade to expand but also brought new traders and a greater degree of competition to the west coast from the 1850s and to the east coast a decade later. As commercial credit became more important, so too did the pressure to create acceptable security in the form of alienable land rights and the need to move towards convertible currencies. These and allied developments produced a 'crisis in commercial organization' on the west coast in the last quarter of the century.[51] Broadly similar trends were set in train on the east coast after the opening of the Suez Canal in 1869 and the arrival of Mackinnon's steamers.[52] It is true that the trade of the region was paltry compared to that of West Africa and that Mackinnon was trying to break into a closed commercial system that was still under the direction of the Sultanate rather than to adjust the management of an already sizeable and partly integrated export sector, as were his counterparts on the west coast. Nevertheless, the steamer held out the prospect of opening up the potential of East Africa by greatly reducing the cost of carriage to Europe, and in doing so increased the incentive for filling cargo space by developing exports on a scale that was far greater than before. What remains unclear at present is how far the commercial system managed from Zanzibar remained robust until it was toppled by foreign influences, and how far it was weakening from the 1850s and had come to the end of its useful life by the 1870s.[53] Until this question is answered, it is impossible to offer a suitably nuanced statement about the relative weight of internal and external causes of economic change in the export sector.

Nevertheless, by the last quarter of the nineteenth century it is clear that tropical Africa had reached the penultimate stage of a long transition, to be completed finally under colonial rule, from slave exports to exports of 'legitimate' products. This process involved structural change arising from the increased commercialization of factors of production in Africa and from the transformation of mercantile functions in the large entrepots. The complexity of the transition ensured that it was protracted and uneven – both through time and across space. Whether it could have been accomplished without external intervention is now a matter of speculation. What can be said is that the increased pace of change, accompanied by the rising ambitions of the Europeans who were promoting it, stepped up the pressure on African societies to conform to external requirements and reduced the tolerance shown towards the intransigent and the slow-moving. The ensuing tensions were greatly sharpened by the difficulties experienced by the leading export crops during the last quarter of the century. The problems faced by exporters of palm produce and ground-nuts in West Africa following the fall in world prices are well known; the crisis felt in Angola as a result of the collapse of the coffee market in the 1870s has been charted as well.[54] But we now have a clearer idea, too, of the acute uncertainties on the east coast: the ivory trade peaked in the 1870s and experienced a serious price fall in the 1890s; the other leading export, cloves, already suffering from the end of the slave trade in 1873, ran into similar difficulties from the beginning of the 1880s, culminating in the indebtedness of many plantation owners in the 1890s; seemingly random phenomena, such as famines, have also been linked to the fluctuating fortunes of the market economy.[55] The story of commercial crisis has even been extended to Madagascar, where it has been connected explicitly to French intervention.[56]

At this point, tropical Africa was judged to be no longer 'well kept' because Britain's grand plan for drawing the region into the new international economic order by way of 'legitimate' commerce was either foundering or heading for the rocks, and the region was no longer 'accessible' because the extension of the market through free trade, railways, commercial law and the adoption of modern currencies was being hampered or at least insufficiently assisted by African rulers who took their independence seriously. The problems of structural transfor-mation, made critical by the downturn in the performance of the international economy during the last quarter of the century, appeared to a growing number of influential European interests to pose a choice between abandoning the 'great transformation' of the nineteenth century or impressing it on the continent by force. Not for the first time, the liberal experiment was implemented by authoritarian means, and 'im-provement' finally reached the interior of Africa by courtesy of colonial rule – a providential outcome, so it was thought, for societies that were unable to play by the rules of the game without paternal guidance from English gentlemen (and their Scots associates) who had been trained from birth to mark out and patrol the frontiers of the second Rome.

Conclusion

This contribution has been pitched at a level of generalization that is close to the edge of credibility, and at points no doubt beyond it. This risky route has been chosen partly because there is no other way of dealing with the wider international setting in the space of one essay, but principally to encourage discussion of the larger issues raised by the nineteenth-century transition in Africa. From this perspective, the transition provides an illustration of Arthur Lewis' proposition that countries on the periphery faced a challenge in the nineteenth century either to industrialize or to trade.[57] The option open to Africa was to trade; the debate over the transition is about how the option was taken up.

As far as the purely African aspects of the story are concerned, my main conclusion relates not to the particulars of the debate (which have been commented on *en route*) but to its importance in the historiography of the continent. Although the subject itself is confined to the nineteenth century, it has obvious implications for interpreting both the era of the slave trade in the seventeenth and eighteenth centuries and the period of colonial rule in the twentieth century, and so provides an outstanding vantage point for viewing the broad sweep of modern African history. The entry point is the route provided by international trade, with its attendant focus on commercial institutions, but the ramifications of the debate extend far into the interior of Africa. In the original formulation, as we have seen, most attention was given to the economics of export production; today, as the essays in the present volume demonstrate, the discussion has broadened to include changes in the ideology of wealth creation, gender relations, and the ties and tensions between the state and private entrepreneurs – a topic that prompts comparison with current international policy-making for African development.[58] These themes are neither temporary products of academic fashion nor confined to just one part of the continent, but relate to central and enduring issues of economic development, social change and political order. The subject is therefore one that can engage historians and social scientists of all persuasions; the debate, accordingly, ought to be more widely known, applied and improved upon by specialists on parts of the continent other than West Africa.

My final observation concerns the wider international context that has been the main subject of this contribution. I have suggested that the transition experienced by West Africa was part of an ambitious programme of modernization that affected, or at least touched, not only the rest of Africa but also the rest of the globe in the nineteenth century. This, the world's first comprehensive development plan, was masterminded by Britain in a long-term venture that was launched after 1815 and pursued through a mixture of 'moral suasion', house-breaking and paternal direction within the empire and beyond it, throughout the Victorian era, into the twentieth century, and right down to the point of decolonization.[59] Fundamentally, this undertaking was designed to protect the British way of life by reproducing it abroad. The idea was to combine progress with stability, to offer a vision of an improved future – economic, political and moral – without upsetting order, privilege and property; by demonstrating, indeed, that the one required the other. This venture, or adventure as it became in imperial novels, was spearheaded by a gentlemanly elite who were explicitly fashioned for that purpose. The representatives of industry had a place in the design but did not draw it up. Standard interpretations of late nineteenth-century imperialism that fasten upon the relative decline of British manufactures and attribute expansionist impulses to foreign rivals have aimed at, and hit, the wrong target. It was not until the second half of the nineteenth century that the dynamic forces of British finance and commercial services began to leave their imprint on other parts of the world – within and outside the empire. The transition in 'oriental' and African societies remained incomplete at this point precisely because Britain had failed to establish an empire of informal sway in these regions. The crises that arose on the frontiers of empire in the late nineteenth century were symptoms not of the breakdown of informal empire but of its belated emergence. In the case of Africa, Britain was not retreating before the advance of more energetic rivals, but expanding beyond frontiers that previously had confined her authority to the coast. If this was not so, how can we explain the fact that, when the dust of Partition had settled, it was Britain, not her rivals, who had secured Egypt and South Africa, the richest parts of the continent, and who, even when only half-exerting herself, took the prizes in tropical Africa?

NOTES

1 It will become apparent that the focus of this essay is on British policy and influence. This limitation is perhaps excusable for reasons of space. A full account would of course deal with the role of other European powers, especially France.

2 Robin Law, 'The historiography of the commercial transition in nineteenth-century West Africa', in Toyin Falola (ed.), *African Historiography: Essays in Honour of Jacob Ade Ajayi* (London, 1993), pp. 91–115. See also Patrick Manning, 'Slave trade, "legitimate" trade, and imperialism revisited: the control of wealth in the Bights of Benin and Biafra', in Paul E. Lovejoy (ed.), *Africans in Bondage: Studies in Slavery and the Slave Trade* (Madison, 1986), pp. 203–33; Paul Lovejoy, *Transformations in Slavery: A History of Slavery in Africa* (Cambridge, 1983), chs. 8–10.

3 At the time, my knowledge of the documentary sources was not as complete as Robin Law has generously suggested ('Historiography', pp. 100–1 and 112, n44). On the other hand, I was greatly helped by two sources of

economic analysis that enabled me to think more clearly about different structures of export production: the first was Hla Myint's perceptive and exceptionally lucid study, *The Economics of the Developing Countries* (London, 1964), which followed his earlier important articles on international trade; the second was the discussion of staple theory by economists and economic historians such as Douglass C. North, J. W. McCarty and Melville H. Watkin in the 1950s and early 1960s. Watkin's essay, 'The staple theory of economic growth', *Canadian Journal of Economics & Political Science*, 29 (1963), was particularly influential in alerting the wider body of historians to the approach and its literature. If I were exploring this question for the first time today I would incorporate recent work on transaction and protection costs, and (following David Richardson's current research) on slaving as rent-seeking activity.

4   A pioneering study in this connection is Susan Martin, 'Gender and innovation: cooking and palm processing in the Ngwa region, south-western Nigeria, 1900–1930', *JAH*, 25 (1984), 411–27. The theme is developed further by Susan Martin and Robin Law in their contributions to this volume.

5   For these reasons distinctions between gathered and cultivated products or between indigenous and introduced crops, though very helpful for a variety of other purposes, tend to minimize the effects produced simply by an increase in the scale of export activities.

6   David Eltis, *Economic Growth and the Ending of the Transatlantic Slave Trade* (Oxford, 1987), p. 229.

7   See esp. Colin Newbury, 'On the margins of empire: the trade of western Africa, 1875–1890', in Stig Forster, Wolfgang Mommsen and Ronald Robinson (eds.), *Bismarck, Europe and Africa: The Berlin Africa Conference, 1884–1885, and the Onset of Partition* (Oxford, 1988), pp. 35–58; and the longer perspective offered by Martin Lynn, 'The profitability of the early nineteenth-century palm oil trade', *AEH*, 20 (1992), 77–97 (and further references given there, particularly to the work of A. J. H. Latham).

8   Equally, of course, evidence of declining performance is not evidence of a changing structure.

9   A. G. Hopkins, 'An economic history of Lagos, 1880–1914', PhD thesis, University of London, 1964.

10 K. O. Dike, *Trade and Politics in the Niger Delta, 1830–1885* (Oxford, 1956).

11 A. J. H. Latham, *Old Calabar, 1600–1891: The Impact of the International Economy upon a Traditional Society* (Oxford, 1973).

12 For example, 'Change and continuity in the British palm oil trade with West Africa, 1830–55', *JAH*, 22 (1981), 331–48; 'From sail to steam: the impact of the steamship services on the British palm oil trade with West Africa, 1850–1890', *JAH*, 30 (1989), 227–45; 'The "imperialism of free trade" and the case of West Africa, c.1800–c.1870', *JICH*, 15 (1986), 22–40; 'Profitability of the early nineteenth-century palm oil trade'; and Lynn's contribution to the present volume.

13 A. G. Hopkins, 'The Lagos strike of 1897: an exploration in Nigerian labour history', *Past & Present*, 35 (1966), 133–55.

14 A. G. Hopkins, 'Economic imperialism in West Africa: Lagos, 1880–92',

EHR, 21 (1968), 580–606. It may be helpful to mention these two articles together and in sequence because some subsequent comment, in criticizing the emphasis laid on the rise of small, free producers and stressing instead the role of slave labour, has been pushing at an open door. The central question, as I saw it, was to understand the relative importance of these different means of producing similar exports and the extent to which they could (or could not) coexist.

15 This is neither the place nor the moment to elaborate an argument advanced twenty-five years ago. However, I would like to re-advertise the value of the data contained in contemporary issues of the *Kew Bulletin*, as these remain an underused source today. The calculations I made on the basis of this evidence helped to convince me that the production of palm oil and kernels for export had become a mass operation as well as a big business. (See, e.g., 'Economic imperialism', p. 588, n3.)

16 A. G. Hopkins, *An Economic History of West Africa* (London, 1973).

17 See, e.g., 'Plantations in the economy of the Sokoto Caliphate', *JAH*, 19 (1978), 341–68.

18 Jan Vansina, 'Towards a history of lost corners in the world', *EHR*, 35 (1982), 165–78; Susan Martin, *Palm Oil and Protest: An Economic History of the Ngwa Region, South-Western Nigeria, 1800–1980* (Cambridge, 1988).

19 For a longer discussion of the British background, see P. J. Cain and A. G. Hopkins, *British Imperialism: Innovation and expansion, 1688–1914* (London, 1993), ch. 2.

20 Canning to Frere, 8 Jan. 1825, quoted in William W. Kaufmann, *British Policy and the Independence of Latin America* (New Haven, 1951), pp. 201, 203.

21 The term came into use in the late eighteenth century, when it was applied mainly to French Canadians and Afrikaners. See James Sturgis, 'Anglicisation at the Cape of Good Hope in the early nineteenth century', *JICH*, 11 (1982), 5–32.

22 Neil Rabitboy, 'The control of fate and fortune: origins of the market mentality in British administrative thought in south Asia', *Modern Asian Studies*, 25 (1991), 737–64.

23 Jeremy Bentham was fascinated by the prospect of realizing a utilitarian utopia in South America and he conducted a weighty correspondence on the subject with leaders of the new states there. See Miriam Williford, *Jeremy Bentham on Spanish America* (Baton Rouge, LA, 1980).

24 The sizeable literature on this subject can now be approached through Eltis, *Economic Growth*. .

25 For recent restatements see Lynn, 'Sail to steam'; Robert V. Kubicek, 'The colonial steamer and the occupation of West Africa by the Victorian state, 1840–1900', *JICH*, 18 (1990), 9–32.

26 The policy was not altered until 1895, when defeat at the hands of Japan forced China into large-scale borrowing for the first time. The chief beneficiary, waiting in the wings, was the City of London.

27 The argument is, of course, that of Ronald Robinson and John Gallagher, *Africa and the Victorians: The Official Mind of Imperialism* (London, 1961). For a recent criticism, see Lynn, 'The "imperialism of free trade"'. The

concept itself both demands and defies definition. A recent attempt to corner the problem is A. G. Hopkins, 'Informal empire in Argentina: An Alternative View', *Journal of Latin American Studies*, 26 (1994), 469–84.

28   G. Liesegang, H. Pasch and A. Jones (eds.), *Figuring African Trade* (Berlin, 1986); Newbury, 'Margins of empire'.

29   C. W. Newbury, 'Credit in early nineteenth-century West African trade', *JAH*, 13 (1972), 81–95.

30   Quoted in M. Chamberlain, *The Scramble for Africa* (London, 1974), p. 36.

31   Quoted in Philip Mason, *The English Gentleman: The Rise and Fall of an Ideal* (London, 1982), p. 214.

32   Newbury, 'Margins of empire', p. 50.

33   This is not, of course, to suggest that the commercialization of the economy was a new phenomenon in Egypt any more than it was elsewhere in Africa. See, e.g., Kenneth M. Cuno, *The Pasha's Peasants: Land, Society and Economy in Lower Egypt, 1740–1858* (Cambridge, 1992).

34   The standard work remains E. J. R. Owen, *Cotton and the Egyptian Economy, 1820–1914* (Oxford, 1969).

35   The use of slaves in Egypt (as opposed to the Sudan) has received relatively little attention. See Gabriel Baer, 'Social change in Egypt, 1800–1914', in P. M. Holt (ed.), *Political and Social Change in Modern Egypt* (London, 1968), pp. 135–61; Baer, *Studies in the Social History of Modern Egypt* (Chicago, 1969), pp. 161–89; and the recent commentary by François Renault, 'La traite transsaharienne des esclaves', *Revue française d'histoire d'outre-mer*, 80 (1993), 467–77.

36   For a case-study of the growth of an entrepot – a more advanced example of developments that were taking place at points on the coast of tropical Africa – see Michael Reimer, 'Colonial bridgehead: social and spatial change in Alexandria, 1850–1882', *International Journal of Middle Eastern Studies*, 29 (1988), 531–53.

37   Gabriel Baer, 'Slavery in nineteenth-century Egypt', *JAH*, 8 (1967), 417–41; and Baer, 'Social change', p. 153; Suzanne Miers, *Britain and the Ending of the Slave Trade* (London, 1975), pp. 75–82.

38   Ehud R. Toledano, *State and Society in Mid-Nineteenth Century Egypt* (Cambridge, 1990); Cuno, *The Pasha's Peasants*.

39   On the final stages, see A. G. Hopkins, 'The Victorians and Africa: a reconsideration of the occupation of Egypt, 1882', *JAH*, 7 (1986), 333–91; and the excellent new study by Juan R. I. Cole, *Colonialism and Revolution in the Middle East: Social and Cultural Origins of Egypt's 'Urabi Movement'* (Princeton, 1992).

40   For amplification and qualification, see Richard Elphick and Hermann Giliomee (eds.), *The Shaping of South African Society* (2nd edn, London, 1989).

41   See, e.g., Norman Etherington, 'African economic experiments in colonial Natal, 1845–1880', *AEH*, 5 (1978), 1–15; Clifton Crais, 'Gentry and labour in three Eastern Cape districts', *South African Historical Journal*, 18 (1986), 125–46; and Crais, *White Supremacy and Black Resistance in Pre-Industrial South Africa: The Making of the Colonial Order in the Eastern Cape, 1770–1865* (Cambridge, 1992); Timothy Keegan, 'Dispossession and accu-

mulation in the South African interior: the Boers and the Tlhaping of Bethulie, 1833–61', *JAH*, 28 (1987), 191–207; Malyn Newitt, 'Economic penetration and the Scramble for southern Africa', in Peter Morris (ed.), *Africa, America and Central Asia: Formal and Informal Empire in the Nineteenth Century* (Exeter, 1984), pp. 35–62. Dr Newitt is one of the very few specialists on southern Africa to have made explicit use of the literature relating to 'legitimate' commerce in West Africa.

42 E.g. Colin Bundy, *The Rise and Fall of a South African Peasantry* (London, 1979); William Beinart, *The Political Economy of Pondoland, 1860–1930* (Cambridge, 1982); Philip Bonner, *Kings, Commoners and Concessionaires: The Evolution and Dissolution of the Nineteenth-Century Swazi State* (Cambridge, 1983); Peter Delius, *The Land Belongs to Us: The Pedi Polity, the Boers, and the British in the Nineteenth-Century Transvaal* (London, 1984).

43 Charles van Onselen, 'Reactions to the spread of rinderpest in southern Africa, 1896–7', *JAH*, 13 (1972), 473–88; Charles Ballard, 'The repercussions of rinderpest: cattle, plague and peasant decline in colonial Natal', *IJAHS*, 19 (1986), 421–50.

44 Hermann Giliomee, 'Western Cape farmers and the beginnings of Afrikaner nationalism, 1870–1915', *Journal of Southern African Studies*, 14 (1987), 38–63; Arthur Webb, 'Early capitalism in the Cape: the Eastern Province Bank, 1839–73', in Stuart Jones (ed.), *Banking and Business in South Africa* (New York, 1988), pp. 47–68; Peter Richardson, 'The Natal sugar industry, 1849–1895: an interpretative essay', *JAH*, 23 (1982), 522–6; Keith Tankard, 'The effects of the "Great Depression" of the late nineteenth century on East London, 1873–88', *South African Journal of Economic History*, 6 (1991), 72–88.

45 For this reason, and to avoid repeating summaries found elsewhere in this volume, West Africa will be dealt with briefly. A guide to the literature can be found in the Appendix to this book.

46 Beyond these examples, generalization becomes difficult: wild rubber was tapped mainly (but not exclusively) by free labour; gum, another gathered product, appears to have been produced largely by slaves (at least in Senegal).

47 The summary by Eltis appears to be faithful representation of the detailed literature on this point: *Economic Growth*, pp. 227–8.

48 Hopkins, 'Economic imperialism'; *Economic History*, ch. 4.

49 See here esp. Joseph Miller, *Way of Death: Merchant capitalism and the Angolan slave trade, 1730–1830* (London, 1988), pp. 138–9.

50 For two well-known examples, see Claude Meillassoux (ed.), *L'esclavage en Afrique précoloniale* (Paris, 1976); Suzanne Miers and Igor Kopytoff (eds.), *Slavery in Africa* (Madison, 1977).

51 Newbury, 'Margins of empire', p. 57.

52 J. Forbes Munro, 'Shipping subsidies and railway guarantees: William Mackinnon, eastern Africa and the Indian Ocean, 1860–93', *JAH*, 28 (1987), 209–30. I would like to take this opportunity to thank Professor Forbes Munro for his helpful comments on this subject over a period of years. A much clearer picture of the precise similarities and differences between the

west and the east coast will emerge when his major study of Mackinnon's activities has been completed.

53   For two different views, see Norman Bennett, *Arab versus European: Diplomacy and War in Nineteenth-Century East Africa* (New York, 1986); Frederick Cooper, *Plantation Slavery on the East Coast of Africa* (New Haven, 1977).

54   On the latter, see David Birmingham, 'The coffee barons of Cazengo', *JAH*, 19 (1978), 523–39; Jill R. Dias, 'Famine and disease in the history of Angola', *JAH*, 22 (1981), 349–78.

55   A. M. Sheriff, 'Ivory and economic expansion in East Africa in the nineteenth century', in Liesegang, Pasch and Jones, *Figuring African Trade*, pp. 415–49; Franz Rudolf Menne, 'Production and export of cloves towards the end of the nineteenth century', ibid., pp. 557–90; James Giblin, 'Famine and social change during the transition to colonial rule in north-eastern Tanzania', *AEH*, 15 (1986), 85–105.

56   Gwyn R. Campbell, 'Toamasina (Tamatave) and the growth of foreign trade in imperial Madagascar', in Liesegang, Pasch and Jones, *Figuring African Trade*, pp. 525–55.

57   W. Arthur Lewis, *Growth and Fluctuations, 1870–1913* (London, 1978), p. 158; and ch. 8 for the response.

58   In the 1980s the World Bank was concerned with 'getting prices right', which meant attacking state monopolies and encouraging private entrepreneurs; today, it is interested in 'bringing the state back in' and with the associated need for 'good governance'. African entrepreneurs and governments were arguing over much the same issues during the nineteenth-century transition and also fashioned ideologies to represent and legitimate their positions.

59   For an interpretation of the colonial period, see P. J. Cain and A. G. Hopkins, *British Imperialism: Crisis and Deconstruction, 1914–1990* (London, 1993), ch. 9.

Appendix
The 'crisis of adaptation': a bibliography

This is not a bibliography of works cited in the contributions to this volume, but a guide to the literature on the commercial transition in nineteenth-century western Africa, including especially the debate on the concept of a 'crisis of adaptation'. It is confined to works which deal wholly or substantially with the history and implications of the transition, rather than those which mention it only casually or briefly, to works which bear upon the African as opposed to the European side of the Atlantic trade (though this distinction is difficult to make in practice), and chronologically, to those which deal with the pre-colonial rather than the colonial period (though, again, this distinction is not always clear-cut); but within these limitations, it is (in intention, though doubtless not in execution) comprehensive.

General studies

Anjorin, A. O. 'European attempts to develop cotton cultivation in West Africa, 1850–1910', *Odu*, 2nd series, 3/1 (1966), 3–15.

Austen, Ralph A. 'The abolition of the overseas slave trade: a distorted theme in West African history', *JHSN*, 5/2 (1970), 257–74.
    African Economic History: Internal Development and Economic Dependency (London, 1987), chs. 4–5.

Brooks, George A. 'Peanuts and colonialism: consequences of the commercialization of peanuts in West Africa, 1830–1870', *JAH*, 16 (1975), 29–54.

Chamberlin, Christopher. 'Bulk exports, trade tiers, regulation, and development: an economic approach to the study of West Africa's "legitimate trade"', *JEH*, 39 (1979), 419–38.

Eltis, David. *Economic Growth and the Ending of the Transatlantic Slave Trade* (Oxford, 1987).
    'The African role in the ending of the transatlantic slave trade', in Serge Daget (ed.), *De la traite à l'esclavage: Actes du colloque international sur la traite des noirs, Nantes, 1985* (Paris, 1988), II, pp. 503–20.

Eltis, David and Walvin, James (eds.). *The Abolition of the Atlantic Slave Trade: Origins and Effects in Europe, Africa and the Americas* (Madison, 1981), Part II.

Flint, J. E. and McDougall, Ann. 'Economic change in West Africa in the nineteenth century', in J. F. Ade Ajayi and Michael Crowder (eds.), *History of West Africa*, II (2nd edn, London, 1987), pp. 379–402.

Hopkins, A. G. *An Economic History of West Africa* (London, 1973), ch. 4.

Jones, G. I. *From Slaves to Palm Oil: Slave Trade and Palm Oil Trade in the Bight of Biafra* (African Studies Centre, University of Cambridge, 1989).

Klein, Martin A. 'Slavery, the slave trade, and legitimate commerce in late nineteenth-century Africa', *Etudes d'Histoire Africaine*, 2 (1971), 5–28.

Latham, A. J. H. 'Price fluctuations in the early palm oil trade', *JAH*, 19 (1978), 213–18.

Law, Robin. 'The historiography of the commercial transition in nineteenth-century West Africa', in Toyin Falola (ed.), *African Historiography: Essays in honour of Jacob Ade Ajayi* (Harlow, 1993), pp. 91–115.

Liesegang, G., Pasch, H. and Jones, A. (eds.). *Figuring African Trade: Proceedings of a symposium on the quantification and structure of the import and export and long-distance trade in Africa 1800–1913* (Berlin, 1986).

Lynn, Martin. 'Change and continuity in the British palm oil trade with West Africa, 1830–55', *JAH*, 22 (1981), 331–48.

'From sail to steam: the impact of the steamship services on the British palm oil trade with West Africa, 1850–1890', *JAH*, 30 (1989), 227–45.

Lovejoy, Paul E. *Transformations in Slavery: A History of Slavery in Africa* (Cambridge, 1983), ch. 8.

Lovejoy, Paul E. and Richardson, David. 'British Abolition and its impact on slave prices along the Atlantic coast of Africa, 1783–1850', *JEH*, 55 (1995), 98–119.

Manning, Patrick. 'Slaves, palm oil, and political power on the West African coast', *African Historical Studies*, 2 (1969), 279–88.

'Slave trade, "legitimate" trade, and imperialism revisited: the control of wealth in the Bights of Benin and Biafra', in Paul E.Lovejoy (ed.), *Africans in Bondage: Studies in Slavery and the Slave Trade in Honour of Philip D. Curtin* (African Studies Program, University of Wisconsin-Madison, 1986), pp. 203–33.

Munro, J. Forbes. *Africa and the International Economy 1800–1960* (London, 1976), ch. 2.

Newbury, Colin W. *The Western Slave Coast and its Rulers: European Trade and Administration among the Yoruba and Aja-Speaking Peoples of South-Western Nigeria, Southern Dahomey and Togo* (Oxford, 1961), chs 2–3.

'Prices and profitability in early nineteenth-century West African trade', in Claude Meillassoux (ed.), *The Development of Indigenous Trade and Markets in West Africa* (London, 1971), 91–106.

'Credit in early nineteenth century West African trade', *JAH*, 13 (1972), 81–95.

Oloruntimehin, 'Tunji. 'The impact of the Abolition Movement on the social and political development of West Africa in the nineteenth and twentieth centuries', *African Notes*, 7/1 (1972), 33–58.

Senegambia

Curtin, Philip D. 'The abolition of the slave trade from Senegambia', in David Eltis and James Walvin (eds.), *The Abolition of the Atlantic Slave Trade* (Madison, 1981), pp. 83–97.

Diouf, Mamadou. *Le Kajoor au XIXe siècle: pouvoir ceddo et conquête coloniale* (Paris, 1990).

Klein, Martin A. *Islam and Imperialism in Senegal: Sine-Saloum, 1847–1914* (Edinburgh, 1968).

'Social and economic factors in the Muslim Revolution in Senegambia', *JAH*, 13 (1972), 419–41.

McLane, Margaret. 'Commercial rivalries and French policy on the Senegal River, 1831–1858', *AEH*, 15 (1986), 39–67.

Searing, James F. *West African Slavery and Atlantic Commerce: The Senegal River valley, 1700–1860* (Cambridge, 1993), ch. 6.

Swindell, Ken. 'SeraWoollies, Tillibunkas and Strange Farmers: the development of migrant groundnut farming along the Gambia River 1848–95', *JAH*, 21 (1980), 93–104.

Webb, James L. A., Jr. 'The trade in gum arabic: prelude to French conquest in Senegal', *JAH*, 26 (1985), 149–68.

Weil, Peter M., 'Slavery, groundnuts and European capitalism in the Walé Kingdom of Senegambia, 1820–1930', *Research in Economic Anthropology*, 6 (1984), 77–119.

Upper Guinea

Bowman, Joye L. ' "Legitimate commerce" and peanut production in Portuguese Guinea, 1840s-1880s', *JAH*, 28 (1987), 87–106.

Goerg, Odile. *Commerce et colonisation en Guinée, 1850–1913* (Paris, 1986).

'Deux modalités d'adaptation à l'abolition de la traite atlantique: le Rio Nunez et le Rio Pongo (actuelle Guinée)', in Serge Daget (ed.), *De la traite à l'esclavage* (Paris, 1988), II, pp. 557–73.

Ijagbemi, E. A. 'The Freetown Colony and the development of "legitimate" commerce in the adjoining territories', *JHSN*, 5/2 (1970), 243–56.

Jones, Adam. *From Slaves to Palm Kernels: A History of the Galinhas Country (West Africa) 1730–1890* (Wiesbaden, 1983).

Gold Coast

McCarthy, Mary. *Social Change and the Growth of British Power in the Gold Coast: The Fante States 1807–1874* (Lanham, Maryland, 1978), chs 3–4.

McSheffery, Gerald M. 'Slavery, indentured servitude, legitimate trade and the impact of Abolition on the Gold Coast, 1874–1901', *JAH*, 24 (1983), 349–68.

Reynolds, Edward. 'Agricultural adjustments on the Gold Coast after the end of the slave trade, 1807–1874', *Agricultural History*, 47 (1973), 308–18.

Trade and Economic Change on the Gold Coast, 1807–1874 (London, 1974).

'Abolition and economic change on the Gold Coast', in David Eltis and James Walvin (eds.), *The Abolition of the Atlantic Slave Trade* (Madison, 1981), pp. 141–51.

'The slave trade, slavery and economic transformation of the Gold Coast in the nineteenth century', in Serge Daget (ed.), *De la traite à l'esclavage* (Paris, 1988), II, pp. 583–602.

Sanders, J. 'Palm oil production on the Gold Coast in the aftermath of the slave trade: a case study of the Fante', *IJAHS*, 15 (1982), 49–63.

Wilson, Louis E. *The Krobo People of Ghana to 1892: A Political and Social History* (Athens, Ohio, 1992), chs 5–6.

Wolfson, Freda. 'A price agreement on the Gold Coast: the Krobo oil boycott, 1858–1866', *EHR*, 6 (1953), 14–25.

Asante

Arhin, Kwame. 'Aspects of the Ashanti northern trade in the nineteenth century', *Africa*, 40 (1970), 363–73.

'The Ashanti rubber trade with the Gold Coast in the eighteen-nineties', *Africa*, 42 (1972), 32–43.

'The economic and social significance of rubber production and exchange on the Gold and Ivory Coasts, 1880–1900', *CEA*, 20 (1980), 49–62.

'Trade, accumulation and the state in Asante in the nineteenth century', *Africa*, 60 (1990), 524–37.

Austin, Gareth. ' "No elders were present": commoners and private ownership in Asante, 1807–1896', *JAH*, forthcoming.

Dumett, Raymond. 'The rubber trade of the Gold Coast and Asante in the nineteenth century: African innovation and market responsiveness', *JAH*, 12 (1971), 79–101.

LaTorre, Joseph Raymond. 'Wealth surpasses everything: an economic history of Asante, 1750–1874', PhD thesis, University of California, Berkeley, 1978.

Lewin, Thomas J. *Asante before the British: The Prempean Years, 1875–1900* (Lawrence, Kansas, 1978), ch. 3.

Van Dantzig, Albert. 'Elmina, Asante and the abolitionists: morality, security and profits', in Serge Daget (ed.), *De la traite à l'esclavage* (Paris, 1988), II, pp. 683–602.

Wilks, Ivor. 'Asante policy towards the Hausa trade in the nineteenth century', in Claude Meillassoux (ed.), *The Development of Indigenous Trade and Markets in West Africa* (London, 1971), pp. 124–41.

Asante in the Nineteenth Century: The Structure and Evolution of a Political Order (Cambridge, 1975), chs 5, 15.

Dahomey

Coquery-Vidrovitch, Catherine 'De la traite des esclaves à l'exportation de l'huile de palmes et des palmistes au Dahomey: XIXe siècle', in Claude Meillassoux (ed.), *The Development of Indigenous Trade and Markets in West Africa* (London, 1971), pp. 107–23.

Law, Robin. 'Royal monopoly and private enterprise in the Atlantic trade: the case of Dahomey', *JAH*, 18 (1977), 555–77.

'Dahomey and the end of the Atlantic Slave Trade' (Centre of African Studies, Boston University, Working Papers in African Studies No. 165, 1992).

Manning, Patrick. *Slavery, Colonialism and Economic Growth in Dahomey, 1640–1960* (Cambridge, 1982), chs 2–3.

Reid, John 'Warrior aristocrats in crisis: the political effects of the transition from the slave trade to palm oil commerce in the nineteenth-century kingdom of Dahomey', PhD thesis, University of Stirling, 1986.

Ross, David A. 'The career of Domingo Martinez in the Bight of Benin 1833–64', *JAH*, 6 (1965), 79–90.

Soumonni, E. A. 'Dahomean economic policy under Ghezo, 1818–1858: a reconsideration', *JHSN*, 10/2 (1980), 1–11.

Yoder, John C. 'Fly and Elephant Parties: political polarization in Dahomey, 1840–70', *JAH*, 15 (1974), 417–32.

Lagos/Yorubaland

Agiri, B. A. 'Aspects of socio-economic change among the Awori, Egba and Ijebu Remo communities during the nineteenth century', *JHSN*, 7/3 (1974), 465–83.

Ajayi, J. F. Ade and Austen, Ralph A. 'Hopkins on economic imperialism in Africa', *EHR*, 25 (1972), 303–6.

Akintoye, S. A. 'The economic background of the Ekitiparapo 1878–1893', *Odu*, 2nd series, 4/2 (1968), 30–52.

Clarke, Julian. 'Households and the political economy of small-scale cash crop production in south-western Nigeria', *Africa*, 51 (1981), 807–23.

Hopkins, A. G. 'The Lagos strike of 1897: an exploration in Nigerian labour history', *Past & Present*, 35 (1966), 133–55.

'Economic imperialism in West Africa: Lagos, 1880–92', *EHR*, 21 (1968), 580–600.

'Economic imperialism in West Africa: a rejoinder', *EHR*, 25 (1972), 307–12.

'Property rights and empire building: Britain's annexation of Lagos, 1861', *JEH*, 40 (1980), 777–98.

Warri/Benin

Ikime, Obaro *Merchant Prince of the Niger Delta: The Rise and Fall of Nana Olomu, Last Governor of the Benin River* (Ibadan, 1968).

Lloyd, P. C. 'The Itsekiri in the nineteenth century: an outline social history', *JAH*, 4/2 (1963), 207–31.

Ryder, A. F. C. *Benin and the Europeans 1485–1897* (London, 1969), ch. 7.

Niger Delta/Old Calabar

Alagoa, E. J. 'Nineteenth century revolutions in the Eastern Delta and Calabar', *JHSN*, 5/4 (1971), 565–74.

Cookey, Sylvanus *King Jaja of the Niger Delta: His Life and Times, 1821–1891* (New York, 1974).

Dike, K. Onwuka. *Trade and Politics in the Niger Delta 1830–1885: An Introduction to the Economic and Political History of Nigeria* (Oxford, 1956).

Hargreaves, Susan. 'The political economy of nineteenth-century Bonny: a study of power, authority, legitimacy and ideology in a Delta trading community from 1790–1914', PhD thesis, University of Birmingham, 1987.

Latham, A. J. H. *Old Calabar 1600–1891: The Impact of the International Economy upon a Traditional Society* (Oxford, 1973), Part 2.

'Palm oil exports from Calabar 1812–1887 (with a note on price formation)', in
    G. Liesegang, H. Pasch and A. Jones (eds.), *Figuring African Trade* (Berlin,
    1986), pp. 265–96.
Nair, Kannan K. *Politics and Society in South-Eastern Nigeria 1841–1906: A
    Study of Power, Diplomacy and Commerce in Old Calabar* (London, 1972),
    chs 2–4.

Igboland

Afigbo, A. E. 'The eclipse of the Aro slaving oligarchy 1807–1927', in *Ropes of
    Sand: Studies in Igbo History and Culture* (Ibadan, 1981), pp. 239–81.
Dike, Kenneth Onwuka and Ekejiuba, Felicia *The Aro of South-Eastern Nigeria,
    1650–1980: A Study of Socio-Economic Formation and Transformation in
    Nigeria* (Ibadan, 1990), ch. 8.
Isichei, Elizabeth. *The Ibo People and the Europeans: The Genesis of a Relation-
    ship – to 1906* (London, 1973), ch. 4.
    A History of the Igbo People (London, 1976), ch. 7.
Martin, Susan M. *Palm Oil and Protest: An Economic History of the Nwa Region,
    South-Eastern Nigeria, 1800–1980* (Cambridge, 1988), ch. 2.
Northrup, David 'The compatibility of the slave and plam oil trades in the Bight
    of Biafra', *JAH*, 17 (1976), 353–64.
    *Trade without Rulers: Pre-colonial economic development in South-Eastern
    Nigeria* (Oxford, 1978), chs 7–8.
Oriji, J. N. 'A study of the slave and palm produce trade amongst the Ngwa-Ibo
    of Southeastern Nigeria', *CEA*, 91 (1981), 311–28.
    'A re-assessment of the organization and benefits of the slave and palm
    produce trade amongst the Ngwa-Igbo', *CJAS*, 16 (1982), 523–48.
    *Ngwa History: A Study of Social and Economic Changes in Igbo Mini-States in
    Time Perspective* (New York, 1991), ch. 5.
Ukwu, U.I. 'The development of trade and marketing in Igboland', *JHSN*, 3/4
    (1967), 647–62.

Cameroon

Austen, Ralph A. 'Slavery among the coastal middlemen: the Duala of Ca-
    meroon', in Suzanne Miers and Igor Kopytoff (eds.), *Slavery in Africa*
    (Madison, 1977), pp. 305–33.
    'The metamorphoses of middlemen: The Duala, Europeans and the Cameroon
    hinterland', *IJAHS*, 16 (1983), 1–24.
Elango, L. Z. 'Trade and diplomacy on the Cameroon Coast in the nineteenth
    century', in Martin Njeuma (ed.), *Introduction to the History of Cameroon in
    the Nineteenth and Twentieth Centuries* (London, 1989).

Sudan/Sahel

Baier, Stephen. 'Trans-Saharan trade and the Sahel: Damergu, 1870–1930', *JAH*,
    18 (1977), 37–60.
Klein, Martin. 'The slave trade in the Western Sudan in the nineteenth century',

in Elizabeth Savage (ed.), *The Human Commodity: Perspectives on the trans-Saharan trade* (London, 1992), pp. 39–60.

Lovejoy, Paul E. 'Plantations in the economy of the Sokoto Caliphate', *JAH*, 19 (1978), 341–68.

Mason, Michael. 'Captive and client labour and the economy of the Bida Emirate, 1857–1901', *JAH*, 14 (1973), 453–71.

West-Central Africa

Birmingham, David. 'The coffee barons of Kazengo', *JAH*, 19 (1978), 523–38.

Dias, Jill R. 'Black chiefs, white traders and colonial policy near the Kwanza: Kabuku Kambilo and the Portuguese, 1873–1896', *JAH*, 17 (1976), 245–65.

'Famine and disease in the history of Angola, c.1830–1930', *JAH*, 22 (1981), 349–78.

Martin, Phyllis M. *The External Trade of the Loango Coast 1576–1870: The Effects of Changing Commercial Relations on the Vili Kingdom of Loango* (Oxford, 1972), ch. 7.

M'Bokolo, Elikia: *Noirs et blancs en Afrique equatoriale: les sociétés côtières et la pénétration française (vers 1820–1874)* (Paris, 1981), ch. 5.

Patterson, K. David. *The Northern Gabon Coast to 1875* (Oxford, 1975), ch. 3.

Index

Other books in the series

Printed in the United States
1527400007B/21